IFIP Advances in Information and Communication Technology

501

IFIP – The International Federation for Information Processing

IFIP was founded in 1960 under the auspices of UNESCO, following the first World Computer Congress held in Paris the previous year. A federation for societies working in information processing, IFIP's aim is two-fold: to support information processing in the countries of its members and to encourage technology transfer to developing nations. As its mission statement clearly states:

IFIP is the global non-profit federation of societies of ICT professionals that aims at achieving a worldwide professional and socially responsible development and application of information and communication technologies.

IFIP is a non-profit-making organization, run almost solely by 2500 volunteers. It operates through a number of technical committees and working groups, which organize events and publications. IFIP's events range from large international open conferences to working conferences and local seminars.

The flagship event is the IFIP World Computer Congress, at which both invited and contributed papers are presented. Contributed papers are rigorously refereed and the rejection rate is high.

As with the Congress, participation in the open conferences is open to all and papers may be invited or submitted. Again, submitted papers are stringently refereed.

The working conferences are structured differently. They are usually run by a working group and attendance is generally smaller and occasionally by invitation only. Their purpose is to create an atmosphere conducive to innovation and development. Refereeing is also rigorous and papers are subjected to extensive group discussion.

Publications arising from IFIP events vary. The papers presented at the IFIP World Computer Congress and at open conferences are published as conference proceedings, while the results of the working conferences are often published as collections of selected and edited papers.

IFIP distinguishes three types of institutional membership: Country Representative Members, Members at Large, and Associate Members. The type of organization that can apply for membership is a wide variety and includes national or international societies of individual computer scientists/ICT professionals, associations or federations of such societies, government institutions/government related organizations, national or international research institutes or consortia, universities, academies of sciences, companies, national or international associations or federations of companies.

More information about this series at http://www.springer.com/series/6102

Yuko Murayama · Dimiter Velev
Plamena Zlateva · Jose J. Gonzalez (Eds.)

Information Technology in Disaster Risk Reduction

First IFIP TC 5 DCITDRR International Conference, ITDRR 2016
Sofia, Bulgaria, November 16–18, 2016
Revised Selected Papers

 Springer

Editors
Yuko Murayama
Tsuda University
Tokyo
Japan

Plamena Zlateva
Bulgarian Academy of Sciences
Sofia
Bulgaria

Dimiter Velev
University of National and World Economy
Sofia
Bulgaria

Jose J. Gonzalez
University of Agder
Grimstad
Norway

ISSN 1868-4238   ISSN 1868-422X (electronic)
IFIP Advances in Information and Communication Technology
ISBN 978-3-319-88611-4   ISBN 978-3-319-68486-4 (eBook)
https://doi.org/10.1007/978-3-319-68486-4

Printed on acid-free paper

This Springer imprint is published by Springer Nature
The registered company is Springer International Publishing AG
The registered company address is: Gewerbestrasse 11, 6330 Cham, Switzerland

Preface

The effects of disasters are very serious and it may take a very long time to recover from the destruction caused. The ensuing damage can be severe and offering relief may lead to expenses in the range of billions of euros. The occurrence of natural disasters has increased in the past few years and it is expected that their frequency will continue in the coming years.

Owing to the multidisciplinary nature of work in the field of disaster risk reduction, people from various backgrounds are included in this field of research and activity. Their backgrounds are likely to include industry, diverse geographical and global settings, not-for-profit organizations, agriculture, marine life, welfare, risk management, safety engineering, and social networking services.

At present, at global and national levels, a wide range of scientific and applied research activity is conducted in the area of disaster risk reduction concerning individual types of disasters. Modern information and communication technologies (ICT) can facilitate significantly the decision-making processes from the point of view of disaster risk reduction.

Following the increasing number of disasters worldwide and the growing potential of both ICT and ICT expertise, at its General Assembly held during October 8–9, 2015 at the Daejeon Convention Center, Daejeon, Korea, the IFIP established the Domain Committee on Information Technology in Disaster Risk Reduction in order to:

- Promote disaster risk reduction within the ICT community
- Provide an additional opportunity for IFIP members to work with other specialized bodies such as the UN, UNISDR, ICSU, ITU, and ISCRAM
- Coordinate the efforts of member societies as well as different Technical Committees and Working Groups of IFIP in the disaster-related field

The disaster support offered by the Domain Committee is based on the following major pillars:

- Information acquisition and provision
- Shelter information management for local governments
- Disaster information systems
- State-of-the-art ICT (such as the Internet of Things, mobile computing, big data, and cloud computing).

IFIP's Domain Committee on Information Technology in Disaster Risk Reduction organized the First IFIP Conference on Information Technology in Disaster Risk Reduction (ITDRR 2016), during November 16–18, 2016, at the University of National and World Economy, Sofia, Bulgaria.

ITDRR 2016 provided an international forum for researchers and practitioners to present their latest R&D findings and innovations. The conference was especially focused on various ICT aspects and the challenges of coping with disaster risk reduction. The main topics included areas such as big data, cloud computing, the Internet of Things and natural disasters, mobile computing, emergency management, disaster information processing, disaster risk assessment and management, and disaster management simulation.

ITDRR 2016 invited experts, researchers, academicians and all others who were interested in disseminating their work to attend the conference. The conference established an academic environment that fostered the dialogue and exchange of ideas among different levels of academic, research, business, and public communities.

The Program Committee received 52 paper submissions, out of which 20 research papers were finally accepted. We are particularly grateful therefore to the members of the Program Committee, and the many reviewers of papers, for their dedication in helping to produce this volume.

August 2017   Yuko Murayama
                                                             Dimiter Velev
                                                          Plamena Zlateva
                                                         Jose J. Gonzalez

Organization

General Chair

Dimiter Velev   University of National and World Economy, Bulgaria

Co-chairs

Yuko Murayama   IFIP Vice President, Japan
Jose J. Gonzalez   University of Agder, Norway

Finance Chair

Eduard Dundler   IFIP Secretary, Austria

Publicity Chair

Jun Sasaki   Iwate Prefectural University, Japan

Steering Committee

Yuko Murayama   IFIP Vice President, Japan
Diane Whitehouse   IFIP TC9 : ICT and Society Chair, UK
Erich Neuhold   IFIP TC5 : Information Technology Application Chair,
                            Austria
Jose G. Gonzalez   University of Agder, Norway
A Min Tjoa   IFIP Honoray Secretary, Austria
Plamena Zlateva   Institute of Robotics, Bulgarian Academy of Sciences,
                            Bulgaria
Dimiter Velev   University of National and World Economy, Bulgaria

Program Committee

Andreas Karcher   Universität der Bundeswehr, Germany
Andreas Prinz   University of Agder, Norway
Bjørn Erik Munkvold   University of Agder, Norway
Chrisantha Silva   Computer Society of Sri Lanka, Sri Lanka
Denis Trcek   University of Ljubljana, Slovenia
Edgar Weipel   Secure Business Austria, Austria
Eliot Rich   University at Albany, USA
Elsa Negre   Lamsade, Université Paris, Dauphine, France
Frederick Benaben   École Nationale Supérieure des Mines d'Albi-Carmaux,
                            France

Contents

Understanding the Importance of Proper Incentives for Critical Infrastructures Management – How System Dynamics Can Help

Denis Trček[1] and Jose J. Gonzalez[2(✉)]

[1] Laboratory of e-media, Faculty of Computer and Information Science, University of Ljubljana, Večna pot 113, 1000 Ljubljana, Slovenia
denis.trcek@fri.uni-lj.si
[2] Centre for Integrated Emergency Management, University of Agder, 4898 Grimstad, Norway
josejg@uia.no

Abstract. Computer and information systems are now at the core of numerous critical infrastructures. However, their security management is by far not a trivial issue. Further, these systems, by their very nature, belong to the domain of complex systems, where system dynamics (SD) is an established method, which aims at modelling such systems, their analysis and understanding. Further, on this basis it enables simulation of various policies to properly manage complex systems. More precisely, through understanding of the basic elements of the whole mosaic and their interplay, proper incentives can be tested. And this is important, because proper incentives can lead to the desired patterns of behavior of such systems, which may often be counter-intuitive. Therefore this paper presents a novel approach by using SD for managing critical infrastructures (more precisely the internet) when it comes to security related incentives. Based on already developed archetypes it provides a template model that bridges these conceptual models with concrete models that are suited to particular environments, and enable quantitative simulations.

Keywords: Critical infrastructures · Policies · Management · Modeling and simulation

1 Introduction

Proper incentives that are implemented through policies or regulation are very vital for complex systems management as they often lead to counterintuitive or even unwanted consequences. History provides many such examples. In 1920, the US government implemented very strict alcohol production, distribution and consumption prohibition legislation. The effects were at least surprising. Strong alcoholic drinks started to flourish (in particular gin), as they were easier to transport and sell secretly than weak alcoholic drinks (for the same effect for consumers). Before this legislation, pubs were almost exclusively visited by men. But when illegal market appeared women often accompanied men at the selling spots – and so they started to consume alcohol, too.

Y. Murayama et al. (Eds.): ITDRR 2016, IFIP AICT 501, pp. 1–8, 2017.
https://doi.org/10.1007/978-3-319-68486-4_1

But probably the most unwanted effect was that black market became increasingly controlled by the mafia. Consequently, its power increased, and the mafia became and remained a very strong player due to this source of income even after 1933 when President Roosevelt banned the legislation of alcohol prohibition [1].

This is by far not the only case of an incentive which has resulted in completely unwanted consequences. Some recent incentives that are likely to result in unwanted effects (based on evidence and lessons learnt in the respective field) are those by the US government where flooding-prone areas are declared as safe despite the evidence of the contrary (being stimulated by a wish to picture "normal" conditions in an endangered areas) [2].

Now getting to critical infrastructures, in particular communications – computer and information systems security incidents are a consequence of interplay of numerous inter-related factors. Among those factors, human based ones are often at the core of related problems. And proper policies – more precisely, proper incentives – may have a strong impact as to the desired outcomes here as well. One widely known example is the case of ATMs security in the banking sector. When it came to a dispute between a customer and a bank because of a fraud, the burden of proof was put on the banks in the US case, while in Europe, the burden was put on customers. Counterintuitively, the final result was that the overall ATM security was better in the US than in Europe (and all this at lower costs). The core of reasoning was that banks are easier to put appropriate prevention measures in place due to their knowledge and economic power. Put another way, those who should knew better and have more power in their hands should be primarily in charge [3].

Therefore proper incentives are clearly important and they should be carefully studied. As this is easier said than done (one should think only about experimenting with various incentives in real, large scale, environments), appropriate methods that could provide steps into the right direction are much desired. Put another way, to foster aligned incentives it is much desired to have tools for their verification, or at least for playing with associated scenarios to figure out what the unwanted effects of these incentives could be. And this is the main contribution of this paper that is focused on critical infrastructures management, more precisely, cybersecurity. The paper builds on System Dynamics (SD) that has a long and proven track record in various areas of complex systems, including their management. Not only that it enables understanding of complex dynamic systems in a very intuitive way (which is very fine for non-experts), it also enables their modeling and validation (to support with scientific rigor appropriate decision making procedures and management).

This paper presents further steps in the direction of using SD to improve critical infrastructures systems security through aligned incentives. Therefore in the second section the basics related to incentives are given. In the third section the further extension of archetypes is given that results in a template model, which can be adapted to particular cases in a quantitative way. Discussion comes next, being followed by conclusions in the fourth section. The paper is concluded by references.

2 Understanding the Battlefield Landscape

Traditional economics and security relationship was pointed at already years ago in the pioneering papers written by Anderson and Moore [4–7]. Summing up the main messages of these works is as follows:

– With current IT technology, attacks are easier than defense. Suppose that a software solution has 1,000 bugs, and for each of those the MTBF is 1,000 h. Suppose further that a defending user of this software wants to patch it as much as possible and invests 10,000 h in testing per year. In one year the defender will therefore find (on average) 10 bugs. On the other hand, the attacker can afford only 1,000 h of testing per year, and will therefore find (on average) only 1 bug. Now one can easily calculate the low odds that this last bug will be one of those 10 ones discovered by the defender.

– Asymmetric information, as applied to ordinary economics by Akerloff, is playing its role also in case of IT solutions [8]. Suppose an experienced vendor offers 10 good security assuring products at 200 EUR each, while another option are 10 weak security products at 100 EUR each. Clearly, a vendor can (or is likely able to) tell the good from bad, but buyers cannot. According to Akerloff, users are rational (which is often not the case cases in reality) giving the starting price at 150 EUR based on the assumption that they are going to get with equally probability a good or a bad product. At this price the seller is motivated to sell only the weak product, so the spiral of negative market selection process is started.

– Network externalities effects stimulate, among others, producers to get on market as soon as possible, which put a pressure on extensive security testing. Thus "get on the market first and do the fixing later" is often a dominant strategy to enable the "get big fast" effect. Further, due to the reinforcing loop of these effects, the winner takes it all situation starts and the landscape becomes more and more uniform. Further, security is often a barrier in usability terms, so even when it is available, the product is configured by default in a rather moderate way. As a consequence, the increasing proportion of systems is becoming susceptible to the same kinds of attacks, so any kind of "epidemics" becomes a natural threat.

To remedy this kind of situation Anderson and Tyler propose avoiding the principle of misaligned incentives, which relate to allocation of security risks. Put simply, those that are most responsible (or in a privileged position) for providing security are usually the least affected by negative consequences. As already mentioned, one typical example where the testing of this claim proved as correct is ATM and credit card frauds.

Based on the above described lessons learned, the following non-technical counter-measures have been proposed:

– Ex ante regulation instead of ex post liability – simply put, involved entities ae liable for their products and services [7].

– Related information disclosure – involved entities should be stimulated to disclose security related information, ranging from found bugs (which is already happening [9]) to aggregated or estimated loss figures (which is yet to be implemented on a wider scale). This issue is closely related to enabling cyber insurance for taking appropriate precautions that would result in better and more consistent data statistics. An interesting variant of this idea is liability in case of Digital Millennium Copyright Act (DMCA). Here in case of a copyright infringement an internet service provider (IS) is not automatically liable. However, it becomes liable if, upon notification, it does not remove or block the distribution of copyrighted material [7].

- Accreditation and education level requirements – software engineers and programmers should become subject to accreditation requirements and related procedures. It is rather surprising that the essence that runs at the heart of today's critical infrastructures (i.e., software) can be designed and implemented by virtually anyone. Something like this is unimaginable in other important domains like medicine, jurisprudence, and civil engineering, to name a few [10].

There are likely other options for counter-measures – see, e.g., [11, 12]. And to further identify them it helps to ask oneself the following question: "Which are the motivations for people that would stimulate them to act in a way that would improve security of the internet?"

3   System Dynamics and Evaluation of Proper Management Policies

System dynamics (SD) is now an established research and application method that has a proven track record in many areas. As briefly described in [13], system dynamics addresses people, processes, material and information flows by emphasizing the importance of feedback loops. These feedback loops are the major cause for the behavior of (mainly non-linear) dynamic systems.

The modelling starts with a qualitative stage where basic variables are identified and linked accordingly. Through iteration stages the model is improved and the above mentioned causal loops emerge in more and more refined form (consequently, these models are also referred to as causal loop diagrams). As to the links among variables, they have positive polarity if an increase (decrease) of causal variable results in an increase (decrease) of the consecutive variable. But if the output variable is decreased (increased) by an increase (decrease) of the input variable, the polarity is negative.

To obtain models that can be simulated one must transition from causal loop diagrams, where one does not distinguish between different kind of variables, and stock-and-flow models. In the stock-and-flow model version, variables are divided into auxiliary ones and accumulators (also referred to as levels or stocks), where levels play special roles in a system. First, they are the source of inertia. Second, they constitute a kind of primitive memory within the system – an aggregate of past events. Third, they serve as absorbers, and decouple inflows from outflows.

The causal loop diagram provides a holistic view of the system, and enables a better understanding of the basic principles of its functioning. As indicated above, such a causal loop model is usually further elaborated to obtain a quantitative stock-and-flow model. In a stock-and-flow model concrete relationships between variables are established through the introduction of appropriate equations. The model at this stage is ready for calibration based on real data, and use for system simulation and policies derivation.

In order to provide additional insights into incentives issues, and enable appropriate counter-measures that would improve critical communications infrastructure security, appropriate conceptual and template model(s) would be useful. This has been shown to be the case with many other areas addressed by SD like market penetration of a product, infections spreading, and so on.

Now as to conceptual models – for our particular domain two key system archetype models have already been developed [10]. However, archetype models are a special category of causal loop diagrams [14, 15]. They are purely qualitative models with an intention to provide only the basic understanding of the core of a phenomenon at hand. But in order to obtain a quantitative model (that is usually at the top of the agenda) one still needs to fill the gap with so called template models, which identify not only the core variables (factors), but also the related complementary variables, and the nature of the involved variables.

3.1   The Template Model Preliminaries

Now which could be the main motivations of people when it comes, in general, to ensuring security of the internet? Among the main motivation groups are those about avoiding bad reputation (being an unreliable partner, a partner causing damage ...), those about avoiding penalties (being charged, being arrested, being disconnected from the internet ...), and those that are about preventing unnecessary or excessive costs (how much to invest in security in order to not to invest too much). This is, of course, not the exhaustive set of possibilities, but it is sufficient to enable derivation of the desired template model.

3.2   The Template Model

In line with the above described reasoning, there are four lines along which the needed SD template model is to be built: The first one is the core of the problem, which is the lifecycle of vulnerabilities and related threats. The second line is the actions line, which is actually in close interplay with the third line, the line of incentives (policies) that are at the core of the analysis. The fourth line is the "final judgment line", i.e., the line that quantifies the success of implemented incentive (policies) in terms of financial gain or loss.

Now the explanation along the horizontal lines follows that sticks with the internal logic of the observed system(s). The vulnerabilities line starts with vulnerabilities production rate. These are vulnerabilities that are a side product of each system design and they remain silent as potential vulnerabilities until they become discovered. Depending on their discovery rate, the appropriate proportion of potential vulnerabilities becomes a recognized fact, i.e., vulnerabilities with an active damage potential. As an active vulnerability is in principle not an isolated one, this active vulnerability typically leads to additional (cascaded) vulnerabilities. These latter vulnerabilities are usually not immediately recognized; therefore they fill the accumulation of the potential vulnerabilities. The vulnerabilities line ends with the sink of active vulnerabilities that are eliminated due to being fixed or becoming irrelevant (e.g., when the technology is changed) (Fig. 1).

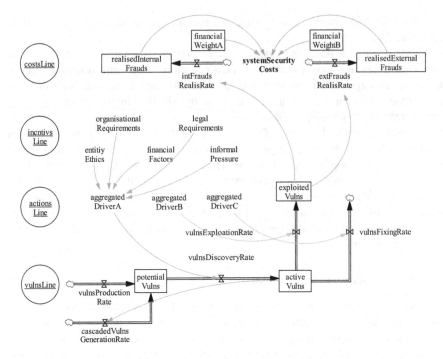

Fig. 1. The template model with the layered factors and their interdependencies

The next line is actions line, where aggregated effects of incentives (from the third, policy line) play the key role. Aggregated drivers are linked to appropriate flows and actually "turn into reality" the dynamics of the observed system (note that for a better clarity only the links for aggregated driver are given). Depending on how successfully we manage the key rates (i.e., the vulnerabilities discovery rate, the vulnerabilities exploitation rate and the vulnerabilities fixing rate) the extent of exploited vulnerabilities is obtained. And using according financial weights the total security cost (that is due to exploits) is obtained. A cautious reader may see that the total security costs could be obtained by taking into account also costs of organizational requirements, informal pressures, and so on (indicated, but not further detailed in the model).

4 Discussion

The above template model per se is still a qualitative one – but with a difference from its archetype counterparts. First, it enables deeper understanding of all variables that are driving the phenomenon at hand within the community. Second, it serves as a building block that can be turned straightforwardly into a full-blown quantitative model, which can be tested – and tuned accordingly – based on real data. Actually, such template models (although they are referred to as template models here for the first time) are crucial parts of system dynamics arsenal. This arsenal contains not only basic models (like, e.g., the core logistic curve model) but also their more elaborated variants (like, e.g., the Bass Diffusion Model) [16]. And this latter is actually a kind of a template model.

The reason for such step by step approach is rather evident – every model needs to be fine-tuned to a specific case with particular variables. But getting real data to obtain quantified cyber-security models is not a trivial task – on the contrary. So making security measurable is high on the agenda for quite some years. Although the situation is still not an ideal one, it should be stated that some notable advancements have been done in this area, mostly due to MITRE Corp. initiative called Making Security Measurable MITRE Corp. [9].

We anticipate that right at this point template models will provide additional advantage. Their elaboration within the community (as this is normally the case) is expected to result in one or more stable representatives, where it will be clearly visible, which variables (still) need to be collected, what the nature of these variables is, and how they can be tested for consistency. Not to mention that such situation would be already very close to automation of related processes, including testing of incentives.

5 Conclusions

It is known for a long time that cyber security is not just a matter of technical issues, but at least as much a matter of issues that include economics elements and agents' motives. These issues are all subject to incentives, and when properly aligned, these incentives may result in effective (although often counterintuitive) consequences that lead to improved security of targeted systems at lower costs. One typical example is the case of ATM frauds as a result of different incentives in the US and EU – while in the first case the burden of proof was put on banks, in the second case it was put on customers. But surprisingly, US banks had lower frauds number, and the total security costs was lower.

The above instructive case is the main motive behind this paper that is about aligned incentives for improving cyber-security. By using system dynamics we have extended the related artefact models with a template model that fills the gap towards quantitative models, which can be calibrated with real data, so the incentives can be verified accordingly. By doing so proper alignment of incentives is enabled through testing of various policies and their consequences before being implemented in reality.

References

1. Bastable, J., Mason, A., Allan, T.: Great Secrets of History. The Reader's Digest Assoc., London (2012)
2. Horowitz, A.: New Orlean's new flood maps: an outline for disaster. The New York Times, Opinion Today, 1 June 2016
3. Anderson, R.: Security Engineering. John Wiley and Sons, New York (2001)
4. Anderson, R.: Why information security is hard? An economic perspective. In: Proceedings of the 17th Computer Security Applications Conference, ASAC 2001, IEEE (2001)
5. Anderson, R.: The economics of information security. Science **314**(AAA), 610–613 (2006)

6. Anderson, R.: Information security: where computer science, economics and psychology meet. Philos. Trans. Royal Soc. **367**, 2717–2727 (2009)
7. Moore, T.: The economics of cybersecurity: principles and policy options. Int. J. Critical Infrastruct. Prot. **2**, 103–117 (2010). Elsevier
8. Akerlof, G.: The market for lemons: qualitative uncertainty and the market mechanism. Quart. J. Econ. **84**(3), 488–500 (1970)
9. MITRE Corp.: Making Security Measurable, https://makingsecuritymeasurable.mitre.org/. Accessed 6th May 2016
10. Gonzalez, J.J., Trček, D.: Proper incentives for proper IT security management - a system dynamics approach, HICSS 2017, Hawai (2017)
11. Arief, B., Bin Adzmi, M.A., Gross, T.: Understanding cybersecurity from its stakeholders' perspective. Secur. Priv. **15**(1), 71–76 (2015). IEEE
12. Arief, B., Bin Adzmi, M.A., Gross, T.: Understanding cybersecurity from its stakeholders' perspective - defenses and victims. Secur. Priv. **15**(1), 84–88 (2015). IEEE
13. Trček, D., Trobec, R., Pavešič, N., Tasič, J.: Information systems security and human behavior. Behav. Inf. Technol. **26**(2), 113–118 (2007). Taylor Francis
14. Senge, P.: The Fifth Discipline. Doubleday, New York (1990)
15. Wolstenholme, E.F.: Towards the definition and use of a core set of archetypal structures in system dynamics. Syst. Dyn. Rev. **19**(7), 7–26 (2003)
16. Sterman, J.: Business Dynamics. McGraw-Hill, New York (2004)

A Proposal on Patient Transport Decision Making in Multiple Hospitals in a Large-Scale Disaster

Jun Sasaki[(✉)]

Faculty of Software and Information Science, Iwate Prefectural University,
Iwate, Japan
jsasaki@iwate-pu.ac.jp

Abstract. In 2011, the Great East Japan Earthquake and Tsunami destroyed three prefectural hospitals in Iwate Prefecture, Japan. The author interviewed officers working in the Iwate Medical Central Office as well as medical doctors working in public hospitals, of which there are 25 in Iwate Prefecture. Based on the interviews and several reports this paper describes the problem of patient transport in a large-scale disaster. In such situations, the decision making process is confusing, making it difficult to transport patients efficiently from hospitals in the disaster areas to supporting hospitals. This paper proposes a new decision making method to solve the problem of patient transport. The simulation results of a risk analysis comparing the proposed method with conventional methods are presented.

Keywords: Disaster information · Emergency management · Patient transport · Medical information · Decision making

1 Introduction

The Great East Japan Earthquake and Tsunami occurred on 11 March 2011. It destroyed many buildings and killed many people in the Tohoku area of Japan [1]. There are many studies on large-scale disasters, including research into disaster communications [2, 3] and information systems [4]. There are also many reports on medical diseases caused by large-scale disasters [5–11]. However, there are few reports on emergency medical activities during large-scale disaster situations. This paper surveyed Iwate Prefectural hospitals' emergency response activities during the Great East Japan Earthquake and Tsunami by interviewing medical doctors of Iwate Prefectural hospitals and officers of Iwate Medical Center and analyzing obtained reports and documents on the disaster affecting. One of the main problems was that the decision making process was confusing, making it difficult to transport patients efficiently from hospitals in the disaster areas to supporting hospitals. This paper proposes a new decision making method for patient transport to solve this problem.

Y. Murayama et al. (Eds.): ITDRR 2016, IFIP AICT 501, pp. 9–19, 2017.
https://doi.org/10.1007/978-3-319-68486-4_2

2 Damage Situation of Iwate Prefectural Hospitals

Iwate Prefecture is the largest prefecture on Honshu, a main island of Japan. The area is approximately 15,280 km^2, spanning 200 km from north to south and 150 km from east to west. Iwate Prefecture is surrounded by mountains and there are few means of public transport within the region. As such, there are 25 public hospitals throughout Iwate Prefecture, the largest number among Japanese prefectures. All 25 public hospitals are managed by the Iwate Prefectural Medical Office.

Figure 1 shows the locations and damage situations of Iwate prefectural hospitals on 14 March 2011. The hospitals can be classified into two groups: inland-area hospitals and seacoast-area hospitals. A large mountainous area, called the Kitakami Sanchi, sits between the two hospital group areas.

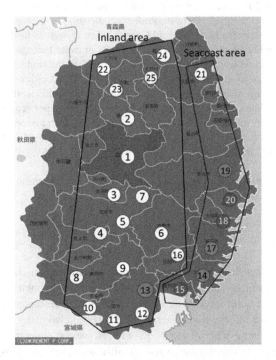

Fig. 1. Damage situation of Iwate prefectural hospitals during the 2011 Great East Japan Disaster

In Fig. 1, each hospital is identified by a number. The seacoast-area hospitals were damaged to various degrees by the large tsunami. Hospitals 15, 18 and 20 were classified as completely damaged, whereas hospitals 13, 14, 17 and 19 were damaged but functional. These functional damaged hospitals accepted and supported patients from completely damaged hospital areas. They needed and received support from surrounding undamaged hospitals; for example, hospital 13 was supported by hospital 12 (see Fig. 1).

The author interviewed two medical doctors, one from a functional damaged hospital (ID = 14) and another from a supporting hospital (ID = 4). They were key person and the two doctors played important roles at the time of the disaster. According to the reports from the Iwate Prefectural Medical Office, functional damaged hospitals had problems with telecommunications, electricity (including fuel for an auxiliary power generator), water, chemical and medical materials, and food; however, those problems were addressed within three days.

In completely damaged hospital areas, there was a need for clothing, gasoline, portable heating units, food, toiletries, blankets, medicine, diapers and oxygen tanks. Most of those needs were eventually met and requested items were provided by the government, as well as volunteer and support groups.

For several minutes after the earthquake on 11 March 2011, all communications to/from seacoast-area hospital 14 were disrupted; however, the hospital was able to use the emergency wireless phone provided by Iwate Prefecture and the satellite phone provided by the Nippon Telephone and Telegram Corporation. Staff at the hospital connected those telephone lines with the hospital's private wireless phone system. The doctor interviewed for this study stated that the temporary telephone system proved useful during the disaster.

In an emergency meeting after the disaster, the doctor's team planned their disaster response strategy using whiteboards, which they filled with text, tables, figures and maps. When the whiteboards were completely covered, the staff took photos of the boards, erased them and filled them with new text. Thus, they created a record of their activities during the disaster. The second interviewee stated that staff at inland-area hospital 4 wrote on building doors and walls, as well as a whiteboard during an emergency meeting; it was important to make a wide space and tools available for writing.

In Japan, most hospitals use the Emergency Medical Information System (EMIS) to access information about disasters [12]. A color-coded map of Japan on EMIS indicates which areas are: experiencing a disaster; in a state of vigilance; receiving disaster assistance; or training for the early disaster response. In the case of a large-scale disaster, Disaster Medical Assistance Teams (DMATs) are immediately dispatched to the damaged area by helicopters or cars. After the 2011 disaster, DMAT members from various countries as well as those from other parts of Japan arrived at the damaged areas. However, inland-area hospital staff could not determine the number of DMATs that had arrived at the seacoast-area hospitals. In fact, at that time, the Iwate Prefectural Medical Office did not know that 19 DMATs (83 members in total) were operating in hospital 14 during the disaster period.

3 Patient Transport from Damaged Hospitals to Supporting Hospitals

In the Japan disaster of 11 March 2011, many patients in seacoast area of Iwate Prefecture were transported to inland-area hospitals, which were better equipped to provide medical care, using ambulances and helicopters.

Figure 2 shows the number of inbound patients per month transported from seacoast-area hospitals to inland-area hospital 4. The number of patients transported decreased rapidly after the disaster. In the early disaster response period, the number of patients transported by helicopter transport was relatively large (50% of ambulance transport).

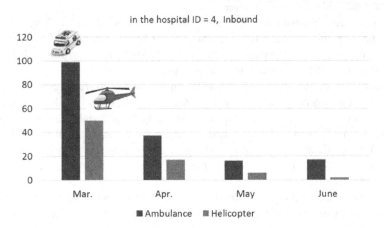

Fig. 2. Number of inbound patients transported from seacoast-area hospitals to inland-area hospital 4.

Figure 3 shows the number of outbound patients transported from seacoast-area hospital 14 to inland-area hospitals. Most of those patients were transported by ambulance in March 2011.

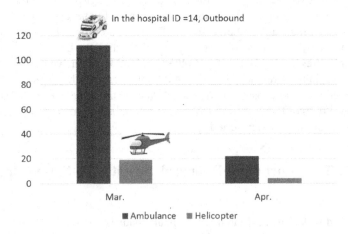

Fig. 3. Number of outbound patients transported from seacoast-area hospital 14 to inland-area hospitals

Table 1 shows the number of patients transported between Iwate prefectural hospitals from 11 March to 31 March 2011. The number of patients transported from sea-coast area hospitals 14, 17 and 19, and the number of received patients at inland-area hospitals 1, 2, 4, 6, 8 and 12 was large (>10). According to the interviewee from seacoast-area hospital 14, the complex arrangement of patient transport was carried out on an individual basis via telephone and facsimile. Ideally, patient transport should be carried out immediately and intensively after a disaster using many ambulance cars and helicopters. Rapid decision making is required to transport patients in large-scale disaster situations. However, it can be difficult to quickly decide on the destinations for patient transport in an emergency case. This study aims to develop a rapid decision making method for patient transport in large-scale disaster situations. The remainder of this paper introduces a case study and the proposed patient transport method for Iwate prefectural hospitals.

Table 1. Number of patients transported between Iwate prefectural hospitals (from a seacoast-area hospital to an inland-area hospital) from 11 March to 31 March 2011.

Seacoast-area hospital ID	Inland-area hospital ID									
	1	2	4	5	6	8	9	12	23	Total
14	3				15	6	3	29		56
15	2		4	4						10
17	16		68	1	56	17	6			164
19	33	11	5							49
20									6	6
Total	54	11	77	5	71	23	9	29	6	285

4 Patient Transport in March 2011

The method of patient transport is usually decided according to the patient condition, transportation time and number of patients able to be accepted by the destination hospital. If the number of patients is large, as is often the case during a large-scale disaster, patients must be transported rapidly to supporting hospitals without thorough consideration of each patient's condition.

Table 2 shows the average transportation time (minutes) by car between seacoast-area hospitals (column) and inland-area hospitals (line) in Iwate Prefecture. The "ID" numbers correspond to the same hospitals as in Fig. 1. Transport time (minutes) was calculated as the shortest distance between hospitals according to Google Maps.

Table 3 shows the number of patients able to be accepted by supporting hospitals.

Figure 4 shows the actual number of patient transfers after the large tsunami. This figure is based on the numbers shown in Table 1. Arrows indicate the destination of the patient transfer, and the arrow thickness indicates the number of transport patients. Hospitals 17 and 14 are relatively large hospitals. During the Great East Japan Earthquake and Tsunami disaster if 2011, medical doctors at the disaster site negotiated with supporting hospitals on patient transfers on a case by case basis. The first problem

Table 2. Usual transportation time (minutes) between seacoast area hospitals (column) and inland-area hospitals (line) in Iwate Prefecture by car.

ID	1	2	4	5	6	8	9	10	12	21	22	23	24
14	118	137	87	74	64	86	79	91	76	208	168	156	172
15	113	135	85	73	61	75	77	72	52	206	166	155	170
17	110	133	83	70	41	94	81	117	106	182	164	152	167
19	123	165	149	136	106	163	147	187	178	97	159	194	138
20	128	170	133	120	91	147	131	159	142	126	188	186	167

Table 3. Usual transportation time (minutes) between seacoast area hospitals (column) and inland-area hospitals (line) in Iwate Prefecture by car.

ID	1	2	4	5	6	8	9	10	12	21	22	23	24
14	118	137	87	74	64	86	79	91	76	208	168	156	172
15	113	135	85	73	61	75	77	72	52	206	166	155	170
17	110	133	83	70	41	94	81	117	106	182	164	152	167
19	123	165	149	136	106	163	147	187	178	97	159	194	138
20	128	170	133	120	91	147	131	159	142	126	188	186	167

with that process was that it required a long time and represented a burden to the doctors who were needed for the decision making regarding patient transport. The second problem was a lack of coordination. As shown in Table 3, for example, although one hospital (ID = 5) had no capacity to accept further patients, 5 patients were transported to that hospital.

5 Proposed Method

In the above case, doctors in damaged hospitals had to negotiate with several hospitals to decide on the hospital to which to transport the patient. As mentioned, this process was time consuming and required considerable effort on the part of the doctors. In the case of a large-scale disaster, this type of negotiation is not feasible because many patients need to be transported.

This paper proposes calculating the risk for each destination hospital, selecting the hospital with the lowest risk, and transporting the patient to that hospital without negotiation. Here, risk is determined based on the transport time and the number of patients able to be accepted by the supporting hospital. The value of risk (r_k) of supporting hospital k is calculated using following equation.

$$r_k = T_{tk}/N_{ak} \tag{1}$$

where Ttk is the transportation time between the damaged hospital and the supporting hospital (ID = k), and Nak is the number of patients able to be accepted by the supporting hospital (ID = k).

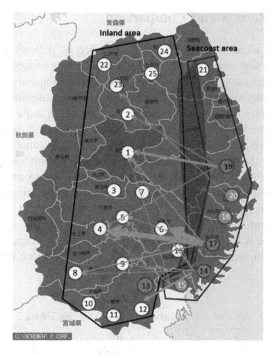

Fig. 4. Map of patient transportation from 11 March to 31 March 2011.

Table 4 shows the value of risk, which is calculated by Eq. (1) using transportation time (minutes) shown in Table 2 and the number of acceptable patient given in Table 3. There are four obviously high-risk hospitals (ID = 2, 5, 9 and 24). These hospitals are removed from the candidate pool of destination hospitals. The number of transport patients (n_{ak}) from the damaged hospital (ID = a) to the supporting hospital (ID = k) can be calculated using the following equation.

$$n_{ak} = \frac{N_a}{r_{ak} \sum_{i=1}^{n} \frac{1}{r_{ai}}} \tag{2}$$

Table 4. Number of patients able to be accepted by supporting hospitals

ID	1	2	4	5	6	8	9	10	12	21	22	23	24	Total
Na	157	5	78	0	12	80	3	64	59	41	40	36	5	580

where N is the total number of patients in the damaged hospitals, n is the total number of supporting hospitals, and r_{ak} is the value of risk of transportation from a damaged hospital (ID = a) to a supporting hospital (ID = k).

6 Simulation Results and Comparison

Table 5 shows the simulation results of the number of patients transported from affected hospitals to supporting hospitals based on the proposed method. The numbers of patients transported using the conventional method are compared with those derived using the proposed method. In previous method, supporting hospitals 2, 5, 6 and 9 had exceeded their capacity for acceptable number of patients. In those hospitals, patients might have had to be transported to other hospitals. In contrast, using the proposed method, patients were transported to hospitals with sufficient capacity to admit them.

Figure 5 shows the simulation results of patient transport using the proposed method. This figure is based on the calculation results shown in Table 4. Arrows indicate the destination of the patient transports, and the arrow thickness indicates the number of patients transported. We can see that the patient transport is distributed more widely among supporting hospitals compared with Fig. 4. If helicopters can be used, the transport distance is less of an issue compared with hospital capacity. Therefore, in the proposed method, acceptable capacity is more highly prioritized than transport distance.

Table 5. Value of risk calculated by Eq. (1) using Tables 2 and 3.

ID	1	2	4	5	6	8	9	10	12	21	22	23	24
14	0.752	27.4	1.115	-	5.333	1.075	26.33	1.422	1.288	5.073	4.20	4.333	34.4
15	0.720	27.0	1.090	-	5.083	0.938	25.67	1.125	0.881	5.024	4.15	4.306	34.0
17	0.701	26.6	1.064	-	3.417	1.175	27.00	1.828	1.797	4.439	4.10	4.222	33.4
19	0.783	33.0	1.910	-	8.833	2.038	49.00	2.922	3.017	2.366	3.975	5.389	27.6
20	0.815	34.0	1.705	-	7.583	1.838	43.67	2.484	2.407	3.073	4.70	5.167	33.4

The number of arrows, indicating transfers to destination hospitals, is greater in proposed model (see Fig. 5) compared with the current method (see Fig. 4). However, in a large-scale disaster situation, there is no time to carry out conventional negotiations. Because the time is the highest priority, patients should be transported from damaged hospitals to supporting hospitals as soon as possible. Before such transfers can take place, supporting hospitals and damaged hospitals must provide information to a control center in the area regarding the number of patients able to be accepted and those to be transported, respectively. The control center would allocate the patients among supporting hospitals based on the proposed method. The proposed method of decision making will thus be more efficient than the conventional method (Table 6).

7 Backup and Sharing of Patient Information

Emergency medical services [12] comprise an organized and collaborative effort among several organizations to provide care in order to transport sick or injured patients to hospital. Although such collaboration is important, there is no time to make

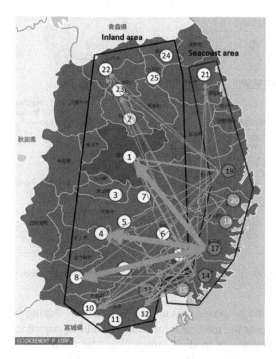

Fig. 5. Simulation results of patient transport using the proposed method.

Table 6. Value of risk calculated by Eq. (1) using Tables 2 and 3.

ID	Supportable hospitals													
	1	2	4	5	6	8	9	10	12	21	22	23	24	Total
Affected hospitals 14	14	-	10	-	2	9	-	7	8	2	2	2	-	56
15	3	-	2	-	0	2	-	1	2	0	0	0	-	10
17	44	-	29	-	9	26	-	17	17	7	8	7	-	164
19	16	-	8	-	1	6	-	4	4	5	3	2	-	49
20	2	-	1	-	0	1	-	1	1	0	0	0	-	6
(a) Proposed method	79	0	50	0	12	44	0	30	32	14	13	11	0	285
Total (a)/Na	50%	0%	64%	-	100%	55%	0%	47%	54%	34%	33%	31%	0%	49%
(b) Previous method	54	11	77	5	71	23	9	0	29	0	0	6	0	285
Total (b)/Na	34%	220%	99%	-	592%	29%	300%	0%	49%	0%	0%	17%	0%	49%
Na	157	5	78	0	12	80	3	64	59	41	40	36	5	580

decisions to transport individual patients in the case of large-scale disasters. In the large tsunami disaster of 11 March 2011 in Japan, three hospitals were completely destroyed, and many patients' medical records disappeared. To provide consistent emergency and long-term medical and health care service in a disaster area, it is important to backup and share patient data.

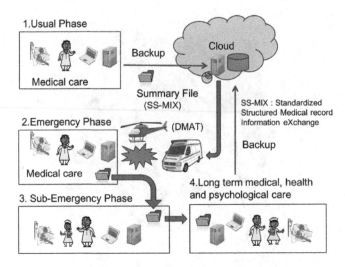

Fig. 6. Proposed backup and information sharing method.

Figure 6 shows the proposed backup and information sharing method.

The author proposes the medical information should be copied to a cloud server for backup purposes. The size of medical information files tends to be large, especially if they include medical image data. The author proposes using the standardized structured medical record information exchange (SS-MIX) system to backup patient data and restart medical care after a disaster. In case of an emergency, the supporting hospital can use the SS-MIX data in the cloud server, and medical care can resume immediately. These data can be used for the patients in the sub-emergency phase, such as those living in shelters or temporary housing. Further, it will be useful in the case of long-term health and psychological care.

8   Conclusions

This paper described the condition and emergency response activities of Iwate pre-fectural hospitals following the Great East Japan Earthquake and Tsunami disaster based on interviews and documents provided by two medical doctors and an officer from the Iwate Medical Central Office. A new method of decision making for patient transportation in the case of a large-scale disaster was proposed. The effectiveness of the proposed method was compared with current methods by simulation.

Patient transportation, medical information backup and information sharing issues in disaster situations warrant further study. The purpose of the study was to propose an efficient decision making process and data storage/sharing system that can be applied in large-scale disaster situations in Iwate Prefecture, other areas of Japan and other nations.

Acknowledgments. The author would like to thank Professor Yuko Murayama of Tsuda College, for fruitful discussions. The author also deeply appreciates the participation of the two doctors from Iwate prefectural hospitals and officers from the Iwate Prefectural Medical Office who provided interviews and significant reports, respectively. The names of the interviewees and hospitals are omitted for anonymity. This research was supported by JSPS KAKENHI Grant Number 15K01950.

References

1. Norio, O., Kajitani, Y., Shi, P., Tatano, H.: The 2011 Eastern Japan great Earthquake disaster: overview and comments. Int. J. Disaster Risk Sci. **2**(1), 34–42 (2011)
2. Murayama, Y.: Issues in disaster communications. J. Inf. Process. **22**(4), 558–565 (2014)
3. Wilensky, H.: Twitter as a navigator for stranded commuters during the great East Japan Earthquake. In: Proceedings of the 11th International ISCRAM Conference-University Park, Pennsylvania, USA, May 2014
4. Van De Walle, B., Turoff, M., Hiltz, S.R. (eds.): Information System for Emergency Management. AMIS. M.E. Sharpe, Inc., Armonk (2010)
5. Aoki, T., Fukumoto, Y., Yasuda, S., Sakata, Y., Ito, K., Takahashi, J., Miyata, S., Tsuji, I., Shimokawa, H.: The great East Japan Earthquake disaster and cardiovascular disease. Eur. Heart J. **33**, 2796–2803 (2012)
6. Yamada, S., Hanagama, M., Kobayashi, S., Satou, H., Tokuda, S., Niu, K., Yanai, M.: The impact of the 2011 Great East Japan Earthquake on hospitalization for respiratory disease in a rapidly aging society: a retrospective descriptive and cross-sectional study at the disaster base hospital in Ishinomaki. BMJ Open **3**, e000865 (2013). https://doi.org/10.1136/bmjopen-2012-000865
7. Ogawa, S., Ishiki, M., Nako, K., Okamura, M., Senda, M., Sakamoto, T., Ito, S.: Effects of the Great East Japan Earthquake and huge tsunami on glycaemic control and blood pressure in patients with diabetes mellitus. BMJ Open **2**, e000830 (2012). https://doi.org/10.1136/bmjopen-2012-000830
8. Takahashi, T., Goto, M., Yoshida, H., Sumino, H., Matsui, H.: Infectious disease after the 2011 great East Japan Earthquake. J. Exp. Clin. Med. **4**(1), 20–23 (2012)
9. Leor, J., Poole, W.K., Kloner, R.A.: Sudden cardiac death triggered by an Earthquake. New Engl. J. Med. **334**, 413–419 (1996)
10. Nohara, M.: Impact of the great East Japan Earthquake and Tsunami on health, medical care and public health systems in Iwate Prefecture, Japan, 2011. WPSAR **2**(4) (2011)
11. Schooley, B., Murad, A., Abed, Y., Horan, T.: A mHealth system for patient handover in emergency medical services. In: Proceedings of the 10th International ISCRAM Conference, Baden-Baden, Germany, May 2013
12. Emergency Medical Information System (Japanese), 9 September 2015. https://www.wds.emis.go.jp/

Urban Disaster Simulation Incorporating Human Psychological Models in Evacuation Behaviors

Tatsuya Yamazaki[1,2(✉)], Hiroyuki Tamai[1,2], Yasunori Owada[3],
Kiyohiko Hattori[3], Shin'ichi Taira[3], and Kiyoshi Hamaguchi[4]

[1] Princeton University, Princeton, NJ 08544, USA
[2] Graduate School of Science and Technology,
Niigata University, Niigata, Japan
yamazaki@ie.niigata-u.ac.jp
[3] Resilient ICT Research Center, National Institute of Information
and Communications Technology, Sendai, Japan
[4] Wireless Networks Research Center, National Institute of Information
and Communications Technology, Yokosuka, Japan

Abstract. Building evacuation simulation provides us with various knowledge and suggestion before a real disaster happens. To date, however, evacuees were often modeled as homogeneous without individual motivation in a large-scale urban simulation model, which is rather different from real human behavior. In this paper, an evacuation simulation model with human psychological models is developed for urban disaster situation. Three psychological models are actually incorporated: normalcy bias, emotional contagion bias, and sympathy behavior bias. Normalcy bias is the initial evacuation delay caused by a belief that abnormal events rarely happen. Emotional contagion is the effect of one person's emotional state on the emotional state of people around him/her both explicitly and implicitly. Simulated experimental results show that the proposed model provides accurate evacuation behaviors than the normal behavior model without psychological consideration.

Keywords: Disaster · Evacuation · Multi-agent system · Psychological model

1 Introduction

As one of the largest disasters, the Great East Japan Earthquake and its following Tsunami are memorable, which resulted in losing about 15,900 lives and missing about 2,900 people [1]. When such disasters including not only earthquakes but also hurricanes, floods, and so on occur at a populated area, damage will become huge and tremendous. Recently, since computing power is available at a low cost and GIS (Geographic Information System) is developed, computer simulations have become a powerful tool to prepare disasters. Namely, computer simulations may enable us to find out a bottleneck point when people are evacuating or to educate people which is a better evacuation way.

Y. Murayama et al. (Eds.): ITDRR 2016, IFIP AICT 501, pp. 20–30, 2017.
https://doi.org/10.1007/978-3-319-68486-4_3

MAS (Multi-agent System) is a popular scheme to simulate a disaster situation on a computer platform. MAS contains an environment, objects, and agents. In MAS, an agent can be a physical or virtual entity that can act, perceive its environment (in a partial way) and communicate with others [2]. The agents are autonomous and relations between the agents as well as a set of operations that can be performed by the agents can be defined.

Agent behaviors can be physically reproduced through computer simulations using MAS. Though evacuation models built on GIS obey physical rules defined on buildings, roads, railways, etc., important psychological parameters are not frequently used [3]. In addition, evacuating agents are often modeled as homogeneous without individual motivation in a large-scale urban simulation model, which is rather different from real human behavior. Modeling psychological variables will enhance prediction of human behavior during evacuations. Apart from MAS, there is a previous research that designs and analyzed evacuation routes in transportation networks in cases of natural disasters [4]. Therein, a method for defining two independent paths from the disaster area to each destined shelters for vehicle flow allocation in evacuation planning, considering both travel time and capacity of the transportation network.

In this paper, an evacuation simulation model with human psychological models is developed for urban disaster situation. We introduce three typical psychological biases: normalcy bias, emotional contagion bias, and sympathy behavior bias.

Firstly, normalcy bias, or the normality bias, is the initial evacuation delay caused by a belief that abnormal events rarely happen. It is one of the most usual psychological biases and can be seen in case of hurricanes, typhoons, Tsunami or floods [5]. Secondary, the emotional contagion bias is the effect of one person's emotional state on the emotional state of people around him/her both explicitly and implicitly. Simply speaking, this bias is to follow to the others and following a person with leadership belongs to this category. Finally, the sympathy behavior bias means that people instinctively take care of others, especially the weak such as elderly persons, injured persons, and so on. Without considering the kindness to others that people inherently have, accurate simulation results cannot be obtained.

Vorst [3] stated as follows: "Most people like to postpone evacuation till more convincing observations are available. Leaving home is very uneasy and risky." His statement exactly tallies with what we call the normalcy bias. Also, Vorst pointed out such evacuation models that reflect the normalcy bias was not represented in simulations of evacuation procedures [3].

We propose human psychological models to realize the above biases. The proposed models have two points mainly. The first point is that a parameter is incorporated in each agent to implement the normalcy bias. The second point is that a function of recognizing the other agents is realized for each agent. Combination of the introduced parameter and the recognition function enables the agent to equip emotional contagion bias. Moreover, we introduce the role of agent such as elderly persons. The agent role in combination of the recognition function is used to realize the sympathy behavior bias.

The proposed models are evaluated by simulation experiments for urban disaster cases. For the experiments, agents with the proposed psychological models are implemented on a simulation system with GIS data. A virtual city area is prepared for the area where the agents walk to find out their shelters. The experimental results show that more accurate human behaviors are realized by the proposed model.

The rest of this paper is organized as follows. Section 2 introduces the related work and the detailed explain of the proposed models is provided in Sect. 3. After the simulation experiment setting is described in Sect. 4, the experimental results are presented in Sect. 5. Finally, Sect. 6 concludes this paper.

2 Related Work

Agents and MAS have been studied in the area of AI (Artificial Intelligence). In the AI area, agents are autonomous entities which observe environments through their sensors and act on the environments using their actuators. Agents are programmed to achieve their goals autonomously by interacting with the environments. When an agent has ability to change its behavior according to the results of action, it is said that the agent can learn. Reinforcement learning is a scheme of learning where agents change their behaviors according to the rewards from the environments. Reinforcement learning was often applied to the case of learning game strategies [6].

When the agent technology was applied to disaster simulations, it is simply called an agent-based simulation or system (ABS) initially. Wu et al. [7] have developed the Dynamic Discrete Disaster Simulation System (D4S2), that is a comprehensive decision support system to simulate the large-scale disaster responses. D4S2 has an interface with a GIS system and a result was visualized on a GIS map. However, the responder agents' operations were regulated by a set of rules.

Chen et al. [8] analyzed real-time cell phone data and developed Dynamic Adaptive Disaster Simulation (DADS), which is a system capable of predicting population movements in large-scale disasters. It unifies diverse modeling concepts and techniques as well as considering cell phone and GIS data. In their simulations, they could predict population movements during a disaster like Hurricane Katrina accurately. The DADS system includes two types of agents: synthetic and predictive agents. In the simulation, the synthetic agents generate a set of real-time data using the real-world cell phone data. The predictive agent is associated with a cell phone user one by one and moves to represent predictions of the cell phone user's future movements.

Yun et al. [9] proposed a swarm-based dynamic disaster evacuation simulation model. Their simulation model was run on a simulated platform for complicated modeling system called Swarm invented by the Santa Fe Institute. In their simulation, every agent had the same property but they could get better performance of evacuation by changing the evacuation command dynamically than the static evacuation plan. Samira and Fatima [10] proposed a multi-agent simulation. Their purpose was to save a heart attack victim, which is different from the disaster evacuation. Therefore, they included three different types of agents in the simulation: victim, environment, and succourer agents. Among them, the succourer agent belongs to BDI (Belief, Desire and intention) type agents and it has beliefs about the world in which it operates, and it must meet the desires by making intentions the behavior of the system, until the emergence of approaches oriented agents. But concrete implementation methods were unclear, so that it is difficult to apply this BDI type to the disaster evacuation cases.

More recently, Mustaphaa *et al.* [11] proposed an agent-based methodological framework for complex system (Supply Chain, Natural Disaster) including GIS database. The framework itself seems to be general and it reflects the organizational structure and policies within the simulation. They also proposed various models in the framework as well as a specification of the translation process between the models. No implementation of simulation models nor simulation results, however, appeared in this paper. Nevertheless, it is true that interest in human factors and psychology is growing in the area of evacuation research [12], where human factors include physical, cognitive, motivational and social variables. Sakellariou *et al.* [13] just implemented an evacuation simulation where the evacuees are the agents with an emotional status instead of human psychological models. It is a subject of great interest that they referred to the emotion contagion.

In common, there is no proposal for evacuation simulation systems including agents with human psychological models in the above works. To construct a evacuation simulation system which reflect real human behaviors, agents have to be equipped with human psychological models.

3 Proposed Model

In order to make the evacuation simulation system for disasters more accurate, three psychological biases are proposed. One parameter is introduced to model the normalcy bias in each agent. Then the agents observe the other agents around him/her to decide the majority behavior that corresponds to the emotional contagion bias. Lastly the sympathy behavior bias is realized by applying roles to some agents.

3.1 Normalcy Bias

The role of the normalcy bias is to delay evacuation even if a disaster really occurs. For this, the parameter of "Level of Anxiety (LoA)" is incorporated in each agent as shown in Fig. 1. Once a disaster occurs, the LoA parameter monotonically increases each time a simulation step proceeds. Then the LoA parameter excesses a pre-defined threshold, the agent starts evacuation. The period between the disaster occurrence and the evacuation start corresponds to the situation under the normalcy bias. The initial value of the LoA parameter can be set as a different value for each agent. Thus it is possible to prepare various agent types from weak normalcy to strong normalcy. In simulation experiments, the initial values of the LoA parameter are provided based on some distribution.

3.2 Emotional Contagion Bias

As mentioned-above, the role of the emotional contagion bias is to let an agent follow to the other agents. For this purpose, we implement a model in which an agent recognizes the other agents around him/her.

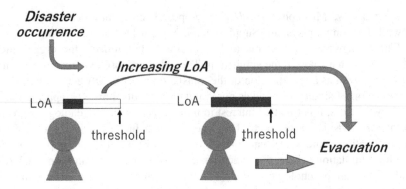

Fig. 1. Level of Anxiety (LoA) parameter for the nomalcy bias

As presented in Fig. 2, an agent (Agent A) can recognize the other agent (Agent B) within the area of circle with radius r. r is a parameter of recognition distance. When Agent A recognizes Agent B, the LoA parameter decreases, and vice versa. It means both agents in the normalcy bias feel relieved more because of existence of another agent. Recognition occurs just once, while the LoA parameter increases according to the simulation step proceeding. As a result, when the LoA parameter attains to the threshold, the agent starts to evacuate.

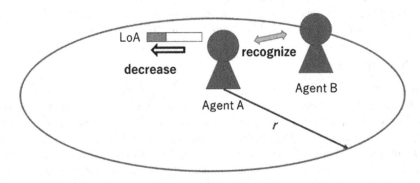

Fig. 2. A model to implement the emotional contagion bias

3.3   Sympathy Behavior Bias

As the targets of sympathy, elderly person agents are introduced. The characteristic of the elderly person agents is that their walking speed is slower than the normal agents that are the agents referred in the previous sections. In addition, when a normal agent recognizes an elderly person agent within the area of the emotional contagion circle of the normal agent (Fig. 2), the normal agent slows down the walking speed to accompany with the elderly person agent.

4   Simulation Experimental Setting

Aiming at urban disaster cases, an MAS with human psychological models has been implemented on a simulation system linked with GIS data. For the evaluation experiments, a virtual city area was selected for the simulation experiments. The size of the virtual city area that is shown in Fig. 3 is about 1.0 km x 1.2 km. In Fig. 3, thin lines running vertically and horizontally represent the roads where the agents have to walk for evacuation. The areas surrounded by the roads represent parks, buildings, and so on. As examples, an area of park and an area of building are directed in Fig. 3, although they may be difficult to be distinguished.

Building   Park

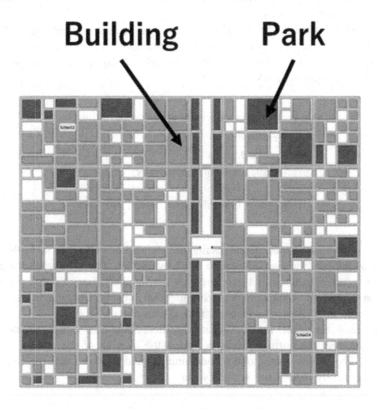

Fig. 3. The virtual city map used for simulation experiments

For the simulation experiments, two shelters that are the agents' evacuation goals are fixedly set at upper-left and lower-right points. The number of agents is 5,000, and all agents are assigned inside any building randomly at the start of each simulation experiment. It is assumed that each agent knows the shelter place which he/she aims to evacuate as the goal.

5   Simulation Results

Using the experimental environment presented in Sect. 4, several simulation experiments were carried out to evaluate the proposed models.

5.1   Simulation Results for Normalcy Bias

Only the LoA parameter is set for each agent to evaluate effect of the normalcy bias modeling. In this simulation experiment, the initial distribution of the LoA parameter was changed. The lower the average of the LoA parameter, the stronger the effect of normalcy bias becomes. The threshold value of the LoA parameter, which is the limit value to start evacuation, was set to 360.

The initial distribution of the LoA parameter was generated according to the uniform distribution. The range of the uniform distribution was changed as shown in Table 1 (b), (c), and (d). The agent model in Table 1 (a) is a comparative model without implementing the LoA parameter.

Table 1. The agent models for normalcy bias simulation

	Agent models
(a)	No normalcy bias
(b)	Normalcy bias only (initial values: 360–240)
(c)	Normalcy bias only (initial values: 300–180)
(d)	Normalcy bias only (initial values: 240–120)

Figure 4 shows the experimental results for the agent models set as in Table 1. The vertical axis presents the elapsed time to finish evacuation, that is to reach the pre-set evacuation goal. The horizontal axis presents the number of agents that completed evacuation. Therefore, when a graph reaches to 5,000 in the horizontal axis, the vertical axis means the time when all agents completed evacuation.

From Fig. 4, the agents finish evacuation earliest in the case without the normalcy bias. The stronger the normalcy bias becomes, the later all of the agents complete evacuation. The results correspond to our intuition and it shows that the simulation system successfully models the normalcy bias.

5.2   Simulation Results for Emotional Contagion Bias

Next, the recognition function is implemented in the simulation system along with the LoA parameter. The recognition distance r is set as 5 m. Again, the initial distribution of the LoA parameter is the uniform distribution as in the experiment of Sect. 5.1. The ranges of the uniform distribution are shown in Table 2 (e), (f), and (g). Again, the agent model without the normalcy bias appears in Table 2 (a) for comparison.

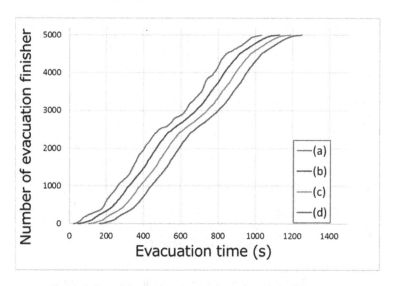

Fig. 4. The simulation results for the agent models in Table 1

Table 2. The agent models for emotional contagion bias simulation

	Agent models
(a)	No normalcy bias
(e)	Normalcy bias only (initial values: 360–240) + emotional contagion (r = 5 m)
(f)	Normalcy bias only (initial values: 300–180) + emotional contagion (r = 5 m)
(g)	Normalcy bias only (initial values: 240–120) + emotional contagion (r = 5 m)

The experimental results for the agent models in Table 2 are presented in Fig. 5. The vertical and horizontal axes are the same as those in Fig. 4. From Fig. 5, the agent evacuation was delayed more than the cases in Fig. 4 because of the emotional contagion bias. It is also shown that the strength of the normalcy bias still has the evacuation delay.

5.3   Simulation Results for Sympathy Behavior Bias

Finally, the simulation experiments for the sympathy behavior bias were evaluated. In these experiments, the elderly person agents are introduced and two comparative cases are tested. The ratio of the elderly person agents was changed and the parameters are shown in Table 3. Table 3 (h) shows the case where 25% of the elderly person agents are replaced for the normal agent. Similarly, Table 3 (i), (j), and (k) show the various cases in which the elderly person agents ratio changed when the agents have the normalcy bias. For comparison, the case with the normalcy bias is shown in Table 3 (d). For these simulation experiments, the range of the uniform distribution is the same as that in Table 1 (d).

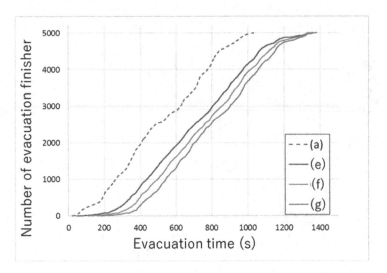

Fig. 5. The simulation results for the agent models in Table 2

Table 3. The agent models for sympathy behavior bias simulation

	Agent models
(a)	No normalcy bias
(h)	No normalcy bias only + elderly persons (25%)
(d)	Normalcy bias (initial values: 240–120)
(h)	Normalcy bias only + elderly persons (10%)
(j)	Normalcy bias only + elderly persons (25%)
(k)	Normalcy bias only + elderly persons (50%)

Figure 6 presents the results based on the model setting shown in Table 3. First of all, by comparing the cases (a) and (h), it can be said that evacuation completion time for all of the agents is almost the same for these two cases. Then we compare the cases of Table (d), (i), (j), and (k). Total evacuation time is almost the same for these four cases. From these experimental results, it is found that the sympathy behavior bias does not show any negative effect in evacuation time. The sympathy behavior is important to support the weak-side people such as the elderly persons. However, comparing the group of (a) and (h) and the group of (d), (i), (j), and (k), there is a gap between these two groups. From these results, it is found that the normalcy bias is a bottleneck to prevent fast-evacuation. We should educate people to remove the normalcy bias to accelerate their evacuation.

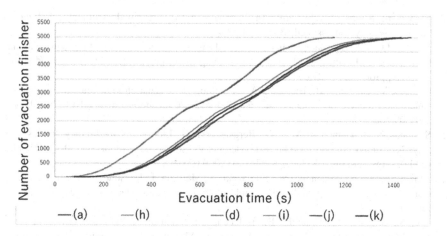

Fig. 6. The simulation results for the agent models in Table 3

6 Conclusions

In this paper, we have proposed the evacuation simulation models with the typical psychological biases: the normalcy bias, the emotional contagion bias, and the sympathy behavior bias. These models have been implemented in an evacuation simulation system based on MAS and GIS for urban disaster situation. Several simulation experiments have been carried out and it is found that the proposed models are reasonable and correspond to our intuition.

The simulation model for evaluation was a virtual city area. Therefore, we are planning to implement these proposed models on the simulation system with a real GIS data. Moreover, other psychological models such as a straight walking bias should be considered to make the simulation system more realistic and more accurate.

It may be useful to learn actual human judgements and behavior from an evacuation drill in order to construct an evacuation model for simulations. For example, de Jong and Helsloot [14] report that the flood risk awareness decreased through an exercise three days. Namely, the risk awareness was 21% on the first day, 18% on the second day and only 10% on the third day in the beginning. This awareness, however decreased on the first day with 9%, while on the other days it increased with respectively 20% and 23%. Although he situation is different that dealt in this research and the results could be different among drills, there must be something to be learned to empower the simulation models.

References

1. Ono, K.: Civil-military medical assistance cooperation after the great east Japan earthquake experiences and lessons. Cent. Excell. Disaster Manag. Humanit. Assist. (COE-DMHA) **5**, 45–52 (2012). Honolulu, LIAISON

2. Ferber, J.: Multi-agent System: An Introduction to Distributed Artificial Intelligence. Addison-Wesley Professional, Boston (1999)
3. Vorst, H.C.M.: Evacuation models and disaster psychology. In: First International Conference on Evacuation Modeling and Management, pp. 15–21, (2010). https://doi.org/10.1016/j.proeng.2010.07.004
4. Campos, V., Bandeira, R., Bandeira, A.: A method for evacuation route planning in disaster situations. Procedia Soc. Behav. Sci. **54**, 503–512 (2012). https://doi.org/10.1016/j.sbspro.2012.09.768
5. Stephens, N.M., Hamedani, M.-Y.G., Bergsieker, H.B., Eloul, L.: Why did they "choose" to stay? perspectives of hurricane katrina observers and survivors. Psychol. Sci. **20**(7), 878–886 (2009). https://doi.org/10.1111/j.1467-9280.2009.02386.x
6. Ishii, S., Fujita, H., Mitsutake, M., Yamazaki, T., Matsuda, J., Matsuno, Y.: A reinforcement learning scheme for a partially-observable multi-agent game. Mach. Lear. **59**(1/2), 31–54 (2005)
7. Wu, S., Shuman, L., Bidanda, B., Balaban, C.: Agent-based discrete event simulation modeling for disaster responses. In: Fowler, J., Mason, S. (eds.) Industrial Engineering Research Conference, pp. 5–12. Society for Computer Simulation International (2008)
8. Chen, F., Zhai, Z., Madey, F.: Dynamic adaptive disaster simulation: developing a predictive model of emergency behavior using cell phone and GIS data. In: Workshop on Agent-Directed Simulation (ADS 2011), pp. 5–12. Society for Computer Simulation International (2011)
9. Yun, J., Zhao, G., Fang, T., Liu, S., Huang, C., Wang, C.: A swarm-based dynamic evacuation simulation model under the background of secondary disasters. Syst. Eng. Procedia **5**, 61–67 (2012). https://doi.org/10.1016/j.sepro.2012.04.010
10. Samira, B., Fatima, B.: Multi-agents simulation of human behavior in a situation of emergency. Adv. Comput. Int. J. (ACIJ) **3**(1), 25–30 (2012). https://doi.org/10.5121/acij.2012.3102
11. Mustaphaa, K., Mcheicka, H., Mellouli, S.: Modeling and simulation agent-based of natural disaster complex systems. In: 4th International Conference on Emerging Ubiquitous Systems and Pervasive Networks (EUSPN-2013) (2013). Procedia Comput. Sci. **21**, 148–155
12. Hofinger, G., Zinke, R., Künzer, L.: Human factors in evacuation simulation, planning, and guidance. Trans. Res. Procedia **2**, 603–611 (2014). https://doi.org/10.1016/j.sepro.2012.04.010
13. Sakellariou, I., Kefalas, P., Stamatopoulou, I.: Evacuation simulation through formal emotional agent based modelling. In: 6th International Conference on Agents and Artificial Intelligence (ICAART 2014), pp. 193–200 (2014)
14. de Jong, M., Helsloot, I.: The effects of information and evacuation plans on civilian response during the national dutch flooding exercise 'waterproef'. Procedia Eng. **3**, 153–162 (2010). https://doi.org/10.1016/j.proeng.2010.07.015

Stalking Resilience

Cities as Vertebrae in Society's Resilience Backbone

Jose J. Gonzalez[1](✉), Magnus Bång[2], Colin Eden[3], Raquel Gimenez[4],
Josune Hernantes[4], Susan Howick[3], Patricia Maraña[4], Igor Pyrko[3],
Jaziar Radianti[1], Amy Rankin[2], and Jose Mari Sarriegi[4]

[1] Centre of Integrated Emergency Management,
University of Agder, Grimstad, Norway
{jose.j.gonzalez,jaziar.radianti}@uia.no
[2] Department of Computer and Information Science,
Linköping University, Linköping, Sweden
{magnus.bang,amy.rankin}@liu.se
[3] Department of Management Science, University of Strathclyde, Glasgow, UK
{colin.eden,susan.howick,igor.pyrko}@strath.ac.uk
[4] Department of Industrial Organization, Faculty of Engineering (TECNUN),
University of Navarra, Donostia/San Sebastian, Spain
{rgimenez,jhernantes,pmarana,jmsarriegi}@tecnun.es

Abstract. This paper presents the EU H2020 project Smart Mature Resilience, which takes advantage of the fact that many cities are committed to become increasingly resilient and have ongoing processes for urban resilience. Smart Mature Resilience develops resilience management guidelines based on a Resilience Maturity Model that engages a growing number of stakeholders and multi-level governance in order for cities to become vertebrae for society's resilience backbone. In a dual approach, employing a systematic literature review of international resilience implementation approaches alongside group processes with experts, the Smart Mature Resilience project has developed a preliminary resilience maturity model consisting of five stages Starting, Moderate, Advanced, Robust and verTebrate (SMART) and a Systemic Risk Assessment Questionnaire. The SMART Resilience Maturity Model suggests two principal processes for the transition to resilience maturity: (1) A process of increasing engagement and collaboration with new stakeholder types, from local, to regional, to national to European in a growing resilience backbone, and (2) a process of quality improvement of policies for transitioning from a Safety-I to a Safety-II perspective (from risk assessment & mitigation to adaption to future surprises as conditions evolve).

Keywords: Resilience · Management guidelines · Critical infrastructures · Natural disasters · Social dynamics · Maturity model · Risk systemicity

1 Introduction

This paper reports findings done during the first year of the European Union's Horizon 2020 project Smart Mature Resilience (H2020-EU.3.7., project ref. 653569). The findings should be considered preliminary, since they will be subject to further refinement during the remaining two years of the project.

Y. Murayama et al. (Eds.): ITDRR 2016, IFIP AICT 501, pp. 31–45, 2017.
https://doi.org/10.1007/978-3-319-68486-4_4

Smart Mature Resilience (SMR) was developed to meet the call "DRS-7-2014: Crisis management topic 7: Crises and disaster resilience – operationalizing resilience concepts". Altogether five out of forty nine proposals targeting this call were funded. SMR started 1 June 2015 and will finish 31 May 2018.

The call adopted the definition of resilience by the United Nations International Strategy on Disaster Risk Reduction (UNISDR): "The ability of a system, community or society exposed to hazards to resist, absorb, accommodate to and recover from the effects of a hazard in a timely and efficient manner, including through the preservation and restoration of its essential basic structures and functions" [1]. Based on this definition, the call stipulated:

- "It is necessary to break down and practically apply the UNISDR definition of resilience to different security sectors. Resilience concepts namely need to be developed for critical infrastructures (supply of basic services like water, food, energy, transport, housing/shelter, communications, finance, health), but also for the wider public to integrate and address human and social dynamics in crises and disaster situations, including the role of the population, the media, rescuers (staff, volunteers and ad-hoc volunteers)."
- "A general resilience management guideline should be developed, linked with the European Union's Risk Assessment Guidelines, and operationalized in one or more of the security sectors, and/or the public."
- "The successful pilot implementation of the developed guideline needs to be demonstrated and tested in an operational environment."

To develop the SMR proposal we took the following stance:

1. To achieve society's resilience one must integrate cities' resilience in the overall perspective. Most people live already in cities, and cities will continue to grow at the expense of rural areas. When man-made or natural disasters happen, cities will always be affected, even if the disaster's epicentre should occur in rural areas.
2. Conversely, cities have the potential to play a key role for society's resilience: they have motivation and resources. Much has been done already and is being done about city resilience. However, the dominant perspective in those approaches is cities as isolated entities. Our project adds the perspective that society's resilience should rest on a resilience backbone with cities as vertebrae in the backbone.
3. Resilience should be seen as a quality improvement process, albeit a highly complex one, guided by a resilience maturity model. In this context a resilience maturity model should be understood as a trajectory through stages of increasing resilience maturity. The resilience maturity stages and the resilience building interventions ("policies") shape the resilience management guidelines required by the H2020's DRS-7-2014 call.

To achieve the goal of delivering a European emergent resilience backbone with cities as vertebrae, the SMR consortium was carefully composed of scientists and practitioner teams. The consortium consists of thirteen partners: four universities, two major non-profit organizations and seven cities.

The seven partner cities of the SMR project have excelled in their commitment as resilient cities or as smart cities. Four of the cities (Bristol and Glasgow – United Kingdom; Rome – Italy; and Vejle – Denmark) were selected by The Rockefeller Foundation as members of the 100 Resilient Cities (http://100resilientcities.org). The other three cities (Donostia/San Sebastian – Spain; Kristiansand –Norway; and Riga – Latvia) have engaged in various smart city activities and networks.

The four universities in the consortium (Agder, Linköping, Navarra and Strathclyde) complement and supplement each other in terms of expertise and methods so as to cover all the relevant aspects of the project research. A major asset for the purpose of conducting pilot implementations of the envisioned resilience management guideline was the fact that three of the universities resided in cities represented in the project consortium (viz. Kristiansand for University of Agder, Donostia/San Sebastian for the University of Navarra and Glasgow for the University of Strathclyde).

Finally, the SMR consortium included two organizations with critical expertise for the success of the project, viz. ICLEI and DIN.

"ICLEI – Local Governments for Sustainability" http://www.iclei.org/ defines itself as «a high-energy, flexible Movement of local governments working together in national, regional and international networks; engaging in global campaigns for sustainability, participating in performance-based programs, advancing through an international exchange of experiences and solutions – a movement which is supported by commitment processes, performance frameworks, programs, networks, strategic alliances and centres of excellence». In the SMR project ICLEI leads the pilot implementation work package. In addition, ICLEI leads the work package that targets dissemination and project impact.

DIN, the German Institute for Standardization, is one of the most active standards organizations in the world. In the SMR project DIN prepares the ground to develop international standards emerging from the project.

The paper continues in Sect. 2 with a discussion of the project's approach in terms of a maturity model. In Sect. 3 we provide an overview of the SMR project's architecture. Section 4 presents the main insights from the project's worldwide literature survey on resilience. Section 5 describes our current understanding of the resilience maturity model. Section 6 concerns the development of the Systemic Risk Assessment Questionnaire. We conclude in Sect. 7 with a brief summing up.

2   Advantages of a Maturity Model for Resilience

Maturity models emerged from quality improvement in software engineering in 1979. In the meantime maturity models have been developed for more than twenty different application areas [2]. To the best of our knowledge, the SMR project embodies the first attempt to develop a maturity model for society's resilience.

Beyond the rationale that a resilience maturity model contains key aspects of the resilience management guidelines required by the H2020 DRS-14-2014 call, proceeding in terms of a resilience maturity model has a key advantage: It facilitates the otherwise extremely difficult requirement to develop and test in an operational environment the pilot implementation of the resilience management guideline.

Achieving resilience within the scope of a three year project that, as a first step, must develop the tools to achieve resilience, is hardly possible. The partner cities in the SMR project were carefully selected so that the cases for demonstrating and testing the resilience management guideline concern cities in different stages of maturity.

First, a preliminary resilience maturity model was developed, shown in Table 1. The SMART acronym maturity model corresponds to the first letters of the maturity stages Starting – Moderate – Advanced – Robust and the T from the last stage Vertebrate.

Table 1. Preliminary resilience maturity model

Maturity stage	Description
Starting	The city has launched policies regarding resilience development. The risk assessment is still fragmented and incomplete with regard to hazards affecting critical infrastructures and man-made threats. The community involvement and the private-public cooperation are incipient. The approach is mainly city centered. A multi-governance approach with a European dimension is dormant. The city is not part of a larger resilience network
Moderate	The city manages resilience development policies, using control measures. The risk assessment with regard to hazards affecting critical infrastructures and man-made threats are been operationalized in cooperation with critical infrastructure providers. Plans to involve communities and develop private-public cooperation have been developed. The city recognizes the relevance of a multi-governance approach with a European dimension and acts to invigorate the approach. The resilience management is still fragmented and siloed. The city has started planning for networking with other European cities with regard to resilience and sustainability
Advanced	The city has developed a framework to manage resilience within an explicit holistic approach that integrates critical infrastructure providers, expertise on man-made disasters and sustainability. Community resilience and private-public cooperation is part of the approach. The nodes in a multi-governance approach with a European dimension are well-linked in the plans, but not yet fully operationalized. The city is member of a major network of European cities with regard to resilience and sustainability
Robust	The city has engaged all relevant agents to its resilience holistic approach. Agents perceive value added by resilience. The multi-governance approach with a European dimension is well developed and operationalized. The city is a member in a major network of European cities with regard to resilience and sustainability, with a proactive posture regarding interdependencies and potential cascading effects
VerTebrate	The city excels with its resilience as part of the ecosystem (regional, national, European) resilience. The city acts as a vertebra in the European Resilience backbone

Note the increase of the cities' capability as functional units ("vertebrae") of the resilience backbone as they progress toward higher resilience maturity levels.

Next, a preliminary assessment of the resilience maturity of the partner cities was done. The outcome yielded that Donostia/San Sebastian was at the resilience maturity stage "Moderate", Kristiansand at the stage "Advanced" and Glasgow at the stage "Robust". The project target is to demonstrate and validate that each city will progress to the next higher stage of resilience maturity. Thus the SMR project is structured so that much of the trajectory toward resilience, from low to high stages, is covered.

3 Overview of the Smart Mature Resilience Proposal

The SMR project was conceived with the perspective of a holistic, multi-level governance perspective of European resilience with cities as vertebrae in a strong European resilience backbone. SMR builds upon the experience, the insights and the practice of on-going endeavours on urban/city resilience (including smart cities), but it approaches risk and resilience in an overall European perspective. The project does not view cities as isolated entities, but rather as interconnected and interdependent units, in the similar situation of vertebrae as interconnected and interdependent parts of a backbone. Cities can be affected directly or indirectly by disasters. Indirect effects can arise from proximity, from interdependencies and cascading effects, or even from sharing the same class of major threats and suggesting common approaches and collaborative arrangements.

Figure 1 illustrates the vision of a resilience backbone in Europe with cities as vertebrae. SMR targets an emergent resilience backbone consisting of the cities in the consortium as a direct project result. Furthermore, the project develops the tools and triggers a process to facilitate growth of the resilience backbone by attracting and consolidating more cities in the resilience backbone.

Figure 2 illustrates that the Resilience Management Guideline rests on three pillar tools (Resilience Maturity Model, Systemic Risk Assessment Questionnaire and Resilience Building Policies). The Engagement and Communication Tool ensures active user participation. The System Dynamics model is a computer simulation that integrates and connects the tools, supporting decision makers to diagnose and monitor with "what-if" analysis the progress to higher resilience maturity levels.

The activities during the first year of the project enhanced the preliminary resilience maturity model presented in Table 1 and a prototype of the Systemic Risk Assessment Questionnaire. In addition, design principles and specification for the Engagement and Communication Tool were derived.

The enhanced resilience maturity model was the outcome of two parallel project activities: (1) a thorough survey of the literature on resilience, followed by a literature synthesis and experts' assessment of the findings using a Delphi process; and (2) workshops with experts on critical infrastructure, climate change, social dynamics and city representatives occurring in Riga, Bristol, Rome and Vejle. The prototype of the Systemic Risk Assessment Questionnaire evolved from activities using Group Explorer (See http://www.strath.ac.uk/media/faculties/business/brochures/GE_Brochure.pdf) during the workshops mentioned above.

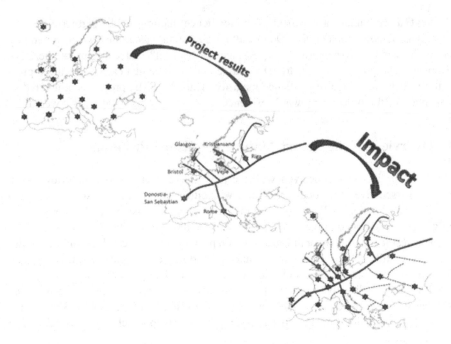

Fig. 1. The vision of an emergent resilient backbone in two stages: as direct project result and as long-term impact of the project

4   Resilience Literature Survey

A worldwide literature survey of state-of-the-art resilience research was carried out to inform the development of the resilience management guideline and ensure common ground of concept, methods and approaches throughout the project. The survey was in part worldwide and general, and in part focused on Europe and specific problem areas. The aim was to identify, synthesize and assess the main challenges and best practice existing today. Further, the survey serves as a repository of policies, metrics and best practices for continued work in the project.

The literature survey encompassed several reviews which can be summarized as follows: (1) a systematic literature review of academic peer-reviewed journal articles on urban resilience (119 articles), (2) a systematic literature review of three problem areas (resilience in critical infrastructure, climate change and social dynamics) (38 articles), (3) a review of EU project reports regarding resilience (170 reports) (4) a review of approaches and methods in relevant organisational bodies and networks (23 reports), (5) a survey of approached used in the SMR project cities (7 questionnaires).

The main findings of the resilience literature survey can be summarized as follows:

4.1   There are Different Perspectives on the Concept of Resilience

An analysis of underlying assumptions and differences in definitions of urban resilience uncover four conceptual "tensions", that is, theoretical concepts which are inconsistent or unclear. (1) "The notion of equilibrium". The concept of an equilibrium makes the distinction between resilience as the ability to "bounce back" or retain functionality in the face of disturbance [3] compared to definitions that have a multi-equilibrium view, or see resilience as adaptive cycles, emphasizing the systems' ability to adapt, learn and change [4, 5]. (2) "Resilience behaviours". Comparisons between the behaviours that characterise resilience uncover different theoretical underpinnings and thus pose a challenge when used concurrently in definitions. For example, "recover" suggests that there is an objective to "get back" to a previous state, "absorb" suggests coping with a disturbance without changing the basic structure and "adapt" suggests a change in structure to cope with new demands. (3) "Temporal aspects", that is, differences in how resilience is described; as something that happens before, during or after some disturbance. The differences imply the need for different types of policies and strategies, e.g., do they focus on building stable structures (before), flexible response teams (during) or re-building (after)? (4) "Urban resilience boundaries". Defining boundaries for the system to be examined presents a challenge which is not well discussed in literature, nor described in the reviewed urban resilience definitions. Boundaries include, for example, geographical (city or region limits), temporal, sectors of inclusion and level of abstraction.

4.2   A Shift in Resilience Tools from Theory to Practice

The literature review shows that frameworks for urban resilience are abstract and far from being a practical tool for operationalization. There is a large variety in the attributes/indicators used in the frameworks, which reflects a lack of consensus and unification on the notion of urban resilience in general and the central concepts is relates to. The findings further reflect the vast number of aspects that are important to resilience in an urban context and that there are many ways to increase resilience, depending on the area of interest. In developing guidelines for resilience it is thus of importance to carefully consider how to go from general concepts to specific applications. Each city that applies the maturity model is unique and thus a model which encompasses a large number of variables is necessarily on a high level. However, guidance on how general concepts can be applied in context may be a useful part of developing guidelines to aid the implementation. This could be, for example, support on how to priorities more/less important parts of the model to a particular context and also to demonstrate how different aspects of the model are interlinked.

4.3   Political and Financial Support and Social Engagement

The literature suggests that the financial and political capital of a city is a critical factor for resilience management. Challenges related to urban resilience are in many cases related to gaining support and financing resilience-supporting measures. Further, as found in the SMR partner city survey, a difficulty is that much of the policy and related decision-making regarding resilience is outside the cities' jurisdiction, which inhibits their response to disasters and crises. The dependencies, numerous stakeholders (subcontractors) and legal frameworks render managing the infrastructures on the local level difficult. A present strategy in the resilience work by the partner cities, as demonstrated in the survey, is to improve communication among different stakeholders and to pool resources locally and regionally. The strategy was echoed in the literature review as a central factor for successful implementation of policies.

Another influencing element of urban resilience is citizens as local communities. Strategies to increase resilience include having well-informed citizens and promoting self-protective behaviour. Involving local stakeholders also has the benefit of building trust in a community and identifying local needs, which in turn may increase the resilience of a community. To create resilience, it is not sufficient to create new policies at a high level, it is also critical to have support from the community in order to make changes. These enabling factors should be considered in the development of the maturity model.

4.4   There is a Need to Link Resilience and Governance

In the literature, resilience is often linked to governance concept although the use and context of governance itself varies among scholars, especially in how it operates in society [6]. However, there are common themes, including adaptiveness, adaptive capacity and multi-level governance [6–9]. Adapting from Commission of Global Governance (CGC), governance is interpreted as "the sum of the many ways individuals and institutions, public and private, manage their common affairs" [10]. Governance is a continuous process, requiring cooperation and capacity to accommodate conflicting or diverse interests. It consists of formal institutions and regimes empowered to enforce compliance, as well as informal arrangements that people and institutions either have agreed to or perceive to be in their interest. In brief, adoption of governance implies several aspects: (1) Institutional pluralism and networks beyond the state established through cooperation of multiple actors and partnerships, distributed responsibilities. (2) No longer single sovereign authority. (3) New form of authority and control based on diplomacy, agreements, and empowerments. (4) Multilevel governance and issues of scale such as how much it is possible to talk on a widespread cross-national shift and trend [6].

The concept of resilience within governance of institutions and organisation is relatively new, and the Hyogo Framework Action (HFA) 2005-2015 has pushed the resilience agenda forward in governance circles. Governance is important because governments often cannot act alone to respond to specific disaster events. When linking governance to the city resilience, it suggests that a resilient city should be capable of sustaining multi-level, multi-stakeholders platform to promote resilience in different levels: regional, national and international. At a more advanced maturity level, organizational capacities of the city to negotiate and make agreement are required. Principles of good partnership are becoming relevant such as shared vision, consensus, participation, negotiation, inclusion, volunteerism, accountability, and trust [11].

4.5   Managing Risk in a Governance Context

Incorporation of resilience into governance means that an increased numbers of actors such as politicians, regulators, businesses, NGOs, media and the public are involved in common affairs. The literature points out the importance of taking into account risks of collaborative practice in governance, and wider social and political context [8, 11]. Risk governance is a comprehensive way of understanding and dealing with risks from different sources of hazards, including all relevant actors and stakeholders, who have to deal with the effects and impacts of the respective risks [7]. When a city adopts multilevel governance approach on a common issue, it should be followed by an understanding of the advantages and disadvantages of this concept such as unclear responsibility or accountability and many other consequences that may follow. Partnership in risk management is considered as a way of risk governance [7]. One strategy is to establish public-private insurance systems against unexpected events such as natural disasters, to enable risk sharing cooperation through public-private partnerships.

5   The Enhanced Resilience Maturity Model

The principal aim of the second work package of the SMR Project is to gather requirements from partner cities regarding resilience based on their current experience and expectations in order to enhance the preliminary version of the Resilience Maturity Model (Table 1) as well as gathering information for the other tools (see Fig. 2).

Fig. 2. Tools supporting the resilience management guideline

The SMR project focuses on resilience on three different topics: (1) risks and problems derived from critical infrastructures and technology dependencies, (2) climate change and the resulting increase of natural disaster risks, and (3) human dynamics such as, immigration, poverty, population aging and dependencies problems. Work-shops on these topics with the partner cities and their stakeholders enabled the project to understand better partner cities' requirements regarding resilience as well as to orient the outcomes of the project to cities' needs. The collected information was used to enhance the preliminary version of the Resilience Maturity Model with indicators and policies.

Four workshops with partner cities and local stakeholders were organized to gather their requirements regarding the resilience building process. The first workshop, held in Riga 26–29 October 2015, focused on the analysis of the partner cities' dependency towards critical infrastructures and technology. The second workshop, held in Bristol 25–28 January 2016, collected information on risks associated with climate change. The third workshop, held in Rome 22–25 February 2016, analysed social problems. Finally, a workshop was held in Vejle 9–12 May 2016 with the aim to explore the partner cities' current experiences, best practices, and difficulties concerning the resilience building process.

In all the workshops the different challenges that the cities are facing were also discussed. Further, the possible policies and actions that could be carried to overcome potential barriers were identified. As a result, a great range of resilience building policies were identified, in addition to useful requirements for the development of the SMR tools.

The workshop sessions were also very helpful to create a collaborative and supportive environment between the scientific partners (universities, ICLEI and DIN) and the cities, building trust among them and therefore, increasing their involvement in addition to giving the opportunity of mutual learning.

Two different methodologies were used during these workshops: Group Explorer (GE) and Group Model Building (GMB). For details on GE see the next section.

Group model building (GMB) is a collaborative methodology that enables integrating fragmented knowledge, initially residing in the minds of different agents, into aggregated models [12]. GMB encourages consensus building among the involved agents. Actually, the GMB methodology has specific exercises where the group of experts is usually divided into small groups, and then the results obtained are exposed in plenary in order to encourage the discussions between different problem perspectives that enrich the process and lead to reach a consensus.

The information collected from the GMB exercises with partner city representatives and stakeholders during the four workshops was analysed and combined with results from the worldwide literature survey on resilience. This enhanced and refined the preliminary Resilience Maturity Model from Table 1. Thereafter, a Delphi process provided additional insights and feedback concerning the Resilience Maturity Model, leading to an even more refined version.

Table 2 shows the high-level structure of the maturity model. The dots indicate text with details about the corresponding entry (e.g. detailed descriptions of the resilience maturity stages and resilience building policies).

The policies contained in the maturity model are generic, bearing in mind that the maturity model will be in charge of supporting activities at a strategic level. Therefore, the policies described in each maturity stage are described using a high-level approach, while in the policy repository tool the policies are particularized for each city. The policies we classified along five resilience dimensions that were elicited from the workshop participants using the GMB method: Robustness of infrastructure & Resources, Preparedness, Leadership & Governance, Cooperation and Learning.

Table 2. Structure of the enhanced resilience maturity model

		Maturity stages				
		Starting	Moderate	Advanced	Robust	verTebrate
Maturity stage description		...	...	...	...	...
Resilience dimensions	Robustness of infrastructure & Resources	Policies corresponding to the Starting Stage Related to the Robustness of infrastructure & Resources dimension	...	...	...	...
	Preparedness	...	...	...	...	...
	Leadership & governance	...	...	...	...	...
	Cooperation	...	...	...	...	...
	Learning	...	...	...	...	Policies corresponding to Vertebrate Stage related to the Learning dimension

While we expect that the project work in the second and the third project year will help improve and refine the content of the model – in terms of the model policies – the overall structure of the Resilience Maturity Model after the first project year as shown in Table 2 is likely to remain quite stable.

Rather than providing a detailed description of the identified policies – which would require much space – we render on Fig. 3 a tentative insight emerging from project work done so far. (Needless to say, the policies and the tentative insight will be subjected to critical analysis during the implementation of the resilience pilot in the second year of the project.)

6 The Systemic Risk Assessment Questionnaire

"Resilience .... requires actively understanding the risk landscape" [13].

This quote highlights that a key element of resilience is an ongoing risk assessment. Cities which are mature with respect to resilience should therefore be actively assessing the different types of risks which impact them and the impact of policies to mitigate such risks. In addition, as cities become more mature, there will be increasing engagement with key stakeholders. Therefore risk assessment and mitigation tools are required that can take account of the perspective of a wide variety of stakeholders involved in city resilience, consider how risks and stresses impact the cities level of resilience and which mitigation policies best support their resilience journey. In addition, the development of city resilience is inevitably constrained by finite resources, and therefore it is important for cites to prioritise risks and stresses in order to get value for money through cost-benefit analysis.

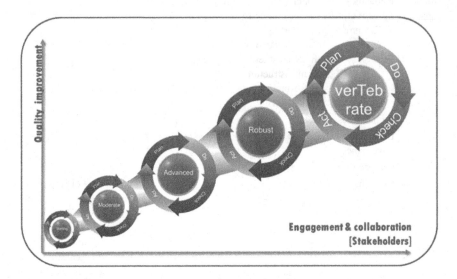

Fig. 3. The contents of the enhanced Resilience Maturity Model with two principal dimensions: x-axis) Engagement and collaboration with more stakeholder categories (local, regional, national, European); y-axis) Continuous quality improvement within each maturity stage, increasing in scope as the city progresses to higher stages of resilience maturity

Recent research [14–17] indicates that it is the interaction and dynamics between different types of risk that can cause the most damage to, for example, a project or a city. Risk and stresses are likely to interact with one another and form a *portfolio* where the impact of the whole is greater than the sum of the parts. When one risk event is triggered, it may reinforce the likelihood and ramifications of other risks or stresses, [16], as well as form interacting vicious cycles where risk consequences mutually feed themselves [18]. In contrast to traditional risk registers where risk are treated as independent [17], by recognising the *systemicity of risks*, it is possible to identify and address those risk or stresses which seem most potent in triggering and reinforcing negative ramifications within the risk landscape.

As a result, the risk systemicity perspective calls for the introduction of new tools and approaches to managing risks, which allow multiple stakeholders to surface and negotiate their understandings of the relationships between relevant risk and stresses with respect to the city [18].

A tool which encompasses the systemic perspective on risks is the Systemic Risk Assessment Questionnaire which has been used successfully in the context of risks assessment in projects within a large company in the private sector [16]. The Systemic Risk Assessment Questionnaire is an interactive questionnaire programmed in Excel using Visual Basic for Applications which comprises a set of questions about the relationships between risks. The questions in the Systemic Risk Assessment Questionnaire seek to gain stakeholders judgments regarding the risks they face. However, the questions are not independent from one another, instead they capture the interdependence between risks through, for example, removing risks that become irrelevant or giving increased weight to some risks due to responses to questions regarding other risks. The output of the questionnaire is a risk score which helps in assessing the risk level of a given project or initiative and provides help in prioritising those areas where most attention is required.

The Systemic Risk Assessment Questionnaire is therefore being developed for the needs of the SMR project. The initial work on the Systemic Risk Assessment Questionnaire construction was grounded in a series of group workshops organised with representatives of the seven European cities involved in SMR. Each of the workshops was dedicated to one of the themes being covered by the SMR project: critical infrastructure, climate change, and social problems. The aim of the sessions was to gather views and opinions from city representatives with regards to risks associated with each theme. These views were gathered using a Group Explorer decision support system to facilitate group discussion and negotiation about risks [19, 20]. The system allowed for surfacing and gathering the perspectives of multiple stakeholders in a fair and structured manner [18]. The entire process was facilitated by an academic representative who, at various stages of the session, invited participants to engage in different types of exercises, such as consideration of risk that may impact their cities, identification and prioritisation of key risk themes, and gathering of policies which address the identified risks. The resulting empirical data formed a risk map including over 2000 concepts and links which depicted complex relationships between risk events and their ramifications, as expressed by city participants.

Drawing on the analysis of the risk map created by workshop participants, the researchers seek to generate a list of risks scenarios which will form the basis of the Systemic Risk Assessment Questionnaire. When using the Systemic Risk Assessment Questionnaire, respondents will be asked to answer questions about the likelihood of the risk scenarios and the risks which trigger them with respect to their own cities. In order to provide an indication of the overall level of risk in a city, risk scenarios will also be weighted with respect to the potential impact of the scenarios if they were to occur. These weights will be informed by the analysis of the maps produced during the workshops and will be validated with city participants in two further workshops.

As indicated above, a key outcome from the Systemic Risk Assessment Questionnaire is to assist in the prioritisation of managing risks and stresses. It will also provide a tool that can be used to engage multiple city stakeholders in considering those risks which impose the greatest threat on a city, creating potential barriers to resilience, and to agree upon the most important areas to prioritise policies.

7   Concluding Remarks

SMR is an ambitious project, but as evidenced in this paper, good progress has al-ready been done in its first year.

The close collaboration between the scientific partners and city partners has al-lowed to create an intellectually stimulating environment which translates into better understanding of resilience.

Following the lessons from the literature, the project partners have aimed to translate the general concepts into practical applications, as well as to address the 'theoretical tensions' around resilience; this is evidenced in the city resilience tools which are described in this discussion. It can be argued that the co-creation of the city resilience tools by both the scientific partners and city partners at the same time helps to achieve the balance between 'the general' (conceptual level) and the 'specific' (operational level).

Whilst the development of tools has proved to be a collaborative process for the SMR partners, it is expected that the same level of collaboration will be sustained as the project enters its second year when the city resilience tools will be implemented in the participating cities.

Acknowledgement. The Smart Mature Resilience research project has received funding from the European Union's Horizon 2020 research and innovation programme under grant agreement no. 653569.

References

1. UNISDR, UNISDR Terminology on Disaster Risk Reduction. International Strategy for Disaster Reduction (ISDR), pp. 1–30 (2009)
2. Wendler, R.: The maturity of maturity model research: a systematic mapping study. Inf. Softw. Technol. **54**, 1317–1339 (2012)
3. Bruneau, M., et al.: A framework to quantitatively assess and enhance the seismic resilience of communities. Earthq. Spectra **19**(4), 733–752 (2003)
4. Walker, J., Cooper, M.: Genealogies of resilience: from systems ecology to the political economy of crisis adaptation. Secur. Dialogue **42**(2), 143–160 (2011)
5. Malalgoda, C., Amaratunga, D., Haigh, R.: Challenges in creating a disaster resilient built environment. Procedia Econ. Financ. **18**, 736–744 (2014)
6. Walker, G., et al.: Risk governance and natural hazards. CapHaZ-Net FP7 Project (2010)
7. Costa, M.M., et al.: Governance indicators for (Un)succcesful MSPs (2013)
8. Renn, O.: Risk governance: coping with uncertainty in a complex world. Nat. Hazards **48**(2), 313 (2008)
9. Crowe, P., Foley, K.: The Turas project: integrating social-ecological resilience and urban planning: TURAS FP7 project, pp. 1–15 (2013)
10. CGG: Our Global Neighbourhood. Oxford University Press, Oxford (1995)
11. McLean, L., Guha-Sapir, D.: Developing a resilience framework. ENHANCE FP7 Project, vol. 2015 (2013)
12. Vennix, J.A.M.: Group Model Building: Facilitating Team Learning using System Dynamics. Wiley, Chichester (1996)
13. Van der Vegt, G.S., et al.: Managing risk and resilience. Acad. Manag. J. **58**, 971–980 (2015)
14. Williams, T.M.: Systemic project risk management - the way ahead. J. Risk Assess. Manag. **1**(1–2), 149–159 (2000)

15. Williams, T.M., Ackermann, F., Eden, C.: Project risk: systemicity, cause mapping and a scenario approach, In: Kahkonen, K., Artto, K. (eds) Managing Risks in Projects, E and FN Spon, London, UK (1997)
16. Ackermann, F., et al.: Systemic risk assessment: a case study. J. Oper. Res. Soc. **58**, 39–51 (2007)
17. Eden, C., et al.: The role of feedback dynamics in disruption and delay on the nature of disruption and delay (D&D) in major projects. J. Oper. Res. Soc. **51**, 291–300 (2000)
18. Ackermann, F., et al.: Systemic risk elicitation: using causal maps to engage stakeholders and build a comprehensive view of risks. Eur. J. Oper. Res. **238**, 290–299 (2014)
19. Ackermann, F., Eden, C.: Using causal mapping with group support systems to elicit an understanding of failure in complex projects: some implications for organizational research. Group Decis. Negot. **14**, 355–376 (2005)
20. Ackermann, F., Eden, C.: Making Strategy: Mapping Out Strategic Success. Sage, London (2011)

Usability Evaluation of Information Technology in Disaster and Emergency Management

Tilo Mentler[(⊠)], Henrik Berndt, Daniel Wessel, and Michael Herczeg

Institute for Multimedia and Interactive Systems,
University of Luebeck, Luebeck, Germany
mentler@imis.uni-luebeck.de

Abstract. Apart from technical reliability, usability is one of the major criteria for safe and efficient usage of interactive information technology in disaster and emergency management. However, in this setting, usability evaluation is difficult due to the heterogeneity and unpredictability of operation conditions, as well as the difficult, usually mobile, context. However, there are ways to conduct usability evaluations in disaster and emergency settings. Thus, in this paper, advantages and disadvantages of empirical and analytical usability evaluation methods for interactive systems in disaster and emergency management are discussed. The importance of formative evaluation measures within an iterative human-centered design process is emphasized. It is illustrated by two case studies dealing with paramedics' and emergency physicians' usage of mobile and wearable devices in mass casualty incidents.

Keywords: Usability · Evaluation · Usability engineering · Human-Centered design · Disaster management · Emergency management

1 Introduction

Representative for many researchers and practitioners, Meissner et al. [1] postulate "a tremendous potential for increasing efficiency and effectiveness in coping with a disaster" by supporting disaster relief forces, aid workers and general public with information technology. However, availability and technical reliability of interactive systems alone will not lead to improved workflows or more pervasive information flows. As any socio-technical system, disaster and emergency management "relies both on human and technical function carriers" [2]. It is characterized by the "reciprocal interrelationship between humans and machines" [2]. Thoughtful human-machine task allocation and user interface design are of utmost importance.

For more than 30 years, usability has been the major criterion for assessing human-computer interaction. It is defined as "the extent to which a product can be used by specified users to achieve specified goals with effectiveness, efficiency and satisfaction in a specified context of use" [3]. Several methods and process models for systematic usability have been developed. Apart from involving users early and designing iteratively, evaluating usability at different stages and with defined measures is one of the basic principles of usability engineering [4–6].

© IFIP International Federation for Information Processing 2017
Published by Springer International Publishing AG 2017. All Rights Reserved
Y. Murayama et al. (Eds.): ITDRR 2016, IFIP AICT 501, pp. 46–60, 2017.
https://doi.org/10.1007/978-3-319-68486-4_5

However, within the context of disaster and emergency management gaining "credible feedback on how well [...] design is working and to how to improve it" [6] is challenging for at least two reasons:

- Time- and safety-critical characteristics of disasters and emergencies put high requirements on users and technology. Even early prototypes might require advanced levels of hardware and software quality.
- Mobile contexts of use allow for unique and often unpredictable operational conditions (e.g. weather, lighting, safety hazards, connectivity). Many influences should be considered but can neither be created intentionally in laboratories nor in the field.

For example, Leitner et al. [7] explain their decision to test a mobile emergency information system under laboratory conditions instead on-site as follows: "Firstly, we didn't want to risk the test being interrupted when an emergency call arrives, resulting in incomplete data. Secondly, we had to consider the ethical aspect that instead of relaxing between emergency cases, the physician would have to participate in our test. This could have influenced his or her performance in a real emergency case. Other reasons were technical ones. For a realistic test it would have been necessary to establish a working wireless infrastructure in the car, which would have tied up too many resources of the development team necessary for other tasks in the project."

In any case, usability must be considered while designing interactive systems for users acting and making decisions under the influence of various stressors. This topic will be addressed by describing background and related work in Sect. 2. Several usability evaluation approaches will be compared with respect to the context of disaster and emergency management (see Sect. 3). In Sect. 4, two case studies about the human-centered design and evaluation of mobile and wearable interactive systems for members of Emergency Medical Services (EMS) in mass casualty incidents (MCIs) will be presented. Conclusions will be drawn in Sect. 5.

2 Background and Related Work

As mentioned before, usability evaluations should be part of systematic approaches to usability rather than a single quality measure at the end of a development project. Therefore, basic principles of usability engineering will be elaborated in Sect. 2.1. Following this, usability evaluation methods will be distinguished with respect to time of conduction and reasoning approaches in Sect. 2.2. Finally, related work to usability evaluation in disaster and emergency management will be outlined.

2.1 Usability Engineering

Usability engineering processes refer to "concepts and techniques for planning, achieving, and verifying objectives for system usability" [8]. They embrace but are certainly not limited to user interface and interaction design. For different stages of development, several methods have been developed or derived from humanities, social or engineering sciences [5]:

- Observing and interviewing users in the field as well as formal task analysis and user research methods in order to understand the context of use.
- Writing scenarios or sketching storyboards as well as working with different kinds of low-fidelity and high-fidelity prototypes (e.g. wireframes, mockups, paper prototypes) as an aid to envision design solutions.
- Testing the suitability of design solutions with respect to users, tasks and operating conditions in the laboratory and in the field (see Sect. 2.2).

Sophisticated process models like Contextual Design [8], Scenario-Based Design [9], the Usability Engineering Lifecycle by Mayhew [10] or the Usability Engineering Lifecycle by Nielsen [11] describe steps and methods to follow in great detail.

2.2 Usability Evaluation

Independently of the process used, there is no guarantee for a certain degree of usability. Therefore intermediate results and the final product have to be tested in order to identify usage problems and room for improvement [12]. Suitable approaches depend, among others, on the

- fidelity of prototype (from paper prototype to fully functional interactive system);
- stage of development (from proof of concept to final test);
- available resources (e.g. budget, time, access to participants, equipment);
- expertise of evaluators (incl. skill in applying different techniques).

Evaluation Approaches. In general, ex ante, formative and summative evaluations can be differentiated. Additionally, we highlight the need for continuous evaluations.

Ex ante evaluations are usually done prior to an implementation to evaluate the concept (e.g. regarding feasibility or costs vs. benefits). They are focused on the current situation and potentials for improvement [13, 14]. Given the high costs and risks of developments for disaster and emergency management, interventions should be planned well and address the issues with the greatest potential for improvement. Ex ante evaluations can help to understand and determine the usage context and specify the requirements for new technology. Given the need of evaluations to have clear goals or comparison standards to objectively determine the quality of a solution, results of this primary assessment can be useful for formative and summative evaluations. Well-formulated and stated standards are crucial in disaster and emergency management because standards might differ between countries and even within different states of a country.

Formative evaluations are conducted several times during the development in order to gain suggestions for improvement. They are a crucial feedback mechanism to ensure the development stays on track and is optimized for the future users, not the developers. It is usually an interactive process with a focus on qualitative data that is helpful for the developers to come up with, implement and justify design decisions [15–17].

A summative evaluation is conducted once at the final stages of development. It is used to evaluate the overall success of the development. Objectivity, impartiality and independence of the evaluator are crucial as the results may be addressed by politicians, the public or funding agencies [15–17].

Combining these approaches is recommended in all of the previously mentioned usability engineering processes. Furthermore, some of them consider user feedback after installation respectively placing a product in the market (e.g. [11]).

Valuable insights regarding usability can be gained by getting feedback from users after several weeks, months or years of using an interactive system in practice (continuing evaluation). These observations can highlight issues not apparent in the usually short-term summative evaluation or reveal the effects of changing conditions (e.g. new standards or technologies are introduced), a changing user base (e.g. generational changes), or new threats (e.g. previously never encountered disasters).

Observing the actual usage in the field over long time periods should be planned during development and implemented. If done well, the results can be used for continuous improvement. Log files can be very useful as they unobtrusively gather actual usage data. Anonymously recorded with the user's knowledge and consent, they can help to identify features or function rarely used. Following this, developers and users could decide either to remove them or to improve their accessibility in the following version or via a short-term update. To go beyond the currently available features, users should be able to express usability problems without any great effort, e.g. via an implemented feedback function.

Interviews, workshops and (online) surveys can also be conducted but they have the disadvantage that users afterwards would have to remember interaction problems or other critical situations that occurred. During disasters or emergencies, they will not even be able to take notes about them. Therefore, it is unlikely that feedback would contain a great deal of actual improvement possibilities. However, log files could be used as memory aids to determine usability problems.

Reasoning Approaches. With respect to reasoning approaches, analytic methods based on models, guidelines or experts' reviews can be distinguished from empirical methods involving tests with actual users or appropriate representatives. While the first ones are often applied at early stages of usability engineering processes, the second ones are usually utilized at advanced stages. Because there is no "silver bullet" to usability evaluations, analytic and empiric methods are often combined in iterative design processes. Guiding empirical tests with results of analytic approaches was named *mediated evaluation* in the domain of education [18]. This term has been adopted by some researchers in the field of human-computer interaction and usability engineering [8].

Evaluation Designs. Data from evaluations have to be seen in context, so the research design of the evaluation matters as well. An *experiment* (i.e. randomly assigning people to either an experimental or a control group while controlling for confounding variables (cf. [19]) allows for determining cause-and-effect relationships. However, this requires a large amount of participants (roughly 30 per condition) and a high degree of control over the setting (see Sect. 3.2).

Quasi-experiments (variation, e.g. two conditions but no control of confounding variables) are more common. A typical example is the implementation of the solution in one workplace and comparing it with the performance in another one without that solution. However, the evidence is weaker as they do not allow casual inferences (there might be other reasons for the performance difference). Correlation studies are easier to conduct, but correlation does not imply causality so the values of conclusions are limited.

At the very least, some context should – and usually can – be provided, either with data from a previous/alternative solution or the current gold standard, or compared to earlier tests (pre-post-tests). While this data might not allow for casual inference, it provides at least some reference points for interpretation. Practical constrains usually determine what is possible, and even if the best design is not possible, the best possible design should be chosen.

2.3   Usability Evaluation in Disaster and Emergency Management

As mentioned before, technical reliability of systems in disasters and emergencies alone would not lead to better outcomes because "when the user interaction with a safety-critical system goes wrong, the result can be catastrophic" [20]. The importance of usability evaluations has not only been recognized by single research groups (e.g. [21–23]) but also by principal organizations dealing with disaster and emergency management. The Sendai Framework for Disaster Risk Reduction 2015-2030 is "the first major agreement" [24] with respect to disaster risk management and has been endorsed by the General Assembly of the United Nations. Although it does not name the term usability (evaluation), several statements in this matter can be found in the document:

- "…taking into account the needs of different categories of users…" [25, p. 14]
- "To support the development of local, national, regional and global user-friendly systems and services for the exchange of information on good practices, cost-effective and easy-to-use disaster risk reduction technologies and lessons learned on policies, plans and measures for disaster risk reduction." [25, p. 16]
- "…develop such systems through a participatory process; tailor them to the needs of users, including social and cultural requirements…" [25, p. 21]

The United Nations Office for Disaster Risk Reduction (UNISDR) adds that "it is imperative to improve the usability of such services [for information dissemination in disasters] by strengthening technological infrastructure in all locations and providing information in a clear and concise way" [26, p. 88].

These statements show that usability of interactive systems is an important aspect of disaster and emergency management. However, terms like "user-friendly systems" and "easy-to-use" have long been challenged by usability and human-computer interaction experts, because they are either "unnecessarily anthropomorphic" [10, p. 23] and can hardly be operationalized [27].

3   Assessing Usability Evaluation Methods and Settings

In the following sections, several analytic and empirical usability evaluation methods and settings will be assessed in their suitability for disaster and emergency management evaluations. They have been selected because they have proven to work in several domains with safety-critical characteristics.

3.1   Methods

Heuristic evaluations, model-based approaches, and cognitive walkthroughs will be outlined as usability evaluation methods in the following sections.

Heuristic Evaluation. In the context of usability evaluations, heuristics address "some basic characteristics of usable interfaces" [10, p. 115] like "Speak the users' language: The dialogue should be expressed clearly in words, phrases, and concept familiar to the user, rather than in system-oriented way" [10, p. 20].

A systematic and individual analysis of an interactive system according to such principles by one or more usability experts is called heuristic evaluation [8, 10]. Well-known and often applied sets of heuristics are Nielsen's 10 Usability Heuristics [10] and Shneiderman's 8 Golden Rules of Interface Design [28].

Because of their context independence, such heuristics cannot be used to evaluate domain-specific and safety-oriented aspects of interactive systems for disaster and emergency management. Furthermore, some recommendations might conflict and products might have different requirements that make it necessary to violate generic heuristics. However, violating a guideline or heuristic should be done deliberately and for good reasons. In general, if applications fail such basic principles of user interface and interaction design, they will hardly be usable in a safe and efficient way, especially under extraordinary circumstances. Therefore, heuristic evaluations by usability experts are an important and helpful method for formative evaluations. They can easily be complemented but not completely replaced by domain-specific inspections by disaster and emergency management experts. If possible, decisions based on guidelines should be tested via empirical data, e.g. in formative or summative evaluations.

Model-Based Approaches. In order to predict and analyze courses of human-computer interaction, task-oriented modeling approaches were developed [5, 12]. They have been applied to safety-critical domains like healthcare [29].

Methods like GOMS (Goals, Operators, Methods, Selection Rules) or KLM (Key-stroke-Level Method) are among the most commonly used model-based approaches [12, 28]. In this regard

- Goals are "simply the user's goals, as defined in layman's language" [30, p. 81];
- Operators are "the actions that the software allows the user to take" [30, p. 81];
- Methods are "well-learned sequences of sub-goals and operators that can accomplish a goal" [30, p. 81];
- Selection Rules are "the personal rules that users follow in deciding what method to use in a particular circumstance" [30, p. 81f].

By predicting the time to complete (TTC) tasks for single operators, overall performance can be estimated. In the case of disaster and emergency management, these estimations might be less precise than in other domains because GOMS specifically "applies to situations in which users will be expected to perform tasks that they have already mastered" [28, p. 84].

Therefore, model-based usability evaluation should be regarded as a valuable complement to other approaches and limited to the most time-critical parts of user interfaces for professional operators.

Cognitive Walkthrough. Cognitive Walkthrough and its variations like Cognitive Jogthrough are other analytic approaches to step-wise analysis of human-computer interaction by system designers and usability experts. It is based on the CE+ theory of exploratory learning [5, 31].

Apart from understanding important characteristics of future users, regular and extraordinary usage scenarios as well as defined sequences for efficient task completion are required [5]. Based on them, an analyst performs each interaction step individually and answers questions whether users would

- try to solve the problem in the right way;
- notice that an appropriate function or feature is available;
- associate available actions with desired effects;
- recognize the progress they made towards their goal [5].

Cognitive Walkthroughs have been applied to safety-critical domains, e.g. air traffic control [32]. With regard to computer-supported cooperative work, some modifications were found to be necessary in order to deal with individual and group tasks [33].

Therefore, cognitive walkthroughs might be especially helpful to improve applications for single non-professional users or individual operators of emergency and rescue services. Cooperation and team aspects characterizing disaster and emergency management to a certain degree could hardly be assessed with this approach.

3.2 Settings

For settings, the typical division of laboratory and field settings will be followed. Each of them will be assessed for its feasibility.

Usability Tests in the Laboratory. In the context of usability engineering, laboratory studies are characterized by users testing an interactive system in an artificial environment intended for evaluations (i.e. not in the users' workplace). The examiner's control of the setting is used to ensure stable testing conditions and to allow the use of standardized benchmarks [5, 8]. Laboratory environments usually allow for detailed unobtrusive data gathering, e.g. when audio and video recording equipment is hidden from view.

The main advantage of laboratory studies is high internal validity. Different users can use the product under the same circumstances, reducing the influence of confounding factors in the environment (e.g. disturbances, variance in environmental conditions, etc.). Given the high degree of control regarding confounding variables, laboratory studies are well-suited for experiments. This way, the improved version can be tested against the current version to determine whether the improved version is actually better.

However, laboratory studies suffer from limited external like ecological validity. The effects determined in the controlled situation in the laboratory might not carry over to actual use in the field. This is the case, if important aspects of the actual use (e.g. stress, environmental factors) were not replicated in the laboratory. For example, a solution supporting voice input and optical head-mounted display output, which is usable under well-defined lighting conditions and low noise level, might be useless while standing next to a highway in the rain under high traffic. This is frequently a problem with experiments —the usual focus on depth (few variables and a high degree of control) is at odds with the breadth of different conditions in disaster and emergency settings.

In summary, usability tests in the laboratory are an important empirical approach to measuring usability of disaster and emergency management systems, but have to consider the critical aspects of future usage scenarios. For example, both noise levels and lighting conditions can be modified with the aid of audio equipment or dimmers. For mobile and wearable devices, users should be requested to stand up or walk around. If necessary, obstacle courses have to be built.

Usability Tests in the Field. As opposed to laboratory studies, field studies are characterized by testing an interactive system in the users' familiar work environment. Preparing, conducting and analyzing results of usability tests in the field is challenging for several reasons:

- Access to critical areas, especially in safety-critical domains, might only be possible to a limited extent or not at all.
- Working conditions can hardly be controlled by examiners, e.g. disruptions by colleagues or environmental conditions.
- Data recording is more difficult than in laboratories. Retrospective interviews might be necessary in order to make sense of certain usage situations.

However, field studies can deliver valuable insights that are hard to get otherwise. The external, e.g. ecological validity is high, although at the cost of internal validity. While field experiments are possible, they typically require large amounts of resources. In general, field studies are useful in summative evaluations. Results of field studies can also be used to improve laboratory studies, e.g. by replicating important environmental factors.

4   Case Studies

In the following sections, two case studies conducted in close collaboration with Emergency Medical Services are outlined. Special respect is given to the applied formative and summative usability evaluation measures.

4.1   Supporting Collaboration in MCIs with Tablet PCs

Mass Casualty Incidents (MCIs) are characterized by "more patients at one time than locally available resources can manage using routine procedures" [34]. Dozens or hundreds of paramedics and emergency physicians have to collaborate in order to treat patients in the best possible way and apply resources efficiently. Incident commanders are in charge of task prioritization and personnel management.

Currently, paper-based artifacts (e.g. forms, tables, charts, maps) and various means of communication (e.g. radio, mobile phone, messengers, face-to-face conversations) are used for record keeping and information management. Situation awareness of incident commanders in MCIs is a demanding challenge [35].

Mobile computer-based tools might help to improve the situation because data can be exchanged and updated within a narrow time frame independent of the incident commanders' locations. Scalable visualizations (e.g. filter functions, summary vs.

detail view) would allow for solving different information needs. Problems because of poor handwriting could be prevented. However, designing such solutions is both a technical and a usability challenge. Incident commanders and other rescue forces are under high physical and mental stress due to the extraordinary circumstances.

Within a two-year user-centered system design project, we developed a prototype of a tablet-based data gathering and information management system in close collaboration with German Emergency Medical Services (cf. [36–38] for more details).

Apart from regular interviews, focus groups and workshops with members of Emergency Medical Services, several specific formative and summative usability methods were applied. They are described subsequently.

First of all, prototypes and single interaction elements were reviewed by usability experts a number of times. The well-established dialogue principles of ISO standard 9241-110 served as heuristics (see Sect. 3.1). For example, error tolerance as one of these dialogue principles was considered by proposing a button-oriented design (see Fig. 1)"offering a choice of valid input values, e.g. for triage categories, diagnoses, drug names, doses or feed rates" [39], "favoring filtering over searching functions" [39] and "searching phonetically when needed" [39].

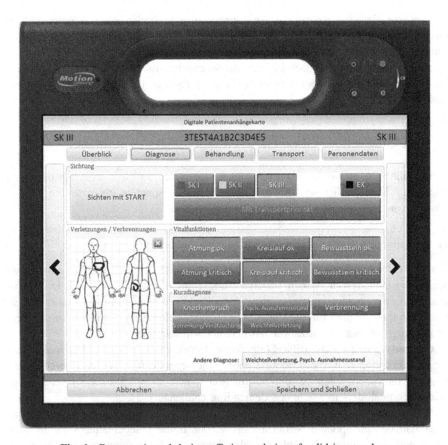

Fig. 1. Button-oriented design offering a choice of valid input values

Furthermore, alternative designs were presented to members of EMS. They were invited to choose their preferred version or to make proposals for better solutions. For example, four different drafts of a bar chart visualizing the number of patients in a specific triage category were discussed by 36 paramedics and physicians (see Fig. 2).

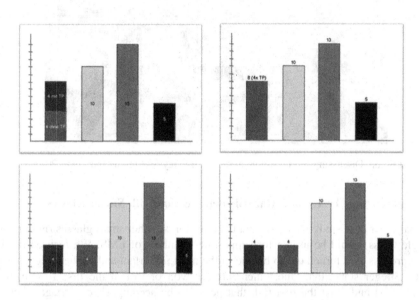

Fig. 2. Alternative design of a bar chart for triage categories [34]

While 5 participants came up with own solutions, the 3 versions preferred most got 9, 6 and 5 votes, respectively. Disregarding minor differences, e.g. exact label positions, one design approach got 14 votes. The drafts were subject of a controversial debate which "enabled us to better match our conceptual model with their mental model beyond the use cases associated with the actual chart" [35].

The advanced prototype was shown to visitors of the leading German professional emergency medicine and rescue fair "akut 2012" at an own booth for two days (see Fig. 3). Although this is not a standard form of formative evaluation, we gained both important feedback from various experts as well as confirmations for our basic approaches [40].

Summative evaluation was performed during an exercise with an EMS and 40 virtual patients represented by cards. "Staging, triage, treatment, transport and assembly areas as well as an emergency control room were in place and equipped with tablet PCs" [40]. Participants were observed by 10 persons (members of the research team and volunteers) and asked to answer the validated ISONORM questionnaire after finishing the test. Following this, debriefing with all parties involved was conducted. Despite some network connectivity problems and minor usability flaws, results support the basic design approach. Based on these findings, we continued our research about usability of mobile and wearable devices in safety-critical domains using the example of EMS.

Fig. 3. Discussing the prototype at the emergency and rescue fair "akut 2012"

4.2   Supporting Triage and Hazard Identification with Smart Glasses

In a half-year case study we dealt with the question whether smart glasses (in our case Google Glass) could be usable for supporting members of EMS. We focused on the triage process as it turned out to be one of the most important and challenging tasks in MCIs. Streger states that "most incidents are won or lost in the first 10 min after arrival" [41] and "that the first task that needs to be accomplished is triage of casualties" [41]. Triage shall ensure the best possible outcome for the casualties by assigning a treatment priority for each of them. Since it has to be done as fast as possible, it is usually conducted by a member of one of the first arriving ambulances. Because MCIs are rare events for individual EMS members, most of them have only little experience in this matter.

The decision for starting research on smart glasses resulted from potential advantages compared to mobile devices (e.g. tablets), e.g. hands-free operation or the display in the user's sight of view. Carenzo et al. [42] and Cicero et al. [43] confirm this assumption. Google Glass supports voice recognition and touch gestures on the right side piece as primary interaction forms. Both of them were considered [44].

A user-centered design process was chosen. Experts from EMS and disaster relief units participated throughout all stages of development. First of all, semi-structured interviews were conducted with ten domain experts. Basic requirements as well as challenges for system design were derived. For example, the usage of algorithms was recommended. There was broad consensus that members of EMS shall not only have a command of the algorithms but also use them mandatory in the triage process [45]. Nevertheless, algorithms for triage in MCIs might not be remembered completely by rescue workers because of their mental load in extraordinary and rare circumstances. A computer-based solution not only could replace paper-based versions but gather data for documentation purposes and exchange it with incident commanders [46].

Before coding, mockups were designed and evaluated with usability and domain experts. Subsequently, two versions of the application with different interface and interaction design were implemented. One of them had to be discarded quickly because of technological flaws and not being consistent with design principles of Google. The other one was implemented iteratively (see Fig. 4).

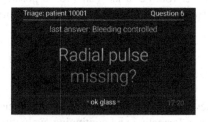 

Fig. 4. Instructions and questions are shown to the user interacting via voice commands. (Color figure online)

The application was evaluated by 14 domain experts [46]. Because one of them saw the display distorted, only 13 EMS test persons could be considered. Participants were given four case descriptions and asked to perform triage. They were observed and notes were taken about usability problems. 11 of 13 users were able to solve all tasks without problems after a short learning phase. 2 participants were uncertain about system's state

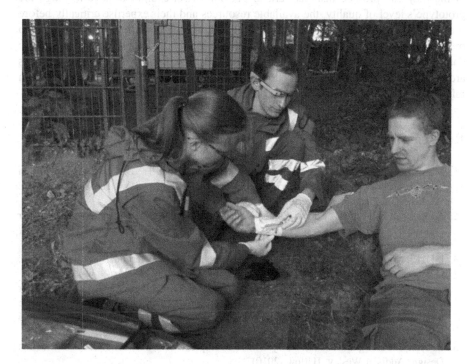

Fig. 5. Triage of a casualty with a heavy bleeding. The user wearing smartglasses helps applying a pressure dressing [46].

and further actions even at the last test case [46]. 8 participants called the triage support system *"useful"* [46] and *"helpful"* [46].

In addition, the usage scenario of two EMS members working together while one of them is using smart glasses was simulated for demonstration purposes (see Fig. 5). Applying a pressure dressing or performing other routine tasks seems to be possible while interacting with the wearable device. However, further research and usability evaluations are necessary.

5   Conclusions

Usability evaluations of disaster and emergency management systems are both crucial and challenging. Focus should be laid on ex ante, formative and continuing evaluation approaches utilizing heuristic evaluations, cognitive walkthroughs, log files and integrated feedback functions.

Usability tests in the laboratory are characterized by a high degree of control regarding confounding variables. When performing them for disaster and emergency settings, critical aspects of future usage scenarios have to be considered. Modifying noise levels, lighting conditions or interrupting users are quite easy measures to derive a certain degree of realism.

On the contrary, usability tests in the field require large amounts of resources. While they can provide insights hard to get otherwise, examiners have to judge the prototype's level of quality, the available resources and their expertise critically before preparing such a test. For example, several persons might be necessary in order to observe different areas of operation and responsible users belonging to just one public authority. Conducting data, analyzing results and drawing appropriate consequences are major challenges under these circumstances. Cost-benefit ratio should be kept in mind.

References

1. Meissner, A., Luckenbach, T., Risse, T., Kirste, T., Kirchner, H.: Design challenges for an integrated disaster management communication and information system. In: First IEEE Workshop on Disaster Recovery Networks (DIREN) (2002)
2. Ropohl, G.: Philosophy of Socio-techical systems. In: Agazzi, E., Lenk, H. (eds.) Society for Philosophy and Technology (1999). http://scholar.lib.vt.edu/ejournals/SPT/v4_n3html/ROPOHL.html
3. ISO: Ergonomic requirements for office work with visual display terminals (VDTs) - Part 11: Guidance on usability (1998)
4. Good, M., Spine, T.M., Whitesid, J., George, P.: User-derived impact analysis as a tool for usability engineering. In: Mantei, M., Orbeton, P. (eds.) CHI 1986 Proceedings of the SIGCHI Conference on Human Factors in Computing Systems. ACM, NY, pp. 241–246 (1986)
5. Benyon, D.: Designing Interactive Systems. A Comprehensive Guide to HCI and Interaction Design. Addison Wesley, Harlow (2010)
6. Butler, K.A.: Usability engineering turns 10. Interactions **3**, 58–75 (1996)

7. Leitner, G., Ahlström, D., Hitz, M.: Usability of Mobile Computing in Emergency Response Systems – Lessons Learned and Future Directions. In: Holzinger, A. (ed.) USAB 2007. LNCS, vol. 4799, pp. 241–254. Springer, Heidelberg (2007). https://doi.org/10.1007/978-3-540-76805-0_20

8. Beyer, H., Holtzblatt, K.: Contextual Design. Defining Customer-Centered Systems. Morgan Kaufmann, San Francisco (1998)

9. Rosson, M.B., Carroll, J.M.: Usability Engineering. Scenario-based Development of Human-Computer Interaction. Academic Press, San Francisco (2002)

10. Mayhew, D.J.: The Usability Engineering Lifecycle. A Practitioner's Handbook for User Interface Design. Morgan Kaufmann Publishers, San Francisco (1999)

11. Nielsen, J.: Usability Engineering. Kaufmann, Amsterdam (1993)

12. Herczeg, M.: Software-Ergonomie. Theorien, Modelle und Kriterien für gebrauchstaugliche interaktive Computersysteme. Oldenbourg Wissenschaftsverlag, München (2009)

13. CORE Consultancy Research Evaluation (n.d.). http://www.evaluation.co.at/evaluation_konzept.htm

14. European Commission: Ex Ante Evaluation. A practical guide for preparing proposals for expenditure programmes (2001). http://ec.europa.eu/smart-regulation/evaluation/docs/ex_ante_guide_2001_en.pdf

15. Wottawa, H., Thierau, H.: Lehrbuch Evaluation. Verlag Hans Huber, Bern (1998)

16. Sarodnick, F., Brau, H.: Methoden der Usability Evaluation. Wissenschaftliche Grundlagen und praktische Anwendung. Verlag Hans Huber, Bern (2006)

17. Sauro, J., Lewis, J.R.: Quantifying the User Experience. Practical Statistics for User Research. Elsevier/Morgan Kaufmann, Amsterdam (2012)

18. Huber, O.: Das psychologische Experiment: Eine Einführung. Verlag Hans Huber, Bern (1987)

19. Scriven, M.: The Methodology of Evaluation. Purdue University, Lafayette (1966)

20. Redmill, F., Rajan, J.: Human Factors in Safety-Critical Systems. Butterworth-Heinemann, Oxford (1997)

21. Fischer, H., Klompmaker, F.: Enriching disaster control management based on human-centered design. In: Proceedings of the 9th International Conference on Information Systems for Crisis Response and Management ISCRAM. ISCRAM, Vancouver (2012)

22. Yang, D., Zhang, D., Frank, K., Robertson, P., Jennings, E., Roddy, M., Lichtenstern, M.: Providing real-time assistance in disaster relief by leveraging crowdsourcing power. Pers. Ubiquit. Comput. 8, 2025–2034 (2014)

23. Li, J., Wilson, L., Stapleton, S., Cregan, P.: Design of an advanced telemedicine system for emergency care. In: Robertson, T. (ed) OZCHI 2006 Proceedings of the 18th Australia Conference on Computer-Human Interaction: Design: Activities, Artefacts and Environments, pp. 413–416 (2006)

24. United Nations Office for Disaster Risk Reduction. http://www.unisdr.org/we/coordinate/sendai-framework

25. United Nations Office for Disaster Risk Reduction: The Sendai Framework for Disaster Risk Reduction 2015–2030. http://www.unisdr.org/files/43291_sendaiframeworkfordrren.pdf (2015)

26. United Nations Office for Disaster Risk Reduction: Progress and Challenges in Disaster Risk Reduction (2014). http://www.unisdr.org/files/40967_40967progressandchallengesindisaste.pdf

27. Cooper, A., Reimann, R., Cronin, D.: About Face 3. The Essentials of Interaction Design. Wiley, Indianapolis (2007)

28. Shneiderman, B.: Designing the User Interface. Strategies for Effective Human-Computer Interaction. Addison-Wesley, Indianapolis (1998)

29. Magrabi, F.: Using cognitive models to evaluate safety-critical interfaces in healthcare. In: CHI 2008 Extended Abstracts on Human Factors in Computing Systems (CHI EA 2008). ACM, New York, pp. 3567–3572 (2008)
30. Bonnie, J.: Why GOMS? Interactions **4**, 80–89 (1995)
31. Rieman, J., Franzke, M., Redmiles, D.: Usability evaluation with the cognitive walkthrough. In: Conference Companion on Human Factors in Computing Systems (CHI 1995). ACM, New York, pp. 387–388 (1995)
32. Novick, D.G.: Using the cognitive walkthrough for operating procedures. Interactions **3**, 31–37 (1999)
33. Ereback, A.L., Höök, K.: Using cognitive walkthrough for evaluating a CSCW application. In: Conference Companion on Human Factors in Computing Systems (CHI 1994). ACM, New York, pp. 91–92 (1994)
34. World Health Organization: Mass casualty management systems - strategies and guidelines for building health sector capacity (2007). http://www.who.int/hac/techguidance/
35. Mentler, T., Herczeg, M.: Interactive cognitive artifacts for enhancing situation awareness of incident commanders in mass casualty incidents. J. Interact. Sci. **3**, 7 (2015)
36. Kindsmüller, M.C., Mentler, T., Herczeg, M., Rumland, T.: Care & prepare - usability engineering for mass casualty incidents. In: ACM EICS4Med 2011: Proceedings of the 1st International Workshop on Engineering Interactive Computing Systems for Medicine and Health Care. ACM, New York, pp. 30–35 (2011)
37. Mentler, T., Herczeg, M., Jent, S., Stoislow, M., Kindsmüller, M.C.: Routine mobile applications for emergency medical services in mass casualty incidents. In: Biomed Tech - Proceedings BMT 2012, vol. 57 (Suppl. 1), pp. 784–787 (2012)
38. Mentler, T., Herczeg, M.: Routine- und Ausnahmebetrieb im mobilen Kontext des Rettungsdienstes. In: Boll, S., Maaß, S., Malaka, R. (eds.) Mensch & Computer 2013. De Gruyter, München, pp. 109–118 (2013)
39. Mentler, T., Herczeg, M.: Applying ISO 9241-110 dialogue principles to tablet applications in emergency medical services. In: Comes, T., Fiedrich, F., Fortier, S., Geldermann, J., Müller, T. (eds.) 10th International ISCRAM Conference, ISCRAM, Baden-Baden, pp. 502–506 (2013)
40. Mentler, T., Herczeg, M.: Human factors and ergonomics in mobile computing for emergency medical services. In: Ahram, T., Karwowski, W., Marek, T. (eds) Proceedings of the 5th International Conference on Applied Human Factors and Ergonomics, AHFE, Krakow, pp. 4149–4160 (2014)
41. Streger, M.R.: Prehospital triage. Emerg. Med. Serv. **27**, 21–27 (1998)
42. Carenzo, L., Barra, F.L., Ingrassia, P.L., Colombo, D., Costa, A., Della Corte, F.: Disaster medicine through Google glass. Eur. J. Emerg. Med. **3**, 222–225 (2015)
43. Cicero, M.X., Walsh, B., Solad, Y., Whitfill, T., Paesano, G., Kim, K., Cone, D.C.: Do you see what I see? Insights from using Google glass for disaster telemedicine triage. Prehospital Disaster Med. **1**, 4–8 (2015)
44. Berndt, H., Mentler, T., Herczeg, M.: Smartglasses for the triage of casualties and the identification of hazardous materials. i-com **2**, 145–153 (2016)
45. Bundesamt für Bevölkerungsschutz und Katastrophenhilfe: In: 6 Sichtungs-Konsensus-Konferenz (2015). http://www.bbk.bund.de/SharedDocs/Downloads/BBK/DE/Downloads/GesBevS/6_Konsensus-Konferenz_Protokoll.pdf?__blob=publicationFile
46. Berndt, H., Mentler, T., Herczeg, M.: Optical head-mounted displays in mass casualty incidents: keeping an eye on patients and hazardous materials. Int. J. Inform. Syst. Crisis Response Manag. **3**, 1–15 (2015)

Formal Methods for Safe Design of Autonomous Systems Dedicated to Risk Management

Sophie Coudert[(✉)] and Tullio Joseph Tanzi

Telecom ParisTech, Sophia Antipolis, France
{sophie.coudert, tullio.tanzi}@telecom-paristech.fr

Abstract. A new generation of Autonomous systems (UAVs, ROVERs, etc.) is coming that will help improve the situational awareness and assessment, especially in difficult conditions like disasters. Rescuers should be relieved from time-consuming data collection tasks as much as possible and at the same time, Autonomous systems should assist data collection through a more insightful and automated guidance thanks to advanced sensing capabilities. In order to achieve this vision, two challenges must be addressed though. The first one is to achieve a sufficient autonomy. The second one relates to the reliability with respect to accidental (safety) or even malicious (security) risks. This however requires the design of new embedded architectures to be more autonomous, while mitigating the harm they may potentially cause. Increased complexity and flexibility requires resorting to modelling, simulation and formal verification techniques in order to validate such critical aspects.

Keywords: Autonomous systems · Formal methods · Safety · Security

1 Introduction

According to Guhar-Sapir et al. [14], in 2012, naturally triggered disasters (earthquakes, landslides, and severe weather, such as tropical cyclones, severe storms, floods) killed a total of 9,655 people, and 124.5 million people became victims, worldwide. Although those numbers were well below the 2002–2011 annual averages (107,000 people killed and 268 million victims), economic damages did show an increase to above-average levels (143 billion USD). When a natural disaster occurs in a populated area, it is mandatory to organize disaster management operations quickly and effectively in order to assist the population, to reduce the number of victims, and to mitigate the economic consequences [9, 14, 22, 23]. A non-optimal organization causes supplementary losses and delays in resuming the situation to normal (http://www.un-spider.org/).

At any time, the rescue teams need immediate and relevant information concerning the situations they have to face: disaster evolution, surviving persons, critical zones, access to refugee camps, spread assistance tools, etc. The required information is provided by a comprehensive data handling system fed with data generally produced by organizations and space agencies involved in the International Charter Space and Major Disasters.

Y. Murayama et al. (Eds.): ITDRR 2016, IFIP AICT 501, pp. 61–76, 2017.
https://doi.org/10.1007/978-3-319-68486-4_6

As explained in [23], new approaches and the use of new technologies are required for a more efficient management, before, during, and after a crisis. Every specific action at each step of the crisis must be specifically taken into account. For that purpose, new dedicated tools and methodologies are required to better handle crisis situations.

We present in this paper a new approach for which a new generation autonomous systems may help improve the response of rescue teams. In particular, we discuss how autonomous systems may support rescue teams and help them to more systematically explore their surroundings. We discuss the important challenges that must be addressed in terms of navigation and detection autonomy, as well as reliability in terms of safety and security, in order to enable the seamless use of such systems by non-experts persons.

1.1 Potential Applications of Autonomous Systems

We have identified three critical fields in the relief missions: (i) communications and coordination, (ii) recognition field, and finally (iii) search operations.

During such an event, maintaining a communication link with the various actors of the response on the one hand and with victims on the other hand is crucial. Unfortunately, when the communication infrastructure has been hit, rescue teams rely essentially on radios or satellite communications. This link remains essential even in the face of non-catastrophic circumstances, like for instance a major black-out in a network (electricity, water, etc.).

Autonomous systems might extend the communication range available as they may be deployed as mobile radio relays. They may also convey messages in a disruption tolerant network (DTN) fashion, during their normal operations, typically between the actors involved. Data sensing results have to be communicated as they are produced, and will serve for the coordination of relief operations. In this sense, the systems should also be autonomous in deciding which data to pre-process and to communicate in order to establish operational priorities.

The detection and the monitoring of the impact of natural disasters on terrain are mainly performed by space borne and air borne relying on radio and optical instruments. Due to limitations in the time window observation attached to optical instruments (i.e. no observation at night or in presence of cloud cover), radio observations are available 24/7 and relatively insensitive to atmospheric conditions: these are therefore particularly useful during the "Response phase" when information must be delivered to the disaster cell with a delay as short as possible delay [18, 26, 27].

Autonomous systems may bring significant improvements with respect to those issues. They can be easily equipped with various kinds of sensors in addition to optical ones depending on their potential mission. Their capacities make it easy to observe below a cloud cover. For example, search and rescue teams may carry UAVs and deploy them upon need on site, for instance to explore some flooded area in order to find a practicable path to victims, or a ruined building. In this respect, UAVs extend the exploration range of rescue teams while at the same time improving their safety in areas that may reveal dangerous for their own safety. The senseFly UAV has for instance demonstrated the automated mapping capabilities of small drones and how they could improve the lives of victims in the aftermath of the Ha"ıti 2010 earthquake, by enabling the authorities to quickly draw maps of devastated areas [4].

After a brief presentation of context and an introduction to safety and security aspects (Sects. 1 and 2), Sect. 3 is a brief high level introduction to formal methods. Section 4 provides some more concrete example of applying them, in the domain of autonomous systems and risk avoidance. Section 5 is a discussion about present and future development followed by conclusion.

2 Reliability: Safety and Security

Legal and ethical constraints arise out of potential risks incurred by the use of an autonomous systems with respect to both victims and rescuers. For instance, a UAV crash may cause damages and harm people; as another example, privacy requires the release of any footage of a disaster to be controlled. Satisfying those constraints requires taking into account the risks linked with fault-tolerance (like for instance in case of the violation of real-time deadlines of safety-critical tasks) and security (sensed data piracy, hijacking, etc.) and to prevent them with adequate countermeasures. Mitigating or preventing those risks involves the introduction of multiple security and safety mechanisms into components as well as in the overall architectural design, which we detail per domain below.

A common way to ensure that a sensor (navigation or payload) has not failed or that its data have not been corrupted by interference, noise or attacks is to perform a plausibility check. Those checks can be done on sensor data in isolation. Many embedded functions also rely on the data produced by several sensors, and checks will consist in ensuring their consistency. Typically, the stabilisation system relies on data issued from the gyroscope, altimeter, etc. Such a verification must be used in our system architecture to improve both the safety of critical function and to limit the impact of attacks.

The deployment of Autonomous systems for such applications will also bring up societal challenges. Indeed, the apparition of a UAV may be terrifying to an unprepared victim (Predator Syndrome), which might reduce the effectiveness of the detection operations. In contrast, victims may not notice UAVs flying at a high altitude and therefore fail to signal their position as they would for an aircraft. New standards will probably have to be defined in this respect.

Furthermore, in critical applications regarding safety, a solution must be validated before it is applied on the field. It is forbidden to test solutions directly on the real system for safety reasons. Any attempt of modification or intrusion of a safety system must be approached with the utmost care. The proposed solutions must be validated, and, if possible, formally validated. It is the case of prevention systems for accidents, installed on highways. They also are in charge of gathering information in the case of an accident actually occurring. In this context, we aim to provide an approach to validate the behaviour of a critical system before its effective realization (rapid pro-totyping). Since the tests are not covering all the possibilities, we then move to formally verifying the critical properties. This formal analysis is made possible by the mathe-matical grounds used.

Regarding the critical applications, meaning the applications for which a system failure could cause important damages to the people and/or the installations, it is possible to gain enough confidence about the systems functioning by imposing suitable development and validating methods. Norms indicating the methods to follow can be found. For instance, the techniques used in a safety functional analysis highlight external specifications defects that may have gone unnoticed during the various stages of the study. The past few years have witnessed progresses made in the field of operating reliability for the technical parts of risky systems. Nevertheless, some issues still remain:

- What level of reliability should we allocate to each component?
- How do we assess this reliability?
- What are the main default risks?
- How do we identify them?
- How do we measure them?
- ...

To conclude this first part, it is necessary to constitute an approach based on formal methodology able to insure the safety of the autonomous system behaviour. Mathematical models and formal methods are tools with interesting features to ensure these objectives.

3 Formal Methods Overview

As pointed by [21] in a chapter about formal methods, mathematical analysis modelling is not new in engineering. The specificity of formal methods is their close relation to computer science, mechanisation and automating. They originate in modern formal logics which characterises reasoning rules as pure shapes and then allow to mechanically check valid reasoning as strict combination of valid rules. The soundness of such reasoning relies on the mathematical proof of each rule—the inference it allows is always true (roughly speaking, in set theory)—and on the mathematical proof of the combination principles: combining valid rules leads to valid deductions or inferences. This kind of approach has then been extended to other way of reasoning on mathematical models such as model checking for example which allows to establish properties on state machines by going through all possible states.

Thus the first historical interest of formal tools was to avoid human mistakes in reasoning. The profit was a very strong guaranty but the cost was very high. Indeed, formal reasoning requires each elementary step be explicit and is thus very complexe. For example, proving that $a + b + c + d + e = e + a + c + b$ requires multiple application of rules $x + y = y + x$ and $(x + y) + z = x + (y + z)$. Model checking is limited by the number of states of FSM (Finite State Machines), etc. On the other hand, formalizing allows some total or partial automating. As computers were slow, it was of limited interest but as computing capabilities increased a lot, things have changed. And the last three decades have seen the development of many enhancements, complementary technics, associated tools, methodologies, etc. (see [5]). Thus, although intrinsic complexity and induced cost remains an obstacle to the substantial use of formal methods in industry, the scope of these methods has extended to more than only guaranteeing critical small systems or small critical parts of systems.

Experience around formal methods leads to the emergence of some keys trends in recurrent difficulties to apply them and solutions to overcome these difficulties. These solutions have led to develop knowledge useful beyond the simple aim to rigorously prove properties. Here we summarise this in three points without claiming to be exhaustive.

Abstraction, refinement and early modelling. The idea is simple: omitting information which does not matter with respect to an expected property makes it easier to establish this property. For example, you can ignore identities of people in a queue if you are only interested in the size of the queue. Abstraction provides simpler models and thus significally simplifies applying formal technics. It reduces the number of states of state machines for model checking. It reduces the number of formulas and makes them simpler for logically specified properties. In brief, it makes checking feasible where it would not be without abstraction. The major issue for a reliable guaranty is then to ensure that omitted information actually doesn't matter. Much scientific results in formal methods address this concern: they characterize reliable relations between abstract and concrete models to ensure good abstractions.

As shown by **Error! Reference source not found.**, refinement is the methodological counterpart of abstraction: mathematical relations are similar and the difference is the order in which models are produced. Abstraction extracts property-relevant information from a more concrete model while refining adds details to an abstract model to move toward complete model (Fig. 1).

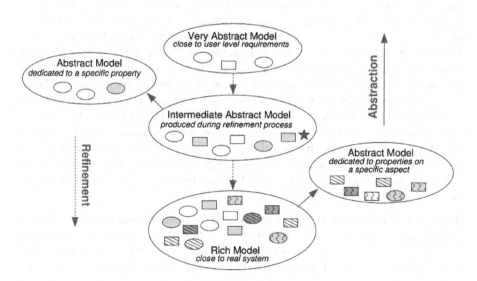

Fig. 1. Abstraction – Refinement

Properties can be checked at each level and mathematical guaranty about relations between models ensures high level properties are inherited by lower levels. Another similar aspect is composition: different parts or agents of a system can be specified separately and these specifications are then combined using specific rules. Preservation (or not) of properties by composition is also mathematically assured but additional verifications are sometime necessary.

The perfect warranty is proof (interactive or automatic, depending of method) but the amount of induced work often leads to compromises. Despite this restriction, experience shows that using techniques of formal methods and the use of abstraction, very early in the design process seriously improves the reliability of the result. Another gain is early detection of high level design errors. It avoids the enormous cost induced by the late detection and long and costly ex-post checks. Formal guaranty applies only in the case of mathematical models. Human expertise is very important both to design the detailed model corresponding to the real system and to specify the required high level properties.

Diversifying the use of formal models. Not everything can be proved, but once formal model have been produced, they are also used to apply a wide variety of techniques taking benefit of rigor and abstraction. Here we just give an idea of some of these approaches. Formal techniques allow rapid prototyping. Formal model can be animated and, for example, used for validation: a human can observe the global behaviour of the system before it is implemented. Using computing and abstraction, rapid simulation can be implemented by optimized algorithms and although all paths and states of the system are not covered, the automatically tested part of the system is then much more substantial compared to previous simulation approaches. Formal specification can also be used to automatically produce test sets with a good understanding of the scope of these sets. As high level specification describe "what" the system does and not "how", they can be used to provide inferred high level results to compare with the expected ones (i.e. they provide an "oracle"). It is well known that confronting two solutions to obtain a safer result is a good approach when these solutions are very different; here the specification plays the role of one solution. Some works exists also about automatic generation of human readable documentation. As development of formal methods is quite recent, complementary tools using their models continue to emerge nowadays and this presentation is not exhaustive. And last but not least, it is widely recognized that formal modelling alone suffices to highly enhance the design process. Indeed as formal specifying is exigent, it forces to make all requirement precise and unambiguous which leads to debugging them at the beginning of the design process, which is very rentable.

Making specification more user-friendly and providing methodologies. Models must properly represent reality and thus be validated by humans. Unfortunately expertise both in application domain and formal notation is rare which compromises the use of formal technics. Tools are developed to overcome this problem. For example, graphical notations are used to describe systems in an intuitive way and the result is then automatically translated into formal description. Previously mentioned animation of models or automatic generation of natural language helps humans to confront formal specifications with their expectations without formal expertise. Such tools are often integrated in environments with associated methodologies combining formal and unformal verifications. Much has been done to make use of formal methods more attractive and convincing and to allow experts of application domain to play their role.

It would be unrealistic to believe that use of formal methods can be done without formal method experts. The way in which specifications are written has a significant impact on the efficiency of the tools or the size of the proofs. Scientific work continues to propose guidelines, methodologies and associated tools for finding good abstraction and structuring. Concrete expertise is also required on tools themselves. For example in some context a semi-automatic theorem prover may be more powerful using a property written "b = a" than using the same property written "a = b". The lack of such expertise is an obstacle but it is an inherent problem as formal methods are recent. The situation is changing and some businesses begin to have their own team of specifiers. For example Parisian metropolitan company (RATP) uses the B method since the nineties and has its own team of specialists.

As formal methods have essentially been developed by mathematicians moving to computer science, they naturally have been initially applied to software engineering. As a paradox, the programmer's world was not familiar with mathematical modelling and it has probably put the brakes on their integration in real practice. Moreover time to market consideration have become more important than safety in this domain and despite all previously presented enhancements, historical cost of formal methods have been dissuasive. Of course, much of these enhancements and specialisations have targeted software engineering. But in general they may be useful for a lot of other disciplines. Logics can not only model software but potentially anything in the world. This appears in recent developments. They have been applied to computer hardware verification and then more generally to hardware–software system design such as embedded systems. Security aspects, i.e. protection against attacks are also addressed. More recently, they are extended to cyber-physical systems [10, 13] and the question of modelling not only discrete time but also continuous aspects arise. And as illustrated in Sect. 4.3 new applications appear, for example to validate human-machine interaction [8].

Today formal methods have attained a certain level of maturity and are relevant to explore new domains and particularly those were safety is crucial. For all these reasons we believe that formal methods may yield interesting benefits to "risk management". And here we focus on autonomous systems in this context.

4 Autonomous Systems Illustrations

Applications of formal methods already exist in relation to risk management and autonomous systems. In this section we present some of them. The examples of the two first subsections are extracted from our previous works concerning various equipments dedicated to the safety road (cf. Sect. 4.1) or autonomous system such as UAV (cf. Sect. 4.2). The third one briefly summarise other works in the literature.

4.1   Transportation Example: Motorway

In this illustration, taken from [24], we adopt a synchronous approach to model and analyse the behaviour of devices related to safety on the highways. This approach provides guarantees on system behaviour and allows you to test its behaviour as soon as the design phases (see **Error! Reference source not found.**). The selected graphic synchronous model, which is based on the concepts of States and transitions, allows more communication with the users of the system, without recourse to the underlying synchronous language explicitly. Associated tools facilitate the implementation and operation of test scenarios. These tests can also be carried out interactively. Even more interesting is the possibility of formally establishing properties of safety. The knowledge acquired during the design phase, i.e. before the actual performance of the system, can be reflected immediately toward the design team.

The goal is the definition of an information system for the technical data necessary to maintain the level of viability and security of a highway network. The studied solution proposes to use private communication network buried along the motorway to transmit information. The network used is a basic emergency call network (RAU). If a user comes to use emergency phone at the same time as relief, its communication becomes a priority at the expense of any other operation. In case of malfunction of the classic RAU, the system must be able to offer an alternative of taking over and relief by routing the message to the next connection point operational (Fig. 2).

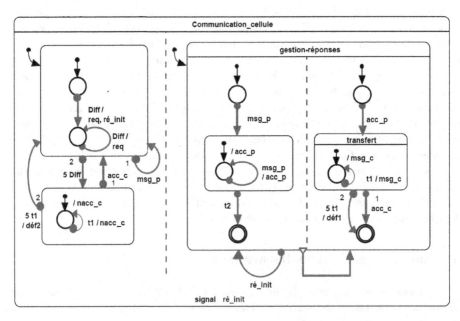

Fig. 2. Example of behaviour modelling

Given the formal nature of the model used, it is possible to prove properties related to the model. The technique that we have adopted is that of symbolic model checking. The idea is to explore exhaustively the State space of the model. This assumes that our model has a finite number of states. However, this space while finite can be so large that the audit programs are unable to analyse it. The use of a symbolic evaluation avoids an explicit construction of the state-space and makes it possible to tackle potentially very large areas.

The models are translated into a system of Boolean equations that represent the control of the program. As there are very effective techniques based on the BDD (Binary Decision Diagrams) to evaluate the systems of Boolean equations symbolically, we can apply techniques of symbolic verification to our models.

In a simplified way, a security property expresses the fact that, no matter how the system changes, we won't get unwanted situations. Being able to prove this kind of property is naturally important in critical systems. In our applications, we distinguish between different classes of safety properties: (i) Combinatorial properties. They express that a predicate is always true for all available states (for example, a mutual exclusion between actions). (ii) Properties of sequential type. These properties are usually expressed by formulas of temporal logics. It comes, for example to show that a dangerous succession of actions will never happen.

In conclusion, we thus have very valuable assistance, because the created scenarios correspond to changes that the tester may not even think about. It is clear that this technique may lead the user to discover anomalies deeply hidden in its specifications or design.

4.2 Autonomous System: Safety Drone Born

We now illustrate some results obtained from the modelling and validation methodology of a mini-drone aimed at autonomously indoor navigating. This drone was implemented on top of an existing drone platform [19]. It uses a 720p monocular camera to capture 2D images. "Corkscrew flight" allows to reconstruct the UAV 3D environment from the captured 2D images. This requires the synchronization between the motion control (MC) subsystem and the payload management (PM) in charge of image acquisition. The UAV deduces from its environment model flight orders that are sent to the flight control agent.

The approach consists in a three-step methodology: (i) model the functions of the system, (ii) capture the candidate hardware architectures, which is defined in terms of processors, buses and memories, and finally (iii) allocate functions and their communications to the resources of the hardware architecture and study the impact of this allocation with respect to the properties assessed.

In the first iterations of the design, the main purpose of validation is not so much to search for possible deadlock situations usually studied on more accurate models than to study the load of processors and platform buses, and the impact of this load on the flight capabilities of the drone.

For instance, one can clearly see that data from the different sensors (video, attitude, altitude) are sent separately to the ComputingNavigationOrders function that fuses them to interpret the scene before sending commands to the FlightControl.

Modelling tools computes the CPU load resulting from a simulation of the different tasks at hand, as well as a simulation of the inter-CPU information flows triggered by function interactions. This can be used to determine that it would be quite safe to run the emergency tasks on the drone CPU for instance. Other simulations about emergency situations have also been successfully performed to verify that this partitioning of functional tasks can support emergency response functions within acceptable real-time constraints.

4.3   Other Works

(A) B-method, metro and railway story. The numerous uses of the B method [2, 11, 12, 17] in the domain of rail transportation [1] is an atypical example of successful early introduction of such a kind of method in industrial practice. Indeed, it relies on interactive proving of set theoretic properties, which requires lot of human expertise and manpower. Thus, thirty years ago, it was difficult to convince industry to move to such approaches. Moreover complete implementation of the method supposes to entirely prove the respect of abstract specifications and required properties by final software. This is particularly demanding and binding unlike model checking, for example, which offers automatic tools and can be applied punctually on some specific aspects of systems. The counterpart is one of the strongest possible guaranties. Success of B method is essentially due to the effort made by its designer for proposing a language closed to programming languages, and also to its first well-known real-size application: METEOR, the first driver-free Parisian metro. As French RATP decided to use formal method to offer strong guaranty, they developed their own team of specifier and this first use of B-method has been followed by other ones. Then B-method provider developed a deep expertise and successfully promotes the use of the method for other railway businesses in the world. A lot of these railway applications concern autonomous and automatic systems (driver-free trains, automatic doors, etc.).

Error! Reference source not found. provides a very simplified view of the B-method, without any technical consideration. At abstract high level main properties and operations are described without any implementation details. For example, moving can be described without speed considerations. Only necessary order between actions is provided and order depending on implementation choices is ignored. Refining consist in adding details on state and operation steps: introducing speed, door control, etc. Last level is fully deterministic (all order choices have been done) and contains all details of relevant state for software implementation. Language changes during process: high level language handles parallelism while implementation language provides programming language constructs. At each level proof obligations are generated, and proving them (with an interactive prover) ensures that all invariants are satisfied and that low level operation behaviour respects high level operation description. Thus high level invariants have not to be re-proved at low level. This relies on proved mathematical (set theoretic) foundations of the method. To have a total confidence in final software, three other conditions must hold: high level specification is well written, code generation does not introduce errors (there are certified generators) and the computer on which it runs is reliable, of course (which is not in the scope of the method) (Fig. 3).

(B) Autonomous vehicle coordination. In this example [6], the addressed problem is coordination of autonomous vehicles and the used technique is "satisfiability decision" (more precisely "satisfying modulo theories"). In mathematical logic, satisfiability and validity are elementary concepts of semantics.

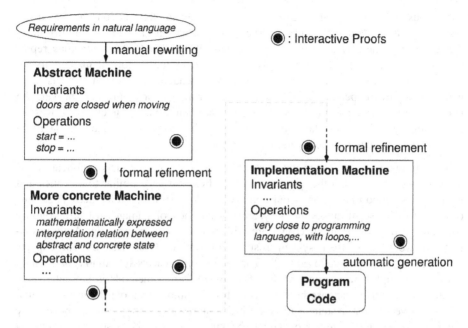

Fig. 3. Intuitive overview of the B method

Driver-less vehicles already exist and the state of Nevada even passed legislation allowing them to operate on public roads. One of the main safety requirements is to avoid collisions. As it would be very expensive to put equipments to all crossing, the chosen solution is a distributed one: decision algorithms are located in vehicles which communicate with each other using messages and message acknowledgments.

Satisfiability is well known in logics. Considering a set of properties (logical formulas), the problem is to decide whether all these properties can be true together. Lots of algorithms have been developed and optimized about this. The goal of the authors is to apply this fully automatic proving technique to the vehicle coordination problem. The presented work evaluates feasibility on a simplified but realistic case.

The applied method consists in providing descriptions by way of usual logical formulas. Descriptions concern both the behaviour of a vehicle and the constraints to respect in order to avoid dangerous situations. Vehicles send requests to access areas of the crossing and the communication protocol together with the vehicle behaviours ensure that only one vehicle can occupy an area at any time. Using the satisfiability as technique is then asking the prover if "not safe" is possible, where "not safe" is described by formulas. Authors had to add some invariants (intermediate properties) to help the prover to automatically establish the expected result using induction. Authors also discuss the scope of the case study and find results convincing despite simplifications (essentially, one single crossing).

This approach is interesting from several points of view. Used proof principles, such as induction, are powerful ones and this does not compromise automating. As considered functions have not to be fully interpreted, the modelling can concern continuous time, infinite and dense data sets. For example, location and speed are expressed with reals and they use abstractions such are "near", "far", "safe-distance" for reasoning. These abstraction are mathematically related to the continuous representation (location, speed, etc.). Applying such technique as formal method to the addressed problem is quite recent and the work is academic. Although proof is automatic, it requires expertise to find the "good" invariants for helping the prover; the language is mathematical logic and no user-friendly environment is evocated. Results are promising and authors claim to be aiming for the integration of the approach in a general tool for vehicular applications in the future.

(C) Confidence in autonomous systems. [15] concerns military application of autonomous vehicles, but the questions they address are very similar to our ones and the paper is a good illustration of our point, with a lot of relevant references. A serious obstacle to the use of autonomous systems is the lack of human trust in autonomy software. Thus most military UAVs are still under remote monitoring. Authors distinguish two kinds of trust: system trust and operational trust. The first one expects system to do what it is supposed to do. The second one expects system to actually help human to complete tasks successfully. The use of formal methods is presented as a solution to seriously increase both kinds of trust. Authors promote the use of formal models to verify that systems satisfy critical requirements. About this purpose, they mention existing intensive use of model checking and also robot's software synthesis from formal models. And about operational trust they use powerful simulation based on these models and also evocate model checking to validate human-machine interaction. For this, they have developed an approach in which cognitive models predict human behaviour [16].

[15] focusses on two main practical problems evocated in Sect. 3: how to produce formal models and how to exploit them in a sufficiently intuitive way to be useful for non-specialists. To solve the first problem, they present a tool which synthesizes models from graphical representations of scenarios (ESC: Event Sequence Charts). As some information is sometime missing in ESCs, the tool interactively asks for it during synthesis. To solve the second problem they developed a 3D simulator for autonomy software. These developments are intended to complete the FORMAL (FOrmal Requirements Modeling and AnaLysis) toolset they use. FORMAL integrates a lot of tools for checking consistency, generating invariants, simulating and checking properties at each simulation step, and also model checkers, theorem provers, automatic test generation and source code synthesis (many references are given in the paper). It is a good illustration of the variety of services formal methods can offer to guaranty autonomy software, and of current developments to make their use easier.

5 Discussion About Present and Future

Presented examples illustrate how existing approaches can be used to guaranty reliability of autonomous systems and in particular autonomous systems for risk management, where safety considerations are not reduced by time-to-market ones. Current methods can be used as they are. But as their development is recent and as they are evolving, future application is promising. From this study we identify some major lines, briefly summarized in the following points. The first two ones are shared with other application domains and the last ones is a short discussion about prospective for the risk area.

Combining methods. All methods are not efficient for the same aspects or properties. For example timed automata may be used for real time constraints but the complexity of timed models leads to avoid them for time independent question. Interactive proof is very powerful but also tedious and costly, thus it should be reserved to chosen aspects. Thus a rich approach would be to combine methods, and also to combine them with non-formal ones. Such approaches already exist. Some merging are easy: for example, as b-method machines are state machine, they can allow some model checking or model animation. Hybrid approaches can strongly enhance confidence in result but require some complementary fundamental research to offer mathematical guaranty of consistence between models of the different methods.

Using formal methods early in design process. As pointed in part 3 experiment shows that using formal methods at requirement and abstract levels is very profitable. A well designed general system (before details are added) is easier to verify, handle and develop. Some approaches such as the B-method or [25] are intrinsically top-down and another main reason for this is that it makes efficient applying of formal methods easier. Another complementary reason is that applying formal methods to already developed systems implies to extract formal models from low-level descriptions and rebuild abstraction where intentional information have disappeared (replaced by operational one). It requires a difficult reverse engineering process. This delicate process is not easy and potentially error-prone.

Prospective. Section 4.3(C) already shows that new application domains lead to new ideas about how to use formal models. Other recent evolving may be very interesting for the risk field. Among them, let us cite the extension of these methods to cyber-physical-systems: systems with sensors and strong interaction with physical environment. And another very relevant aspect is that formal methods may not only be used to model computing systems but also environment and physical systems. As the B-method presented above is used to develop software, a more recent version targets system modelling [3]. Theory is similar but methodology is different: operations are replaced by events; high level specifies the problem and low level specifies the solution. As example, [3] presents the behaviour of traffic lights controlling the access to an island. The high level specification only says that no more than x cars can be on the island at a same time. The high level property is the real safety one and totally abstracts the way to obtain it. Then refinement gradually introduces a bridge, lights, sensors, etc. And only last level introduces the controlling software driving the lights, and its communications with sensors. This approach allows to prove that a solution correctly solves a problem expressed at a pure user level (see also [7]). Its implementation remains difficult today as efficient decomposition (avoiding that adding an event leads to redo all proofs) is not easy. However guidelines are studied for this [20] and experience shows that with good decomposition the amount of proofs is easily balanced by the benefit of the analysis: proofs can be relatively direct without a lot of distortions to cope with the formalism.

It results that beyond designing autonomous systems, it is particularly interesting to explore specialisation of formal methods to risk issues, as people in this field do not have the same needs and the same culture as those working in software development, and as domain requires strong guaranty about multiple aspects.

In order to conceive a risk-sharing system, one must answer those questions well before their exploitation. In this context, it is important to have access to tools allowing the assessment of production and support policies about reliability and efficiency and the systems operational performances, especially its availability, safety, robustness, etc. Using a simulation is part of this process. It allows to support the technological approach upstream and to help overcoming various kinds of difficulties: (i) complexity of the system: dynamic, multiple resources interacting, gradual deployment; (ii) lack of feedback; (iii) necessity of multiple and partial approaches.

6 Conclusion

The design of autonomous systems, such as Drones for example, intended to carry out complex missions is an important challenge. The realisation of such a stand-alone system designed to evolve in its post-disaster conditions is still more demanding, mainly in the design of the architecture that must support this autonomy with a very good level of security and efficiency.

The use of the techniques of simulation on test cases, coupled with mathematical proof techniques allow to size and check the properties and safety features. The analysis focuses on functional and non-functional properties for safety and performance aspects. This new approach allows us to find the limits and to validate the consistency of complex systems without having to build real prototypes. It also lets us collect information on a new system, low-cost and at an early stage of the project. A lot of dysfunction, when using the system, appears when the operational conditions are different from those defined for the design. Checking and verifying all options in a design is not always possible before its realisation.

Complex systems are difficult to test and validate in extreme conditions. Designers can provide the use of a prototype to refine their approach. However, the prototype can hardly be comprehensive and fully representative of the final behaviour. It goes the same for test conditions. By building a virtual prototype, able to model more critical behaviours, it is possible to reproduce a functioning according to operational conditions. This process integration from the early stages of the project, allows having retroactive effect immediately on the design.

Tools of modelling and verification are an important improvement to the mastering of complexity. This allows to improve confidence in performance, safety and security properties needed by the real operational conditions. Moreover, present evolution of formal techniques and recent applications to risk management issues are promising attractive opportunities. Benefits for risk field must be increased and diversified in the future.

References

1. Sil4 railway software (2016). http://www.clearsy.com/en/our-specific-know-how/b-method/
2. Abrial, J.R.: The B-Book: Assigning Programs to Meanings. Cambridge University Press, New York (1996)
3. Abrial, J.R.: Modeling in Event-B: System and Software Engineering, 1st edn. Cambridge University Press, New York (2010)
4. Ackerman, E.: Drone adventures uses UAVs to help make the world a better place. IEEE Spectrum, May 2013
5. Almeida, J.B., Frade, M.J., Pinto, J.S., de Sousa, S.M.: An Overview of Formal Methods Tools and Techniques, 1st edn. Springer, London (2011). https://doi.org/10.1007/978-0-85729-018-2_2. Chapter 2
6. Asplund, M., Manzoor, A., Bouroche, M., Clarke, S., Cahill, V.: A formal approach to autonomous vehicle coordination. In: Giannakopoulou, D., Méry, D. (eds.) FM 2012. LNCS, vol. 7436, pp. 52–67. Springer, Heidelberg (2012). https://doi.org/10.1007/978-3-642-32759-9_8
7. Banach, R.: The landing gear case study in hybrid event-B. In: Boniol, F., Wiels, V., Ait Ameur, Y., Schewe, K.-D. (eds.) ABZ 2014. CCIS, vol. 433, pp. 126–141. Springer, Cham (2014). https://doi.org/10.1007/978-3-319-07512-9_9
8. Bolton, M.L., Bass, E.J., Siminiceanu, R.I.: Using formal verification to evaluate human-automation interaction: a review. IEEE Trans. Syst. Man Cybern.: Syst. 43(3), 488–503 (2013)
9. Chatterjee, R., Fruneau, B., Rudant, J., Roy, P., Frison, P., Lakhera, R., Dadhwal, V., Saha, R.: Subsidence of Kolkata (Calcutta) city, India during the 1990s as observed from space by differential synthetic aperture radar interferometry technique. Remote Sens. Environ. 102(1–2), 176–185 (2006)
10. Drechsler, R., Khne, U.: Formal Modeling and Verification of Cyber-Physical Systems. 1st International Summer School on Methods and Tools for the Design of Digital Systems, Bremen, Germany, September 2015. Springer, Heidelberg (2015). https://doi.org/10.1007/978-3-658-09994-7
11. Fantechi, A.: Twenty-five years of formal methods and railways: what next? In: Counsell, S., Núñez, M. (eds.) SEFM 2013. LNCS, vol. 8368, pp. 167–183. Springer, Cham (2014). https://doi.org/10.1007/978-3-319-05032-4_13
12. Fantechi, A., Fokkink, W., Morzenti, A.: Some Trends in Formal Methods Applications to Railway Signaling. Wiley, Hoboken (2012). pp. 61–84
13. Fitzgerald, J., Gamble, C., Larsen, P.G., Pierce, K., Woodcock, J.: Cyber-physical systems design: formal foundations, methods and integrated tool chains. In: FormaliSE 2015, Florence, Italy, 18 May 2015, pp. 40–46. IEEE (2015)
14. Guha-Sapir, D., Hoyois, P., Below, R.: Annual disaster statistical review 2012: the number and trends. CRED, Brussels, Belgium (2012)
15. Heitmeyer, C.L., Leonard, E.I.: Obtaining trust in autonomous systems: tools for formal model synthesis and validation. In: FormaliSE 2015, pp. 54–60. IEEE Press, Piscataway, NJ, USA (2015)
16. Heitmeyer, C.L., Pickett, M., Leonard, E.I., Archer, M.M., Ray, I., Aha, D.W., Trafton, J.G.: Building high assurance human-centric decision systems. Autom. Softw. Eng. 22(2), 159–197 (2015)
17. Lecomte, T., Burdy, L., Leuschel, M.: Formally checking large data sets in the railways. CoRR abs/1210.6815 (2012)

18. Lefeuvre, F., Tanzi, T.: International union of radio science, international council for science (ICSU), joint board of geospatial information societies (JBGIS). United Nations office for outer Space Affairs (OOSA) (2013)
19. Ranft, B., Dugelay, J.L., Apvrille, L.: 3D perception for autonomous navigation of a low-cost MAV using minimal landmarks. In: Proceedings of IMAV'2013, Toulouse, France, 17–20 September 2013 (2013)
20. Sato, N., Ishikawa, F.: Separation of considerations in event-B refinement toward industrial use. In: Proceedings of FMSEE&T 2015, Co-located with FM 2015, Oslo, Norway, 23 June 2015, pp. 43–50 (2015)
21. Sommerville, I.: Formal methods. In: Software Engineering, 9th edn. (Teaching Book). Pearson Education (2011). Chapter 27
22. Tanzi, T., Lefeuvre, F.: Radio sciences and disaster management. C. R. Phys. **11**, 114–224 (2010)
23. Tanzi, T., Perrot, P.: T´el´ecoms pour ling´enierie du risque. editions herms, ed. Collection Technique et Scientifique des T´el´ecoms (2009). (in French)
24. Tanzi, T., Andr, C.: Mod´elisation synchrone appliqu´ee la suˆret´e de fonctionnement. In: 12ˆeme Colloque National de Suˆret´e de Fonctionnement, 28–30 mars 2000. Montpellier - France (2000)
25. Tanzi, T., Apvrille, L., Dugelay, J.L., Roudier, Y.: UAVs for humanitarian missions: autonomy and reliability. In: 2014 IEEE Global Humanitarian Technology Conference (GHTC), pp. 271–278. IEEE (2014)
26. Tanzi, T.J., Lefeuvre, F.: The contribution of radio sciences to disaster management. In: Gi4DM 2011, Antalya, Turkey, May 2011
27. Wilkinson, P., Cole, D.: The role of the radio sciences in the disaster management. Radio Sci. Bull. **3358**, 4551 (2010)

Using the Scorecard Approach to Measure Seismic Social Resilience in Nablus, Palestine

Vania Cerchiello, Paola Ceresa, and Ricardo Monteiro[✉]

Scuola Universitaria Superiore Pavia, Pavia, Italy
{vania.cerchiello, paola.ceresa,
ricardo.monteiro}@iusspavia.it

Abstract. Social vulnerability helps to explain why communities experience the consequences of an earthquake differently, even though they are subjected to similar levels of ground shaking. The differential impacts of an earthquake can be a consequence of social vulnerability and, for this reason, it is a critical element for fostering mitigation plans and developing policies to reduce earthquake risk. Measuring resilience is not an easy task and, in this study, is performed through the Scorecard Approach. The latter is a self-assessment and participatory tool that measures resilience with qualitatively derived information at two different urban levels: population and local administration. The case study is the city of Nablus in the Palestinian region which is not only affected by seismic events but also by political conflicts. The provided results enable the resilience assessment of different districts of Nablus concerning several themes of disaster risk reduction. These will help to better understand how different variables – such as gender, age, educational level, monthly income and membership neighbourhood influence the vulnerability assessment.

Keywords: Vulnerability · Resilience · Palestine · Scorecard Approach

1 Introduction

During the assessment of seismic risk, a great deal of effort is usually dedicated to the analysis and evaluation of the hazard and physical vulnerability components, supported by the deep knowledge and research in the engineering seismology and earthquake engineering fields. Nevertheless, for a more comprehensive evaluation of urban risk, it is increasingly becoming clear the important role played by the community during extreme events. Populations have different capacities to prepare for an event, react in different manners and recover from damages disproportionately, if they occur [1]. The evaluation of all these aspects, combined with the physical dimensions of a disastrous event, will lead to the overall assessment of urban risk. Certainly, earthquake safety begins with the compliance to the technical and engineering rules to build safe structures. However, great emphasis should also be placed on fostering disaster resilient communities. Indeed, a resilient population can better withstand adversity and recover more quickly when earthquakes occur. Resilience, as defined by the United Nations International Strategy for Disaster Reduction (UNISDR), is "the ability of a system, community or society exposed to hazards to resist, absorb, accommodate to and

© IFIP International Federation for Information Processing 2017
Published by Springer International Publishing AG 2017. All Rights Reserved
Y. Murayama et al. (Eds.): ITDRR 2016, IFIP AICT 501, pp. 77–92, 2017.
https://doi.org/10.1007/978-3-319-68486-4_7

recover from the effects of a hazard in a timely and efficient manner, including through the preservation and restoration of its essential basic structures and functions" [2].

It is not simple to both measure and develop plans to enhance the resilience of communities, which is crucial not only to assess the starting conditions of the community, but also, as a first step in disaster risk management. Knowledge of gaps and vulnerable factors leads communities to the enhancement of their capacities to respond to and recover from an event. Different techniques can be employed to give a measure of resilience: selection of variables highly connotative for the society [3], computation of indicators and indices [4] or participatory processes, as the one used in the present research. The Scorecard Approach is a self-evaluation tool empowering city stakeholders to quantitatively assess risk and resilience parameters based on qualitatively derived information at multiple levels [5]. This methodology was applied for the first time as a pilot study in Lalitpur [6], Nepal, in 2014, and a year later in the Quito (Ecuador) as case study for South America [7].

This paper describes the application of this approach to the Palestinian context within the activities of the EC-funded research project SASPARM 2.0 (Support Action for Strengthening PAlestine capabilities for seismic Risk Mitigation). This project promotes the training of scientists, practitioners, students, citizens, stakeholders and increases the awareness of the seismic risk concept in the city of Nablus (see Fig. 1).

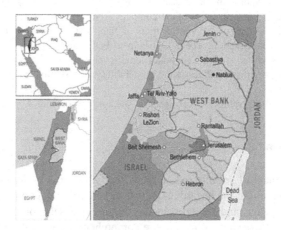

Fig. 1. The West Bank and Nablus 8

A consortium of three institutions manages the project: EUCENTRE (European Centre for Training and Research in Earthquake Engineering) and IUSS (Institute for Advanced Study) in Pavia (Italy), and ANNU (An-Najah National University) in Nablus (Palestine). One of the major outcomes of the SASPARM 2.0 initiative is the development of an integrated seismic risk model for Palestine, based on a state-of-the-art hazard model and in-situ collected vulnerability and exposure data [9, 10]. The city of Nablus, the first Palestinian city to join the UNISDR's *Making city resilient campaign*, constitutes the case study area for the implementation and calibration of the model.

2 Sources of Social Vulnerability in Palestine

Palestine is exposed to various natural hazards including earthquakes. The entire region around Palestine faces ongoing small to mid-scale disaster risks and a large-scale urban disaster is potential [11]. Specifically, the seismic risk is associated with the tectonic plate boundary in the Jordan Valley known as the Dead Sea Transform (DST). Historical records show that major earthquakes have caused severe damage and many hundreds, and sometimes thousands, of fatalities. The most recent earthquake (ML 5.2) took place on February 11, 2004 [12]. The possibility of a major destructive earthquake is part of all contingency plan scenarios [13].

The vulnerability conditions of Palestine can be classified as high to very high, driven by the following issues: access restriction, population fragmentation, infrastructure, physical, social and economic vulnerabilities. All these sources increase the consequences of a disaster event. Therefore, measures need to be planned and put in action to reduce the risk impact on population and exposed assets. The negative factors that mainly affect the population are the movement restrictions due to the checkpoints, barriers and permit requirements placed on Palestinians. These current political restrictions greatly constrain the potential for economic and job growth in Palestine, · generally, and in Nablus, in particular. Moreover, economic restrictions, globalization and poor labour laws have also negatively affected employment and made the cost of living too expensive for Palestinians to have healthy, sustainable lives [8]. The restrictions are not only delineated in movements setting, but even concern the work permit requirements, which prevent Palestinian population from freely working within the West Bank and Israel.

For all these reasons, Palestinian communities are subjected to policies make them more vulnerable in case of an earthquake strikes. Moreover, the territorial fragmentation leads to controlled access to land, water, gas, electricity and other resources. These kinds of resources are of crucial importance during an emergency state and negatively affect the management of a seismic crisis due to lack of independence and self-sustenance.

Social structures also constrain livelihoods and sharpen the social vulnerability. In Nablus, local traditions and customs prevent some women from publically entering the work force. Some women work, but only informally as street vendors during holidays or as shop workers at home [8]. Despite that, changes are in place; young women in the labour force remind us that society is moving towards their acceptance [8]. In the light of such evaluations, the present research takes into consideration the gender distribution as a variable that would affect vulnerability. Indeed, the new active role of women could lead the community to a more resilient capacity and to a faster reaction and recovery from disasters.

3 Methodology for Social Vulnerability Assessment

Social vulnerability assessment can be performed with different methods. The most commonly employed tool makes use of composite indicators, such as Human Development Index, Environmental Sustainability Index, Prevalent Vulnerability Index (sum of Exposure and Susceptibility, Socio-Economic Fragility and Lack of Resilience) and Social Vulnerability Index [14]. The indicator is a quantitative or qualitative measure derived from observed facts that simplifies and communicates the reality of a complex situation [15]. Social vulnerability indicators are potentially powerful tools because they summarize complexity and provide quantitative metrics to compare places and track progress [16]. Moreover, these indicators are relatively easy for non-experts to interpret. Although indicators are increasingly recognized as useful tools for policy-making and public communication, because they can be used as performance measures, they can be misleading if poorly constructed or misinterpreted. Furthermore, indicators can lead to overly simplistic and inappropriate conclusions if dimensions of resilience are ignored because difficult to measure or just simply unknown. The good quality of an indicator lies in the accessibility to information that are representative of the local knowledge, condition and context. Often, this kind of data is not accessible or not available from publically databases (national censuses). As such, for the Palestinian particular context, the design of targeted surveys is preferred with respect to the above-mentioned methodology.

3.1 Scorecard Approach

Palestinian areas are largely affected by difficulties and lack of data, which are not often representative of the reality. A proper questionnaire, the so-called Scorecard Approach, is a good alternative method, mostly for its participatory characteristic. This approach describes better the context because it is adapted to the Nablus situation and citizens are the main actors of the assessment because the population directly replies to the proposed questions.

The purpose of the Scorecard Approach is to build a tool that can capture the key functional and organizational areas for urban resilience. The concept of resilience has found its way into disaster risk management as mentioned in the Hyogo Framework for Action (HFA) [17], which establishes the goal of "building resilience in nations and communities". More recently, even the United Nations started the campaign for urban disaster reduction with the banner "Making Cities Resilient". The UNISDR defined the so-called 10 Essentials, representing a set of indicators in the form of a checklist by which resiliency can be measured [18]. The Scorecard Approach encompasses the ten essentials into six key dimensions that mainstream Disaster Risk Reduction (DRR) into planning and decision-making processes (see Fig. 2). The dimensions and the related main questions are summarized in Table 1.

The implementation of the Scorecard Approach in Nablus required a preparatory process to capture the local context into the design of the indicators (questions) and targets (answer schemes). The questionnaire preparation benefits of academia feedback, in particular from the Opinion Pools and Survey Studies Center of ANNU. In this way, the development and implementation of the initial Scorecard Approach have been carried out in a collaborative effort between the European and Palestinian Institutions, leading to the final questionnaire, subsequently spread among population and the local administration.

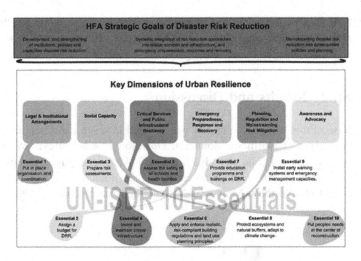

Fig. 2. Key dimensions of urban resilience 5

Table 1. Six dimensions/themes of Scorecard Approach

Dimensions/themes	General questions
Awareness & Advocacy	What is the level of awareness and knowledge of earthquake disaster risk?
Social capacity	What are the capacities of the population to efficiently prepare, respond and recover from a damaging earthquake?
Legal and institutional arrangements	How effective are mechanisms to advocate earthquake risk reduction in your quarter?
Planning, regulation and mainstreaming risk mitigation	What is the perceived level of commitment and mainstreaming of DRR through regulatory planning tools?
Emergency preparedness, response and recovery	What is the level of effectiveness and competency of disaster management including mechanisms for response and recovery?
Critical services and public infrastructure resiliency	What is the level of resilience of critical services to disasters?

The challenge of the approach is the self-assessment of the population able to understand its own vulnerability and identify opportunities for resilience enhancement.

Moreover, the results will enable local policy makers and communities to establish priorities for more in-depth analysis, allocate funds and develop emergency and disaster management programs more effectively. Even though the case studies in Lalitpur and Quito foresaw local workshops to have the opportunity of interaction between population, representatives of the Municipality and experts in the development of the approach, this exchange was not possible in Nablus for safety reasons and even for language constraints. In order to overcome these challenges, the questionnaires were translated in Arabic and university students were properly trained to support the filling in of the questionnaire. The questionnaires were spread in different areas of Nablus and the population was involved in an active way.

4   Case-Study Results and Discussion

For the purpose of this study, Nablus city was divided in seven main neighbourhoods: Old City, Southern and Northern Mountain, Downtown, AlMakhfeya, Western and Eastern Areas (see Fig. 3). The city also includes Palestinian refugee camps (Balata, 'Askar and 'Ein Beit el Ma' – red markers in Fig. 3), including 6% of participants, mostly located in the Northern Mountain, Western and Eastern Areas [19].

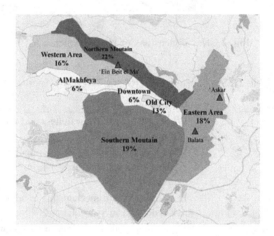

Fig. 3. Questionnaires distribution in Nablus (Color figure online)

The total number of collected questionnaires was 526, out of which 433 were filled by general population and the remaining 93 by local administration staff. When compared to the previous initiatives (e.g. the Lalitpur case-study 6 that featured 43 participants in the workshop), the sample size in Nablus was much larger. The absence of a specific seminar may have led to error in the questionnaire's completion, however, it is expected that it is balanced by a large number of collected questionnaires.

The gender distribution of the respondents is homogeneous: 51% male and 49% female, whereas the local administration features a higher percentage of men (56%). Preliminary quantitative measurements were performed regarding age, educational level and monthly income, as shown in Figs. 4, 5 and 6. Respondents' ages range mostly between 20 and 30 years (53%) whilst a non-negligible percentage (27%) is between 30 and 40 years old (Fig. 4). This information is closely correlated to the educational level (Fig. 5), particularly when referring to university students (38%) and

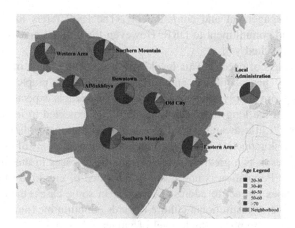

Fig. 4. Age distribution

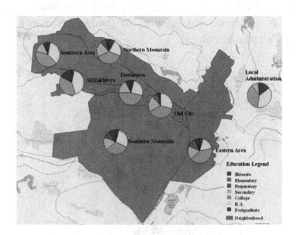

Fig. 5. Education level distribution

bachelor degrees (27%). Very aggregated answers were obtained for the monthly income (Fig. 6): about 47% of respondents declared 1500–3500 NIS (1NIS = 0.26 USD), 17% stated about 0–1500 NIS whilst 18% did not answer at all.

4.1 Score System

A scheme of answers was established to track progress on the mainstreaming of risk reduction. The answers were defined by using five main scores, from 1 to 5 [20]:

1. **High:** "Full integration". This level refers to a situation where risk reduction is fully absorbed into planning and development processes as well as core services. This level describes a situation where DRR is "institutionalized". However, this is not to suggest that an optimum level of attainment has occurred: there is still a need for further progress.

2. **Moderate:** "Engagement and commitment". The level refers to a high level of engagement and commitment to DRR. However, the policies and systems have not been fully established yet.
3. **Low:** "Awareness of needs". This level refers to an early stage of awareness. The institutions may have activities and dedicated efforts for preparedness, however these initiatives are simply limited to response. This level is expected not to result in risk reduction in the long term and vulnerability is expected to increase.
4. **Almost none:** "Little awareness". There is no institutional policy or process for incorporating risk reduction within the functions and operations of the organization. The probable result is a great vulnerability and high losses in the future.
5. **No awareness:** Population is not aware or informed of any kind of processes and municipality does not act to address problems. In some cases, there is an adverse attitude and adverse institutional culture towards adopting measures to reduce risk. The not-awareness implies a high level of vulnerability and lack of resiliency.

Six of the total 39 questions had less possible answers, which led to just three corresponding scores: 1 (High), 4 (Almost none) and 5 (Not awareness). The different scheme for those 6 questions was adopted to render the questionnaire easier to understand by the Palestinian citizens.

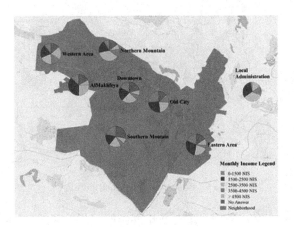

Fig. 6. Monthly income distribution

4.2   Global and Detailed Results per Theme

The global results for population and administration staff, divided by score, are shown in Fig. 7. Most of the answers belong to the range of "moderate" to "almost none" awareness for both groups. Moreover, the mean scores per theme show a similar trend for the citizens and the municipality representatives (see Fig. 8).

The population mean scores range between 2.7 and 3.6, the latter being found for the theme of "Planning, Regulation and Mainstreaming Risk Mitigation". As expected, the local administration group exhibits a lower score *i.e.* demonstrates a better perception of risk, its management and reduction with respect to the citizens. However, the

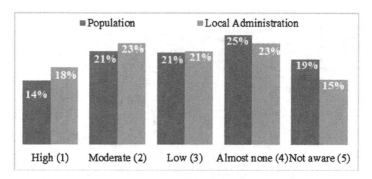

Fig. 7. Scores distribution

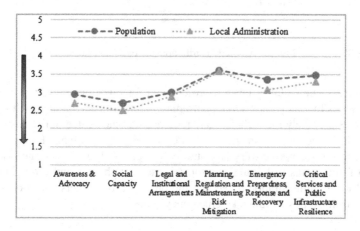

Fig. 8. Mean score distribution per theme

difference is not so remarkable, which means a low level of resilience even in decision making bodies.

Figure 9 illustrates the distribution of answers for all the questions of each theme. The highest scores for the population group belong to the "Emergency preparedness, response and recovery", "Planning, regulation and mainstreaming risk mitigation" and "Legal and Institutional Arrangements" themes. For the latter two themes, the mean score for local administration group shows three higher peak values (q3.1, q4.1, q4.2).

There are seven peak scores denoting particularly high vulnerability:

- "Emergency preparedness, response and recovery" – recovery and food provision (q5.8);
- "Planning, regulation and mainstreaming risk mitigation" – availability of safety areas for both citizens and administration (q4.1, q4.2) and availability of insurance (q4.5, q4.6);
- "Legal and Institutional Arrangements" – existence of ordinances and regulation for earthquake safety and risk reduction (q3.1, q3.2).

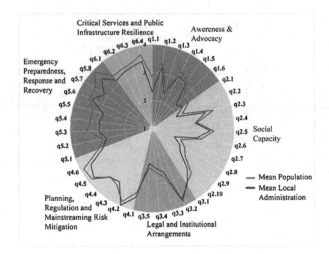

Fig. 9. Answers distribution per each question

The highest vulnerability levels were denoted for questions related to retrofitting measures, plans for emergency and repair/replacement, laws and regulatory framework. These themes are likely too technical and require deep knowledge in risk management that often lacks at the administration level as well. In addition, "Emergency preparedness, response and recovery" questions were generally related to the availability of human force, funds and material resources, such as shelters and food [21]. Population and local administration agree that the provision of shelters and food is essentially lacking for a post-earthquake emergency (q5.8).

4.3   Normalized Resilience Index

A linear max-min normalization has been computed per theme and per neighbourhood according to Eq. 1. The Normalized Index, $NI_{i,j}$, is the score of the neighbourhood i and theme j; max corresponds to the maximum score for the theme (5); min corresponds to the minimum score for the theme (1); and avg corresponds to the average of the participants' results per neighbourhood.

$$NI_{i,j} = \frac{avg_i - min_j}{max_j - min_j} \tag{1}$$

By using this normalized scale (illustrated in Fig. 10) general considerations among themes have been performed. Furthermore, the comparison of results coming from the different neighbourhoods and the local administration group has been carried out. As for the absolute score, values close to 0 represent very high resilience whereas values close to 1 represent very low resilience (almost none).

The results in Fig. 10 denote a low resilience level for "Planning, regulation and mainstreaming risk mitigation", "Critical services and public infrastructure resilience" and "Emergency preparedness, response and recovery", with the local administration group exhibiting peaks of 0.64, 0.57 and 0.53, respectively. When evaluating the percentage of results by ranges of resilience (Table 2), the most representative range from local administration and population corresponds to a "low-almost none" level of resilience. Indeed, most of indices vary between "low" (75%) and "almost none" (21%). In this context, it is relevant to prioritize "Planning, regulation and mainstreaming risk mitigation", "Critical services and public infrastructure resilience" and "Emergency preparedness, response and recovery" topics in order to improve the capacity of the city and of local administrators to respond to, react and recover from emergency state.

Table 2. Percentage of answers by ranges of resilience

Ranges of resilience		Percentage of answers
High	0.0–0.1	0%
	0.1–0.2	0%
Moderate	0.2–0.3	0%
	0.3–0.4	4%
Low	0.4–0.5	33%
	0.5–0.6	42%
Almost none	0.6–0.7	17%
	0.7–0.8	4%
Not aware	0.8–0.9	0%
	0.9–1	0%

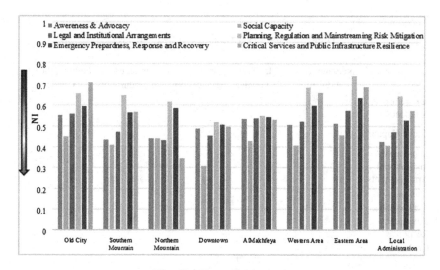

Fig. 10. Normalized scores

4.4 Statistical Dependence of Variables

Further statistical post-processing of the data has been performed to assess which variables have a higher effect in the citizens' answers. MANOVA (multivariate analysis of variance) was employed, as it allows to analyse data involving more than one dependent variable at a time. MANOVA allows testing hypotheses regarding the effect of one or more independent variables on two or more dependent variables [22]. In this particular study, the dependent variables were the questions of each theme, whereas the independent variables were the neighbourhoods, gender, age, educational level and monthly income. The results are illustrated in Tables 3, 4 and 5.

Table 3. MANOVA results with single variable

	Neighbourhood	Gender	Age	Education	Income
Awareness & Advocacy	●	●	●	●	●
Social Capacity	●			●	●
Legal and Institutional Arrangements	●	●			
Planning Regulation	●			●	
Emergency Response	●				●
Critical Services	●				

Table 4. MANOVA results with two variables

	Neighbourhood+ Education	Income+ Gender	Income+ Education	Income+ Neighbourhood	Neighbourhood+ Gender
Awareness & Advocacy	●	●	●		
Social Capacity	●		●	●	
Legal and Institutional Arrangements					
Planning Regulation	●				●
Emergency Response	●				
Critical Services	●				

Table 5. MANOVA results with three and four variables

	Education + Income + Age	Education+ Income + Gender	Education + Income + Neighbourhood	Education + Income + Gender + Age
Awareness & Advocacy	●	●		●
Social Capacity			●	

It is evident that the neighbourhood variable plays a major role in all the themes (the largest is the circle, the more the variable affects the theme – Table 3). Furthermore, the membership neighbourhood has a strong influence on the topics in combination with educational level variable (Table 4).

A smaller relevance can be observed in neighbourhood – gender combination for "Planning, Regulation and Mainstreaming Risk Mitigation" theme and in neighbourhood – income for "Social Capacity" (Table 4). On the other hand, educational level, which plays an active role in increasing awareness towards disaster risk, demonstrates a significant influence on the respondents in three topics only (Table 3). The education level is very representative when combined with just neighbourhood, as mentioned before (Table 4). The couple education – monthly income has influence in two cases: "Awareness & Advocacy" and "Social Capacity" (Table 4). This confirms how educational empowering in association with socioeconomic status increases the level of awareness, knowledge about risk and recovery potential [23].

Moreover, a non-negligible interdependence has been observed between educational level, income, age and gender (Table 5), even if specific to the "Awareness & Advocacy" theme. This result instead denotes how the ability of people to understand information, access to recovery and resources depends on a combination of several variables.

Furthermore, following the estimation of the most relevant variables, linear regression analyses have been computed and tested through ANOVA to find the model that best explains each theme [24]. ANOVA computes the analysis of a variance table for different linear model fits and tests whether the more complex model with two or three independent variables is significantly better or not with respect to a simpler one with just one independent variable. In addition, the validity of the model has been verified considering if the variance of the residuals was constant across the indices, that results in points distributed around the mean (Homoscedasticity - Constant Variance), and the examination of normal distribution of the residuals (normality of errors).

According to Table 6, the analysis on linear models performed with ANOVA agrees with the MANOVA results. The reported p-values in Table 6 were used to check the level of significance for the several tested models. The smaller the p-value, the stronger the relationship is between dependent and independent variables.

Three themes are well correlated with neighbourhood in combination with educational level factor. "Planning, Regulation and Mainstreaming Risk Mitigation" relates highly to educational level and "Critical Services and Public Infrastructure

Table 6. Linear models per theme tested through ANOVA

	Neighbourhood	p-value	Neighbourhood+ Education	p-value	Education	p-value
Awareness & Advocacy			●	$6.36 \cdot 10^{-3}$		
Social Capacity			●	$2.79 \cdot 10^{-4}$		
Planning and Regulation					●	$1.61 \cdot 10^{-6}$
Emergency Response			●	$1.84 \cdot 10^{-2}$		
Critical Services	●	$3.967 \cdot 10^{-6}$				

Resilience" with neighbourhood. The only exception concerns the "Legal and Institutional Arrangements" topic. It is not driven by any of the examined variables and models. This is probably due to that fact that this topic is at a very underdeveloped stage in Palestine.

5 Conclusions

Nablus city is facing the theme of disaster risk management and reduction only from the last decade, many times based on the collaboration between local researchers and European institutions. The presented methodology is useful to evaluate the status, gaps and current achievements of key resilience dimensions in the city. The Scorecard Approach provides a useful diagnosis tool and denoted, for this particular case, a low level of resilience of the city and lacking strategies in DRR.

Training will help the dissemination of guidelines and policies for fostering good habits in risk prevention and preparation. Indeed, several activities have been and will be developed in Nablus and in Palestine to contribute to the enhancement of the capacity of the cities to respond to earthquake events. Great effort is dedicated to the youngest layers of the population, who will be the new generation of civil protection volunteers and will implement future processes of vulnerability mitigation measures.

However, in the light of the questionnaires' responses, improvements should be foreseen, especially in local centres for emergency response and plans. In order to assure informed decisions, results about risk scenarios and planning should be communicated in an appropriate language to the population, promoting effective systems of information for disaster risk management. Moreover, society should be involved in the decision processes through mechanisms of participation. On the other hand, local administrators' results show a low capacity of the administration staff itself in risk management. For this reason, administration should strengthen the regulation for the implementation of seismic requirements of public infrastructure and propose incentives for the private one. In addition, special training for municipality personnel could be a key measure for improvement of the society resilience.

The performed assessment will enable local policy makers and communities to establish priorities for more in-depth analysis, to allocate funds and to develop emergency and disaster management programs more effectively. The development of the "citizens' science" will be possible only with the strong synergy and collaboration between stakeholders, policy makers and society, aware on the importance of the prevention in the development of urban resilience strategies.

Acknowledgements. This research has been carried out under the project "ECHO/SUB/2014/694399 SASPARM 2.0 Support Action for Strengthening PAlestine capabilities for seismic Risk Mitigation". Project Co-funded by ECHO–Humanitarian Aid and Civil Protection. The authors would also like to thank Dr. Christopher Burton for his invaluable input.

References

1. Civiletti, G., Camassi, R., Monteiro, R.: Italian seismic sequences: year 2000, the emergency phase in Romagna. Procedia Eng. **161C**, 2088–2092 (2016)
2. UNISDR: UNISDR Terminology on Disaster Risk Reduction, Geneva (2009)
3. Jones, B., Andrey, J.: Vulnerability index construction: methodological choices and their influence on identifying vulnerable neighbourhoods. Int. J. Emerg. Manag. **4**(2), 269–295 (2007)
4. Freudenberg, M.: Composite indicators of country performance: a critical assessment. Organisation for Economic Co-operation and Development, Paris (2003)
5. Anhorn, J., Khazai, B., Burton, C.G.: The risk and resilience scorecard: benchmarking disaster resilience in cities. A monitoring & evaluation tool to engage local stakeholders. In: ICLEI (2014)
6. GEM, SAI, Heidelberg University, CEDIM, NSET, USAID: Participatory evaluation of earthquake risk and resilience in Lalitpur sub-metropolitan city. Workshop report (2014)
7. GEM, South America Risk Assessment. https://www.globalquakemodel.org/what/regions/south-america/
8. Catholic Relief Services Jerusalem, the West Bank and Gaza: Urban Livelihoods in the West Bank City of Nablus – A rapid livelihoods assessment using the Integral Human Development conceptual framework (2012)
9. Monteiro, R., Ceresa, P., Cerchiello, V., Dabeek, J., Di Meo, A., Borzi, B.: Towards integrated seismic risk assessment in Palestine – application to the city of Nablus, In: ECCOMAS, Crete Island, Greece, vol. VII (2016)
10. Grigoratos, I., Dabeek, J., Faravelli, M., Di Meo, A., Cerchiello, V., Borzi, B., Monteiro, R., Ceresa, P.: Development of a fragility and exposure model for Palestine – application to the city of Nablus. Procedia Eng. **161C**, 2023–2029 (2016)
11. Al Dabbek, J.: An assessment on disaster risk reduction in the occupied Palestinian territory. An-Najah Univ. J. Res. – Nat. Sci. **24**(1), 1–46 (2010)
12. USAID MERC Project Team (M18-057): Earthquake Hazard Assessment and Building Code, Final report, Earth Sciences and Seismic Engineering Center at An-Najah University (2004)
13. UNDAC: Disaster Response Preparedness Mission to the State of Palestine (2014)
14. Cutter, S.L., Boruff, B.J., Shirley, W.L.: Social vulnerability to environmental hazards. Soc. Sci. Q. **84**(1), 242–261 (2003)

15. Nardo, M., Saisana, M., Saltelli, A., Tarantola, S.: Handbook on constructing composite indicators: methodology and user guide. Organisation for Economic Cooperation and Development, Paris (2008)

16. Tate, E.C.: Social vulnerability indices: a comparative assessment using uncertainty and sensitivity analysis. Nat. Hazards **63**, 325–347 (2012)

17. UNISDR: Hyogo Framework for Action 2005–2015: Building the Resilience of Nations and Communities to Disasters, World Conference on Disaster Reduction, Kobe, Hyogo, Japan (2005)

18. UNISDR: Ten-point checklist for local governments – ten essentials for making cities resilient. http://www.unisdr.org/campaign/resilientcities/toolkit/essentials

19. The applied Research Institute: Nablus city profile, Jerusalem (2014)

20. Khazai, B., Bendimeard, F., Cardona, O.D., Carreño, M.L. Barbat, A.H., Burton, C.B.: A guide to measuring urban resilience. Principles, tools and practice of urban indicators. Earthquake Megacities Initiative (2015)

21. Vecere, A., Monteiro, R., Amman, W.: Comparative analysis of existing tools for assessment of post-earthquake short-term lodging needs. Procedia Eng. **161C**, 2217–2221 (2016)

22. Multivariate Analysis of Variance. http://www.statmethods.net/stats/anova.html

23. Burton, C.G., Silva, V.: Assessing integrated earthquake risk in OpenQuake with an application to Mainland Portugal. Earthq. Spectra **32**(3), 1383–1403 (2015)

24. Chambers, J.M.: Linear models. In: Chambers, J.M., Hastie, T.J. (eds.) Statistical Models in: S. Wadsworth & Brooks/Cole (1992). Chapter 4

Better Access to Terminology for Crisis Communications

Mikael Snaprud[1], Jaziar Radianti[2(✉)], and Dag Svindseth[3]

[1] Tingtun AS, Lillesand, and University of Agder, Grimstad, Norway
mikael.snaprud@uia.no
[2] Centre for Integrated Emergency Management, University of Agder, Grimstad, Norway
jaziar.radianti@uia.no
[3] Fire Chief at East Agder Fire Department, Arendal, Norway
dag@oabv.no

Abstract. Crisis management depends on efficient communications with professional staff and with people who are affected by the crisis. The correct interpretation of general language and technical terms is crucial to take good actions and to save valuable time. To reduce the risk of misunderstandings we need a well-established crisis management terminology. Several collections of terms have been prepared for hazard areas such as pollution, radiation, fire safety, and dangerous goods. Today such terminologies can be provided on different websites, depending on how the national crisis management is organised. This distribution and a variation of different formats and user interfaces can make them hard to use. In this paper, we propose a novel approach to enable the term definition retrieval from a selection of terminologies directly from the text where the term is used. Initial experiments show that this approach can save time both for the retrieval and for the maintenance of terminologies. People involved in training and planning can benefit from access to definitions directly from the text of online documents. Terminology maintainers can benefit from the automated generation of internal links in the terminology so that the terms used in the definition of the other terms are automatically linked.

Keywords: Terminology · ICT - supported crisis communication · Crisis glossary

1 Introduction

Most literature in crisis management as well as in practice among crisis management practitioners, underline the importance of crisis communications to respond to small or large-scale incidents [1–8]. Therefore, the specific terms used in crisis communication must be precise, to be understood in the same way both by professionals responsible for handling a crisis and by the general citizens who need to stay in-formed about the crisis development. Precise terminology for crisis communication will reduce the risk of misunderstandings [9] among those who are responsible for responding the crisis. Communications to general citizens may also rely on their understanding of terms to ensure that they take appropriate actions in emergency situations. Unfortunately, even

Published by Springer International Publishing AG 2017. All Rights Reserved
Y. Murayama et al. (Eds.): ITDRR 2016, IFIP AICT 501, pp. 93–103, 2017.
https://doi.org/10.1007/978-3-319-68486-4_8

though crisis terminologies often are provided freely online, the existence of such resources remains unknown to the people in general and limitedly used among professionals for preparations or in operations. On the other hand, the use of Information Communication Technology (ICT) for preparedness, during the crisis or in the recovery period is greatly adopted, especially in developed countries. The ICTs have been the main reason for recent shifting of the nature of crisis communication [10] from a centralized command structure to multidirectional communication between a range of actors from various sectors and background (language, culture, knowledge). In such urgent and complex interaction with multiple stakeholders, the risk of communication misunderstanding may increase, and the actual (meaning) of the message may not be properly conveyed. A shared conceptual meaning and understanding are as crucial as the crisis communication model or technologies to enhance the common understanding and improve the effectiveness of disaster response.

The navigation in the jungle of terms to assure correct understanding is a pressing challenge. Taking Norway as an example, this is prevalent for most of the crucial crisis management services including police, fire service, medical service and for the media. Misunderstandings caused by misinterpreted terms are often only clarified in the evaluation phase, after the crisis response is carried out. Given the organisation of crisis management agencies into different services, the solution may not be one singular set of terms with an ambition to cover all aspects and services. However, as a preferred minimum solution the different actors should have thorough knowledge about internal terms and how others use them. For the wider audience, the media has a special responsibility to use specific terms to describe crisis events. The media al-ready has style guides and tools in place for how to spell foreign names or for words to use or avoid. But they do cannot cover crisis management in a consistent way without sources of reference. This situation underlines the need to raise the crisis management terminologies in the research agenda.

This paper argues that in current ICT-based crisis communication practices there is little attention to how crisis terminology can be maintained and used efficiently for training and operations as a part of preparedness and response in the crisis management cycle. To support the earlier claim, the authors conduct a literature survey and several documentations on practices for communicating crisis response, to explore how crisis terminologies are used and maintained. In this paper, we also provide examples and sources for crisis terminology in different fields and countries and examine the current use of these technical terms. To this end, we propose a concept and a novel solution to harmonize and to integrate crisis-related terminologies. We also outline how the approach can support a robust, accessible, and more human-centric ICT-based crisis communication. The suggested approach is based on an online service demonstrated on the website for the Norwegian Association for firefighters' terminology (http://www.kbt.no).

2   Previous Studies and Paper Scope

As indicated by Mayner and Arbon [11], the need for harmonisation of the definition of disaster terms is evident as a solid basis for building more unitary research, policy, and practice. They provide an example of analysis of the term "disaster" in a source with

110 glossaries containing disaster terminology, but only 52 contained the definition of the disaster. They point out that, even for one word, "disaster" there is very little consensus, what the disaster actually means. Mayner and Arbon [11] found at least 128 different disaster definitions. Likewise, Hagelsteen and Becker [5] raise the concern regarding the potential discrepancies in how individuals or organisations perceive the key disaster concepts. They use the essential concepts related to the "disaster risk reduction (DRR)" and "capacity development" as a test case using groups of international experts as respondents and examining documents from nine capacity development projects for DRR. Their research finds significant differences concerning how the respondents define DRR concepts. This finding strengthens the earlier study conducted by Lipson and Warren [12] that common definition of "capacity building" is not homogeneous among their respondents that covered NGOs from 18 countries.

Hagelsteen and Becker [5] point out the tendencies of people's attitude to underestimate the importance of using terminology correctly and assume that two different parties have the same understanding as a reason for this inconsistencies. In addition, Thywissen [9] argues that the definitions of the same terms were developed simultaneously and homogeneously in multiple disciplines and results in variation of definitions for the same term, causing the so-called "Babylonian Confusion." Thywissen [9] further suggests a common vocabulary of unique, well-formulated definitions and concepts, to avoid misunderstandings in the communication between different ac-tors.

Some efforts have been initiated to harmonise the crisis management terms using various approaches such as by using taxonomies [13–17], terminologies-vocabularies [18, 19], domain ontology [20–23], semantic integration [24] or developing interoperability framework [25–27]. Despite the recognizing of some limitations in the use of crisis terminology issues, how to increase the adoption of such resources in an easy way and make them accessible, is not so much studied as the existence of such resources and how to use them in day-to-day practices are still two separate issues. Reuter et al. [18], for example, address the same concern as our research, i.e. how to deal with terminology ambiguities in collaborative systems. This study, however, is exploratory in essence, while the technical approach discussed in this work is more about the conceptual and requirement level than suggesting concrete ICT solution.

Crisis glossaries are an agreed set of terminologies formally issued by the government, public agencies or associations covering different countries, intended to use for harmonising and enhancing crisis management terms. Traditionally, the use of these terms is more scholarly-education oriented, and ensuring that professionals can find and access different disaster-related glossaries uniformly, and never fully used for the more practical-oriented purpose. As a result, this domain is often overlooked, especially, how enable people to quickly find and use them whether they are needed for training, crisis communication or in crisis management operations.

For the sake of clarity, we outline several boundaries that define the scope of this paper, i.e. which ones are not part of this paper's goals, and. what is the actual contribution of this paper.

Firstly, the notion of establishing the better human-centric approach and integrated crisis glossary is to be applied in the local, general crisis management practices. The idea is neither for solving multilinguistic issues nor for proposing a method for achieving agreed terms in the context of international humanitarian missions where multi-actor, multi-national responders may be involved in the affected area within a single country. However, our proposed approach can potentially be expanded into this type of international, multi-actor humanitarian mission, if relevant glossaries exist for serving humanitarian actions.

Secondly, this paper is neither intended to make new crisis glossaries which should consider non-homogeneous vocabularies, standardisation such as NIEM (www.niem. gov), conversion or translation to semantic mapping nor to analyse different understandings that may occur between organisations.

Thirdly, this paper is neither about proposing terminologies, taxonomies, vocabularies or domain ontology, nor solving technical interoperability issues. These fields have been thoroughly scrutinized through massive efforts e.g. in European projects such as DISASTER (disaster-fp7.eu), SecInCoRe (www.secincore.eu), EPISECC (www. episecc.eu), or CRISP (www.crispproject.eu), in addition to some papers cited earlier.

This paper is about the current issues hindering efficient access to terminologies for crisis communications, and a proposed approach to resolve them.

3   Methodology and Examples of Terminologies

In this article, a qualitative method is applied, especially document collection and literature review, and a simple technical implementation of integrated glossary service as a proof of concept for our suggested solution. The verification from a practitioner adds the confidence towards the need on the proposed notion.

We surveyed documents containing to obtain a sample of official information on glossaries used for crisis management worldwide. The goal is to provide a concrete illustration on the domain discussed in this paper. The glossary document examination is not intended for an exhaustive search, but instead to point out exemplary cases of the weaknesses of current presentation of emergency management glossaries, making it hard for users to find them, as explained in Sect. 4.

While ICT-based support or websites inform public the best practices intended for all in responding to hazard, they rarely include the terminology. The Table 1 below is to show some examples.

In this paper, we propose a novel approach to support disaster communication through an innovative glossary service, integrated into the ICT-based solution, which is more human-centric oriented and accessible. This approach could be used to provide access to relevant terminologies from the resources in Table 1. The weaknesses of the current search method of these crisis terminologies and proposed and implemented technology to support more human-centric crisis glossary services are illustrated further in Sects. 4 and 5 respectively.

There are several initiatives across government to collect terms related to their sector of responsibility related to crisis management. The following sections present a selection of them from Norway, Indonesia and international ones from Europe. Most of them are presented in different record formats. The modes for access also vary widely from PDF documents to access via application programming interface.

Table 1. Examples of practices for responding/alerting disasters in different countries

Country	Practice	Glossary on site	Languages covered
Japan	Emergency warning System	Not found	English, Japanese
Queensland Australia	Standard Emergency Warning Signal (SEWS)	Not found	20 language translation service via phone call
The Netherlands	NL-alert	Not found	Dutch only
Norway	Kriseinfo	Not found	Norwegian and English but only Norwegian up to date.
US	Integrated Public Alert & Warning System (IPAWS)	Not found	17 languages on the site

In Norway, we have located three groups of sources featuring government agencies like:

1. The Norwegian Directorate for Civil Protection (DSB) or Miljøkommune (www. miljokommune.no = environment municipality).
2. Environment Agency and clusters of organisations like the KBT (a cluster for fire safety) or AFTERM (a cluster for coastal hazard terms).
3. The law, regulations and guidance notes to the law, and standards.

All of these agencies manage their own set of terms. Some of them have an international collaboration to manage translations. The KBT has a collaboration with the Federation of the European Union Fire Officer Associations with 25 languages (FEU, see Table 2). The European Environment Agency is another relevant European source covering more than 30 languages. The coverage of terms in different languages seems to vary. Globally, the United Nations Office for the Coordination of Humanitarian Affairs (OCHA) has only one glossary with five terms related to Pauses During Conflict. Most of the disaster-related terms in UN agency are maintained in UNISDR (The United Nations Office for Disaster Risk Reduction), and available in all official United Nations languages (https://www.unisdr.org/we/inform/publications/7817).

We also examine Indonesia, one of the countries that is considered by UNISDR to be among the most disaster-prone countries in the world. Indonesia faces multiple hazards such as earthquake, tsunami, volcanic eruption, flood, landslide, drought, and forest fires, and terrorism [28]. The National Disaster Management Authority of Indonesia provides a limited collection of technical terms derived from the Act Number 24 of 2007 on Disaster Management. Apparently, the terms are limited compared to the disaster risks faced by this country in different likely disaster scenarios.

In Australia, Emergency Management Australia publishes the glossary as a pdf form, as a part of Australian Emergency Manual series. The glossary is intended for different organisations: public, private and community organisations. This is an example of a glossary document that has clear intended users.

Table 2. Examples of technical term collections from different countries

Country	Example	Remark/name
Norway	DSB	Norwegian Directorate for Civil Protection (DSB)
	Miljøkommune	A website with resources for municipalities
	Environment agency	National environment directorate
	Law and regulations	Norwegian legal documents
	Standards	Standards Norway, responsible for national standards
	KBT	Federation of national agencies related to fire safety
European/international	FEU	The Federation of the European Union Fire Officer Associations
	Prevention web	UN Office for Disaster Risk Reduction (UNISDR)
	EIONET	European Environment Information and Observation Network
Indonesia	National Disaster Management Authority	
Australia	Emergency Management Australia	
US	US Department of Health And Service	

The most comprehensive collection of glossaries is gathered by the US Department of Health and Human Services. It covers a wide range of disasters, emergency managements and humanitarian relief glossaries across agencies in the US and worldwide. The summary and links to the sources can be seen in Table 2.

4   Current Use of Collections of Terms

The ways to retrieve the definitions are very varied, but all of them will require the user to carry out some navigation to locate the relevant definition. We are aware of five online approaches available for users:

1. General search engine (possibly use the "define:" option);
2. Search for term in general dictionary (requires user to find e.g. dictionary.com.);
3. Search for term in a relevant term source (requires user to find e.g. KBT.no);
4. Search for term in the law/regulation (requires user to find and browse lovdata.no [access to a collection of online legal resources] in Norway e.g.).
5. The user uses a built-in functionality like "Define" on an iPad or Kindle device, or a browser extension to retrieve Wikipedia definitions.

The approaches 1 and 2 will require the user to switch context from the text where the term appeared and often return many irrelevant hits. Approaches 3 and 4 require that the user is aware of the specific sources. Approaches 1-4 all have in common that the user must change context and carry out a search on some other webpage. In some cases, user typos will be caught and corrected, and some services simply do not return any hits for mistyped terms. The 5th approach can keep the user in the context but will not give access to the specific crisis terminologies.

5 Current Representations of Collections of Terms

We note two challenges with the current practice, namely that the definitions of terms can be scattered across many sources, and that they are only available in for-mats that do not well support re-use in terms of machine-readability, such as tables on webpages or PDF documents. Tim Berners Lee proposed a Five-star deployment scheme for open data, to indicate the level of applicability for further use of the data (http://5stardata. info/en/).

As an example, we can look at the two Norwegian data sources KBT and AFTERM dealing with fire hazards and coastal area pollution hazards respectively. The data in both sources are stored in a database and published on HTML pages. So, the format is open and non-proprietary, URIs can be used to point to specific definitions of terms in the KBT source, and some of the external sources are provided as hyperlinks. This would award 5 out of 5 stars for the KBT representation. This will allow for efficient re-use and projection of these resources on other texts as indicated in the following section.

6 A Novel Approach to Access Term Definitions

The novel approach will allow the user to stay in the context where the term occurs and retrieve term definitions in a pop-up. Figure 1 shows an example from reading a Norwegian text about fire safety in buildings. The example shows the definition of the Norwegian term antennelse (set fire to/ignition).

Fig. 1. Example retrieval of the Norwegian term "antennelse" [ignition]. The text is part of a legal regulation about fire safety in buildings, and the definition is retrieved from KBT.

There are some services provided on the iPhone and Kindle that can deliver a similar output. However, these are limited to their hardware platforms and do not support users with other platforms.

Important difference compared to such solutions is the crucial narrowing of scope. The selection of terms will be limited to the disaster management area to allow the user to focus on the communication and not have to wade in long lists of irrelevant search hits. Images or video clips added to the term definitions can also help to con-vey the meaning more efficiently and overcome language barriers.

The approach can also support multiple terminologies. In this way, one click can replace the time consuming exercise to send the user off to multiple websites and to locate and query the individual terminologies for the requested definition. The pro-posed solution can also provide a ranking among multiple terminology sources if needed.

A similar approach can be used to support translations of a selection of relevant terms into additional languages. Please not that this will not replace a complete translation but can yet help non-native speakers to grasp the message.

The solution is designed in such a way that it is accessible for all regardless of disabilities, conforming to the Web Content Accessibility Guidelines (WCAG 2.0). This means that people using a mouse and a web browser like Firefox, Chrome or Internet Explorer, will get a similar user experience like those using a screen reader like Jaws or NVDA using the keyboard to navigate among definitions of terms. The approach is also designed to work across all common web browsers and platforms including mo-bile devices and tablets. These capabilities taken together forms the basis of a tool to support learning [29], for disaster preparedness.

We also expect that the simplified retrieval of definitions can support the termi-nology maintainers in their work, e.g. to harmonize the content among the different terminologies. A time-consuming part of the maintenance of terminologies is also the bookkeeping of internal links where one term that is defined is used in the definition of another term. Changes in the glossary can have far-reaching cascading effects that are currently manually maintained. Our approach will support the automated generation of internal links as shown in Fig. 2.

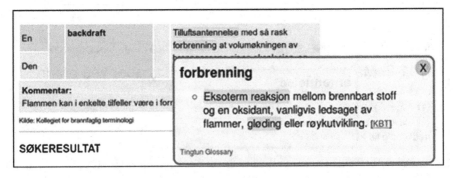

Fig. 2. Example retrieval of term definition from KBT backdraft. The definition of "forbren-ning" (combustion) refer to the definition of "gløding" (glowing).

The definitions can be shaped with simple formatting like bullets or emphasized text and can contain images. Figure 3 shows an image to illustrate the definition of the term "oljeforurensning" (oil pollution). To support the training for oral communications, the definitions can also be read aloud with an integrated text to speech solution.

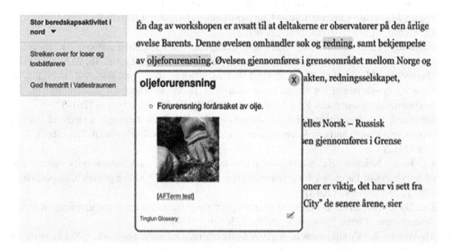

Fig. 3. Example to show definition of the term "oljeforurensing" (Oil pollution) illustrated with an image

The definitions can link in external references with additional information. This way the definition can link supporting materials or further illustrations e.g. in the form of content from Wikipedia, sound files for correct pronunciation, or video clips.

7   Conclusions and Future Works

In this paper, we have argued that in the current improvement of crisis communication technologies, the importance of shared understanding regarding the main concepts in the messages being exchanged is often overlooked. Even though terminologies are available and well-made, they are not necessarily well integrated into the communication resources or easy to use. A novel approach to unify the access to multiple terminologies and to improve the retrieval functionality has been introduced. The approach has been implemented for the terminology maintained by the Norwegian Firefighters Association (KBT) and has already demonstrated contributions to improved usability both for the terminology users and for the maintainers.

Future steps will include to enhance the capabilities of the approach to make it more robust and to seek collaboration with forward-looking crisis response organisations to carry out further experiments both for terminology maintenance and for crisis training initiatives.

References

1. Iluzia Iacob, A., et al.: Strategy map for the crisis communication. Procedia Econ. Financ. **23**, 1119–1124 (2015)
2. Coombs, W.T.: The value of communication during a crisis: insights from strategic communication research. Bus. Horiz. **58**(2), 141–148 (2015)
3. Drake, J.L., et al.: Communicating Climate-Change and Natural Hazard Risk and Cultivating Resilience. Springer, Heidelberg (2016)
4. Edworthy, J., et al.: Passing crisis and emergency risk communications: the effects of communication channel, information type, and repetition. Appl. Ergon. **48**, 252–262 (2015)
5. Hagelsteen, M., Becker, P.: A great babylonian confusion: terminological ambiguity in capacity development for disaster risk reduction in the international community. In: 5th International Disaster and Risk Conference (IDRC), Global Risk Forum (2014)
6. Johansen, W., Aggerholm, H.K., Frandsen, F.: Entering new territory: a study of internal crisis management and crisis communication in organisations. Public Relat. Rev. **38**(2), 270–279 (2012)
7. Ki, E.-J., Nekmat, E.: Situational crisis communication and interactivity: usage and effectiveness of Facebook for crisis management by fortune 500 companies. Comput. Hum. Behav. **35**, 140–147 (2014)
8. Liu, B.F., Fraustino, J.D.: Beyond image repair: suggestions for crisis communication theory development. Public Relat. Rev. **40**(3), 543–546 (2014)
9. Thywissen, K.: Components of Risk: A Comparative Glossary, pp. 1–48. UNU Institute for Environment and Human Security (UNU-EHS), Bonn (2006)
10. Tapia, A.H., Moore, K.A., Johnson, N.J.: Beyond the trustworthy tweet: a deeper understanding of microblogged data use by disaster response and humanitarian relief organisations. In: ISCRAM (2013)
11. Mayner, L., Arbon, P.: Defining disaster: the need for harmonisation of terminology. Australas. J. Disaster Trauma Stud. **19**, 21–25 (2015)
12. Lipson, B., Warren, H.: 'Taking Stock'–A Snapshot of INGO Engagement in Civil Society Capacity Building. INTRAC International NGO Training and Research Centre, Oxford (2006)
13. Barthe, A.M., Truptil, S., Bénaben, F.: Towards a taxonomy of crisis management simulation tools. In: ISCRAM 2015 Conference Proceedings – 12th International Conference on Information Systems for Crisis Response and Management. Kristiansand, University of Agder (UiA), Norway (2015)
14. Pottebaum, J., Marterer, R., Schneider, S.: Taxonomy of IT support for training emergency response and management. In: ISCRAM 2014 Conference Proceedings – 11th International Conference on Information Systems for Crisis Response and Management, pp. 374–378 (2014)
15. Addams-Moring, R., Kekkonen, M., Zhao, S.: A simple taxonomy for mobile emergency announcement systems. In: Proceedings of ISCRAM 2005 – 2nd International Conference on Information Systems for Crisis Response and Management. Royal Flemish Academy of Belgium, Brussels (2005)
16. Grant, T., Van der Wal, A.J.: A taxonomy of market mechanisms for information sharing in crisis response coalitions. In: Proceedings of the 9th International ISCRAM Conference (2012)
17. Shamoug, A., Juric, R.: Addressing interoperability through the semantic of information highway in managing responses in humanitarian crises. In: Proceedings of the 8th International ISCRAM Conference-Lisbon (2011)

18. Reuter, C., et al.: Dealing with terminologies in collaborative systems for crisis management. In: Proceedings of the 9th International ISCRAM Conference. Simon Fraser University, Vancouver, Canada (2012)
19. Temnikova, I., Castillo, C., Vieweg, S.: EMTerms 1.0: a terminological resource for crisis tweets. In: ISCRAM 2015 Proceedings of the 12th International Conference on Information Systems for Crisis Response and Management (2015)
20. Malizia, A., et al.: Emergency alerts for all: an ontology based approach to improve accessibility in emergency alerting systems. In: Proceedings of ISCRAM 2008 – 5th International Conference on Information Systems for Crisis Response and Management. Information Systems for Crisis Response and Management, Washington DC (2008)
21. Galton, A., Worboys, M.: An ontology of information for emergency management. In Proceedings of 8th International Conference on Information Systems for Crisis Response and Management (2011)
22. Liu, S., Shaw, D., Brewster, C.: Ontologies for crisis management: a review of state of the art in ontology design and usability. In: Proceedings of the ISCRAM 2013 - Information Systems for Crisis Response and Management conference (2013)
23. Javed, Y., Norris, T., Johnston, D.: Ontology-based inference to enhance team situation awareness in emergency management. In: Proceedings of the ISCRAM 2011 - 8th International Conference on Information Systems for Crisis Response and Management, Lisbon (2011)
24. Barros, R., et al.: Edxl-rescuer ontology: conceptual model for semantic integration. In: Proceedings of the ISCRAM 2015- 12th International Conference on Information Systems for Crisis Response and Management (2015)
25. Gatial, E., Hluchy, L.: Data interoperability approach during major accidents. In: Conference Proceedings ISCRAM 2016 – 13th International Conference on Information Systems for Crisis Response and Management. Federal University of Rio de Janeiro, Rio de Janeiro, Brasil (2016)
26. Park Jr., J.S.: Enabling cross-organisation interoperability through dynamic directory integration. In: Proceedings of ISCRAM 2005 – 2nd International Conference on Information Systems for Crisis Response and Management. Brussels: Royal Flemish Academy of Belgium (2005)
27. Buscher, M., et al.: A new manhattan project?: Interoperability and ethics in emergency response systems of systems. In: Proceedings of ISCRAM 2013 -10th International ISCRAM Conference, Baden-Baden, Germany (2013)
28. AIPA: Indonesia's country report on disaster response management in AIPA caucus report. ASEAN Inter-Parlementary Assembly-AIPA, Manila, Philippines (2011)
29. Snaprud, M.H., Helmikstøl, G.R.: A Socratic E-learning approach. Int. J. Adv. Corp. Learn. 8(2), 44–46 (2015)

Towards European Dimensions of City Resilience

Jaziar Radianti[(✉)]

Department of ICT, Centre for Integrated Emergency Management,
University of Agder, Grimstad, Norway
jaziar.radianti@uia.no

Abstract. Disaster resilience is becoming more important and raises the highest concerns worldwide, including in Europe. Cities have a vital role for resilience because a majority of the population resides in the cities. Despite the recognition of the importance of city resilience, there is no strong consensus what city resilience is and its dimensions, and how the resilience concept should be transferred into management practice in the cities. In this paper, we conduct a survey of EU sectorial approaches in terms of EU-funded projects related to climate change and critical infrastructure, where urban or city resilience are in focus. The goal is to obtain an overview of how the resilience concept is interpreted, used, and applied in different EU sectors or in cross-sectorial areas. The aim of this paper is to devise a set of schemes on components that should exist as pillars for supporting the European dimension of city resilience. The paper presents three models derived from the concepts, definitions, and applications in different EU-funded research projects. How "urban" resilience has been considered in the European context so far, and how a "resilience backbone" for Europe can be established, are among the issues examined in this paper.

Keywords: City resilience · Resilient dimensions · European dimension of resilience · Disaster resilience

1 Introduction

Disaster resilience is becoming more important and raises the highest concern world-wide, especially in Europe, where resilience is a top priority and a subject to an active campaign, putting city and community resilience in the core [1]. The frequently cited definition of resilience from UNISDR suggests it as "The ability of a system, community or society exposed to hazards to resist, absorb, accommodate to and recover from the effects of a hazard in a timely and efficient manner, including through the preservation and restoration of its essential basic structures and functions" [2]. Currently, however, the city resilience as a unit for analysis is still not well defined. Besides, there is no single, agreed-upon definition. The network of 100 Resilient Cities, for instance, defines urban resilience as "the capacity of individuals, communities, institutions, business, and systems within a city to survive, adapt, and grow no matter what kinds of chronic stresses and acute shocks they experience." The example of the

© IFIP International Federation for Information Processing 2017
Published by Springer International Publishing AG 2017. All Rights Reserved
Y. Murayama et al. (Eds.): ITDRR 2016, IFIP AICT 501, pp. 104–118, 2017.
https://doi.org/10.1007/978-3-319-68486-4_9

chronic stress in urban areas can originate from critical infra-structure problems (such as inefficient public transport system, food shortages); climate change (water scarcity, heatwaves) or social problems such as a high rate of unemployment. In Europe, the needs to incorporate resilience into the city plan are evident [3–5], as more and more cities have formulated their city resilience strategies such as in London [6], Copenhagen [7], or Rotterdam [8]. Despite the development of resilience networks worldwide or at European level, there is no strong consensus what city resilience is and its components or dimensions, and how far resilience concept has entered, and been interpreted and implemented in different policy areas. Besides, ideas on how to subsume resilience into management practices are still vague, as diverse problem areas require different definitions of resilience, and in turn, result in various designs of practicing it (See publications of Resilient Cities Series on various urban resilient strategies and experience worldwide in http://resilient-cities.iclei.org/.). How the European dimension should interact in the city resilience context adds complexities of how this concept should be discerned.

One way to understand the fragmented discussions and approaches to resilience in various sectors in Europe is by conducting a desk survey of EU funded projects as done in this paper. This paper examines various resilience conceptual and practical point of view with respect to climate change and critical infrastructure, with urban or city resilience in the core. The goal is to obtain an overview of how the resilience concept is interpreted, used and applied in different EU sectors or a cross-sectorial area. The main contribution of this paper is to devise a set of schemes identifying components that should serve as pillars of a city, that can further be a backbone for supporting European resilience. The paper presents three models derived from the concepts, definitions, and applications in different EU-funded research projects.

In Sect. 2 we describe how cities have been represented and projected within EU policies. In Sect. 3 we propose methods to extract concepts and applications of resilience in different EU-funded research projects. Section 4 summarizes the "keywords" of the general definitions of resilience, filtered from EU project literature and proposals that provided the working definitions of different resilience dimensions. This section also elaborates and discusses the proposal to strengthen the EU dimension of city resilience. Section 5 concludes and summarizes the findings in this article.

2 Existing City Elements in EU Policies

There are various programs, initiatives and policies to provide a vision for "cities" in Europe. We identify that urban areas have been projected as Green Cities, as Open Cities, as Resilient Cities, as Innovative Cities and Creative Cities. By recognizing this, we ensure that the contribution of this article can be relevant and fills the gap between existing policies and approaches to the cities in Europe. In the next section, we summarize the perspective on Green Cities, Open Cities, Innovative-Creative Cities, and Resilient Cities—which is this paper's focus.

Green Cities represent ideas, policies, initiatives and projects within sustainable urban mobility environmentally friendly cities targeting zero CO_2 emissions (See http://ec.europa.eu/transport/themes/urban/urban_mobility/; ELTIS, http://www.eltis.

org/, and CIVITAS, http://www.civitas-initiative.org/). Thus, the focus lies upon measures and policies on controlling urban pollution, improving the air quality, promoting urban sustainability and intelligent mobility, and increasing the amount of green spaces in cities. The use of environmentally friendly transport and sustainable products is highly emphasized. The establishment of targets and limits for different pollutants can be used as a tool to control air quality, as well as waste management and urban wastewater treatment. Initiatives at city level have been started; for example, the Covenant of Mayors (www.covenantofmayors.eu) aims to significantly limit CO_2 emissions. Energy efficiency for mobility, and other areas that consume significant amounts of energy have been introduced.

Open cities focus on how to make buildings, cities and environments more age-friendly (to all age groups) (See EU policy for active and healthy ageing http://ec.europa.eu/eip/ageing/actiongroup/index/d4). In addition, open cities also focus on the implementation of EU integration policies (See EU policy for integration, (https://ec.europa.eu/migrant-integration), since cities are responsible for a wide range of services provided to migrants, and they play a major role in shaping the interaction between migrants and the society that welcomes them. Rome is a unique example of this case (See EU and Roma, http://ec.europa.eu/justice/discrimination/roma/).

Innovative and creative cities highlight the richness and diversity of European cultures as a part of EU's aim for smart, sustainable and inclusive cities and stimulus for dynamism, creativity, and social inclusion. Smart cities (See http://ec.europa.eu/eip/smartcities/) and communities European Innovation Partnership, iCapital (See https://ec.europa.eu/research/innovation-union/index_en.cfm?section=icapital&pg=home), European Capital of Culture (See European Capitals of Culture (https://ec.europa.eu/programmes/creative-europe/actions/capitals-culture_en), European heritage label (See https://ec.europa.eu/programmes/creative-europe/actions/european-heritage-label_en) are among examples of initiatives under this category.

Resilient cities emphasize how to make cities in Europe more resilient against unexpected events. In April 2013, the EU strategy on adaptation to climate change also committed to making Europe more climate resilient. The effects of climate change will have far-reaching consequences across Europe, and climate adaptation is needed to protect people, buildings, infrastructure, businesses, and ecosystems. We have seen that policy, strategy and actions have been proposed or formulated. However, there is still a lack of clarity regarding how city resilience is operationalized and serves as a backbone across Europe. An EU-funded project Smart Mature Resilience (SMR) is an example of a project extending city resilience toward overall European resilience. In this paper, relevant concepts that can be useful to extend city resilience into over-all European Resilience are gathered, using the method explained in Sect. 3.

3   Methods

A desk survey was conducted to examine how resilience was applied and used in different EU sectors and to extract necessary elements that can be adapted for shaping the city resilience. The search targeted projects related to Critical Infrastructure (CI) and Climate Change (CC). Systematic mapping study was applied, encompassing the examination of relevant EU policies, EU funded project deliverables, and corresponding journal articles [9–11]. Catalogues of FP7 and H2020 projects were examined, i.e., (1) Catalogue of EU funded projects in Environmental Research 2007-2011 FP7 Theme 6– Environment (including climate change); (2) Catalogue of R&I Projects 2014 Climate action, environment, resource efficiency and raw materials Horizon 2020; (3) Catalogue of Security Research Projects under the 7th Framework Programme for Research, EU Research for a Secure Society: (4) EU policy documents, especially related to CI and CC policies.

The following procedure was performed when searching for relevant EU sectorial projects: (1) Identifying projects where the resilience issues are very likely to be addressed, both under FP 7 and Horizon 2020 calls; (2) Filtering project titles and abstracts using keyword "resilience"; and then "city" or "urban"; and lastly using "critical infrastructure", "protection", or "climate change"; (3) manual filtering by going through the project websites to verify if the identified projects were relevant, e.g. if the project actually is about resilience, or only mentioned it as a part of another irrelevant context; (4) examining more closely the project reports and deliverables to be included in the review. In total, 13 projects related to Environment (Climate Change) FP7, 18 projects under Secure Societies FP 7 calls, 3 projects under Climate Action environment H2020 and 4 projects under Secure Societies H2020 were reviewed. In total, we looked at 170 documents (reports, deliverables and scientific reports of each project, if any). We created a framework for review prior to examination, organized the relevant information into the framework and extracted further content that potentially can contribute shaping understanding of city resilience. In this paper, we only present the most important elements of resilience found in our survey, i.e. the synthesis of the resilience definitions has been applied in various unit of analysis in different research projects, and resilience elements that are transferred into three models of resilience dimensions in Sect. 4.

4 City Resilience Dimensions and Definition

4.1 Resilience Dimensions and Definitions

Note, the goal of this section is not to discuss deeply the various definition of resilience in the literature. We rather try to identify the unit of analysis when the resilience concept is applied, which is then called "dimensions" in this paper. Through the review efforts, we have collected and filtered different definitions of resilience both from different authors and projects' operational definition that have been cited in the selections of EU project deliverables.

There is a batch of definitions, with many coming from the same sources, and some try to adapt in accordance with the context (i.e. resilience to what? for example, the resilience to flooding). The definitions compiled in this section are presented as the collection of main keywords that are frequently used and become the main essence of the resilience concept. We extract the main concepts from the definitions and try to find the occurrence of a set of keywords in all identified definitions from literature, to understand the common words describing resilience. We present two collections of keywords summarized in two charts in Fig. 1: the left figure is the keywords derived from CI literature and the right figure derived from CC literature. We collected 111 definitions from CI literature and 58 definitions in CC literature. From the charts, we have seen that the terms ability/capability, adapt, recover, absorb, change, and resists are the most popular words to capture resilience (to hazards, disturbances, unexpected events, abnormal situations). The following terms have been used in the literature as a unit of analysis when applying resilience concept:

- Urban/city resilience. The terms such as space or spatial resilience are also found to refer to a city or urban area. It also covers urban built infrastructure resilience.
- Ecological, socio-ecological resilience.
- Critical infrastructure, smart grid, technical, communication resilience [12–16].
- Cyber-security resilience [17].
- Chemical, biological, radiological, nuclear and explosive (CBRNE) resilience [18–20].
- Economic resilience [16].
- Organisational/local government resilience [21].
- Community/societal resilience/public/neighbourhood resilience [22–25].
- Individual resilience, psychosocial, psychological resilience [26].

The summary of this tentative definition of each dimension is shown in Table 1. Note that these definitions are squeezed out of a cluster of definitions on a specific unit of analysis or dimension. In other words, the definitions have been grouped and categorized before they are merged and extracted, both definitions stemming from CI and CC literature.

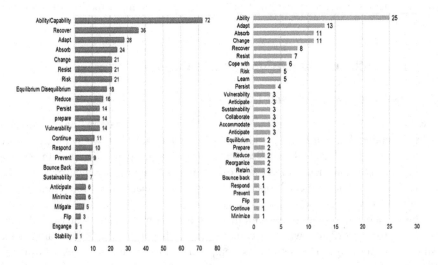

Fig. 1. Common keywords of resilience definitions cited in EU-CI literature (left) and EU-CC literature (right).

Table 1. The summary of the definition of each resilience's dimension.

Definitions
Urban or City Resilience consists of a mixture of resilient built-in environments, resilient design, resilient citizens, and resilient organisations. Resiliently built environments should be designed, located, built, operated and maintained in a way that maximizes the ability of built assets, associated support systems (physical and institutional) and the people that reside or work within these built assets, to withstand, recover from, and mitigate the impacts of extreme natural hazards and human-induced threats. The citizens in the city should be able to handle and respond to unexpected situations resulting from malfunctioning CIs, changes of social, economic and environmental stresses, and also be proactive during a crisis and have the ability to recover by themselves. The organisations at the city level have the capacity to support any transformations by rapid changes taking place in urban key areas.
CI resilience: Resilient infrastructure can resist damage and loss of function, absorb, adapt to, or rapidly recover from a potentially disruptive event, can quickly restore its continuity and support the city's CI-based services. It also covers the ability and reliability of the CIs to cope with the potential damage from extreme weather events, and the capacity to manage the CC impacts on the variability in the available resources.
Community and Social Resilience refers to the capacity of individuals, communities or societies potentially exposed to hazards to adapt, be flexible, and bounce-back by resisting or changing behaviour, taking-up innovations, organising itself to continuously exist, reach and maintain an acceptable level of functioning and structure. This capacity also covers the capability to combat social vulnerability, enhance perceived risk and sense of responsibility, and learn from the previous hazards. This capacity can be improved through education and training.
Socio-ecological system Resilience can be interpreted in two ways: The time it takes for recovering to a quasi-equilibrium state following a disturbance ('engineering resilience' or 'elasticity'), or the capacity of ecosystems to absorb disturbance without collapsing into a qualitatively different state that is controlled by a different set of ecological processes. It is the ability to learn from catastrophic events and to adapt reactively and proactively to changing environmental conditions, to learn what disturbance, inherent discontinuities, and uncertainties that can be tolerated so that the system can be adapted and adjusted so that it still functionally persists.
Organisational Resilience covers all management capacities such as planning, leadership, training, experience, and information management. It includes the capacity to improvise, innovate and expand the operations between impact and early recovery and the capability to conduct a proper risk assessment and risk management.
Local Government Resilience is the capability of an organisation to coordinate and sustain on multiple levels, a multi-stakeholders platform to promote disaster risk reduction. It also includes the capability to engage local communities and citizens in disaster risk reduction activities; the capability to strengthen the institution, capacities and implement practical disaster risk reduction actions; and the capacity to implement tools and techniques for disaster risk in the prevention, preparedness, response, and recovery.
Individual Resilience is a person's own resilient capabilities; the adaptive capacity of individuals to react or adapt positively to hazards or unexpected events.
Economic resilience is the capacity to reduce direct and indirect losses, maintaining functions such as continuous production. It is also the ability of society to adapt to the impacts of e.g. climate change, and damages from hazards which also depend on wealth in addition to society, culture, norms, and practices. It should be able to maintain economic vitality and meet climate targets.
CBRNE resilience is the capability of the responders to detect CBRNE events, to respond and to recover from occurring incidents.

It is worth to mention that we also found the terms "Holistic resilience" and "Pan-European" resilience. However, the notions of these two terms are not fully well defined as units of analysis. Yet, in this paper, we argue that to attach cities onto future European resilience backbones, resilience in all abovementioned dimensions should be accomplished, which then can be considered as holistic resilience. When a holistic city resilience is transmitted, replicated and referred as a role model across regions and nations, then Pan-European resilience will gradually be attained. Note, as the essence of this article, is exploration; at this point, we do not propose a single new definition of city resilience. We are also aware of the scientific literature on resilience [27–36], but we only focus on reports and works on resilience that have been applied for EU research projects. We utilize the aforementioned synthesized definitions and related concepts to propose three upcoming models of European dimensions of resilience in the next sub-section.

4.2   Model of Resilient Dimensions

As mentioned earlier, concepts and relevant elements of resilience in the literature were collected, categorized and grouped. In this section, we have synthesized some findings from the literature and try to propose them as a model of resilient dimensions. Frequently used concepts and definitions to describe resilience are reused for proposing three different models containing elements to achieve European City Resilience.

1. Model of Capacity: ensuring all elements in a city, country, and Europe (actors, entities, environment, physical buildings, and infrastructures) are resilient. In this model, the crucial issue is capacity needed in different resilience dimensions.
2. Model of Adaptive and Risk Governance: Ensuring that risks, institutional arrangement, tasks, and responsibilities are distributed across sectors, actors, entities, and in different resilience dimensions, and geographical boundaries.
3. Model of Networking and Learning: ensuring that spread of resilience across dimensions, entities, actors and geographical boundaries are granted through networking, learning, and sharing circles.

The dimensions incorporated in these three proposed resilient models are based on the lists that have been identified earlier in Sect. 4.1. The models are shown in Figs. 2, 3 and 4. It is essentially an interaction of resilience of different components of the city's system that eventually will be reflected as overall city resilience. In this model, the local government organisations are central as transition hubs towards resilience within the different dimensions of a city. All three models encompass the same elements. In the left side, there is an arrow depicting the efforts for establishing holistic resilience as we have defined earlier in Sect. 4.1. The three blocks in the middle represent different levels of governance: city level, national level, and international level. They also represent different stages of resilience: in the preparedness, response, recovery, and mitigation, as these emergency management stages are highly related to resilience. The ellipse above each block represents the continuous process of designing frameworks for managing, implementing, monitoring and improving resilience in each emergency management stage. During the desk survey, various themes linked to resilience has been explored such as public-private partnerships [12, 37, 38], socio-ecological environments [39] and vulnerabilities [22–25], multilevel governance, adaptive governance, social capacity, risk governance, risk communication and education, collaboration, mutual learning from experience, interdependencies between critical infrastructures, mobilization of social capitals, collaborative decision making, and more. In our models, we map necessary elements and their interactions found in the literature above and locate them in these three frameworks. These elements are represented by small arrows, which link different blocks of governance levels. We will explain further each specific model in the next sub-sections.

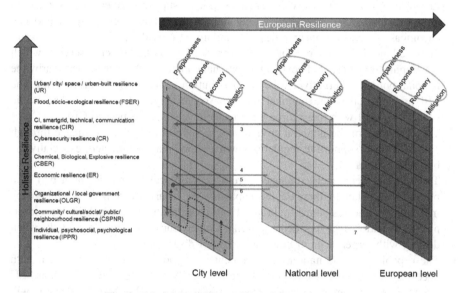

Fig. 2. Model 1: resilience dimensions and capacity

Model of Capacity highlights the capacity as a prerequisite for transforming resilience from cities to Europe. In this model, the capacity refers to the ability to receive, hold or absorb unexpected events in all elements (individuals, private and public entities, physical environments, buildings, and infrastructures) in a city, country, and Europe. Capacity is apparently an important notion that to a certain degree captures the essence of resilience, as also seen in the charts in Fig. 1. In model 1, the capabilities to withstand hazards should be developed in each unit listed on the left side of Fig. 2. The role of local government in the city level is very central and functions as glue for the resilience of other units. The numbered arrows in Fig. 2 show the resilience elements linking cities, nations, and Europe. The number of each arrow represents the following ideas:

1. Representing the capacities that should be built and nurtured in each dimension. The arrow 1 is located in the "preparedness" column as these capacities are instituted in the cities, which can be unique from place to place depending upon each city's risk pictures. Examples of capacities found in the literature are summarized in the capacity matrix (see Table 2).

2. Representing the continuous interaction process between a local government with the community and the individual in all disaster phases: preparedness, response, recovery, and mitigation. The local government educates community and individuals about disaster preparedness and risk perception. Individuals develop self-resilience, ability to collaborate with neighbours and community, or even provide support to the local government. Community can help mobilizing resources and communicate among important entities in crisis.

3. Capability to understand CI dependencies, interdependencies and cascading effects within and across the sectors. The arrow 3 is linked through the national and European level, as CI services such as power supply and energy production, transportation, water are often closely link to the national government and can encompass several European cities. The failures at providing CI services can result in cascading disasters across other services that rely on this specific service, which geographically can spread beyond the national border, e.g. between cities nearby the national border. Alternatively, the water pollution in a city, for instance, with time will probably cross the national border. Accordingly, arrow 3 also depicts the capacity to deal with these three governance levels with respect to CIs.

4. The capability of the national government to support economic resilience through various robust, supportive regulations where cities may be affected, especially the business entities.

5. Training and personnel exchanges across geographical boundaries as a part of a preparedness plan to increase the capability of local government in emergency management and resilience building. It can be enhancing the capability to coordinate with national government as well as other European cities especially when dealing with larger scale or cross-boundary of disasters.

6. The capability of the national government to support the local government with necessary regulations, and to convey the EU strategies and guidelines such as "EU Domestic action on resilience" into action at the city level. This element will support further the city's preparedness, as represented by the arrow 6.

7. The capability of national government to follow the development at the EU level and to bring local initiative and interest into EU policies; capacity to make international agreement in the area of resilient cities; capability to harmonise resilience policy with other EU member states.

We notice mutuality or reciprocal relations between each dimension in terms of capacity; and therefore, a matrix of resilience capacity is introduced here, which is again derived from elements extracted from literature identified in Sect. 2. The capacity matrix mentioned in point 1 (Table 2) shows the required capabilities in different dimensions, (from, to or within the dimension itself). The heading "Capacity from Dimension" in the left part of the Table illustrates the capacities needed in different resilience dimensions included in model 1. The heading "To Dimension" in the upper part of the table represents the intended focus or application area of the resilience capacity building. For example, the box linking OLGR (Organizational/Local Government Resilience) dimension column and UR (Urban Resilience) dimension row, contains "Regulations, resilience budget, technology". It is read as the capacity of organization or local government to provide regulations, resilience budget and technology that will strengthen the resilience of the urban environment.

Table 2. Capacity matrix

		UR	FSER	CIR	CR	CBRNE	ER	OLGR	CSPNR	IPPR
						TO DIMENSION				
	UR	Adapt built- environment	Adaptive to extreme weather	Less hazard prone CI location	Secured by design Urban CIs	minimizes CBRNE events	Urban economy keep adapt to threats	Built assets support institutional	Built assets support Community	Built assets support safe environment
	FSER	Robust to flood or other natural and ecological threats	Adaptive to ecological threats and dependencies	Resilient CIs to ecological threats		Recover from CBRNE events that affect environment				
	CIR	Robust ICT support		dependency			Robust ICT support	Robust ICT support	Robust ICT support	Robust ICT support
	CR	Robustness to cyber-attacks on ICT-based CIs		Robustness to cyber-attacks on ICT-based CIs	Minimize dependency, cascading effects		Robust to cyber-attacks on ICT-based CIs	Robustness to cyber-attacks on ICT-based CIs		
	CBRNE	Capacity to detect event						Robust tech to provide alerts		
	ER	Adaptive to economic stress					Cost and losses	Adaptive to economic stress	Adaptive to economic stress	Adaptive to economic stress
	OLGR	Regulations, resilience budget, technology	Technology support, robust spatial design, Advice for resilient technology usage	Minimize interdependency risk and impacts, Sustainable CIs, Securing CIs	CR events or know resource to contact	Detect and respond CBRNE event or Know resources to respond CBRNE	Regulations	Support relevant entities Establish PuP, Collaborate, share, learn, network, leadership	DRR education PPP Awareness education	Risk education Support counselling Advice for resilient technology usage
	CSPNR	Proactive to urban events	Adaptive to ecological threats	Securing CIs	Prevent, respond and recover from CR events	Detect and inform abnormality	Adapt and recover from economic events	Mobilise resource To inform local authorities	Risk and resilient culture, learn, share, self- organise	Cooperate, support individuals
	IPPR	Risk perception, self-resilience	Risk perception, self-resilience	Risk perception, self-resilience	Inform abnormality	Inform abnormality		Support, engage, volunteering	Build cohesion, Inform abnormality	Self-resilience

UR: Urban Resilience; FSER: Flood, Socio-Ecological Resilience; CIR: Critical Infrastructure Resilience; CR: Cyber Security Resilience; CBER: Chemical, Biological, Explosive Resilience; ER: Economic Resilience; OLGR: Organisational/ Local Government Resilience; CSPNR: Community, Cultural, Public, Neighbourhood Resilience; IPPR: Individual, Psychosocial; Psychological Resilience

Model of Adaptive and Risk Governance. This second model in Fig. 3 captures the adaptive governance, risk governance, and multilevel governance. The upwards arrow on the left side represents the actors and networks in each corresponding resilience, while the right arrow dimension captures the notion of risk governance, and multilevel governance at a different level. Governance is basically a continuing process through which conflicting or diverse interests may be accommodated, and co-operative action may be taken. It includes formal institutions and regimes empowered to enforce compliance, as well as informal arrangements that people and institutions either have agreed to or perceive to be in their interest (CGC). Risk governance looks at the complex networks of actors, rules, conventions, processes and mechanisms concerned with how relevant risk information is collected, analysed and communicated, and how management decisions are taken. Multilevel governance refers to a creative process in which both authority and policy making influences are shared across multiple levels of government. Similarly to the Fig. 2, the numbered arrows (Fig. 3) depict relevant elements found in the literature with respect to governance. The number of each arrow represents the following ideas:

1. The arrangement of risk and responsibility sharing among various local stake-holders at different dimensions. The arrow 1 is located in the "preparedness" column as an arrangement in a city can be established in and between different actors in different dimensions of resilience. The common interest could be the basis for this, with the common goal to increase preparedness.
2. Participations among actors in different groups (city, national, European levels) and communications among them on the arrangement as represented by each arrow in each governance level covers all different identified stakeholders, in various stages of emergency management.
3. Risk perception, and sharing of responsibilities among local actors and stakeholders to minimize the potential negative impacts of the risks.
4. Trust to the regulatory framework for governance.
5. Risk perception, communication and sharing of responsibilities with national stakeholders and international stakeholders to minimize the potential negative impacts of the risks. Governance, Multilevel governance, Public-private partnership (PPP) and Public-public Partnership are ways to deal with the risk, which will be further discussed in the third model.
6. Representing facilitation for international agreement with respect to governance and shared responsibilities, particularly if the risks will involve international networks. International agreements, cooperation between nations, regional, and local networks.

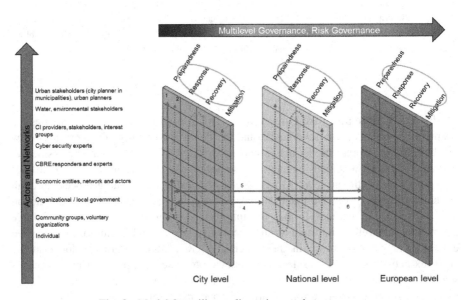

Fig. 3. Model 2: resilience dimensions and governance

Model of Networking and Learning. This model captures the networks of actors establishing the learning and sharing links in different parts of the resilience dimensions. One of the networking models discussed in the literature is public-private partnerships (PPP) where the aim is to establish a kind of cooperation with respect to financing, constructing, renovating, managing and maintaining important infrastructures for society. The partnerships are keys for implementing multilevel governance where the numbers below refer to the numbered lines in Fig. 4:

1. Networking between local government and CI stakeholders-providers as well as economic entities through PPP. The partnership is voluntary but enforceable commitments between public authorities and private enterprises, which can be short-term or long-term. The partnerships are essentially founded on the principle of sharing the same goal in order to reduce risk and gain mutual benefit. Good partnerships comprise the integration of activities, shared vision, consensus, negotiation, participation, collective action, representation, inclusion, accountability, volunteerism, and trust.

2. Public-public Partnership (PuP), where the focus is the partnership between public authorities and citizens in general, aiming at strengthening resilience through community engagements. It is represented by arrow 2. The form could be the community helping the local government through resource mobilization, or the local government updating and educating the community with respect to the resilience practices and actions.

3. Local community networks for emergency preparedness. These are kind of self-organized communities, between neighbourhoods, special interest groups and other local organizations initiated by and for the community. It is represented by arrow 3 that links the CSPNR and IPPR columns.

4. PPP in CI areas at European level, as represented by arrow 4. In this case, in the literature, CIs often have interdependencies with other CIs, which are sometimes located geographically outside a country. Failure in one component or one CI can result in cascading failures in all other CI components or other CI sectors in other countries. Therefore, PPP does occur not only locally, but also nationally and internationally within the European region.

5. Facilitation from the national government to the local administration for networking with national actors. It connects economic sectors at local and national levels. The networking is intended for strengthening economic entities and businesses in various levels of government.

6. International and European resilient city networks, best practice sharing, as so far have been promoted through e.g. Durban Adaptation Charter [40], Mayor Adapt [41], world mayors council [42], Compact of Mayors [43].

7. Networking with national actors for emergency preparedness to increase resilience especially in facing of an escalated unexpected event, which is too big to be handled by local resources.

8. Facilitation from the national government for international networking, e.g. through various regulations, or training on agreement making and diplomacy.

The three models proposed earlier suggest different elements as capacity, governance, and learning-networking which have been extracted from different EU funded research projects to improve resilience. The elements of resilience presented in this paper is exploration in nature but to be able to be applied as a part of the city resilience, the applicability of each element in the city level should be validated so that they are accepted as valid component of resilience, and a backbone of European resilience.

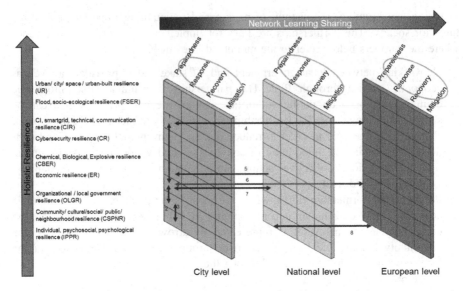

Fig. 4. Resilience dimension and learning-sharing network

5 Conclusions

In this paper, we summarize elements from various EU projects to contribute towards the area of Resilient Cities and propose a "resilience backbone" for Europe. Our contributions are twofold. First, we summarize and synthesize the definition of resilience in different dimensions found in the CI and CC literature to ensure that current approaches to resilience are captured in our EU sectorial approach review.

Second contribution is the proposal to tie together different elements of resilience found in the literature, which can be incorporated as parts of a city resilience framework. We have proposed three different models of European City Resilience, i.e. Model of Capacity, Model of Adaptive and Risk Governance, and Model of Networking and Learning. These provide an overview that can be used as input to operationalize further the resilience concept. These three models and each component are intertwined and will contribute to the spread of the city resilience building to the state, and European level. Eventually, the European backbones for resilience are fully established, and resilience of a city can be measured.

As the identification of elements of European backbones for resilience is based on literature, for the next step, the triangulation with other parallel efforts such as experts' opinion collections in a series of workshops can be a method to harmonize and confirm the results from this literature review.

Acknowledgments. This article is based on the author's contribution to a report for Smart Mature Resilience (SMR) project. This project has received funding from the European Union's Horizon 2020 research and innovation programme under grant agreement no. 653569.

References

1. UNISDR: Building resilience to disasters in Europe: connect and convince to reduce impact of vulnerability. In: UNISDR Europe Annual Report 2012. UNISDR, Geneva, Switzerland (2012)
2. UNISDR: UNISDR terminology on disaster risk reduction. In: International Strategy for Disaster Reduction (ISDR), pp. 1–30 (2009)
3. EEA: Urban adaptation to climate change in Europe, pp. 1–146 (2012)
4. EEA: Adaptation in Europe - addressing risks and opportunities from climate change in the context of socio-economic developments—European Environment Agency, pp. 1–136 (2013)
5. Swart, R., et al.: Europe Adapt to Climate Change: Comparing National Adaptation Strategies, in PEER Report. Partnership for European Environmental Research, Helsinki (2009)
6. Greater-London-Authority: Managing risks and increasing resilience. The Mayor's Climate Change Adaptation Strategy, pp. 1–42 (2011)
7. City-of-Copenhagen: COPENHAGEN Climate Adaptation Plan (2011)
8. Van Peijpe, D., et al.: Rotterdam: climate change adaptation strategy (2013)
9. Budgen, D., et al.: Using mapping studies in software engineering. In: Proceedings of PPIG. Lancaster University (2008)
10. Kitchenham, B., et al.: Systematic literature reviews in software engineering - a systematic literature review. Inf. Softw. Technol. 51, 7–15 (2009)
11. Kitchenham, B.A., Budgen, D., Brereton, O.P.: Using mapping studies as the basis for further research–a participant-observer case study. Inf. Softw. Technol. 53(6), 638–651 (2011)
12. McLean, L., Guha-Sapir, D.: Developing a resilience framework. ENHANCE FP7 Project (2013)
13. Lange, D., Sjöström, J., Honfi, D.: Losses and consequences of large scale incidents with cascading effects, pp. 1–43 (2015)
14. Tilsner, D., Arouca, D.: Deliverable: D2.2: desktop study – contingency planning methodologies and business continuity. EURACOM FP7 Project (2009)
15. Mäki, K., Forssen, K., Vangelsten, B.V.: Factors contributing to CI vulnerability and resilience. INTACT Deliverable D3.2. In: Project Co-Funded by the European Commission Under the 7th Frame-Work Programme, Tampere, Finland (2015)
16. Pursiainen, C., Gattinesi, P.: Towards testing critical infrastructure resilience, pp. 1–39, Luxembourg (2014)
17. Choras, M., et al.: Comprehensive approach to increase cyber security and resilience. In: 10th International Conference on Availability, Reliability and Security (ARES). IEEE, Toulouse (2015)
18. Breivik, H., et al.: D2.3 Critical Event Parameters (2012)
19. Endregard, M., et al.: D2.2 Reference Set of CBRN Scenarios (2012)
20. Endregard, M., et al.: D2.2 reference set of CBRN scenarios. Practice FP7 Project (2012)
21. Rigaud, E., et al.: Conceptual approach to resilience of local governments, pp. 1–117 (2015)
22. Kuhlicke, C., et al.: Social capacity building for natural hazards: a conceptual frame. In: CapHaz-Net FP7 Project, pp. 1–50 (2010)
23. Tapsell, S., et al.: Social vulnerability to natural hazards. In: CapHaz-Net FP7 Project, pp. 524–524 (2010)
24. Kuhlicke, C.: Resilience: a capacity and a myth: findings from an in-depth case study in disaster management research. Nat. Hazards 67, 61–76 (2013)

25. Kuhlicke, C., et al.: Toward More Resilient Societies in the Field of Natural Hazards: CapHaz-Net's Lessons Learnt, pp. 1–76 (2012)
26. Seynaeve, G.: Pycho-Social Support in situations of Mass Emergency: A European policy paper concerning different aspects of psycho-social support for people involved in major accidents and disasters (2001)
27. Carpenter, S., et al.: From metaphor to measurement: resilience of what to what? Ecosystems **4**, 765–781 (2001)
28. Walker, B., Salt, D.: Resilience Thinking: Sustaining Ecosystems and People in a Changing World. Island Press, Washington (2012)
29. Walker, B., Westley, F.: Perspectives on resilience to disasters across sectors and cultures. Ecol. Soc. **16**, 2–5 (2011)
30. Holling, C.S.: Resilience and stability of ecological systems. Annu. Rev. Ecol. Syst. **4**, 1–23 (1973)
31. Holling, C.S.: Engineering resilience versus ecological resilience. Eng. Ecol. Constraints **31**, 32 (1996)
32. Adger, W.N.: Social and ecological resilience: are they related? Prog. Hum. Geogr. **24**, 347–364 (2000)
33. Adger, W.N.: Vulnerability. Glob. Environ. Change **16**, 268–281 (2006)
34. Adger, W.N., et al.: Assessment of adaptation practices, options, constraints and capacity. In: Parry, M.L., et al. (eds.) Climate Change 2007: Impacts, Adaptation and Vulnerability. Contribution of Working Group II to the Fourth Assessment Report of the Intergovernmental Panel on Climate Change, pp. 717–743. Cambridge University Press, Cambridge, UK (2007)
35. Adger, W.N., et al.: New Indicators of Vulnerability and Adaptive Capacity, vol. 122. Tyndall Centre for Climate Change Research, Norwich (2004)
36. Folke, C.: Resilience: the emergence of a perspective for social–ecological systems analyses. Glob. Environ. Change **16**, 253–267 (2006)
37. Costa, M.M., et al.: Deliverable 2.3 working paper: governance indicators for (un)successful MSPs. In: ENHANCE FP7 Project (2013)
38. Carmona, M., et al.: Deliverable 4.1: Working paper: Risk perception and risk cultures in Europe (2014)
39. Crowe, P., Foley, K.: The Turas project: integrating social-ecological resilience and urban planning. In: TURAS FP7 Project, pp. 1–15 (2013)
40. Durban Adaptation Charter (2016). http://www.durbanadaptationcharter.org/
41. Mayors Adapt (2016). http://mayors-adapt.eu/
42. World Mayors Council on Climate Change (2016). http://www.worldmayorscouncil.org
43. Bloomberg, M.R.: Compact of Mayors Guide (2015). https://www.compactofmayors.org/

Climate Deterrence: Disasters and Security After COP 21

Raul Kleber de Souza Boeno[1,2(✉)] and Viriato Soromenho-Marques[2]

[1] Brazilian Army, Brasília, Brazil
raulboeno@campus.ul.pt
[2] University of Lisbon, Lisbon, Portugal
viriatosmarques@netcabo.pt

Abstract. The Paris Agreement (COP 21) indicates an effort of nations towards the creation of a worldwide mechanism to control climate. Estimated to enter into force in 2020, the Agreement recognizes that countries may be affected not only by climate changes, but also by the impact of the actions taken in response to those changes. The objectives of this paper are: to excite the discussion about securitization of climate change, discussing its relation with disasters and conflicts; and to identify items which have constructed the current *status* of climate change in political and security agendas, highlighting the contribution of COP 21. For that purpose, a *corpus* formed by 51 items, produced between the beginning of the Cold War (1945) and July 2016, has been examined according to the analysis units proposed by the Copenhagen School, mainstream for this research. The results obtained indicate: (i) construction of climate change as a threat to international security (linked to conflicts and disasters); (ii) building of financial mechanisms, among others, to align the conduct of countries in a political agenda; and (iii) increase of military sector participation in the debate about climate change and preparation for increased action in disasters. This study makes two contributions to the existing literature. First, it provides a framework of items which clarify the securitization process of climate change and its relation with security, disasters and the armed forces. Second, through this analysis, it underlines the inclusion of the military sector in the relation between climate change, security and disasters.

Keywords: Securitization · Conflicts · Disasters · Climatic deterrence · Armed forces

1 Introduction

The United Nations Climate Conference (COP 21) ended with the adoption of a global climate agreement, estimated to enter into force in 2020 (On 5 October 2016, the threshold for entry into force of the Paris Agreement was achieved. The Paris Agreement will enter into force on 4 November 2016.). With ample support from the international community and member States, the Paris Agreement represents an effort to limit the increase of the planet's surface temperature. However, questions arise: What would be the implications of the Agreement for the climate change securitization

© IFIP International Federation for Information Processing 2017
Published by Springer International Publishing AG 2017. All Rights Reserved
Y. Murayama et al. (Eds.): ITDRR 2016, IFIP AICT 501, pp. 119–138, 2017.
https://doi.org/10.1007/978-3-319-68486-4_10

process? How would the relation between security and disasters be included in the securitization process?

The objectives of the present work are: to excite the discussion about the securitization of climate changes [1] - before COP 21, discussing its relation with disasters and conflicts; and to identify items which have constructed the current status of climate change in political and security agendas, highlighting the contribution of COP 21. Thus, the aim is to contribute to the proposed questions, which have been insufficiently discussed at the conceptual and operational levels.

2 Methodology

In order to answer the proposed questions, a corpus was gathered from western centres for security studies composed of official and academic documents on the following subjects: climate change (CC), security, disasters and armed forces (AF). The time frame established ranges from the beginning of the Cold War (1945) to July 2016; for the conceptual basis, however, the time frame was extended.

The criteria/filters used to select the final corpus were: (i) adhesion to the objective; (ii) to be a future bearing fact (repercussion in the public and political agendas); and (iii) to have impact on the security agenda. The selected mainstream was the Copenhagen School approach to securitization, taking into consideration the collectivity and the environment [2–4]. The analysis units selected for the study were those proposed by Buzan et al. [3]: referent objects, securitizing actors and functional actors. The international system was maintained as level of analysis. To conclude, considerations will be presented on the results obtained, as well as suggestions for future approaches.

3 Results

The final corpus, composed by 51 items, comprises speech acts (discourses/documents) which support the securitization process phases, where CC is pointed out as a threat to referent objects linked to security. Some items do not fully correspond to the above mentioned nexus, but contributed to raise the debate on climate change, as a potential threat, and generated favourable conditions for the speech act to receive attention. Some disasters catalyzed by climate change were also included in the corpus.

Table 1 - Climate Change and Securitization shows the topics that were selected and examined. Besides intersection (CC, security, disasters and AF), elements such as the nexus between referent objects (OR) (It refers to what the securitizing actors declare to be existentially threatened and for which protection is sought. Normally it is the State, its sovereignty, economy, among others [2–4].), securitizing actors (SA) (The securitizing actors initiate the speech act calling attention to the fact that emergency measures are needed [2–4].) and functional actors (FA) (These are those capable of influencing the final decision in the field of security [2–4].) were also considered.

Table 1. Climate Change and Securitization. Source: the Authors, expanded from Boeno et al. [1].

N°	Nexus with OR, AS and AF	Intersection with CC, security, disasters and AF
1	Cold War (1945–1991)	New non military threats, including CC. Widening of the security concept with environmental issues and awareness [5–9]
2	Limits to Growth Report (1972)	Economic growth will depend on factors such as peace and stability. Comprehensive search for raw materials leads to social disruption, triggering conflicts. Alerted about the finitude of planet resources [10, 11]
3	Stockholm Conference (1972)	Global consensus on development and the finite nature of world reserves of natural resources [12]
4	Independent Commission on Disarmament and Security Issues (1982)	Concept of environmental security, distinction between common and collective security. Non military threats: shortage of resources and environmental destruction [13]
5	New Political Thinking Gorbachov (1985)	Introduces the concept of comprehensive security linked to human survival. Associates non military threats to economic and environmental issues [13]
6	The Brundtland Report (1987)	Broadens "security" through the environmental aspect. Environmental stresses may foster political tensions and conflicts, thus becoming a security issue [14]
7	Toronto Conference (1988)	First big meeting of scientists and political decision makers to discuss climate changes. Presented a proposal to contain global warming and reduce emissions of greenhouse gases (GHG). Motivated the creation of the Intergovernmental Panel on Climate Change
8	Intergovernmental Panel on Climate Change (IPCC) (1988)	These reports became a reference for the international community because they expressed consensus and uncertainties about CC. Its first report (1990) unveiled the scientific consensus that CC has an anthropogenic origin [15]
9	United Nations Framework Convention on Climate Change (in Eco 1992)	Increases participation of Non Governmental Organizations (NGOs) in environmental and CC issues [16]
10	United Nations Development Programme (1994)	The Human Development Report introduces the notion of human security, adding new dimensions to the security concept, such as economic, food, environmental and personal security, among others [17]

(*continued*)

Table 1. (*continued*)

N°	Nexus with OR, AS and AF	Intersection with CC, security, disasters and AF
11	I Conference of Parties (COP) (1995)	Global negotiation of Greenhouse Gases (GHG) reduction targets. Twenty COP were held until 2014, with different approaches to CC
12	Kyoto Protocol (1997) (entered into force in 2005)	Agreement for the reduction of GHG that was not ratified by the USA. Europe, the only party to achieve the set targets, receives the largest number of immigrants [18, 19]
13	II World Conference on Disaster Reduction (2005)	Risks of disasters, threats related to geological phenomena and CC should be included in sector-specific development plans [20]
14	New Orleans Disaster (Hurricanes Rita and Katrina) (2005)	Natural disasters comparable to terrorism as a threat to the United States of America (USA) - "Militarization of natural disasters" [21]. This war on "natural disasters" undermined trust in the institutions [22]
15	Establishment of the Emergency Military Unit (UME) (2005)	It was created by Spain after AF action in natural disasters. The UME is an organized military force specifically trained and provided with the necessary means to operate during natural disasters [23]
16	Documentary: An Inconvenient Truth (2006)	Documentary about CC, specifically about the average increase of global temperature; won the Oscar for Best Documentary that year. In 2007, Al Gore, the author of the documentary and former US vice-president, shared the Nobel Peace Prize with IPCC
17	Stern Report (2007)	Mitigating global warming is less costly to world economy than adapting to it. Pressures will increase resulting in conflicts around basic resources [24]
18	UN Security Council (SC) (2007)	Unstable climate fuels migratory pressures and the competition for resources. The SC did not keep CC in its agenda, and it was just useful to impart visibility to the subject [25]
19	Oslo Guideline (2007)	Because of the increased deployment of the AF, the UN issued the Guideline on the Use of Military and Civil Defense Assets in Disaster Relief [26]
20	Solana Report (2008)	Inclusion of CC in Foreign Affairs and Security (European interests). Policies evidencing resentment towards the countries that caused CC. Warning scenario for Europe, the destination of large migrations [27]

(*continued*)

Table 1. (*continued*)

N°	Nexus with OR, AS and AF	Intersection with CC, security, disasters and AF
21	Department of Energy and Climate Change (DECC) (2008)	The United Kingdom (UK) recognized that CC will contribute to escalate the environmental risk and the occurrence of extreme environmental events, increasing the humanitarian crises requiring contribution from the UK Armed Forces (United Kingdom, 2008). Establishment of the DECC to become the leading institution in the government program to change the United Kingdom into a low carbon economy [28]
22	Statement by the UN Secretary General (2009)	CC constitutes a poverty-derived "threat multiplier". The document mentions the poor performance of institutions in organizing resources and solving conflicts [29]
23	European Security Strategy (2009)	Identified global warming as an element of concern, with the potential to aggravate resource scarcity (namely water) and intensify confrontations, creating migratory movements in various regions [30]
24	Central Intelligence Agency US (CIA) (2009)	Establishment of the Center for Climate and Security to provide advice to decision makers on the effects of climate on security
25	Strategic Concept for the Defense and Security of the North Atlantic Treaty Organization (NATO)	Terrorist attacks, CC and shortage of water will shape the future security environment in areas of interest to NATO. The AF need to develop competencies to tackle international crises and humanitarian missions [31]
26	Defense Policy Guidelines Germany (2011)	CC is a threat to German security. CC compromises the subsistence of human beings, causing migrations and conflicts. CC will be critical to the future of Germany and Europe [33]
27	Report of the Department of Defense US (2011)	Issues guidelines aimed at increasing the capacity of the United States Africa Command (AFRICOM) and of the United States Southern Command (SOUTHCOM) to deal with conflicts catalyzed by CC, and to act during natural disasters [34]
28	Security and Defense Policy of the European Union (2012)	Migrations caused by natural disasters exacerbated by CC fuel conflicts and saturate regions. Civil-military cooperation is critical to respond to disasters. The European Security Academy should investigate the reflexes of CC on security [35]

(*continued*)

Table 1. (*continued*)

N°	Nexus with OR, AS and AF	Intersection with CC, security, disasters and AF
29	White Paper on Defense and National Security France (2013)	Recognizes CC as a threat capable of aggravating and increasing extreme events, further weakening vulnerable regions. Current Arctic Ocean ice decrease has strategic consequences, such as the opening of new navigation routes [36]
30	Portugal Strategic Concept of Defense (2013)	Natural disasters and CC were included in the list of threats to security. Increased awareness of losses and that major disasters require global support [37]
31	IPCC Report (2013)	Increase of scientific consensus that CC has an anthropogenic origin and has potential to increase the rivalry between countries, not taking directly to war [38]
32	XXX Conference of the American Armies (2013)	The effects of CC (AF and disasters) were one of the subjects discussed by the military commanders. Extreme climate may impact the civil population, influencing latent social tensions [39]
33	Typhoon Haiyan (2013)	Showed what the AF will be required to do in the future because of climate effects. The capability of the Association of Southeast Asian Nations as a regional security actor was called into question. European and USA Forces were deployed [40, 41]
34	Creation of the Logistics Support Units (2014)	Portugal crates general and emergency military support Forces prepared to provide national response to disaster situations [42]
35	Center for Naval Analyses Reports (CNA) (2007 e 2014)	In seven years the status of CC went from concern to conflict catalyst. An increasing number of catastrophic events will create additional demands for American troops in distinct regions of the globe [43, 44]
36	Emergency Response Military Units (UMRE) (2014)	Argentina equipped 13 UMRE to support the community in emergencies related to fire, floods, among others, which overcome the support capacity of Civil Defence [45]
37	III Conference on Disaster Risk Reduction (2015)	CC exacerbates the frequency and intensity of disasters, halting the progress of sustainable development [46]
38	The National Security Strategy of the United Kingdom (2015)	CC is potentially the greatest challenge to global stability and security, and therefore to national security. CC is increasingly a risk to the UK, with the full effects on UK national security more likely to be seen after 2035 [32]

(*continued*)

Table 1. (*continued*)

N°	Nexus with OR, AS and AF	Intersection with CC, security, disasters and AF
39	National Security Strategy of the United States of America (2015)	CC (a risk to American interests) is connected to natural disasters, migrations, terrorism and conflicts for international resources [47]. Approved the end of academy clearance for access to the CIA climate change database (Feb 15)
40	Conference of the American Armies (2015)	The objective was to discuss procedures for the Aid Operation in Case of Disaster by the Mexican AF [48]
41	Seminar on Humanitarian Aid (2015)	The Brazilian Army sponsored the Seminar on the Humanitarian Aid Force; capacity building proposals for Humanitarian Aid Operations were presented [49]
42	Encyclical: On Care For Our Common Home (2015)	Approaches the internationalization of the Amazon, CC, wars for natural resources, sovereignty of States, conflicts and migrations, among others [50]
43	European Climate Diplomacy Day on 17 June	EU delegations and EU Member State Embassies all over the world join forces to emphasise the importance and benefit of climate action on the Climate Diplomacy Day. The sense of urgency is unmistakable as the decisive UN Climate Conference COP 21 in Paris would take place later that year
44	Resolution 427/NATO Parliamentary Assembly (2015)	Weeks before COP 21, NATO issues the resolution Climate Change and International Security. Urge to fully recognise climate change-related risks as significant threat multipliers in their foreign and security policies; to subsequently increase the frequency of military and political consultations on climate change within NATO, including at NATO summits [51]
45	2030 Agenda for Sustainable Development (2015)	Goal 13. Take urgent action to combat climate change and its impacts – to integrate CC related measures in national policies, strategies and plans. UNFCC is the main forum to negotiate the global response to climate change [52]
46	Global Risks (2015)	The Global Risks Report 2015, by the World Economic Forum: Extreme weather events are 2nd top risk in terms of Likelihood; and Failure of climate-change adaptation is 5th top risk in terms of Impact [53]

(*continued*)

Table 1. (*continued*)

N°	Nexus with OR, AS and AF	Intersection with CC, security, disasters and AF
47	United Nations Climate Change Conference COP 21 (2015)	Maintains the "principle of common but differentiated responsibilities". Creates financial, technology transfer/development, and capability development mechanisms as incentive for the Parts to comply with the terms: financing and payment based on results [54]. (Paris Agreement)
48	Global Risks Report (2016)	The Global Risks Report 2016, by the Word Economic Forum: Extreme weather events are 2nd top risk in terms of Likelihood; and Failure of climate-change adaptation is 1st top risks in terms of Impact [55]
49	Shock Waves: Managing the Impacts of Climate Change on Poverty (2016)	The World Bank in collaboration with research institutions across the globe did the report with innovative analyses to provide insights on the relationship between climate change and poverty. It concludes that climate change and natural disasters are closely linked to poverty [56]
50	International Law Commission (2016)	Third report on the protection of the atmosphere: States have the obligation to protect the atmosphere from atmospheric pollution and atmospheric degradation [57]
51	Inter-American Defense Board (2016)	Panel: Focus Defense on Environmental Protection and Climate Change - better understanding the effects of climate change and identifying potential future participation of the Armed Forces in this regard (February); Conference - The Mechanisms of Attention, Response and Management of Disasters - identifying the gaps and opportunities in the hemispheric mechanisms of response to natural disasters (May) [58, 59]

4   Discussion

4.1   Climate Change and Security

Climate change of anthropogenic origin is understood as a process related to global (systemic and cumulative) changes, of which the most visible aspect is the rise of the average temperature on the surface of the planet. The most significant human influence on Earth's climate system is the emission of greenhouse gases (GHG) [61].

Securitization, understood as a speech act (discourse), generates the awareness that a threat exists, and allows the adoption of urgent and exceptional measures to fight this threat. A given theme would be securitized by entering the security agenda as a threat to a referent object, and as of the moment it is accepted as an abnormal situation by the general public [3]. Desecuritization, then, would be the inverse process, i.e. to prevent the securitization of the theme [2].

The first component of securitization is the belief that a threat exists [61]. To that end, the securitizing agents need to persuade their audience (significant political actors) that CC is a concrete threat to the security – of humanity or of the State. The adoption of emergency actions characterizes the second component of securitization, when the debate indicates a point of disruption of the normal situation and several actions and measures may be taken to mitigate the presented threat. Afterwards, when decision power is concentrated by the securitizing actor, the last component arises, which is the legitimization of actions against the threat, including the use of military force [2].

About the use of military force, Soromenho-Marques [19] alerts that the end of the Cold War did not mean the end of the nuclear threat (mitigated, nevertheless, by the success of the nuclear deterrence strategy). The arms race model, which occurred during the Cold War, did not lead to a central conflict between the two superpowers of the time (USA and USSR), but to a "cooperation among enemies", which would ultimately impose a political abolishment of the risk of central war through successful agreements in all categories of atomic armament. That was possible only because Washington and Moscow understood that, in the frame of a Mutual Assured Destruction which would derive from the use of the respective nuclear warheads, the possibility of victory (obtainment of political gain by military ways) was materially impossible, due to the ensuing generalized catastrophe which would result in Day After (The Day After is a American film, that first aired on November, 1983, on the ABC television.). In other words: the peaceful end of the Cold War (contradicting the inertia of thousands of years of previous history) is the first example of a true "compulsory cooperation" between strategic opponents, united by the imperative of self-preservation. The fundamental question which arises nowadays is that of knowing if, analogously, we will see a similar model of "compulsory cooperation" between the major greenhouse gases (GHG) emitting countries. Is climatic deterrence, similar to nuclear deterrence, possible? Will major countries from the current international system be able to understand, in due time, that climatic collapse is another form of Mutual Assured Destruction, and therefore that wanting to extend large levels of GHG emissions is absurd, in a very short term strategic selfishness perspective? Without the widespread acceptance of the meaning of this compulsory cooperation, to which the climatic deterrence notion rationally leads, it will be very difficult to believe in the possibility that adopting a new international policy for the protection of global climate (in this case, the Paris Agreement) will be able to confer, in fact and lastingly, greater stability to the international system.

In the examined items, Table 1, some securitizing discourses link ideas of abundance and scarcity of resources to CC, as well as to conflicts arising from those resources (food, drinking water, fertile soil). Similarly, other discourses establish a connection between CC and disasters. This second connection has larger scientific support. Meanwhile, its securitization is more complex, especially if the securitizing agent is part of the problem (country with large GHG emissions). Therefore, as far as agents' interests are concerned, caution is needed both when linking CC with conflicts arising from resources, and when linking CC with disasters.

By analyzing the corpus, it can be inferred that CC appears in political and safety agendas as adjuvant, initially linked to the environmental issues and the shortage of resources [12, 19]. However, as a result of the efforts of the scientific community that reduced the uncertainty about the anthropogenic origin of CC and its connection with disasters, they started to be seen as a threat to global security, thus prompting the world to delve into the subject [60, 62]. Bearing that in mind, there is an increase in securitizing discourses which intend to construct climate changes as a threat.

4.2   Referent Object, Securitizing Actor and Functional Actor

In the corpus, CC is presented to the audience as a threat to the existence of the referent object. CC is described both as a military and as a non military threat, endangering areas linked to the survival of humanity. Its most serious impacts would be felt on global economy and international security [24, 27].

As a military threat, CC may become a catalyst of existing social conflicts and tensions, which in view of the fragile management capability of institutions and States, could evolve into armed conflicts [38, 63]. The UN [29] predicts that CC will impact the primary sectors of the economies of the different countries, as well as their respective indicators of income levels and quality of life, contributing to possible conflicts.

In the case of a successful securitization, CC is accepted as a military threat and probably there will be a military participation in conflicts arising from resources. In that case, it is reasonable to consider that, depending on the acceptance by the audience, the threat could be a social construct to benefit the securitizing agents who wish to legitimize their actions and decisions.

As a non military threat, CC is associated to natural disasters such as heat waves, droughts, rising sea level, torrential rain, floods, hurricanes, and other events. CC is capable of increasing the intensity and frequency of natural events, giving rise to colossal human and material damages [20, 40, 64].

In that approach, the threat presents itself as real. It would cease to depend on the acceptance of the audience, but it would depend on the social perception of the risk (For more information, see Beck [69, 70]). In this path, the scientific community plays a decisive role to diminish uncertainty about the link between CC and disasters. The participation of the military sector will take place in disaster management, such as in New Orleans [22] and in the Philippines [40, 65], where conflicts and violence streaks occurred and the armed forces were employed in the "during" and "post-disaster" stages.

The United States of America [47], the North Atlantic Treaty Organization [31], the European Union [30, 35], France [36], the United Kingdom [32] and Germany [33], among others, have included CC in the list of major threats (both military and non military) in their security strategies and defence documents. It is worth noting that the preparation and training of a nation's defence means are oriented according to the threats listed in the respective strategic security documents. On that subject, Brzoska

[66, 67] argues that uncertainties about climate change are going to affect military planning in the future.

Most of the discourses studied originate from the political agenda, confirming the necessary legitimacy of the securitizing actor to voice the political discourse (speech act or political decision) about the existence of the threat [4].

In the present paper, the main referent object identified was the State. On this issue, it was evidenced that economic and political interests have been linked to the above mentioned referent object to reinforce CC as a direct or indirect threat to security (national and international), to economy (regional and global) and to sustainable development. Two examples are the Stern [24] and Solana [27] Reports, where concern about the negative impacts of CC on European economic interests and on those of other economic blocks can be evinced.

As to the functional actors, a trend can be detected to initially assign to military capacity the responsibility of "acting in face of the threats" and, later on, to a partnership between military and civil capacities. In the case of CC as a military threat, guidance from NATO and the USA, among others, was found about the need to increase the capacity of military sectors (military bias). As a non military threat, CC is related to more destructive disasters, requiring the expansion of military capacity to act more frequently in the event of disaster in the future [1].

Some Latin American countries have been developing studies on the subject of CC and security, especially on the AF, departing from the traditional procedure of importing European and United States security models and theories [68]. Goods examples of this fact are the events, such as seminars and congresses, organized by the AF and the academic communities that contribute to further the studies on CC, disasters and the AF.

Some Iberian-American Armed Forces, such as Spain [23] Portugal [37] and Argentina [45] have supplied military units to act specifically in the event of disaster, indicating a possible trend to militarize disasters from the beginning of this century.

On this subject, it is relevant that, weeks before COP 21, NATO (the largest military alliance in the world) directed its members to increase the frequency and participation of military consultations, inside NATO, in CC related matters [51]. Following that path, through NATO Science for Peace and Security Programme, the workshop Implications of Climate Change and Disasters on Military Activities: Building Resiliency and Mitigating Vulnerability in the Balkan Region [71] was held in Sofia/Bulgaria, in July 2016, reinforcing and demonstrating a greater involvement of the military sector in this issue.

After COP 21, the Inter-American Defence Board (2016) held two significant events about climate change and disaster management, with the purpose of better understanding the effects of climate change and to identify possible opportunities to strengthen regional response mechanisms to natural disasters [58, 59].

4.3 Future Legitimization

Securitization will only happen when the subject enters the security agenda, thus rendering the emergency actions to face the threat legitimate and acceptable (including the use of military force), excluding the normal mechanisms that would be used to handle it.

As a result, securitization enables total concentration of decision making powers in the hands of the securitizing agents, which are normally government actors [2].

As previously mentioned, CC was included into the leading Western security strategies, both as a military and a non military threat. CC was placed at the same level of threat as weapons of mass destruction and terrorist attacks (NATO, Germany, European Union, France, United Kingdom, and USA, among others). Thus, it seems reasonable to suggest that a possible alignment between the leading Western political and armed blocks of the North hemisphere came into being in the process of climate change securitization.

The USA directed the United States Africa Command (AFRICOM) and the United States Southern Command (SOUTHCOM) to increase their military capacity to act in conflicts catalyzed by CC and to use their AF in natural disasters (USA 2011). This guidance suggests the existence of an increased concern about Africa and South America, coinciding with the warnings issued in the CNA [43], Stern [24] and Solana [27] reports. The same inference applies to NATO [31].

The CNA Military Advisory Security reports [43, 44] drew increased attention of the USA to Africa. The report issued in 2014 states that CC added environmental stress factors to ethnical conflicts in Africa, increasing the burden on fragile governments. As a result, the Al Qaeda in the Islamic Maghreb, which had been previously confined to the North of Africa, managed to expand its area of action. In its reports, this agency rates CC as a catalyst of conflicts, and alerts that an increasing number of catastrophic weather events will provoke disasters, generating an increased demand for deployment of American troops in different regions of the globe.

This has already occurred in the Philippines, after typhoon Haiyan (2013), when armed forces from different countries were called to act in the region. Questions were raised about the capacity of the Association of Southeast Asian Nations (ASEAN) to act as regional security agent, calling attention about the future demand for AF action in disasters [40, 64].

As for future demands, one of the challenges of the Paris Agreement (COP 21) was to deal with the "principle of common but differentiated responsibilities", due to the fact that there are historically different GHG emission rates and different levels of industrial development, among other indicators, which foster the debate about past, current and future responsibility among countries.

COP 21 brought new elements to the debate about CC and security. The Agreement recognizes that countries may be affected not only by climate change, but also by the impact of the measures taken in response to those changes [54]. Which measures and which impacts?

The answer to these questions is not clear in the Paris Agreement. Meanwhile, the recognition that CC represents an urgent and potentially irreversible threat to human societies and to the planet generates the expectation of ample cooperation of all countries and of their participation in an international response against that threat [54]. In that sense, the Agreement reinforces the perception that we are dealing with the belief in a transborder threat and that the response should be based on strengthening mutual help and strengthening conflict solving mechanisms.

With estimated values of around US$100 billion a year, the Agreement creates three mechanisms: financial; technology transfer and development; and capability development. These mechanisms present themselves as tools to align the conduct of countries in the fulfilment of the established terms in the areas of mitigation and adaptation [54]. From a reductionist point of view, it can be inferred that financial resources will be paid only after results are demonstrated. However, projects that may want to apply to available resources must align with the goals described in the Agreement.

The concern about the applicability of those instruments would lie in the use of a Veiled Coercing Climate Action, internationally inculcated in several forms of political and economic pressure. The third report on the protection of the atmosphere (International Law Commission), after COP 21, strengthens this concern [57].

After COP 21, the Council of the European Union [72] informed that the Agreement of Paris constitutes a legally bound agreement. It argues for several reasons that "the EU looks forward to the UN Security Council continuing its work on Climate Change". It defines the role of environmental diplomacy as the defender of public and private financial flows with the aim of reducing GHG emissions. On the other hand, it also proposes to strengthen mutual aid between the European block and other organizations in the search for solutions to the climate and security issues, establishing strong alliances to create opportunities and prevent conflicts.

There is something which is worth noting at this point: the main forum to negotiate the global response to CC is the UNFCC [54], and not the UN Security Council. This stance from the European block seems to be an attempt to take the debate to the security agenda, securitizing the issue and facilitating the legitimization of future actions. We underline that the UN Security Council has had meetings in 2007, 2011 and 2013 to deal with CC, and that three of the five permanent members of the Council are part of the problem - group of the largest GHG emitting countries in the planet (USA, China, Russia) [73].

4.4   The Role of Technology in Securitization

The technological imperative, together with great powers politics, events, the internal dynamics of academic debates and institutionalisation, constitute the five driving forces of international security studies. Specifically about technology, it is worth highlighting that with every technological innovation the need arises to assess its impacts on security and the stability of strategic relations [61, 74] - and consequently on the securitization of issues.

The focus on technology in the field of security is not recent. One example was the impact of nuclear technology in various areas, such as strategy, medicine, energy and economy, among others [62]. Related to this subject, it is relevant that recent nuclear tests, performed during the second semester of 2016 in Asia, have alerted the international community that the nuclear threat is still an active piece on the board of international relations.

As stated before, CC has been presented as a non military threat, associated with disasters, increasing the intensity and frequency of natural events, and provoking enormous human and material damage [20, 40, 46, 53, 55, 64]. Bearing that in mind, technology provides important instruments for disaster management and reduces uncertainties in the relation between CC and disasters [20, 46, 75].

On the other path indicated, where CC is presented as a military threat, technology has also a fundamental role to play. By changing the conditions for the armed forces to act, technology will be indispensable to provide equipment which is more resistant, and possesses better mobility, capable of enduring greater temperature variation and severe meteorological conditions, apt to operate both in deserts and tropical forests, responding to the demands of military troops in different parts of the globe [76, 77].

For both paths described, the role of technology will be determinant. There is, however, a paradox at this point. The technologies to be developed will probably have a dual use, being used both in war conflicts and in disaster management. This is what has happened with the internet (initially for exclusive military use) and what is happening with new generation drones, which can be used for locating targets and also to map flooded regions, among other things.

The argument is that technology is relatively neutral (To deepen the knowledge on technological determinism and the relation of human nature with technology see LEVY [78] and MARTINS [79], respectively.). Despite important debates about the technological imperative, the use given to a certain tool is what will indicate its impact on security and other areas. By way of example, a research (currently being developed by the Authors) done with armed forces from five countries of the Iberian-American context has identified different technological tools available (Public, private, paid and free) to help communication in disaster management, from which mobile phone apps, website tools, databases, social media, radios, satellites and hardware stand out, among many others. These are some tools which were created for different purposes and which are used for military activities.

At this point it seems relevant to remind the Paris Agreement [54]. With the purpose of improving resilience to CC, reduce greenhouse gases and their impacts on international security, the Paris Agreement financially supports the Development and transfer of technologies and implementation of the Technology Mechanism, boosting technology as a decisive factor for solving CC related problems.

This mechanism emphasizes the importance of technology as a way to involve the international community in climate issues (UN 2015), increasing the management capacity of states, especially in developing countries under all kinds of pressures. About these pressures, Brundtland [14] refers that most technological research is dedicated to creating and processing innovations with commercial value.

Based on this, one can infer that, by financing the development of technologies for the adaptation and mitigation of CC and its impacts, such as disasters, the implementation of the Technology Mechanism may reduce economic pressures on research, as well as on the implantation and dissemination of technologies, strengthening cooperative action about technology development and transfer [54].

The CC securitization process, focus of the present paper, has reserved a special role for technology. Technology will probably be one of the most important decision factors for "Gatekeepers", who will make humanity migrate from a fossil fuel based economy to a Renewable Energy (RE) based economy.

At this point it is relevant to refer the importance of academic debate (one of the driving forces of security studies, alongside technology), which has the power to decisively influence political decision makers about the path to take to desecuritize the climate change issue.

5   Conclusion

Climate change has been given an ostensibly higher status in Western discourses in the second decade of the 21st century, being characterized as one of the most serious threats to humanity. In the analysed items, the inclusion of this issue in the list of threats in the leading Western security strategies is perceivable, indicating an international alignment to fight climate change. This process has constructed climate change as a threat to international security, connected to conflicts and disasters.

By establishing the financial mechanism, the mechanism of technology transfer and development, and the mechanism of capability development, the Paris Agreement creates tools to direct the conduct of countries in the fight against climate change. In the future, the way those mechanisms are employed will allow or prevent the binding of the Agreement with a Coercing Climate Action, internationally instilled in several forms of political and economic pressure.

The securitization process of climate change has followed two paths. The first, as a military threat, has influenced countries and economic blocks to consider future conflicts over basic resources (food, water and energy, among others), highlighting the importance of the military sector to be alert to participate in those possible conflicts. The second path indicates that climate change has influenced the quantity and intensity of extreme weather events (droughts, floods and hurricanes, among others), alerting to the need of enlarging military sector capabilities to act in the event of disaster in different planet regions.

The creation of specialized military units to act in the event of disaster and the organization of several academic and governmental events on climate change, armed forces and disasters, indicate that the participation of the military sector in the debate about climate change aligns more with the second path. Meanwhile, considering that several countries have sought to securitize this issue, the military sector may also be conducted to the first path. That will depend from future decisions and international agreements, considering that the result of the clash between climate deterrence and environmental diplomacy will influence the legitimization of actions against climate change.

The role of technology may be that of guarantor of the Paris Agreement, for the technology transfer and development mechanism may direct the conduct of countries in the combat to climate change and its impacts. For that to happen, the model adopted in order to apply that mechanism will need to operate in harmony with the financial mechanism and with the capacity development mechanism, allowing access to and the expansion of new technologies, which will counterbalance political and economic pressures, respecting the sovereignty of states.

Technologies amplify management capacity and reduce the frailty of states, simultaneously increasing the capacity of armed forces to act in disasters, thus constituting a fundamental link between the human factor and nature.

Last, it must be said that climate change linked to disasters seems more credible than climate change linked to conflicts over resources – situation where several interests are inserted in the securitization discourse, resulting in the need to deepen the conceptual and empirical analysis. Environmental diplomacy, by opting to maintain the issue in the public and political agendas and by describing it as a common and transborder threat, has better conditions to strengthen the mutual aid mechanisms and the mechanisms to solve conflicts. That will allow more countries to agglutinate around the new world agreement to control world climate.

As for future approaches, the Authors suggest discussing the possible implications of the UK's withdrawal from the EU, should that situation be confirmed, in the CC securitization process.

References

1. Boeno, R.K.S., Boeno, R.K., Soromenho-Marques, V.: Climate change and securitization: the construction of climate deterrence. Coleção Meira Mattos - Revista das Ciências Militares **9**, 11 (2015). Rio de Janeiro. http://hdl.handle.net/10451/22441. Acesso em: 10 fev. 2016
2. Wæver, O.: Securitization and desecuritization. In: Lipschultz, R.E. (ed.) On Security. Columbia University Press, New York (1995)
3. Buzan, B., Wæver, O., Wilde, J.: Security: a new framework for analysis. Lynne Rienner Publisher, Colorado (1998)
4. Buzan, B.: Change and insecurity reconsidered. Contemp. Secur. Policy **20**(3), 1–17 (1999). https://doi.org/10.1080/13523269908404228. Accessed 25 June 2015
5. Carson, R.: Primavera Silenciosa (in Portuguese). Melhoramentos, São Paulo (1965)
6. Ullman, R.H.: Redefining security. Int. Secur. **8**, 129–153 (1983)
7. Mathews, J.T.: Redefining security. Foreign Aff. **68**, 162–177 (1989)
8. Myers, N.: Environment and security. Foreign Policy **74**, 23–41 (1989)
9. Guzzini, S.: A história dual da securitização (in Portuguese). In: Barrinha, A., Freire, M.R. (eds.) Segurança, Liberdade e Política. Pensar a Escola de Copenhaga em Português. Imprensa de Ciências Sociais, Lisboa (2015)
10. Meadows, D.H., et al.: Limites do Crescimento (in Portuguese). 2a. São Paulo: Perspectivas (1972)
11. Nye, J.S., Lynn-Jones, S.M.: International security studies. In: Conference on the State of the Field. International Security, vol. 12, n° 4, pp. 5–27. The MIT Press, Spring (1988)
12. Schmidt, L., Nave, J.G., Guerra, J.: Eucação Ambiental. Balanço e perspectivas para uma agenda mais sustentável (in Portuguese). Imprensa de Ciências Sociais, Lisboa (2010)
13. Cunha, L.V.: Segurança Ambiental e Gestão dos Recursos Hídricos (in Portuguese). Nação e Defesa. Europress, Lisboa, n° 86, 2 Série, pp. 27–50 (1988)
14. Brundtland, C.: Comissão Mundial sobre Meio Ambiente e Desenvolvimento: o nosso futuro comum (in Portuguese), ONU (1987)
15. Garcia, R.: Sobre a Terra: Um guia para quem lê e escreve sobre ambiente (in Portuguese), 2nd edn. Público Comunicação Social, Lisboa (2006)
16. ONU (Organização das Nações Unidas): Annex 1 - Rio Declaration on Environmet and Development (in Portuguese). Report of the United Nations Conference on Environment and Development, 25 p., New York (1992)
17. UNDP (United Nations Development Programme): Human Development Report: New Dimensions of Human Security. Oxford University Press, New York (1994)
18. Soromenho-Marques, V.: Alterações Climáticas (in Portuguese). In: Gouveia, J.B., Santos, S. (Coor.). Enciclopédia de Direito e Segurança, pp. 25–37. Almedina, Coimbra (2015)
19. Soromenho-Marques, V.: Segurança Ambiental (in Portuguese). In: Gouveia, J.B., Santos, S. (Coor.). Enciclopédia de Direito e Segurança, pp. 384–396. Almedina, Coimbra (2015)

20. UNISDR (United Nations Office for Disasters Risk Reduction): Marco de Acción de Hyogo para Redução de Desatres 2005–2015. In: Conferencia Mundial sobre la Reducción de los Desastres, Hyogo (2005)

21. García, A.: Informe sobre Huracán Katrina (in Spanish). Curso en Escuela Nacional de Proteccíon Civil (ENPC) y Centro Europeo de Investigación Social de Situaciones de Emergencia (CEISE), Madrid (2005)

22. Tierney, K., Bevc, C., Kuligowski, E.: Metaphors matter: disaster myths, media frames, and their consequences in Hurricane Katrina. Ann. Am. Acad. Polit. Soc. Sci. **604**, 57–81 (2006)

23. España: Ley Orgánica que regula la defensa nacional y establece las bases de la organización militar conforme a los principios establecidos en la Constitución (in Spanish). Ley Orgánica 5/2005, de 17 de noviembre de la Defensa Nacional. Madrid, pp. 37717–37714 (2005)

24. Stern, N.: The Economics of Climate Change: The Stern Reviewn. Cambridge University, London (2007)

25. UN (United Nations): 5663rd meeting (1) - Security Council of the United Nation. UN Documentation Dag Hammarskjöld Library, New York, vol. 1, 36 p. (2007). http://research. un.org/en/docs/sc/quick/meeting/2007. Accessed 15 July 2015

26. UN (United Nations): Oficina de Coordinación de Asuntos Humanitarios. Directrices de Oslo - Directrices para la utilización de recursos militares y de la defensa civil extranjeros en operaciones de socorro en casos de desastre (in Spanish), 42 p., Ginebra, (2007)

27. Solana, J.M.: Alterações climáticas e segurança internacional (in Portuguese). Documento do Alto Representante da Comissão Europeia para o Conselho Europeu, 16 p. (2008). Disponível em: www.consilium.europa.eu. Acesso em: 15 jun. 2015

28. UK (United Kingdom): Department of Energy and Climate Change: Baseline Assessment. London, 15 p. (2009)

29. UN (United Nations): El Cambio climático y sus posibles repercusiones para la seguridad - Informe Del Secretario General (in Spanish) (2009)

30. EU (European Union): Estratégia européia em matéria de segurança: uma Europa segura num mundo melhor (in Portuguese). Council of the European Union. Serviço das Publicações da União Europeia, Luxemburgo, 43 p. (2009)

31. NATO (North Atlantic Treaty Organization): Strategic Concept for the Defense and Security of the North Atlantic Treaty Organization. Summit in Lisbon. NATO Public Diplomacy Division, Brussels, 40 p. (2010)

32. UK (United Kingdom): National Security Strategy and Strategic Defence and Security Review 2015. Williams Lea Group, London, 96 p. (2015)

33. Germany, Ministry of Defence: Defence Policy Guidelines. Berlin, 17 p. (2011). http://www. bmvg.de. Accessed 13 Jan 2015

34. USA (United States of America): Department of Defense. Report of the Defense Science Board Task Force on Trends and Implications of Climate Change for National and International Security. Washington, D.C. (2011). www.acq.osd.mil/dsb/reports/ ADA552760.pdf. Accessed 15 June 2015

35. EP (European Parliament): Relatório sobre o papel da Política Comum de Segurança e Defesa em matéria de crises provocadas pelo clima e catástrofes naturais (2012/2095) (in Portuguese) (2012)

36. France, Ministry of Defence: White Paper - Defence and National Security. Pôle graphique de Tulle, Paris, 137 p. (2013)

37. Portugal, Conceito Estratégico de Defesa Nacional (in Portuguese): Resolução do Conselho de Ministros n.º 19/2013. Diário da República, Lisboa 1ª série, nº 67, 5 de abril de (2013)

38. Adger, W.N., et al.: Human security. In: Climate Change 2014: Impacts, Adaptation, and Vulnerability. Part A: Global and Sectoral Aspects. Contribution of Working Group II to the Fifth Assessment Report of the Intergovernmental Panel on Climate Change, pp. 755–791. Cambridge University Press, Cambridge (2014)

39. OEA (Organização dos Estados Americanos): A CEA e sua contribuição para as Operações de Manutenção da Paz (desenvolvidas sob o mandato da ONU) e em Operações de Ajuda em Casos de Desastre, por meio da criação e a aplicação de mecanismos e procedimentos que permitam melhorar as capacidades coletivas de seus membros e sua interoperabilidade (in Portuguese). XXX Conferência dos Exércitos Americanos, México (2013)

40. Routledge TFG: Asian disaster relief: lessons of Haiyan. Strateg. Comments **20**(1) (2014)

41. IISS (International Institute for Strategic Studies): Climate change, HADR, and Security in the Asia-Pacific. In: Proceedings of the 13th International Institute for Strategic Studies (IISS) Asia Security Summit: the ShangriLa dialogue, 30 p. IISS, Singapure (2014)

42. Portugal: Decreto-Lei n.º 186/2014, de 29 de dezembro de 2014 (in Portuguese). Diário da República, 1ª série, nº 250, 29 de dezembro de 2014, Lisboa (2014)

43. CNA (Center for Naval Analyses - Military Advisory Board): National Security and the Threath of Climate Change. CNA Corporation, Alexandria (2007)

44. CNA (Center for Naval Analyses - Military Advisory Board): National Security and the Accelerating Risks of Climate Change. CNA Corporation, Alexandria (2014)

45. Argentina: Ministério de Defensa. Informe de getión 2014 (in Spanish): Secretaría de Coordinación Militar de Asistencia en Emergencia. Buenos Aires, 32 p. (2014)

46. UNISDR (United Nations Office for Disasters Risk Reduction): Sendai Framework for Disaster Risk Reduction 2015–2030, Sendai, Japan (2015)

47. USA (United States of America): White House: National Security Strategy USA. https://www.whitehouse.gov/sites/default/files/docs/2015_national_security_strategy.pdf. Accessed 15 June 2015

48. Brasil: Centro de Doutrina do Exército Brasileiro. Notícias: 1º trimestre. In: Conferência Especializada sobre ajuda em caso de desastre da CEA (in Portuguese) (2015). Disponível em: http://www.cdoutex.eb.mil.br/index.php/atividades-doutrinarias/2015/1-trimestre/576-noticias-do-c-dout-ex/353-conferencia-especializada-sobre-ajuda-em-caso-de-desastre-da-cea. Acesso em: 15 jul. 2015

49. Brasil: Centro de Doutrina do Exército Brasileiro. Apresentações. Ajuda Humanitária (in Portuguese). In: Simpósio de Força de Ajuda Humanitária (2015). http://www.cdoutex.eb.mil.br/index.php/palestras/forca-humanitaria. Acesso em: 15 jul. 2015

50. Francisco: Carta Encíclica Laudato Si': Sobre o cuidado da casa comum (in Portuguese). Tipografia Vaticana, Vaticano, 192 p. (2015)

51. NATO (North Atlantic Treaty Organization): Resolution 427 on Climate Change and International Security. NATO Parliamentary Assembly, 2 p. P. Stavanger, Norway (2015)

52. UN (United Nations): Transforming our world: the 2030 Agenda for Sustainable Development. Resolution adopted by the General Assembly on 25 September 2015, 35 p., New York

53. WEF (World Economic Forum): Global Risks 2015. In: World Economic Forum, 10th edn., p. 69, Geneva (2015)

54. UN (United Nations): Acordo de Paris. Convenção Quadro das Nações Unidas sobre Mudanças do Clima, Nova York (2015)

55. WEF (World Economic Forum): The Global Risks Report 2016. In: World Economic Forum, 10th edn., p. 69, Geneva (2016)

56. Hallegatte, S., et al.: Shock Waves: Managing the Impacts of Climate Change on Poverty, 207 p. World Bank Group, Washington, D.C., (2016)

57. UN (United Nations): Third report on the protection of the atmosphere - International Law Commission. In: Sixty-eighth session, 52 p., Geneva, (2016)
58. IADB (Inter-American Defense Board): Focus Defense on Environmental Protection and Climate Change. Panel on February 29th, Inter-American Defense Board, Washington, D.C. (2016)
59. IADB (Inter-American Defense Board): The Mechanisms of Attention, Response and Management of Disasters. In: Conference on May 11th and 12th, Inter-American Defense Board. Washington, D.C. (2016)
60. Santos, F.D.: Alterações Globais - Os desafios e os riscos presentes e futuros (in Portuguese). Fundação Francisco Manuel dos Santos, Lisboa, 214 p. (2012)
61. Buzan, B., Hansen, L.: A evolução dos estudos de segurança internacional (in Portuguese). Ed. Unesp., São Paulo (2012)
62. Santos, F.D.: Os Desafios Ambientais Criados pela Grande Aceleração do Pós-Guerra (in Portuguese). Nação e Defesa, **122**(4), 61–78 (2009). Europress, Lisboa
63. Barnett, J., Adger, W.N.: Climate change, human security and violent conflict. Polit. Geogr. **26**(6), 639–655 (2007)
64. Alcantara, P.: Lessons learned from the Philippine government's response to Typhoon Haiyan. J. Bus. Contin. Emerg. Plan. **7**(4), 335 (2014). Summer
65. Le Mière, C., et al.: Climate change, HADR, and Security in the Asia-Pacific. In: 13th International Institute for Strategic Studies (IISS) Asia Security Summit, 30 p. The Shangri-La Dialogue, Singapure (2014)
66. Brzoska, M.: Climate change and the military in China, Russia, the United Kingdom, and the United States. Bull. Atomic Sci. **68**(2), 43 (2012)
67. Brzoska, M.: Climate change and military planning. Int. J. Clim. Change Strat. Manag. **7**(2), 172 (2015)
68. Herz, M., Lage, V.C.: Complexos regionais de segurança: possibilidades para se repensar a América Latina (in Portuguese). In: Barrinha, A., Freire, M.R. (eds.). Segurança, Liberdade e Política. Pensar a Escola de Copenhaga em Português, 306 p. Imprensa de Ciências Sociais, Lisboa (2015)
69. Beck, U.: La Sociedad del Riesgo Global (in Spanish). Siglo Veintiuno, Madrid (2002)
70. Beck, U.: Emancipatory catastrophism: what does it mean to climate change and risk society? Curr. Sociol. **63**(1), 75 (2015)
71. CMDR (Crisis Management and Disaster Response Centre of Excellence): Implications of Climate Change and Disasters on Military Activities: Building Resiliency and Mitigating Vulnerability in the Balkan Region. NATO Science for Peace and Security Programme. Crisis Management and Disaster Response Centre of Excellence, Sofia, BG (2016)
72. EU (European Union): Council conclusions on European climate diplomacy after COP 21. Council of the European Union. Brussels, 9 p. (2016)
73. Gilley, B., Kinsella, D.: Coercing climate action. Survival **57**(2), 7 (2015)
74. Buzan, B., Hnasen, L.: The Evolution of International Security Studies. Cambridge University Press, Cambridge (2009)
75. IPCC (Intergovernmental Panel on Climate Change): Cambio climático 2014: impactos, adaptación y vulnerabilidad - Resumen para responsables de políticas. Contribución del Grupo de trabajo II al Quinto Informe de Evaluación del Grupo Intergubernamental deExpertos sobre el Cambio Climático (in Spanish). Organização Meteorológica Mundial, Genebra, 74 p. (2014)
76. USA (United States of America): Department of Defense. FY 2014 Climate Change. Adaptation Roadmap. Office of the Deputy Under Secretary of Defense for Installations end Environment. Alexandria/VA (2014)

77. USA (United States of America): Department of State. Quadrennial Diplomacy and Development Review (2015). http://www.state.gov/documents/organization/241429.pdf. Accessed 15 Aug 2015
78. Levy, J.S.: The offensive/defensive balance of military technology: a theoretical and historical analysis. Int. Stud. Q. **28**(2), 219 (1984). http://www.jstor.org/stable/2600696
79. Martins, H.: Experimentum Humanum. Civilização Tecnológica e Condição Humana, Relógio d'Água, Lisboa (2011)

Urban Planning with the Combined Method of Perception-Driven Joint Learning Approach (PeDJoLA) and Geographic Information Systems (GIS) Model for Disaster Mitigation

Rahmat Widia Sembiring[1(✉)], Benny Benyamin Nasution[1],
M. Syahruddin[1], Afritha Amelia[1], Bakti Viyata Sundawa[1],
Zulkifli Lubis[1], Prayudi Nastia[2], Suhaili Alifuddin[1], Junaidi[1],
Handri Sunjaya[1], Ismael[1], and Gunawan[1]

[1] Politeknik Negeri Medan, Medan, Indonesia
rahmatws@polmed.ac.id
[2] STIKOM Tunas Bangsa, Pematangsiantar, Indonesia

Abstract. This paper is aimed at disaster risk management in urban government. The combined method of Perception-Driven Joint Learning Approach (PeDJoLA) and Geographic Information Systems (GIS) model and were developed for disaster risk management in urban government purposes. The PeDJoLA model served as the basis for investigating disaster vulnerability of existing settlements and identifying areas for new settlements in cities. This method has six main elements of the development process of risk management capacity, dynamic process based on the cities perception, and leading to shape the understanding and assessment of geospatial information. The use of GIS model is only as an additional tool so that data and detailed. In fact, disaster risk management activities require a very high cost. The measurement of the level of expertise of municipal especially in relation to disaster risk management should be developed.

Keywords: Urban · PeDJoLA · Disaster management · Geospatial information · GIS

1 Introduction

Natural disasters can cause damage that is not controlled, especially in certain seasons. Damage such as damaged roads, residential areas, farmland and other sectors of life. This requires scientists and the government to find a solution in the form of modeling to cope with natural disasters with appropriate management to reduce fatalities [1]. The process of disaster management involves many interacting elements such as a person, a team of authorities, emergency, resources, procedures, random environmental situation and others which are complex. Benefits of a model of knowledge and communication are also functioning in the planning and management of different disaster region [2].

Limitations of remote sensing in the disaster management sector are still experiencing certain problems have run faster in agriculture, geology, cartography,

Y. Murayama et al. (Eds.): ITDRR 2016, IFIP AICT 501, pp. 139–146, 2017.
https://doi.org/10.1007/978-3-319-68486-4_11

meteorology, and natural resource management of the urban analysis and research. On the one hand, the use of ArcGIS software for the policies and management of natural disasters [3]. The process of drafting a classification scheme for Landsat imagery that can be applied to urban areas in generating quality index caused by natural disasters. Data measured as the number of population, urban growth charts, and land use. Urban environment, population abundance and distribution of vegetation play an important role in minimize impact of disasters [3]. The dynamics of complex urban environments can be observed several key variables that describe a city from the physical environment. Variables such as air temperature, surface temperature, wind speed and direction, rainfall, humidity and particle concentration. This situation has a direct impact on human health and the comfort level is still not well understood in some cities. Remote sensing is a way to make an indirect measurement as a proxy for much of this amount [3].

GIS models for the prediction of the degree of vulnerability before and after a natural disaster proposed using spatial data from geological and topographical factors in the linear combination of variables [4]. One empirical model that the authors examined in this article about remote sensing and geographic information systems (GIS) techniques have made significant contributions to the prediction of the damage caused by floods, forest fires, tsunamis, diseases, pandemics or earthquake [1].

2   Complexity of Disaster Management

Viewed from the side of the nature of the disaster, to collect relevant information, make the right decisions, and generate the appropriate action plan. Disaster management is a very complex and difficult influenced decision makers hardly feel the phenomenon of how the disaster spread within complex network systems. Water supply network, gas, electricity, roads and communication networks. Network disruption will have a direct impact on the community and the development of science and technology [5]. The advantage of remote sensing observations is able to design a very large area so as to provide spatial variations in the physical quantity. Some areas can be combined with measurements in providing spatial and temporal resolution that is better than the amount provided by the measurement of the internal aspects of the course. Remote sensing can be calibrated with measurements in the core area. Type of satellite-based remote sensing is capable of measuring a physical quantity in large areas with different temporal and spatial scales. The spatial resolution offered a variety of sensors useful for observations of the urban environment [3].

Spatial data derived from a remote sensing capacity of policy makers to provide spatial information that can be used to measure the condition of the urban environment at the time of the case, before and after a disaster occurs from time to time. Forces a site area of natural disasters in urban areas can be reviewed by using a spatial data from IKONOS, Quickbird, SeaWiFS, Landsat 7 and ASTER. The specification and information are available online in http://sedac.ciesin.columbia.edu/remote/. The combination of the sensor with high spatial resolution (1 m) and high temporal resolution (day) allows the different phenomena can be monitored at different levels in detail. Expected extreme events that have or spatial distribution of components, such as natural disasters (floods, storms, and hurricanes), extreme rainfall, changes in wetlands, population shifts are quick, and the extension informal settlement can be described with the prediction results of remote sensing [3].

Information, communication and technology (ICT) is a group of digital tools and resources used to communicate, generate, distribute, store and make information management. The role of information communication technology in disaster management activity has been demonstrated in the rescue, relief, and restoration of community. Technology has a risk that communities potentially affected by the implementation such as GPS (Global Positioning System), EWS (Early Warning System) and GIS (Geographical Information Systems). This technology also as a platform to launch rescue work in the event of a disaster and transmission precautions to society [6].

Factors of natural disasters that affect the lives of humans and other living creatures. Indonesia as a country that is in a positioning ring of fire is very vulnerable to natural disasters that can eliminate human life. Academia, government, private, and researchers in the field of meteorology, geology, environment, computer, and other disciplines have contributed and attempt to predict the time, location and severity of disasters area. Various predictions on aspects of weather forecasting models, data mining models have been used for the same purpose. New discoveries and concentrated research on disaster management and analysis of the needs of victims affected by natural disasters [7].

There are three categories in the classification of the purpose of the task in the response to natural disasters, namely:

- Prediction: This sets the task involves the prediction of natural disasters, disaster-prone areas and the different attributes of natural disasters that may occur. Basically, this task involving prediction or forecasting of time, place and magnitude of the disaster.
- Detection: This sets the task involves the detection of natural disasters soon after it has happened. Literature study shows that social censorship and other social media sites reported a lot faster to natural disasters from the observatory.
- Disaster management strategy: this method handles the identification of the different entities that take part in the fight against disaster so that communication improved, the right attention from people who are affected are identified and distribution of relief items is optimized [7].

Some progress in the transition system of emergency management and disaster risk reduction, emergency management agencies remain reluctant to adopt proactive management for natural disasters [8]. Material losses and economic impact or environmental exceed the ability of communities affected by the disaster. In the event of a natural disaster in an emergency is very important to minimize losses, damages, and build mental resilience population. The distribution of the resources immediately following the disaster, aid agencies need access to information about the size of the event, the location where the affected population, population dynamics, and distribution resources and infrastructure [9].

The latest European research project aims to support the development of products and tools repair of disaster response when crises occur, especially through the provision of mapping capacity, and for the delivery of services before and after the operation of the crisis [10]. Residents need to be equipped with knowledge and evacuation drills. Education and public awareness have influenced the development of emergency plans, evacuation routes and safe area in the event of a disaster [11]. Disaster mitigation is not only buildings to be reinforced or kept away from the danger zone at all, but the government must have a plan in place to deal with disaster by organizing and training the necessary personnel, making evacuation plan, have an emergency medical facility and make arrangements to provide food, clean water, clothing and other necessities required population [12].

GIS data used in detecting damage caused by a disaster. A remote sensor that varies in space contains a type of optical data, SAR, LIDAR, and vector map with the number of the resolution of 10 m to 0.3 m. Research shows data at a resolution of 10 m can only identify damage at the block level while the detection of damaged buildings individual requires a resolution of at least 1 m by 0.5 m to obtain detailed results [13]. Lack of emergency planning, limited resources (money, energy, medical care unit, etc.), the uncertainty and variability in demand, response time, a reliability of structures and delays in the arrival of aid [14].

The relevant government must have the authority and have a list of industrial energy, water, food, health, finance, transportation, chemical industry, telecommunications and other research facilities during natural disasters where it is required by the population [15]. Spry disaster areas tend to have good institutions, effective early warning, disaster preparedness, and response system. The resulting level of risk is most hazards are increasing over time. Disaster risk of harmful leads to economic losses much faster than the risk of death. In developing countries, the economic conditions and governance, in general, improve vulnerability decreases but not fast enough to offset the increase in foreign exchange. It is inversely proportional to the poorer countries which haveproportionately higher death and the risk of economic losses than developed and developing countries [16].

3   Capacity Development Model

The methodology used in this paper is a GIS software for mapping and the remaining information layers which are listed below were entered into the GIS [12]. The model reviews the model perception driven joint learning approach (PeDJoLA) is a model of the development of the capacity of disaster risk management simpler used in this paper has six main elements of the development process of risk management capacity and dynamic process based on the perception of the country (capacity deficit) on one side (top to bottom) and the people on the other side (bottom up). This perception explains that the state and society have a duty to take action (intervention project) in the capacity building process. Environmental factors play a key role in shaping the process of capacity building [17] (Fig. 1).

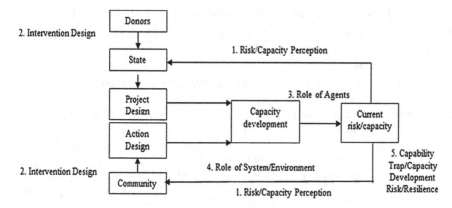

Fig. 1. PeDJoLa capacity development model (Tiwari [17])

4 Discussion

4.1 Perception of Risk and Capacity

Risk perception and capacity of disaster so far are still in good condition by the government and society, but most of the group assumes the risks and different capacities. Subjective disaster risk raises the probability that something bad will happen. Communications planning strategies appropriate to inform the public and understand the situation during emergencies and stress. Lack of understanding of risk perception translate into capacity building efforts such as the possibility that something bad will happen and that is where the subjective risk of bad assumption may not be the same as what other people think is bad. The perception that society, in general, can be used to plan capacity building efforts.

4.2 Intervention Design

Model risk and capacity deficits in perception with capacity building measures. Based on the assessment of disaster risks in the targeted sectors or areas, the existing capacity, and capacity Deficit (comparing what should be there for what is), the government and donors propose capacity building measures. At the same time, based on their own risk perception and capacity deficits to meet the level of acceptable risk in the community to take steps to build capacity.

4.3 Role of Agents

The role of an agent of an area affects change in the level of leadership as the national level of the government sector, non-profit leaders, and NGOs, representatives of donor organizations, community leaders, political leaders and government officials. Environmental work with tension, imperatives and incentives continuing into awards or hamper innovation. Here, the role agents can help reduce disaster risk management (Table 1).

Table 1. Components and sub-components of the PeDJoLA model

Capacity components	Sub components	Application in disaster risk management field
Government capacity		
Institutional	Enabling policies	DRM laws, DRM programs and projects at national, state and local levels
Organizational	Administrative structures	Clear roles and responsibilities in DRM emergency planning
		Risk mapping and mitigation planning, monitoring, DRM data collection
	Coordination	Before, during, and after disasters
		Coordination plans or protocols between departments and agencies, coordination plans
	Publicity	DRM plan publicly available, meetings, periodic DRM material made available
	Awareness	Public awareness plan
Implementation	Enforcement	Building codes, master plan, risk reduction, emergency plan implementation
Technical	Skills and resources	Trained staff, access and motivation for
	Experience	In handling emergency
Political	Leadership	Awareness and interest in DRM
	Publicity	Public campaigns on DRM
	Community participation	Community involvement in prevention and response planning
	Citizen committees	On DRM and response planning
Community capacity	Skills	On safer house, knowledge of disasters
	Coordination	With different community groups
	Cooperation	Trust and help during disasters
	Leadership	Many community leaders
	Inclusion	Minority, women, poor

4.4   Systems and Environment

Government and public sector there is a dynamic system. This measurement system can go through several stages such as transparency, information flow, and relationships between the parts and the whole. Consists of the environmental aspects of economic, political, administrative, social and cultural. Capacity development imposed on the enabling environment as a passive element which may affect the capacity of the development process, the system in disaster risk management efforts. Four factors are important for system management:

- Flexibility to adapt to changing circumstances: It is possible to generate innovatively.

- Flexibility in the relationship between parts and wholes: Risks should be shared the whole system to improve the safety of its members and the entire system. As part of the interconnected systems, weakness in one part of the system requires other parts to adjust and reduce the weaknesses throughout the greater system.
- Interactive exchange between the system and its environment: an ongoing process where the exchange generates a growing form so that it becomes a complex adaptive system.
- Exchange of information: the flow of information between the constituents and external the environment determines the capacity of the system to reduce the risk in the future and create an ongoing relationship with the elements in the environment.

4.5 Capacity Development Implementation

Community development and government in achieving preparedness and disaster resilience, in general, depend on the ministries that deal with the environment, agriculture, construction, planning, and municipal governments. The Ministry is responsible for emergency management, disaster risk management, and urban development.

5 Conclusion

This paper describes the disaster risk management planning at the municipal level. Perception Model-driven joint learning approach (PeDJoLA) used in this paper has six main elements of the building capacity process management and dynamic process based on the perception of a country. This model can be a guide to reducing the risk of natural disasters, leading to shape the understanding and assessment of geospatial information. Research shows PeDJoLA to integrate spatial thinking in local government, cannot approach that focuses only GIS-oriented applications. The use of GIS is only as an additional tool so that data and detailed and accurate geospatial information. Challenges of the city government to reduce the impact of disaster risk by preparing the evacuation area Kordan, physical facilities, counseling and training the public on preventive measures during natural disasters occur. In addition, the measurement of the level of expertise of municipal officials, especially in relation to disaster risk management should be developed. In fact, disaster risk management activities require a very high cost.

References

1. Tehrany, M.S., Pradhan, B., Jebur, M.N.: Flood susceptibility mapping using a novel ensemble weights-of-evidence and support vector machine models in GIS. J. Hydrol. **512**, 332–343 (2014)
2. Othman, S.H., Beydoun, G.: PT US CR. Expert Syst. Appl. (2016)
3. Miller, R.B., Small, C.: Cities from space : potential applications of remote sensing in urban environmental research and policy. **6**, 129–137 (2013)

4. Guo, J., Mason, P.J., Yu, E., Wu, M., Tang, C., Huang, R., Liu, H.: Geomorphology GIS modelling of earthquake damage zones using satellite remote sensing and DEM data. Geomorphology **139–140**, 518–535 (2012)
5. Jin, L., Jiong, W., Yang, D., Huaping, W., Wei, D.: A simulation study for emergency/disaster management by applying complex networks theory. J Appl. Res. Technol. **12**(2), 223–229 (2012). https://doi.org/10.1016/S1665-6423(14)72338-7
6. Rahman, S., Mansoor, S., Deep, V., Aashkaar, M.: Implementation of ICT and wireless sensor networks for earthquake alert and disaster management in earthquake prone areas. In: Procedia - Procedia Computer Science, (CMS), vol. 85, pp. 92–99 (2016)
7. Goswami, S., Chakraborty, S., Ghosh, S., Chakrabarti, A.: A review on application of data mining techniques to combat natural disasters. AIN Shams Eng. J. (2016)
8. Raikes, J., Mcbean, G.: Responsibility and liability in emergency management to natural disasters: a canadian example. Int. J. Disaster Risk Reduction **16**, 12–18 (2016)
9. Cinnamon, J., Jones, S.K., Adger, W.N.: Geoforum Evidence and future potential of mobile phone data for disease disaster management. Geoforum **75**, 253–264 (2016)
10. Casagli, N., Cigna, F., Bianchini, S., Hölbling, D., Righini, G., Del Conte, S., Bianchi, M.: Author's accepted manuscript. Remote Sens. Appl.: Soc. Environ. (2016)
11. Fakhruddin, S.H.M., Chivakidakarn, Y.: Author's accepted manuscript. Int. J. Disaster Risk Reduction (2014)
12. Alparslan, E., Ince, F., Erkan, B., Aydöner, C., Özen, H., Ero, I., Özkan, M.: A GIS model for settlement suitability regarding disaster mitigation, a case study in Bolu Turkey. **96**, 126–140 (2013)
13. Dong, L., Shan, J.: A comprehensive review of earthquake-induced building damage detection with remote sensing techniques. ISPRS J. Photogrammetry Remote Sens. **84**, 85–99 (2013)
14. Hoyos, M.C., Morales, R.S., Akhavan-tabatabaei, R.: Or models with stochastic components in disaster operations management : a literature survey. Comput. Ind. Eng. (2014)
15. Kulawiak, M., Lubniewski, Z.: SafeCity - a GIS-based tool profiled for supporting decision making in urban development and infrastructure protection. Technol. Forecast. Soc. Change (2013)
16. Kamat, R.: Planning and managing earthquake and flood prone towns (2014)
17. Tiwari, A.: The Capacity Crisis in Disaster Risk Management. EH. Springer, Cham (2015). https://doi.org/10.1007/978-3-319-09405-2

The Planning of Smart City to Mitigate the Impacts of Natural Disaster in North Sumatera

Dedy Hartama[1,3(✉)], Herman Mawengkang[3], Muhammad Zarlis[3],
Rahmat Widia Sembiring[2], Benny Benyamin Nasution[2],
M. Syahruddin[2], Prayudi Nastia[1], Abidin Lutfhi Sembiring[3],
Saifullah[1], Eka Irawan[1,3], and Sumarno[1,3]

[1] STIKOM Tunas Bangsa Pematangsiantar, Pematangsiantar, Indonesia
dedyhartama@amiktunasbangsa.ac.id
[2] Politeknik Negeri Medan, Medan, Indonesia
[3] Universitas Sumatera Utara, Medan, Indonesia

Abstract. This article introduces the smart urban planning in the mitigation of natural disasters in urban areas in Indonesia especially North Sumatera. A smart city is a city-based social development, capital, citizen participation, transportation and information technology, natural resources and quality of life. Frequency and socio-economic impacts of natural disasters frequent in recent decades due to climate change and the environment. The approach used in this paper is a combination of Geographic Information System (GIS) and mobile IT in the form of geospatial information. Mobile services sector in which the city government is involved in the formation of smart cities. This article reviews the growth of smart cities and considers how a systems can improve mitigation and adaptation approaches to these risks and to recovery from the natural disasters.

Keywords: Smart city · GIS · Mobile IT · Natural disasters · Mitigation

1 Introduction

Climate change is happening derived from natural processes and human activities. The increase in temperature of the earth, the sea surface, natural temperature variability and global warming led to a dry, crop failure, disturbed ecosystems, water scarcity, degradation of biodiversity, forest fires, and disease. Climate change is part of the economic problems [1]. Activity detects natural disasters are a disaster management [2]. A natural disaster has become a serious problem in urban areas around the world due to worsening ecological factors tend intensified heat effect and global warming [3]. Carbon reduction potential for the buildings and transport [4]. Potential changes are transformative in the decision-making role of disaster risk management [5].

While in Indonesia, natural disasters were recorded until the month of August 2016 is the number of effects for 1512, the dead and missing totaled of 322 people, victims suffer and displaced as many as 2,086,769 inhabitants and the level of damage caused by the disaster as many as 21,537 residential units [6]. Flood disaster was recorded as

Y. Murayama et al. (Eds.): ITDRR 2016, IFIP AICT 501, pp. 147–154, 2017.
https://doi.org/10.1007/978-3-319-68486-4_12

the highest 31.4%, 20.5% climate change and landslides 16.7% and followed by various other natural disasters. Data from the years 1815–2015 in the province of North Sumatra recorded deaths totaled to 2,078 people, missing totaled of 234 people, wounded amounted to 29,206 people, and displaced as many as 332,924 people. From the above data, it is necessary to natural disaster risk management plan to minimize the number of victims affected, especially to build smart city.

Smart cities are meant to be able to handle or reduce unexpected natural disasters through high efficiency. Process optimisation of resources, energy supply, waste management, mobility and urbanisation and population growth. Comprehensive intelligent city model that includes all activities related to natural disasters while keeping the size and complexity of the model is maintained very desirable in order to successfully meet the increasing energy needs of a city of the present and future [7]. Various measures of disaster management and planning have been shown to enhance the emergency management capacity and reduce vulnerability to natural hazards [8].

A smart city is a city-based social development, capital, citizen participation, transportation and information technology, natural resources and quality of life. This understanding is based on a deterministic technology from the control room to the city, providing an overview of the architecture and technology-based information on all activities in the city as well as tools to interact with the infrastructure or adjusting the optimal parameters that have been set [9]. While people around the world have had some degree of adaptation to disaster nonetheless there are a number of victims is likely to increase over time. Effect of an urban morphology affects the size of the resulting impact of the disaster e.g. slope of the land, the location of the geographic area of climate and other factors. Increasing population, the density of buildings and population activities directly impact the disaster [1], for improve decentralised governance of natural disaster need extra effort in highlighting the responsibilities and the role of local government as a key unit in disaster management [10].

In some cities that have a large area tend to be dependent on the government, the system changes involving related parties, strengthening the city's drainage systems, building walls of urban disaster and others [11]. According to the actual facts and new data sources, the gap increases the risk of misuse of information due to limitations of mobile data sources are not well understood. Opportunities for improving disaster management does not guarantee the benefits of the data resulted in less recognised. In helping to address gaps in the use of technology, opportunities, limitations and constraints disaster context [5].

Smart city planning system is the use of a sensor generated data and analysis purposes when decision-making. The resulting smart city government authorities can analyse the data future disasters [12]. The main challenge of how spatial data network can be used to build a smart city based technologies in disaster risk management. Increasing the efficiency of the smart city can be done by providing data related to air temperature, discharge rain, humidity, pressure, wind speed and height of water [12].

This article reviews the growth of smart cities and considers how a systems approach can improve mitigation and adaptation approaches to these risks and to recovery from the natural disasters.

2 Importance of Smart City Disaster Planning

Researchers and scientists have proposed an approach to sustainable urban planning and development. Limit physical growth of uncontrolled exploitation of resources and the need for alternatives. The resulting potential associated with big data, networks, and urban planning. Innovation smart city starts with thinking metabolism urban, produce citizenship intelligent, strengthen human capital, develop collective intelligence of society, facilitating the needs of the population, and the individual gains derived [13] from the availability of new technologies, cities that adopt smart city solutions and communications and information technology organizations usually develop and provide solutions to the technology [14].

Development and population growth in urban areas exacerbate the risk of a possible severity and frequency of natural disasters due to climate change. The need for a strategy to limit the impact of disasters and reduce the possible consequences of a much larger [15] and more destructive in the future. Factors increasing residential population and growing, demanding to be sensitive and prepared to natural disasters such as typhoons and hurricanes, earthquakes, tsunamis, floods, droughts, and forest fires. Climate change can create extreme weather conditions with consequent damage to property and human safety [16].

Simulation of emergencies of natural disasters is essential to minimize the losses, damage and build the resilience of the population. The distribution of emergency resources immediately following the disaster, the need for access to relief agencies information about the magnitude of the disaster, the affected location, characteristics and population dynamics, as well as the distribution of aid resources and infrastructure [5]. In addition, information security for the smart city-related to personal privacy or autonomy of individuals such as secret copyright, patent or trade needs to be enhanced where the information is used to control the system from the electrical grid to medical care when a disaster [17] occurs is very important. Integration of policy always happens at a regional and national level and not at the local level. The area may often be a more relevant scale to address and manage the issues of climate change [18].

The number of institutions responsible for disaster management reduces the effectiveness of disaster management, including the Ministry of Environment (provides guidance on the rules and not national regulations); the regional council (responsible for policy frameworks or regional scale catchment area); territorial authorities (city and county councils are responsible for a particular land use and decision); a group of civil defense emergency management (disaster preparedness and response); and group life line engineering (infrastructure management), hold the responsibility for free. Cooperation between the agency for very important in the flow line and a national holistic approach to natural disaster planning [19]. Urban authorities need to prepare a plan for urban disaster risk management to improve disaster resilience and developing an institutional framework that is effective in improving the resilience of cities and climate change adaptation. Early warning of disasters and geographical mapping needs to be undertaken before natural disaster strikes. Gaps rate of urban growth with the provision of services is increasing rapidly. The city government has set up a disaster management plan, creating early warning systems, emergency response mechanisms, capacity building, disaster, climate change, mitigation, evacuation plans, early recovery systems, and coordination of government agencies [20].

Lack of data information in the event of a disaster can lead to slow access, ineffective and negligent in post-disaster recovery. Decision-making and recovery phase of the response can be strengthened the level of vulnerability for the prevention and preparedness phase of the cycle where data management can support disaster management. Big data actively and passively generated through mobile phone communication that attention from the academic and human population is a source of data that is underutilized in disaster management [5]. Results showed of human learning and application-centric still put a secondary focus on data preparation and exploration of the impact of disasters [21].

3 Smart City Disaster Scenario

The approach used in this paper is a combination of Geographic Information System (GIS) and mobile IT [15] in the form of geospatial information. Geospatial information is a geospatial data that has been processed and can be used to facilitate the planning, decision-making, and activities that are relevant to the location detected natural disasters. Development of geospatial information useful to survey the land such as photogrammetry, remote sensing using very high-resolution satellite imagery, and mapping [22] (see Fig. 1).

4 Discussion

Urban residents worldwide are already depressed because of social and political instability, urbanization, and migration [23] in which the greater frequency of natural disasters. Lifestyle threatens greater impact of natural disasters and residents should consider opportunities through science and technology. The most important projects to government develop local is natural disaster mitigation interventions [24] such as the provision of open land and buildings where the high evacuation can accommodate many people.

Mitigation is a series of efforts to reduce disaster risk, either through physical development as well as awareness and capacity building is facing the threat of disaster. The program aims to reduce or even avoid the impact of catastrophe risk posed by natural disasters. Either before, during and after the disaster. A structured approach to managing uncertainty related to a threat; a range of human activities including risk assessment, developing strategies to manage and mitigate disasters. Basic engineering and natural sciences are essential examined in disaster mitigation planning. In addition, the traditional focus on technology solutions in the life of society affect the evacuation in the event of natural disasters such as outreach to the community about the dangers and help disaster victims. Event organizing and managing a wide range of humanitarian issues related to disaster mitigation in a planned, concerted, integrated, and sustainable so that it becomes an ideal formula in solving various problems of the disaster in the national and local scales. The role of communities in disaster mitigation training and

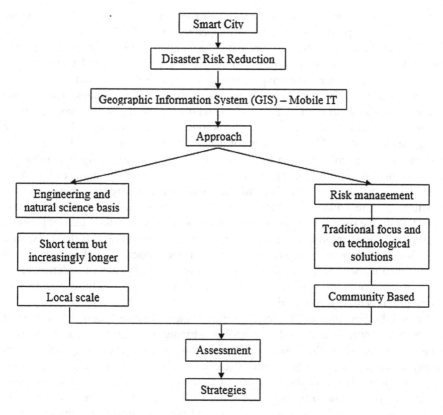

Fig. 1. Smart city system implementation scenario based GIS-mobile IT

community-based and region-based and disaster preparedness and (flood preparedness training, fire preparedness training, eruption preparedness training, earthquake preparedness training).

Smart urban planning provides support for collective action in the evacuation of a natural disaster. Mobile-GIS provides a real-time visualization of spatial risk and resources as well as analyzing the evacuation routes to safe areas. People are expected to know the evacuation routes via social media platforms and twitter. Formulation of dynamic decision support system that transmits data to a place where the population is a social media network for the detection, mitigation, and the resilience of the population against the dangers of natural disasters [25]. Smart urban planning technologies that are environmentally friendly planning a collaboration of agencies involved in the planning process, for example through integration, the division information, and reach the space environment interact city [26].

Smart cities can be built using the data network system in spreading the sensor. Willingness is the most important dataset of data floods that have occurred in worldwide, the temperature of the smart home, vehicles, vehicle parking, pollution, social media, weather and other data [12]. Several approaches need directing for smart city development of equipment and infrastructure facilities. Smart city as a whole can contribute to improving mitigation of natural disasters that can help in situations where policymakers plan proposing methods of cooperative and effective technologies [27].

The main challenge in the development of smart cities is the analysis of real data to make actions [12]. Benefits of building smart cities not only provide benefits to government authorities, but it can help people to guard against disasters and manage them efficiently to achieve the objectives. Natural disaster preventive measures, residents can determine the threshold level of a type of natural disaster has been designated a city. If the predetermined limit then a warning or a warning signal is transmitted to the public through social media [12]. The concept of disaster or hazard mitigation is one way of tackling the rising costs of disaster impacts across the world. Mitigation strategies identified and implemented in an attempt to prevent or minimize harm to the social system, economy, and ecology [28]. Adaptation to climate change is a method for the reduction and prevention of natural disasters. Disaster management and adaptation depending on the role of local government how to establish a policy, plan or program flood management, information and awareness to the community, and flood response [29]. Hazard perception is determined factors of age, education and income, but it depends on a number of factors such as the intensity and frequency of occurrence, the extent of damage to the population and its assets, experience, tradition and way of natural phenomena is recognized [30].

Natural disasters around the world have an impact on public safety and welfare of the urban economy is mainly due to global warming and climate change. Develop techniques in assessing the impact of natural disasters comprehensively and systematically allow nothing extra to catastrophic events [31]. The source of electric power and infrastructure is part of the backbone of modern society. Potential climate change impact and put a low probability on natural disasters Development systems are designed and operated to be reliable under conditions of normal and abnormal [32] should be increased, especially in areas prone to natural disasters due to factors geography.

The sensor system can generate large data disaster data, people, environment, and so on from the smartphone device has great potential to transform urban communities [33]. Social media is consumed by the public can submit relevant information to the spatial characteristics such as geographical information and social hotspot locations. In the event of natural disasters, seismic waves take to propagate away from the epicenter could serve as an early warning system for large-scale incidents. The system was built to predict the mobility of the population or evacuations in various municipalities affected by the disaster can inform disaster management strategy in the future [33]. However, the shortcomings of this system are that if there is an error of the transmitter Global Positioning System (GPS) alone.

5 Conclusion

Big data sensor system in urban environments and applications for monitoring and disaster management using statistical analysis techniques and the major challenges in the development of smart cities is the analysis of real data to make actions. Benefits of building smart cities not only provide benefits to government authorities, but it can help people to guard against disasters and manage them efficiently to achieve the objectives. The sensor system can generate large data disaster data, people, environment, and so on from the smartphone device has great potential to transform urban communities via social media is consumed by the public can submit relevant information to the spatial characteristics such as geographical information and social hotspot locations. In the event of natural disasters, seismic waves take to propagate away from the epicenter could serve as an early warning system for large-scale incidents. The system will built to predict the mobility of the population or evacuations in various municipalities affected by the disaster can inform disaster management strategy in the future.

References

1. Gravitiani, E., Antriyandari, E.: Willingness to pay for climate change mitigation: application on big cities in central Java, Indonesia. Procedia – Soc. Behav. Sci. **227**, 417–423 (2016)
2. Goswami, S., Chakraborty, S., Ghosh, S., Chakrabarti, A.: A review on application of data mining techniques to combat natural disasters. Ain Shams Eng. J (2016)
3. Yamashita, S., Watanabe, R., Shimatani, Y.: Smart adaptation to flooding in urban areas. **118**, 1096–1103 (2015)
4. Adil, A.M., Ko, Y.: Socio-technical evolution of decentralized energy systems: a critical review and implications for urban planning and policy. Renew. Sustain. Energy Rev. **57**, 1025–1037 (2016)
5. Cinnamon, J., Jones, S.K., Adger, W.N.: Geoforum evidence and future potential of mobile phone data for disease disaster management. Geoforum **75**, 253–264 (2016)
6. Disaster Statistic of Badan Nasional Penanggulangan Bencana (BNPB): Laporan Pusat data Informasi dan Humas – BNPB, Jakarta (2016)
7. Calvillo, C.F., Villar, J.: Energy management and planning in smart cities. Ren. Sustain. Energy Rev. **55**, 273–287 (2016)
8. Rumbach, A.: Decentralization and small cities: towards more effective urban disaster governance? Habitat Int. **52**, 35–42 (2016)
9. Walravens, N.: Qualitative indicators for smart city business models : the case of mobile services and applications. Telecommun. Policy 1–23 (2015)
10. Bae, Y., Joo, Y., Won, S.: Decentralization and collaborative disaster governance : evidence from South Korea. Habitat Int. 1–7 (2015)
11. Yamashita, S., Watanabe, R., Shimatani, Y.: Smart adaptation activities and measures against urban flood disasters. Sustain. Cities Soc. **27**, 175–184 (2016)
12. Rathore, M.M., Paul, A., Ahmad, A., Rho, S.: US CR. Computer Networks (2016)
13. Battarra, R., Gargiulo, C., Pappalardo, G., Boiano, D.A., Smeralda, J.: Planning in the era of information and communication technologies. Discussing the "label: Smart" in South-European cities with environmental and socio-economic challenges. JCIT **59**, 1–7 (2016)
14. Paroutis, S., Bennett, M., Heracleous, L.: A strategic view on smart city technology: The case of IBM smarter cities during a recession. Technol. Forecast. Soc. Change **89**, 262–272 (2013)
15. Forino, G., Von Meding, J., Brewer, G., Gajendran, T.: Disaster risk reduction and climate change adaptation policy in Australia. Procedia Econ. Finan. **18**(September), 473–482 (2014)

16. Steiner, F.: Landscape and urban planning frontiers in urban ecological design and planning research. Landscape Urban Plann. **125**, 304–311 (2014)
17. Elmaghraby, A.S., Losavio, M.M.: Cyber security challenges in smart cities: safety, security and privacy. J. Adv. Res. **5**(4), 491–497 (2014)
18. Heidrich, O., Reckien, D., Olazabal, M., Foley, A., Salvia, M., Hurtado, S.G., Tiwary, A.: National climate policies across Europe and their impacts on cities strategies. J. Environ. Manage. **168**, 36–45 (2016)
19. Saunders, W.S.A., Kilvington, M.: Innovative land use planning for natural hazard risk reduction: a consequence-driven approach from New Zealand. Int. J. Disaster Risk Reduction **18**, 244–255 (2016)
20. Shaw, R., Surjan, A., Parvin, G.A.: Urban Disasters and Approaches to Resilience (2016)
21. Granell, C., Ostermann, F.O.: Beyond data collection : objectives and methods of research using VGI and geo-social media for disaster management. CEUS 1–13 (2016)
22. Sutanta, H., Aditya, T., Astrini, R.: Smart city and geospatial information availability, current status in Indonesian cities. Procedia - Soc. Behav. Sci. **227**, 265–269 (2016)
23. Harrison, C.G., Williams, P.R.: A systems approach to natural disaster resilience. Simul. Model. Pract. Theory 0 1–21 (2016)
24. Tironi, M., Farías, I.: Geoforum building a park, immunising life : environmental management and radical asymmetry. Geoforum 1–9 (2015)
25. Ai, F., Comfort, L.K., Dong, Y., Znati, T.: A dynamic decision support system based on geographical information and mobile social networks : a model for tsunami risk mitigation in Padang, Indonesia. Saf. Sci (2015)
26. Yeo, I., Yee, J.: Automation in construction development of an automated modeler of environment and energy geographic information (E-GIS) for ecofriendly city planning. Autom. Constr (2016)
27. Kobayashi, T., Ikaruga, S.: Development of a smart city planning support tool using the cooperative method. Front. Architectural Res. **4**(4), 277–284 (2015)
28. Pine, J.C.: Enhancing the resilience of coastal communities : dealing with immediate and long-term impacts of natural hazards. In: Treatise on Estuarine and Coastal Science, vol. 12, Elsevier Inc. (2011)
29. Ghozali, A., Benny, R., Ulfa, B.: A comparative study of climate change mitigation and adaptation on flood management between Ayutthaya city (Thailand) and Samarinda city (Indonesia). Procedia – Soc. Behav. Sci. **227**, 424–429 (2016)
30. Nedelea, A.: Floods and public perception on their effect. Case study : Tecuci plain (Romania), year 2013. **32**, 190–199 (2016)
31. Abaker, I., Hashem, T., Chang, V., Badrul, N., Adewole, K., Yaqoob, I., Chiroma, H.: The role of big data in smart city. Int. J. Inf. Manage. **36**(5), 748–758 (2016)
32. Espinoza, S., Panteli, M., Mancarella, P., Rudnick, H.: Multi-phase assessment and adaptation of power systems resilience to natural hazards. Electr. Power Syst. Res. **136**, 352–361 (2016)
33. Ang, L., Phooi, K.: Big data research big sensor data applications in urban environments. Big Data Res. **1**, 1–12 (2016)

Forecasting Natural Disasters of Tornados Using mHGN

Benny Benyamin Nasution[✉], Rahmat Widia Sembiring,
Bakti Viyata Sundawa, Gunawan, Afritha Amelia, Ismael,
Handri Sunjaya, Suhaili Alifuddin, Morlan Pardede, Junaidi,
Muhammad Syahruddin, and Zulkifli Lubis

Politeknik Negeri Medan, Medan 20155, Indonesia
benny.nasution@polmed.ac.id

Abstract. Lots of damages, losses, and costs have been the major concern, why handling natural disasters of tornados is very important. Several attempts using different approaches have been carried out, but up to now the results are not yet satisfactory. More promising approaches through a kind of artificial intelligent forecaster have been started for a while, but the results are still not satisfactory either. The capability of mHGN as a pattern recognizer has opened up a new possibility of recognizing a pattern of tornado many hours earlier. Therefore, it can be used to forecast a tornado more efficiently. The results taken from a simulated circumstances of a multidimensional pattern recognition have shown, that the 91% of accuracy can be regarded as satisfactory. Though, several modifications related to the data representation within the mHGN architecture need to be implemented. The deployment of mHGN in several risky areas of tornados can then be expected as a tool for reducing those damages, losses, and costs.

Keywords: Graph neuron · Hierarchical Graph Neuron · mHGN · Natural disaster forecast · Tornado forecast

1 Introduction

Different types of natural disasters have struck many countries since millions of years and caused various problems. Natural disasters have caused not only financial problems but also casualties. Yet, people living in those hit areas have not found effective and efficient ways how to cope with it. Developed countries such as USA [1] and Japan [2] are not excepted. Those countries face natural disasters every year [3] and suffer from them. The situation is worse in some developing countries, such as Nepal and Tahiti, where people generally do not know what to do before, during, and after a natural disaster has occurred.

The most difficult part to handle natural disasters is that they come in random times. Although some natural disasters such as volcano eruptions, earthquakes are not coming every day or every month, people cannot prepare the best way to face them. Two tsunami disasters in 2004 (Indonesia) and in 2011 (Japan) are two evidences that people are not adequately nor properly prepared. Due to the randomness of occurrences

Y. Murayama et al. (Eds.): ITDRR 2016, IFIP AICT 501, pp. 155–169, 2017.
https://doi.org/10.1007/978-3-319-68486-4_13

of natural disasters, it becomes more difficult to handle those frequent ones like tornados, landslides, and flooding. Not only handling natural disasters is difficult, predicting how bad the damages and costs is still a very challenging task.

To reduce damages, losses, and costs after such unpredictable occurrences people have tried to be prepared as good as possible. Disaster management is the general terminology researchers use for the activity of preparing a number of things before, during, and after a natural disaster has occurred. Additionally, since a few centuries back, researchers have been interested in discovering ways to forecast the upcoming of a natural disaster. Some of them are still at the stage of now-casting [4–8], not yet forecasting. According to their methodologies, the most difficult part of forecasting natural disasters lies in the mathematical formulas. At the moment, the success-rate of such forecasters is around up to 80%.

As it is still difficult to have a measure of disaster forecast based on mathematical formulas, it is a great opportunity to figure out other solving methods, such us through utilizing artificial intelligent technologies. Although mathematical functions that can determine the condition of a natural disaster are not yet discovered, air-temperature, wind-speed, wind-direction, and air-pressure that constitute a natural disaster, such as tornado, are all caused by physical states [9]. It means that the condition of a tornado is generally determined by particular physical patterns. So, time-series of several physical values of air-temperature, wind-speed, wind-direction, and air-pressure will determine particular tornado condition.

Multidimensional Hierarchical Graph Neuron (mHGN) has been proven to be capable of working as a pattern recognizer. The latest architecture to prove its capability was the one that uses five-dimension $5 \times 5 \times 5 \times 15 \times 15$ neurons. The architecture has been tested to recognize 26 patterns of five-dimensional alphabetical figures. Despite of 10% of distortion of the figures, the architecture was able to recognize in average more than 90% of those distorted patterns. This experiment result is a positive indication that mHGN has a potential to be developed as a disaster forecaster. The architecture can then be used as an additional tool for reducing the number of damages, losses, and costs when a tornado strikes.

2   Natural Disaster Forecast

Several countries have faced natural disasters more than the others. Every year, the US suffers from tornado more than other countries do. The number of tornados occurred within a year varies, so is the severity of damages, losses, and costs. However, this does not mean that only the US must concern with the occurrence of tornados. When the circumstances of developing a tornado in an area have reached, it is very likely that the area will be hit by a tornado. The likelihood of the occurrence of a natural disaster varies, but the possibility is still there in most parts of the world. For instance, the tsunami that hit Indonesia in 2004 had never been experienced by Indonesians for hundreds of years. This situation applies for other natural disasters.

Many countries under the coordination of the United Nation's UNISDR have worked together to handle natural disasters around the world. This means that any disaster that strikes a country is no longer the concern of the country itself, but it is automatically the world's concern. Such situation has helped researchers in gaining data from various sensors spread around the world. Many researchers have started investigating new approach in forecasting natural disasters. Several issues related to this need to be discussed further.

The randomness of the occurrence of a natural disaster is not only in terms of the location, but also of the time and the severity. Two obvious examples are the tsunami in Indonesia in 2004 and the blizzard in Afghanistan in 2008. A number of researchers in opinion that the severity and the average magnitude of natural disasters have increased since the last decade. However, it is still not clear how severe future natural disasters might be. The impossibility to measure, or to predict the severity of natural disasters, that potentially will occur in the future, has been the major cause of the difficulties in anticipating their occurrences. Several other researchers have come up with the idea that, one way to deal with the randomness of the occurrence of natural disasters is through a disaster forecaster.

Several researchers have investigated natural disaster forecasting through a kind of early warning system [3] and now-casting [1, 4, 6, 7, 9, 10]. The forecasting approach that they [2, 5, 8] have attempted is able to forecast the disaster within one hour time frame. SuzukiI et al. [8] have shown their success in predicting Haneda's gust wind disaster of April 18, 2008. Despite the difficulties in finding appropriate equations, Sorensen [3] admits that his early warning system has been built utilizing a number of fields of science. He [3] further advises that early warning systems will be effective if they integrate the subsystems of detection of extreme events, management of hazard information, and public response.

It seems to be that researchers have tried to find an appropriate approach for working on three areas: natural disaster forecaster, now-casters, or early warning systems. However, they [3, 9, 11] also still integrate their system with disaster management systems. Even Doong et al. [11] suggest that the success of a disaster mitigation concept lies in the quality of the disaster management. This shows that their approach alone is not yet adequate to handle natural disasters. The potential reason to this case is the fact that a system for handling natural disaster requires very complicated mathematical analysis. So many parameters and values need to be considered and included in their calculation [1, 5, 6], and it is time consuming [10], but the system must run fast [1]. The other thing that needs to be considered when deploying such systems is the cost of using high quality sensors [5]. This causes the condition that gaining important measured data in several important areas is challenging [5].

Despite those efforts of researchers, Sorensen [3] argues that in terms of prediction and forecasting, no radical breakthroughs have occurred in the past twenty years. Most natural disaster researchers are working on current technologies that are not focusing on the forecasting techniques. Rather, they are concerned with how natural disaster alerts can be disseminated to the public [3]. While investigating natural disaster issues, special attention has been taken for people with disabilities. Most difficult part in facing a natural disaster is about how to handle people when a natural disaster occurs. Additionally, most common recommendation for an early warning system is "how to evacuate."

Although the randomness of the occurrences of a natural disaster has caused difficulties in handling it, the development of every natural disaster still follows natural science characteristics and rules. Each part of a natural disaster—for example a tornado—owns specific patterns and characters. For instance, a tornado develops its twist through hot and cold winds that move from the opposite directions. Not only the opposite winds play a role in developing a tornado, specific air pressure and air temperature are also significant contributors for a tornado's development.

The steps that a tornado builds its strong winding wind can be treated as a pattern. So, the recorded data from previous tornado disasters must be kept properly. The data is the important source of clue for researchers to analyse the pattern of a tornado. When patterns of tornados can be recorded, it is a strong possibility that when one of the patterns turns up, a system that can recognize patterns can be used to recognize a tornado early before it becomes a strong and destructive one. Such patterns are the most important part of mHGN for forecasting tornados hours before they strike.

3   Multidimensional Hierarchical Graph Neuron (mHGN)

The need to solve multidimensional problems has been discussed since a long time ago. People are aware that to handle complex problems, values taken from numerous dimensions must be considered and calculated. Otherwise, the result that comes up after the calculation analysing just a few parameters cannot be considered correct. In most cases, such a condition has produced very high false positive and true negative error rate. Another issue related to solving multidimensional problems is the solving method that will be implemented. In a complex system, not only the number of dimensions is large, but how all the dimensions are interrelated to each other, or independent on one another, is often not clear.

Natural disaster system is a good example as a multidimensional system. Therefore, forecasting natural disasters is also a type of solving a multidimensional problem. Not only the location or the latitude determines the condition of natural disasters, air-temperature, air-pressure, air-humidity, wind-direction, and wind-speed also play a big role in causing natural disasters of tornados. A problem that still exists is the interdependency amongst those tangible and intangible values (industrial development, people movement, etc.). It is cto figure out a formula that constitutes such interdependency. This is a strong indication that such multidimensional problems may be solved using artificial intelligent approaches such as mHGN.

3.1   Experiment Results

For the experiment, each GN is operated by a thread. Various 2D-, 3D-, 4D- and 5D-pattern recognition have been scrutinized. The compositions used in the experiment are: 15×15 mHGN, $5 \times 15 \times 15$ mHGN, $5 \times 5 \times 15 \times 15$ mHGN, and 5×5 $5 \times 15 \times 15$ mHGN respectively. For instance, in the 15×15 pattern recognition the composition requires: $225 + 195 + 165 + 135 + + 105 + 75 + 45 + 15 + 13 + 11 + 9 + 7 + 5 + 3 + 1 = 1009$ neurons per value of data. As for creating patterns, binary data is used, then two values (i.e. 0 and 1) of data are required. Therefore, 2018 neurons are deployed in the 15×15 mHGN composition. So, 2018 threads have been run in parallel during this 2D pattern recognition. By using threads, the activity of neurons is simulated so that the functionalities are close to the real neuron functionalities.

The experiment has worked on all the patterns of 26 alphabetical figures. Following the composition of the neurons, the alphabet patterns consist of 15×15 pixels. For the training purpose, the mHGN is first fed one-cycle with all the 26 non-distorted patterns. The order of the patterns during the training phase has been determined randomly. Then, to acquire the recognition results the mHGN is fed with a lot of randomly distorted patterns of alphabets. The recognizing accuracy is taken by calculating the average value of the results.

For the sake of the experiment, 20 distorted patterns for each alphabetical figure have been prepared. After acquiring the results, the experiment is repeated 10 times with the same steps, but each time the mHGN is trained with 26 patterns of alphabetical figures with randomly different order. So, for each alphabetical figure for particular percentage of distortion, in total 200 distorted patterns have been prepared as testing patterns.

There are 7 levels of distortion that have been tested, they are: 1.3%, 2.7%, 4.4%, 6.7%, 8.0%, 8.9%, and 10.7%. These levels have been so chosen based on the number of distorted pixels. The sizes of pixels represent the factor and the non-factor of the dimension of the patterns. By doing so, we can observe all the possibilities of distortion. So, in total there are 5200 ($26 \times 20 \times 10$) randomly distorted testing patterns. The following Fig. 1 shows 5 samples of different orders of the patterns:

1	E	N	W	L	I	S	P	G	H	J	D	Y	A	X	Q	R	C	M	F	V	O	T	U	K	Z	B
2	R	P	J	S	O	Q	D	V	C	K	L	E	F	G	X	Y	A	T	Z	B	U	W	T	H	M	N
3	G	B	H	R	Z	C	I	Y	X	S	J	K	D	A	N	T	Q	V	E	W	F	U	P	O	L	M
4	L	N	I	F	R	X	B	K	O	C	T	Z	A	Y	G	V	U	H	P	J	Q	S	W	E	D	M
5	C	E	T	U	N	R	H	Y	G	D	B	K	F	M	I	X	V	S	Q	J	Z	W	O	A	L	P

Fig. 1. Five different randomly ordered alphabets.

The following shows some results taken from testing 4.4% randomly distorted patterns, and the mHGN was previously stored with alphabetical figure patterns, and the order was IEFXMQYJHPDKTORZCUALBGVWNS. The value on the right side of each alphabet show the portion (percentage) of the pattern that is recognizable as the corresponding alphabet (see Fig. 2.).

The following shows 10 samples of distorted patterns of the alphabetical figure of "A" taken from the experiment t of recognizing 5.8% randomly distorted patterns (see Fig. 3.).

After collecting the results taken from testing 5200 patterns we can summarize how accurate the mHGN is, in recognizing different levels of distortion of 26 alphabets. The summary is taken based on the average accuracy values from all the steps. The following shows the summarized result taken from testing distorted patterns using five-dimensional $5 \times 5 \times 5 \times 15 \times 15$ mHGN (see Fig. 4.).

PATTERNS RANDOMLY DISTORTED 4.4 %

Patterns Stored	Distorted Pattern	Recognised patterns and their recognized portion (%) from 20 different randomly distorted patterns																				Recognised Correctly
		1	2	3	4	5	6	7	8	9	10	11	12	13	14	15	16	17	18	19	20	
I	A	A 9A	8A	8A	54A	13A	3A	8A	13A	16A	6A	15A	14A	15A	14A	14A	2A	1A	54A	17A	15	20
E	B	B 3B	4B	36B	37B	11B	36B	11B	37B	10B	5B	36B	13B	10B	12B	11B	6B	9B	11B	36		20
F	C	C 40C	7C	38C	15C	8C	39C	8C	7C	7C	8C	15C	7C	0C	14C	15C	40C	14C	1C	14C	39	20
X	D	D 26D	10D	4D	27D	9D	10D	10D	2D	12D	25D	11D	5D	12D	6D	9D	9D	10D	10D	11D	10	20
M	E	E 10E	6E	30E	29E	12E	11E	11E	11E	10E	10E	29E	11E	10E	10E	11E	12E	29E	31E	6E	10E	9	20
Q	F	F 20F	4F	19F	3F	20F	9F	7F	8F	4F	1F	7F	21H	19F	22H	8F	9F	21F	8F	4F	8	19
Y	G	G 51G	14G	51G	13G	15G	51G	14G	50G	7G	51G	14G	15G	6G	15G	15G	7G	3G	14G	6G	7	20
J	H	H 8H	14H	14H	14H	15H	56H	15H	14H	7H	54H	13H	3H	16H	54H	9H	15H	55H	54			20
H	I	I 54I	6I	1I	53I	6I	14I	14I	55I	15I	15I	54I	14I	14I	15I	54I	6I	15I	14I	16I	5	20
P	J	J 54J	5J	5J	14J	15J	13J	54J	14J	55J	6J	55J	15J	6J	54J	55J	14J	13J	3			20
D	K	K 4K	7K	8K	8K	6K	6K	8K	5K	8H	22K	9K	6K	7K	6K	4K	2H	22K	9K	7K	5	18
K	L	L 9L	11L	5L	38L	11L	11L	11L	39L	6L	40L	12L	10L	6L	5L	10L	7L	10L	12L	38		20
T	M	M 22M	19M	21M	4M	21M	22M	8M	4M	8M	6M	7M	6M	5M	7M	5M	4M	7M	7M	6M	7	20
O	N	N 19N	4N	3N	7H	19N	8N	8N	4N	7N	6N	7N	8N	18N	6N	7N	8N	5N	7N	5		18
R	O	O 54O	16O	15O	14O	14O	7O	56O	14O	54O	8O	3O	16O	14O	16O	55O	54O	8O	15O	7O	54	20
Z	P	P 10P	32P	10P	9P	10P	5P	6P	5P	33P	10P	0P	8P	10P	10P	32P	5P	9P	11P	11		20
C	Q	Q 44Q	15Q	4Q	15Q	45Q	15Q	16Q	13Q	14Q	13Q	6Q	14Q	15Q	15Q	45Q	6Q	44Q	14Q	45		20
U	R	R 11R	12R	12R	5R	12R	11R	38R	5R	6R	10R	10R	7R	37R	10R	37R	37R	38R	11R	2R	12	20
A	S	S 14S	15S	8S	14S	13S	13S	3S	7S	13S	14S	46S	45S	13S	15S	46S	7S	7S	13S	14S	15	20
L	T	T 14T	15T	14T	15T	16T	13T	7T	15T	55T	15T	14T	15T	55T	16T	54T	55T	54T	14T	14		20
B	U	U 4U	7U	10U	7U	10U	11U	11U	9U	11U	5U	30U	4U	10U	10U	10U	11U	2				20
G	V	V 56V	14V	54V	15V	54V	8V	55V	55V	6V	14V	14V	9V	2V	15V	1V	56V	16V	14V	16V	15	20
W	W	W 6W	14W	14W	30W	29W	13W	13W	13W	14W	6W	12W	14W	11W	13W	54V	7W	30W	11W	12		20
W	X	X 15X	53X	16X	15X	15X	14X	15X	14X	14X	14X	7X	6X	16X	54X	15X	14X	54X	14X	13X	54	20
N	Y	Y 15Y	18Y	15Y	13Y	14Y	51Y	8Y	2Y	51Y	13Y	15Y	14Y	13Y	62Y	51Y	15Y	15Y	5Y	15		20
S	Z	Z 7Z	15Z	15Z	14Z	13Z	14Z	16Z	17Z	0Z	51Z	14Z	51Z	50Z	7Z	6Z	7Z	7Z	51Z	14Z	51	20

(Order Type 0)

Fig. 2. The result of al the 26 alphabetical patterns that are twenty times 4.4% randomly distorted.

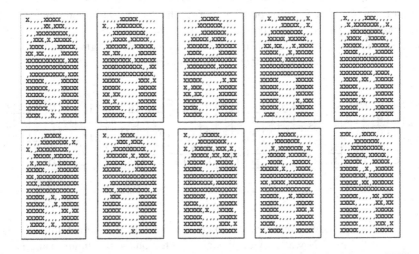

Fig. 3. Ten different randomly 5.8% distorted patterns of alphabetical figure of "A"

It can be seen from Fig. 4 in the last column that the mHGN is able to recognize 91% of the 10.7% distorted patterns of 26 alphabetical figures. Some alphabetical figures of A, C, E, G, I, J, L, O, S, T, U, V, X, Y, Z, are even 100% recognizable. Other patterns of alphabetical figures of H, K, M, N, are not very well recognized because they are visually and physically very similar. In fact, if this architecture is used to recognize different states of the same alphabet, such as regular-A, bold-A, and italic-A as the same alphabet, then mHGN will be able to gain better accuracy values.

The following figure shows the differences of recognition accuracy amongst 15×15, $5 \times 15 \times 15$, $5 \times 5 \times 15 \times 15$, and $5 \times 5 \times 5 \times 15 \times 15$ mHGN architectures when recognizing 10.7% distorted patterns of alphabets (see Fig. 5.).

5X5X5X15X15 Patterns		Distortion (%)						
		1.3	2.7	4.4	6.7	8.0	8.9	10.7
Recognition Accuracy for Each Pattern (%)	A	100	100	100	100	100	100	100
	B	100	100	100	100	98	97	94
	C	100	100	100	100	100	96	100
	D	100	100	100	100	100	100	98
	E	100	100	100	100	100	100	100
	F	100	99	94	89	83	85	74
	G	100	100	100	100	100	100	100
	H	100	100	89	67	48	50	55
	I	100	100	100	100	100	100	100
	J	100	100	100	100	100	100	100
	K	100	100	98	81	70	72	67
	L	100	100	100	100	100	100	100
	M	100	100	93	76	55	66	49
	N	100	100	97	77	63	60	55
	O	100	100	100	100	100	100	100
	P	100	99	87	79	80	81	81
	Q	100	100	100	100	100	94	99
	R	100	100	100	95	100	99	95
	S	100	100	100	100	100	100	100
	T	100	100	100	100	100	100	100
	U	100	100	100	100	100	100	100
	V	100	100	100	100	100	100	100
	W	100	100	100	100	99	98	92
	X	100	100	100	100	100	100	100
	Y	100	100	100	100	100	100	100
	Z	100	100	100	100	100	100	100
Average		100	100	98	95	92	92	91

Fig. 4. The summary of the result using $5 \times 5 \times 5 \times 15 \times 15$ mHGN [12].

Comparison Result		Distortion = 10.7 %			
		15X15	5X15X15	5X5X15X15	5X5X5X15X15
Recognition Accuracy for Each Pattern (%)	A	99	100	100	100
	B	58	69	92	94
	C	67	93	94	100
	D	78	92	94	98
	E	85	80	100	100
	F	61	71	81	74
	G	87	98	100	100
	H	23	63	69	55
	I	95	100	100	100
	J	77	95	100	100
	K	68	59	84	67
	L	50	80	100	100
	M	38	36	35	49
	N	53	42	63	55
	O	100	100	100	100
	P	61	59	75	81
	Q	63	73	73	99
	R	79	90	95	95
	S	78	97	100	100
	T	93	95	100	100
	U	89	84	85	100
	V	100	100	100	100
	W	75	82	98	92
	X	85	100	100	100
	Y	100	100	100	100
	Z	99	100	100	100
Average		75	83	90	91

Fig. 5. Differences of recognition accuracy amongst four different architectures

3.2   Time-Series in Pattern Recognition

Recognizing patterns of time series problem utilizes data that have previously been recorded regularly in timely manner [12]. For instance, if the parameter that needs to be recorded is a single value, and the recording step is every six hours, then there will be 4 values recorded every day. In order to constructs the recorded values as a pattern, the data representation of the recorded values need to be developed so, that they can fit into a pattern recognition architecture. The following Fig. 6 shows two ways of representing recorded data for 8 levels of measurement.

0	00000000	0	00000000
1	10000000	1	00000001
2	11000000	2	00000011
3	11100000	3	00000111
4	11110000	4	00001111
5	11111000	5	00011111
6	11111100	6	00111111
7	11111110	7	01111111
8	11111111	8	11111111

Fig. 6. Two examples of data representation for 8-bit value

It can be seen from Fig. 6 that the data is represented using binary values. The bit difference (distance) between adjacent levels is 1. Additionally, the number of bit differences between any two levels is linear with the value difference between the two levels. However, such data representation will not maximally utilize the binary combination. With 3-bit data, only 3/8 or 0.375 is the occupation rate. For 4-bit data is the occupation rate 4/16 or 0.25. The occupation rate is 5/32 or 0.15625 for 5-bit value. This shows that the above data representation will produce less occupation rate, the more bits is used. This is an indication that due to such an occupation rate the pattern recognizer will have less recognition accuracy the more bits in it is used. The following is a better data representation.

In Fig. 7 it is shown that the number of bit differences between adjacent levels is 1. Between any two levels the bit difference is 2, and 3 between any three levels. This data representation is cyclic. It means that, if it is required the order of binary representation can be modified circularly without affecting the bit differences (distances). Using such a better data representation, for any bit data is the occupation rate constantly 0.75. With such a constant occupation rate the pattern recognizer will have constant recognition accuracy, any number of bits in it is used. The following figure shows an example of recorded data taken from a single value measurement and each value has 8 levels.

It can be seen from Fig. 8 that the recorded values from parameter of 8 levels data construct a two-dimensional pattern of 30 × 8 architecture. Utilizing these recorded data, the pattern recognizer can forecast a tornado 6 h earlier. when the same tornado will occur again. It means that if values have been recorded and the same pattern is recognized by the pattern recognizer, then the tornado is forecasted to occur again within 6-h time.

So, to predict what will occur in 6-h time using 30×8 mHGN architecture, the recognizer need to be fed with data measurement recorded from 7 days and 6 h ago until now. Not only forecasting something that will occur in 6-h time, the 30×8 mHGN architecture can also be used to forecast something that will occur in 12-h time. But, for this purpose the recognizer is fed with data measurement recorded from 7 days only. In this case, the pattern is not fed with 30×8 binary data, but with only 29×8 binary data. This is the same case when a pattern recognizer is fed with incomplete data (only 97% data), but the recognizer still has the capability to recognize the pattern. Similarly, to forecast something that will occur in 18-h time, the recognizer is fed with data measurement recorded from 6 days and 18 h ago (only 93% data). This case is shown in Fig. 4, that after stored with 26 patterns, $5 \times 5 \times 5 \times 15 \times 15$ mHGN architecture is able to recognize 89% incomplete/distorted patterns with 91% of successful rate.

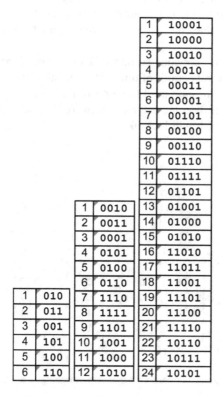

Fig. 7. Three examples of a better data representation for 3-, 4-, and 5-bit value

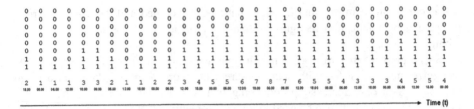

Fig. 8. Data of 8 level value build a 2D-Pattern

4 Multidimensional Graph Neuron for Tornado Forecasting

In the previous section, time series value is described and represented so, that it can be forecasted through utilizing a pattern recognition, such as mHGN. In case of tornado forecasting, single parameter in a location, such as air-pressure, is not the only value that determine the occurrence of a tornado in the location within 6-h time. Several other parameters, such as air-temperature, wind-speed, wind-direction, and air-humidity, play a big role in the occurrences as well. It means that the number of levels or a measured value will increase according to the number of parameters. In case 5 parameters need to be measured and each value contains 8 levels, the required pattern structure would be 30×40.

Also described in the previous section that measuring a parameter at particular point of location for several periods of time will generate a two dimensional pattern. If a series of points of the location need to be measured for several period of time, then the measured values will become a three dimensional pattern. The following Fig. 9 depicts how some part of it will look like.

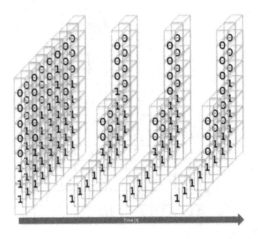

Fig. 9. A row of data of 8 level value build a 3D-Pattern

Also described in the previous section that measuring parameters at particular point of location for several periods of time will generate a two dimensional pattern. If a series and linear of locations need to be measured for several periods of time, then the measured values will become a three dimensional pattern. If the location that need to be measured is an 2D area, then the measured values will generate a 4D pattern. Furthermore, if the location that need to be measured is a 3D area, then the measured values will generate a 5D pattern.

4.1   The Architecture of mHGN for Time-Series Tornado Data

The utilization of mHGN has introduced a new approach that a local tornado forecast can be operated using small and cheap components. The values of air-temperature, air-humidity, air-pressure, wind-speed, and wind-direction can be gained through ordinary sensors. The area that is covered by those sensors can be a 3D area, because such small sensors can be easily mounted in valleys or hills, or even vehicles. The sensors can be embedded in a tiny computer, such as Raspberry Pi. The tiny computer will be responsible to run several GNs. The values taken from the sensors will then be worked out within the GNs. The connectivity of neurons is developed within a tiny computer and through the interconnectivity of the tiny computers.

During mHGN experiments, each neuron and its functionalities is operated by a thread. However, the number of thread will be tremendous, especially when the mHGN is used to work on multidimensional patterns. For example, 15 × 15 architecture of mHGN requires 2018 neurons. This means that the number of threads that need to be run is also 2018. Such a number of threads would be difficult to be run if the computer used for the project is a Raspberry Pi. The new approach to run neurons is through utilizing threads in which the number of threads is only the same as the size of neurons on the base level. The following Fig. 10 shows that instead of utilizing 25 threads the new approach to implement mHGN architecture only requires 9 threads.

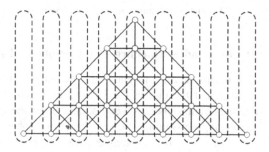

Fig. 10. The number of threads (dashed line) is the same as the neuron size on the base level

In short, to build a tornado forecast for particular location, five parameters need to be measured. They are: air-temperature, air-humidity, wind-speed, wind-direction, and air-pressure. So, if one parameter is represented through 8-bit binary data, then for the measurement of 5 parameters 41-bit data is needed (the dimension must be odd number). For the time series, 21 series of measurement will be carried out. For an area that needs to be protected by mHGN, 3 × 3 × 3 measurement points will be deployed. So, the mHGN dimension will be 3 × 3 × 3 × 41 × 21.

The positions of the 3 × 3 × 3 GNs will form a cylinder shape. In the cylinder, there will be three layers of circles. Each layer contains 9 GNs, in which 8 GNs will be on the border of the circle, and one GN will be located in the centre of the circle. The following Fig. 11 shows the architecture of the positions of the sensors.

The cylinder shape of the architecture has been chosen so, that mHGN still has an ability to recognize the same tornado pattern but developed with the direction different from the ones already stored. For the purpose of training, patterns from the previous tornados will be stored in the mHGN. Each pattern of a tornado will then be stored in mHGN eight times, following the number of eight major compass directions. It will look like as if the mHGN has stored 8 patterns of tornados. By having eight patterns for each tornado stored in mHGN, whenever the same characteristics of a tornado turn up but from different direction from the already stored ones, mHGN will be able to recognize it.

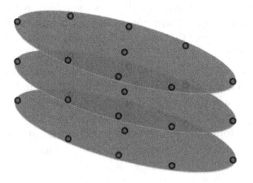

Fig. 11. The architecture of 3 × 3 × 3 sensors

4.2 Case Studies: Joplin's and Hackleburg–Phil Campbell's Tornados

Two deadliest tornados occurred quite recently are the tornado that struck Joplin, Missouri on May 22, 2011 and the one in Hackleburg–Phil Campbell, Alabama on April 27, 2011. To store the circumstances, several parameters in these areas need to be stored in mHGN. Fortunately, the National Oceanic and Atmospheric Administration (NOAA) provides lots of data of: air-temperature, air-humidity, air-pressure, wind-speed, wind-direction in most areas of the US. These data will be the major source for mHGN to store previous occurrences of tornados. In the case of Joplin, the following are several locations of stations that have recorded those data from their sensors including the map in the state of Missouri (see Figs. 12 and 13).

1	Boonville	10	Excelsior Springs
2	Branson	11	Farmington
3	Branson West	12	Fort Leonard Wood
4	Camdenton	13	Hannibal
5	Cape Girardeu	14	Jefferson City
6	Chillicothe	15	CRN: Joplin
7	CRN: Chillicothe	16	Joplin
8	Clinton	17	Kaiser Lake Ozark
9	Columbia		

Fig. 12. Several weather stations in the state of Missouri

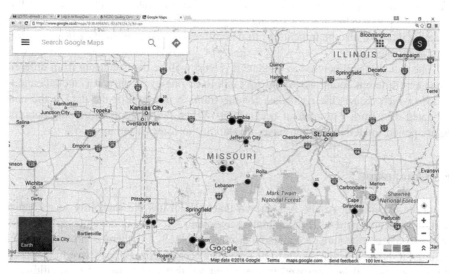

Fig. 13. The locations (bold circles) of several weather stations in the state of Missouri

```
Hourly Obs
Month/Year: 05/2011
Station Location: JOPLIN REGIONAL AIRPORT (13987)
Lat: 37.146
Lon: -94.502
Elev: 980 ft. above sea level
WBAN,Date,Time,StationType,SkyCondition,SkyConditionFlag,Visibility,VisibilityFlag,WeatherType,WeatherTypeFlag,DryBulbFarenheit,DryBulbFaren
heitFlag,DryBulbCelsius,DryBulbCelsiusFlag,WetBulbFarenheit,WetBulbFarenheitFlag,WetBulbCelsius,WetBulbCelsiusFlag,DewPointFarenheit,DewP
ointFarenheitFlag,DewPointCelsius,DewPointCelsiusFlag,RelativeHumidity,RelativeHumidityFlag,WindSpeed,WindSpeedFlag,WindDirection,WindDire
ctionFlag,ValueForWindCharacter,ValueForWindCharacterFlag,StationPressure,StationPressureFlag,PressureTendency,PressureTendencyFlag,Pres
sureChange,PressureChangeFlag,SeaLevelPressure,SeaLevelPressureFlag,RecordType,RecordTypeFlag,HourlyPrecip,HourlyPrecipFlag,Altimeter,Al
timeterFlag
13987,20110521,0053,11,OVC038, ,10.00, , ,64, ,17.8, ,62, ,16.4, ,60, ,15.6, , 87, ,10, ,160, , , ,28.74, , , , , ,29.76, ,AA, , , ,29.78,
13987,20110521,0130,11,BKN025 OVC032, ,10.00, , , ,64, ,18.0, ,62, ,16.7, ,61, ,16.0, , 90, , 9, ,160, , , ,28.72, , , , , ,M, ,SP, , , ,29.77,
13987,20110521,0153,11,OVC023, ,10.00, , , ,65, ,18.3, ,62, ,16.6, ,60, ,15.6, , 84, ,10, ,170, , , ,28.71, , , , , ,29.74, ,AA, , , ,29.76,
13987,20110521,0253,11,BKN023, ,10.00, , , ,63, ,17.2, ,61, ,16.2, ,60, ,15.6, , 90, ,10, ,180, , , ,28.72, , , , , ,29.75, ,AA, , , ,29.77,
13987,20110521,0324,11,SCT023, ,10.00, , , ,63, ,17.0, ,62, ,16.5, ,61, ,16.0, , 93, , 8, ,180, , , ,28.74, , , , , ,M, ,SP, , , ,29.78,
13987,20110521,0353,11,CLR, ,10.00, , , ,61, ,16.1, ,60, ,15.4, ,59, ,15.0, , 79, , 5, ,170, , , ,28.72, , , , , ,29.75, ,AA, , , ,29.77,
13987,20110521,0453,11,CLR, ,10.00, , , ,60, ,15.6, ,59, ,14.9, ,58, ,14.4, , 93, , 5, ,150, , , ,28.74, , , , , ,29.76, ,AA, , , ,29.78
13987,20110521,0553,11,CLR, ,10.00, , , ,60, ,15.6, ,59, ,15.2, ,59, ,15.0, , 97, , 6, ,150, , , ,28.75, , , , , ,29.78, ,AA, , , ,29.80,
13987,20110521,0653,11,BKN012, ,10.00, , , ,64, ,17.8, ,62, ,16.7, ,61, ,16.1, , 90, ,15, ,180, ,.22, ,28.75, , , , , ,29.78, ,AA, , , ,29.80,
13987,20110521,0753,11,OVC014, ,10.00, , , ,67, ,19.4, ,64, ,17.7, ,62, ,16.7, , 84, ,15, ,190, , , ,28.76, , , , , ,29.79, ,AA, , , ,29.81,
13987,20110521,0812,11,OVC016, ,10.00, , , ,68, ,20.0, ,65, ,18.2, ,63, ,17.0, , 84, ,13, ,200, ,.25, ,28.77, , , , , ,M, ,SP, , , ,29.82,
13987,20110521,0853,11,OVC018, ,10.00, , , ,69, ,20.6, ,65, ,18.1, ,62, ,16.7, , 79, ,14, ,190, ,.24, ,28.78, , , , , ,29.80, ,AA, , , ,29.83,
13987,20110521,0926,11,SCT018, ,10.00, , , ,72, ,22.0, ,66, ,19.0, ,63, ,17.0, , 73, ,16, ,210, ,.23, ,28.78, , , , , ,M, ,SP, , , ,29.83,
13987,20110521,0953,11,FEW021, ,10.00, , , ,73, ,22.8, ,66, ,18.9, ,62, ,16.7, , 69, ,16, ,200, , , ,28.78, , , , , ,29.80, ,AA, , , ,29.83,
13987,20110521,1053,11,CLR, ,10.00, , , ,75, ,23.9, ,67, ,19.6, ,63, ,17.2, , 66, ,14, ,190, , , ,28.77, , , , , ,29.80, ,AA, , , ,29.82,
13987,20110521,1153,11,CLR, ,10.00, , , ,79, ,26.1, ,70, ,21.0, ,65, ,18.3, , 62, ,14, ,190, ,18, ,28.76, , , , , ,29.78, ,AA, , , ,29.81,
13987,20110521,1253,11,CLR, ,10.00, , , ,80, ,26.7, ,70, ,20.8, ,64, ,17.8, , 58, ,18, ,180, ,23, ,28.74, , , , , ,29.77, ,AA, , , ,29.79,
```

Fig. 14. An excerpt of the data taken from a weather station in the state of Missouri

In order to collect the suitable data that fit with the architecture of mHGN, the locations of the chosen weather stations that the data will be taken from, must build a figure like a circle, and the middle weather station must be located in the area in which a tornado has hit. The following is an excerpt of the data taken from a weather station Joplin in the State of Missouri (see Fig. 14).

5 Discussion

As is the case with pattern recognition of alphabets, patterns are more or less different to one another. However, in time series measurement data patterns, which are constructed from the measured values of the sensors, can be very similar to one another. Therefore, data representation of measured values before data is fed to the architecture of mHGN plays a big role in having very accurate results. False positive and true negative rate will also be indications to determine the quality of mHGN in forecasting natural disastesr.

The data that will be used to validate this work will be the data taken from different cities and different countries. As mHGN is trained one-cycle only, it is a challenge to choose which data is the right data for the training purpose, or the data is the consolidated data from a number of occurrences. When the appropriate training data has been applied, mHGN will then have a capability to forecast the tornado.

6 Conclusion

From the experiment results it is shown that mHGN has the capability to recognize multidimensional patterns. For simulating a tornado forecast, we have presented results of up to 5D architecture. As already discussed in [13, 14] there is no modification required if the architecture needs to be extended to bigger sizes of patterns. In the future this capability will be improved to the extent so, that multi oriented of multidimensional patterns will also be recognizable. At this stage it is also observed that mHGN still use a single cycle memorization and recall operation. The scheme still utilizes small response time that is insensitive to the increases in the number of stored patterns.

References

1. Cheng, R.T., Smith, R.E.: A nowcast model for tides and tidal currents in San Francisco Bay, California. In: Ocean Community Conference, Baltimore, USA (1998)
2. Ogasawara, J., Tanimoto, K., Imaichi, O., Yoshimoto, M.: Disaster prevention and response support solutions. Hitachi Rev. **63**(1), 236–243 (2014)
3. Sorensen, J.H.: Hazard warning systems: review of 20 years of progress. Nat. Hazards Rev. **1**(2), 119–125 (2000)
4. Kirschbaum, D.B., Adler, R., Hong, Y., Kumar, S., Peters-Lidard, C., Lerner-Lam, A.: Advances in landslide nowcasting: evaluation of a global and regional modeling approach. Environ. Earth Sci. **1**(1), 1–14 (2011)

5. Bellaire, S., Jamieson, B.: Nowcast with a forecast – snow cover simulations on slopes. J. Something **1**(1), 1–7 (2012)
6. Li, P., Lai, E.: Applications of radar-based nowcasting techniques for mesoscale weather forecasting in Hong Kong. Meteorol. Appl. **11**(1), 253–264 (2004)
7. Roy, S.S., Lakshmanan, V., Bhowmik, S.R., Thampi, S.: Doppler radar based nowcasting of cyclone ogni. J. Earth Syst. Sci. **119**(2), 183–199 (2009)
8. SuzukiI, Y., Michihiro, Y., Honma, M.: Development of strong wind nowcasting system. In: International Symposium on Extreme Weather and Cities, Tokyo, Japan (2013)
9. Winterrath, T., Rosenow, W.: The radar-based precipitation nowcasting system RADVOR of Deutscher Wetterdienst for the support of meteorological and hydrological alert systems. In: 8th European Conference on Radar in Meteorology and Hydrology, Germany (2014)
10. Kryvasheyeu, Y., Chen, H., Obradovich, N., Moro, E., Hentenryck, P.V., Fowler, J.: Nowcasting disaster damage. In: arXiv preprint arXiv:1504.06827 (2015)
11. Doong, D.J., Chuang, L.Z.H., Wu, L.C., Fan, Y.M., Kao, C.C., Wang, J.H.: Development of an operational coastal flooding early warning system. Nat. Hazards Earth Syst. Sci. **12**(1), 379–390 (2012)
12. Nasution, B.B., Sembiring, R.W., Sundawa, B.V., Gunawan, Amelia, A., Ismael, Sunjaya, H., Alifuddin, S., Pardede, M., Junaidi, Syahruddin M., Lubis, Z.: Realtime weather forecasting using multidimenssional Hierarchical Graph Neuron (mHGN). In: The 16th International Conference on Neural Networks (NN 2015), Rome, Italy (2015)
13. Nasution, B.B., Khan, A.I.: A hierarchical graph neuron scheme for real-time pattern recognition. IEEE Trans. Neural Netw. **19**(2), 212–229 (2008)
14. Nasution, B.B.: Towards real time multidimensional Hierarchical Graph Neuron (mHGN). In: The 2nd International Conference on Computer and Information Sciences 2014 (ICCOINS 2014), Kuala Lumpur, Malaysia (2014)

Enhancing Regional Digital Preparedness on Natural Hazards to Safeguard Business Resilience in the Asia-Pacific

Yanling Lee[1(✉)], Kenji Watanabe[2], and Wei-Sen Li[1]

[1] National Science and Technology Center for Disaster Reduction,
Taipei, Taiwan
sophiancdr@gmail.com, li.weisen@ncdr.nat.gov.tw
[2] Nagoya Institute of Technology, Nagoya, Japan

Abstract. In March 2015, the Sendai Framework for Disaster Risk Reduction (SFDRR) enforced during the Third UN World Conference on Disaster Risk Reduction. The SFDRR does not just succeed spirits and values of the Hyogo Framework for Action, but also leads the world entering a new phase of disaster risk reduction through stakeholders at national, regional and global levels. Among all regions around the world, the Asia-Pacific is the most vulnerable to natural hazards and climate changes. Disaster risk reduction (DRR) is critical concerned in terms of national security, economic quality growth, environmental sustainability and people's livelihoods. For regional consideration, a large-scale disaster could direct and indirect impact more than one countries due to the damaged or interrupted supply chain. Therefore, regional efforts on DRR have been a focal issue. After the 2011 Great Japan Earthquakes and Tsunami, an emergent global trend of developing strategy to strengthen global value chain or supply chain resilience via business continuity planning (BCP) approach engages the small and medium enterprises (SMEs) and the multinational or international corps to limit interruption and enhance cross border manufacturing, trade and investments. Base on the practical DRR project implementations and experiences over the years, the Asia-Pacific Economic Cooperation (APEC) identifies several key factors to promote disaster resilience in business sectors. The SFDRR also encourages innovation, science and technology DRR approaches i.e. big data and open day can help sharing the value-added information on enhancing capacity building of SMEs' disaster resilient capacity via decent risk communication tools for raising the risk awareness and level of digital preparedness. This paper describes to what extend the business sectors involved in and how to safeguard the cross-border trade and investments with safer and smarter regional strategies in the digital age with large-scale disasters.

Keywords: Business continuity plan (BCP) · Regional digital preparedness · Small and medium enterprises (SMEs) · Big data · Asia-Pacific Economic Cooperation (APEC)

1 High Vulnerabilities of Natural Hazards in the Asia-Pacific

Asia is one of the most competitive marketplaces in the world. Within the region, the struggle on compromising profits on supply chain interruption while disasters. Thus, the fruitful profits come from the significant economy growth via highly supply chain

© IFIP International Federation for Information Processing 2017
Published by Springer International Publishing AG 2017. All Rights Reserved
Y. Murayama et al. (Eds.): ITDRR 2016, IFIP AICT 501, pp. 170–182, 2017.
https://doi.org/10.1007/978-3-319-68486-4_14

integrated operations in the region of high vulnerabilities and exposures to natural hazards of Asia. From 2003–2013, the annual economic loss reach up to some US$68 billion in the Asia-Pacific Region [1]. The critical issues drawn by the average loses call upon the action plans for enhancing disaster resilience at regional level. Disasters not just adversely impact people's livelihoods, but also could interrupt regional or even global business operations, due to the direct impact on commodity shortage. In today's highly globalized and regionalized integration on production activities, more and more business units take advantages to governing global value chains for pursuing ultimate profitability, i.e. to navigate cross-border business networks of public and private sectors to coordinate the manufacturing, operations, financing, marketing and logistics on multiple product line suppliers and subcontractors in order to outreach the end consumers in various parts of the world.

Asia-Pacific Economic Cooperation (APEC) is one of a kind Asia-Pacific economic forum target to uphold the regional economic growth and prosperity. Twenty-one APEC member economies occupied 44% of global trade ($16.8 trillion) and 53% of world real GDP in purchasing power parity (PPP) terms ($35.8 trillion) created by 40% of world population (2.7 billion people) [2], (see Fig. 1).

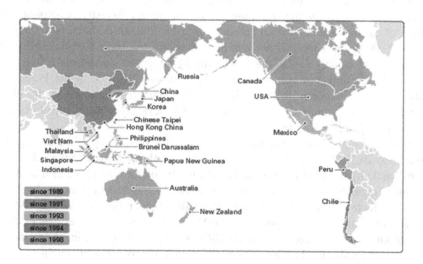

Fig. 1. APEC twenty-one member economies

2   Regional and Global Efforts on Promoting Business Continuity Since 2011 in the Asia-Pacific

Business Continuity Plan (BCP) is not an emergent idea in business management. A conventional BCP usually copes with threats of financial crisis, information interruptions and manufacturing accidents, instead of natural hazards. Learning experiences from the 2011 Great Japan Earthquakes and Tsunami, and the Floods in Thailand that clearly identify high vulnerabilities in business sectors and reminds business owners to develop traditional business continuity plan and include adverse impacts caused by natural disasters. Though interruptions, originated from business operations, cash flows or inconsistency of information, have been taken into serious consideration, but those setbacks are listed as daily-basis check-up items and most business units has plans to respond to the emergency by Standard Operation Procedures (SOPs). However, after a major disaster, chain effects of business interruptions would probable affect the whole supply chain domestically or even internationally. For example, the severe floods in Thailand caused ripple effects of business interruptions to automobile production line and PC manufacture activities in the Asia-Pacific. Likewise, the 2011 earthquakes and tsunami in Japan also brought down ICT industry and auto parts. Counting casualties and losses aftermath, economic loss exceeded 1.7 Billion Yen (equal to 3.4% GDP of Japan), death toll number (or missing) around twenty thousand, direct loss (including damaged households, manufacturing utilities, highways and bridges).

Beside the tangible damage and losses in Japan, it strongly impact the global markets of the supply chain interruption, especially from global supply chain viewpoint. In the 2011 earthquakes, the semi-conductor manufacturing and automobile industries were severely affected and interrupted in the Tohoku read in Japan. The consequences shown on the declining production in car industry. Comparing the number of car manufactured from February of 2011 (800,000), March (400,000) and April (290,000), the supply chain interruption shows the impact of the large-scale disaster toward Japan's global strategy on highly integrated operations. It may attributes to the declining of car productivity in Thailand (19.7%), in the Philippines (24.0%), and in Indonesia (6.1%). Likewise, manufacturers involved in the global value chain such as computer, smartphone and ICT device faced shortage of essential chips produced or supplied by Japan.

Therefore, a trend of enhancing preparedness for private sector by adding new elements to BCP has become an essential issue of disaster management. In 2012, International Organization for Standardization has introduced the ISO 22301 as a new standard to regulate disaster management activities for business operations. An APEC survey conducted by the Asia Disaster Reduction Center shows that over 79% of companies including large corporations and SMEs that these companies neither didn't have nor know business continuity plans (BCPs), (see Fig. 2) [3]. From observation of the trend, obviously, the business owners think that the governments ought to take a major proportion of disaster management and responsible to help them reduce losses and overlook certain obligations shouldered by the business owners themselves. To better enhance the whole society disaster resilience, how to motivate active participation and border engage the involvement from private sectors are the essential backbone supporting to succeed the public-private partnerships. BCP with factors of natural hazards is an ideal vehicle to transport concepts of disaster risk reduction, capacity building and emergency preparedness to business operations via robust preparation.

The main purposes to introduce BCP to business are:

1. Raise businesses' awareness and knowledge to develop disaster reduction/disaster preemptive mechanisms and responding teams.
2. Establish a process to help business develop tailor-made plan for solving foreseen challenges.
3. Help individual company in quickly resuming operation to strengthen business competitiveness and keep promises to clients and employees.

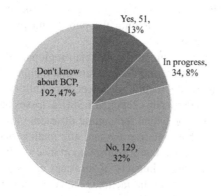

Fig. 2. Survey of adoption and awareness of BCP by the ADRC

More and more industries and corporations taking it seriously of the impacts brought by natural disasters as risks and threats to their employees, suppliers and customers after the 2011 earthquakes and tsunami in Japan. Hence, both public and private sectors recognize the importance of BCP, which can help formulating plans on the potential risks and scenario to further identifying internal, and external vulnerabilities with disaster risk awareness while disasters to ensure the business continuity, industry development and economies sustainability.

3 Primary Targets for Introducing Business Continuity

Australia and Thailand co-host the 2010 "APEC Workshop on Public Private Partnerships and Disaster Resilience" address the need to develop a whole society approach on enhancing disaster resilience and outline the common objectives with scope of collaborative partnerships.

After the Great East Japan Earthquakes and Tsunami in 2011, the Asia Disaster Reduction Centre (ADRC) survey on 267 large and small-medium enterprises within 17 APEC member economies shows the averaged statistic of 67% - "Don't know about BCP" or "Don't have BCP". Exclude the large enterprises, the percentage for SMEs' jumps high to 83% [4]. With limited BCPs availability, the high disaster risk ranking of the economic activities, business operations and product manufacturing in the disaster-prone areas show the vulnerability of global supply chain while natural hazards. Without proper BCPs in positon to go through risk identification, preparedness, emergency response and business resumption phases, disaster can lead the situations toward business and supply chain interruptions and even cease to exist. Compare with those enterprises with BCPs, the quicker recovery from the disaster can quick resume the business operations, which contribute to the regional supply chain connectivity to uphold the regional economic sustainability. However, with limited risk awareness, local knowledge and disaster risk reduction capacity building or training program, business units tend not to prepare in advance. In views of business continuity after disasters, this research depict how to define the information source and utilize the communications tools (ICTs) to better raising the general risk awareness and enhancing disaster resilience as well as encouraging the public and private sectors to develop BCPs for managing risk or impact.

SMEs make great contributions to the national, regional and global economy and trade. Nevertheless, the SMEs are fragile in nature that hampered global supply chains and business operations while natural disasters especially large-scale ones. From coverage of news media, the repeating reports of SMEs' losses occupied headlines year after year. It highlights to some extent the natural disasters impact SMEs in great deal and induce severe supply chain interruption and aftermath economic losses.

A few tangible existing facts confirm the importance of disaster resilience to the SMEs' operations. Firstly, direct impacts of disasters can stop the whole or partial production lines' operations due to the facilities damages, raw materials contaminated or even workforce casualties. Secondly, accompany by the inconvenient situations for SMEs to recover while interruption on water/electricity supply and transportations/logistics occurred. Thirdly, indirect impacts on slow economic and livelihood recovery to some extent cripple business operations especially SMEs'.

Without doubts, flexibility is the key strength of SME to rapidly adapt to the changes of competitive marketplace. SMEs, compared to the large corporations, have relatively little and limited finical support, knowledge and human resource to cope with the risk and exposure to natural hazards. In global economic lifecycle, SME is the fundamental unit to contribute to the local community incomes and regional business economic growth. By reviewing other issues related to disaster management on public private partnership (PPP), disaster resilience and emergency preparedness, it is shown a common trend and demands of SME on mitigating potential disaster risk. As consequence, BCP is an ideal approach to linkage among business people, key stakeholders and disaster managers jointly to work on improving disaster resilience.

The ten easy steps for building up SME's BCP, developed base on ISO22301 Business Continuity Management Standard System, have been introduced to the Asia-Pacific region since 2012 by training workshops and document circulation. The ten steps are composed [5]:

1. Determine BCP purpose, scope and team.
2. Prioritized activities and Recovery Time Objective.
3. What do you need to resume key activities?
4. Risk assessment – know your tragic scenarios.

5. Do not forget pre-disaster protection and mitigation.
6. Emergency response to disaster.
7. BC Strategies to early resumption.
8. Be financially prepared.
9. Exercise makes your plan functional.
10. Ongoing review and improvement.

4   Integrated Big Data Sets for Coordinating Digital Preparedness for Natural Hazards

Case studies from the recent large-scale disaster in the Asia Pacific clearly identify the emerging demands on big data and open data application in time of disasters for emergency preparedness. As a whole society from public services, private industries and general publics, a verified reliable information through the revolution concept of big data and open data is critical for formulating the dynamic DRR strategies and BCPs, deploying emergency relief missions, ensuring global supply chain resilience and maintaining quality growth and livelihoods security. Asia is one of the disaster-prone region, cross-border capacity building and training program, scenario-based drills and exercises on big data and open data on enhancing disaster-resilient manufacturing, trade and investment can direct benefit both of the regional economic sustainability and of human security.

Recent projects of business resilience and global chain resilience, conducted by APEC Small and Medium Enterprises Working Group (SMEWG) and APEC Transportation Working Group (TPTWG) respectively, emphasize importance of applying data and information for achieving smarter investments and building up safer trade environment. For twenty-one member economies of APEC to share the synergies of economic prosperity, regional capacity building and public-private partnership, it is vital to broadly adopt the big data and open data information sharing on emergency preparedness approach to concrete solid and sound foundation for global value/supply chain resilience to artery connect and support business and economic activities in the Asia-Pacific region.

Digital preparedness is a cornerstone of evidence-based DRR approach, which offers value-added knowledge for emergent response while decision-making, process from big data and open data to information intelligence. However, there are technical and policy barriers for developing countries to utilized crowdsourcing, ICTs or Internet of Things (IoT) technology to build up an analytical database and integrated systems with proper telecommunication tools for cross-border BCPs or regional emergency preparedness from data collection to applications, especially for a cross-border or large-scale disasters. Taking into account of the diverse social-economic data sets of demographic characteristics, economic activities, educational background, gender, level of public awareness etc., it is essential to carefully interpret and identify the social vulnerability with gaps for enhancing regional capacity building as a whole society. These parameters from social science perspectives help capacity building at community level and reshaping actionable information from "big data and open data" approach for sustainable economic and business activities.

5   Best Practices on Digital Preparedness in Taiwan Through Public-Private Partnership

Taiwan is a highly disaster-prone country and how to mitigate disaster risk is an essential issue catching attentions from both government and the public. However, due to extreme weather events and potential large-scale earthquakes, risk exposures to land and population increase and become more diverse than ever. In past two decades, the Ministry of Science and Technology has been investing resources on fundamental scientific and technological researches related to characteristics of natural hazards and knowledge for disaster management that helps to pave the basis developing disaster risk reduction and emergency preparedness. Nowadays, emerging technologies speed up the telecommunications development and shorten the lead time from data to deliverable messages in the digital age. In information age, big data and open data not just facilitate trades and business, but also benefit disaster management as a whole.

In case of the lessons learnt from the 2011 Great Japan Earthquakes and Tsunami, specific big datasets can provide a dynamic view on human behaviors and reactions to the shakings and warnings as well as the traffic flow in different phases. From Pre-disaster to post disaster phase, from data to reliable information or message is critical for raising public awareness. An updated information with better risk communication approaches can mitigate the disturbance while emergency respond and level up the quality DRR assessments with higher public awareness of emergency situations. Applying open data principles to big data, it will enhance social preparedness and resilience. Since 2013, Taiwan has introduced the Common Alerting Protocol (CAP) to standardize disaster information for dissemination though multiple channels. Google Crisis Map is one of the platforms in building up the last mile to connect people living in Taiwan and one of the easy access tools to adopt in sending the demanding information in times of disasters. Later, in 2016, five system operators of the fourth-generation (4G) telecommunications officially join to provide the Cell Broadcasting Service (CBS) to mobile phone users. It is an innovative approach to facilitate raising public awareness and ensure wide coverage of the dissemination of information during emergency with in time collaborations among public and private sectors.

In 2009, Typhoon Morakot brought record-breaking rainfalls which caused massive floods and large-scale landslides in the southern Taiwan. The tremendous casualties and losses pushed forward a restructure of disaster management framework and the full commitment of improving emergency operation via information integration. The improvement on meeting the quality information demands for decision-making required to tackle of what we have been exposed to when Typhoon Morakot strike - no adequate collaborations and synergies among respective governmental agencies and authorities at all level to disseminate and interpret the just-in-time effective integrated information for proactive emergency preparedness and response.

One of the key reasons for formulating an integrated information framework on decision-making support is that too many existing individual systems operated independently by each government authority and provided only fragment of information in different time span. Hence, an efficient coordinated emergency preparedness and response countermeasure cannot be deployed in time without the holistic views and pictures of the real situations and the impact assessments on Typhoon Morakot prior to the disasters hit. To cope with the incompatibility of data sets, file structures and value-added information via the social media related to typhoons, floods and precipitation-triggered landslides, the remedial countermeasures request decisive decisions to acquired and incorporated science and technology efforts for integration - 'one Taiwan one respond'. The evidence-based emergency operation needs the implementation of applying improved numerical ensemble models to forecast trajectories and rain of typhoons, producing potential risk maps of inundation for scenario simulation, integrating real-time monitoring data for further decision making. All the outcomes and collective verified information are displayed on GIS-Web-based platform for discussion and decision-making at all level of the government authorities and Emergency Operation Centers (EOCs). Without doubts, big data is the core behind the scene to support the emergency preparedness and operations.

In recent years, the scope of information sharing has extended from central to local governments and NGOs to help enhancing information preparedness at grassroots levels. For local governments, delayed or inadequate information hampers and slows down the process of decision making. Information dissemination and sharing from central to local governments fill in the gap of miss-links information and provides a common operation picture to bring meaningful discussions-speak on the same page. Collaborations with NGOs on helping them to allocate resources in advance, governments can benefit from receiving the NOGs feedbacks as the reliable on-site data source for information and data collection. The mechanism of big data integration is shown in Fig. 3 [6].

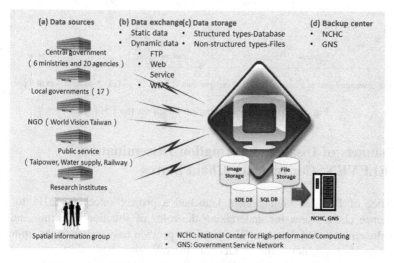

Fig. 3. Integration mechanism of big data [6].

It is always a challenging question to answer - how many and where are people staying - or - when will the next destructive earthquakes hit? For the number of the affected people, through an averaged estimation of population distribution, allocating population proportional to floor areas based on census statistics and taxation data could calculate it. However, it presents a static status of population distribution but real time facts, which does not fully reflect people's dynamic movements in urban districts or national wide around the clock while disasters. As scenario analysis for seismic risk reduction in urban areas, locations, population density and distribution are the key factors, which shape the strategic approaches on how to mitigate possible casualties claimed by a large-scale earthquake.

To resolve the situation, National Science and Technology Center for Disaster Reduction (NCDR) collaborated with the Chunghwa Telecom (CHT), a major telecom service provider occupies 37.90% of the mobile service in Taiwan [7], to tracing mobile signals for collecting numbers of mobile users at specific grids to estimate population distribution pattern. The scope of the pilot project covers three major metropolitan areas in north Taiwan, Taipei City, New Taipei City and Keelung City with numbers of population at 2,695,007, 3,959,855 and 373,721 respectively. The CHT provides data updates three times; at 9 am, at 3 pm and 9 pm; every day that roughly reflects dynamic characteristics of urban population flow and allocation pattern in the urban area as illustrated in the Fig. 4.

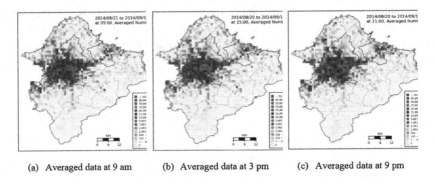

(a) Averaged data at 9 am   (b) Averaged data at 3 pm   (c) Averaged data at 9 pm

Fig. 4. Population distribution based on the CHT data

6   Channels of Disaster Information Dissemination - 7-ELEVEN, Convenience Chain Stores

The Office of Disaster Management launched a project since late 2011 to recruit convenience chain stores for undertaking the roles of situation reporting and information dissemination if disasters. The aim is to provide easy access to the up-to-dated information if emergencies and to facilitate the efficiency and effectiveness of emergency response at township level. The Uni-President Corporation, the holding company of 7-ELEVEN in Taiwan, is the first one of the partners to join the above-mentioned project. Uni-President, one of the largest consumer product manufacturers, runs 7-ELEVEN chain stores numbering over 4,800 retail outlets with comparably wide coverage of in-land logistics networking in Taiwan.

To facilitate the efficient and effective information dissemination, each 7-ELEVEN is well equipped with a LCD panel at cashier displayed possible risks or threats with relevant emergency information on site at local level as illustrated in the Fig. 5. During the 2012 typhoon season (usually from May to October), 7-ELEVEN has piloted a successful story on public private partnership. Their customers including drop-by tourists are well informed and benefit from the real-time typhoon and weather related information via these LCD panels to avoid the possible impact on floods in the immediate areas. In the case of floods, the person in charge of the disaster reporting at 7-ELEVENs will direct report their observations on water levels in real-time basis to the Water Resource Agency(WRA), the government authority of floods. The WRA will relay the confirmed flood cases to the emergency operation center at central or local level for further emergency response i.e. road closure or search and rescue (SAR) deployment.

Fig. 5. Updates on Typhoon displayed on 7-ELEVEN LCD Panel

7 Open Data on the Common Alerting Protocol (CAP)

For further expand coverage on information dissemination during typhoon season, Google starts to offer its services on displaying and disseminating the real-time warning messages by Google Crisis Map, Google Alerts and Google Now. The data sources of warning messages, follow the CAP - an international standard, are come from nine government authorities and public transportation servicing sectors. Messages in CAP format are open to the internet service providers, APP developers, research institutes and industries as open data for them further develop disaster related researches/systems or the innovative DRR APPs and etc. from the free-of-charge information.

Smartphone is another ideal handy device to catch warning messages in the sense of point to point and end to end services, direct to the end users concept. With introducing the 4G mobile technique, a cell broadcasting system (CBS) project is ongoing to send alerts and warnings by the Public Warning System (PWS), which put through the sound of the sirens or alarms as top priority emergency messages from Mobile Network Operator (NNO) to the smartphone users, if earthquakes or any immediate emergency.

8 Conclusion to Move Forward – Enhancing Digital Preparedness on Natural Hazards for Sound and Smarter Investments

The cross-border movements of goods, services and workforce grow rapidly and rather dynamically in the Asia-Pacific. The natural disaster warnings and alerts from big data and open data approach can provide the best and holistic common pictures to effectively integrate the information flow with partnership between public and private sectors to mitigate the impacts. For particularly note, the newly emerging technology accelerate the development of telecommunications technology and shortens the lead time of data processing and information dissemination. Wide coverage of disaster related information dissemination contributes by social media, 7-Eleven chain store, smartphone, MNO etc. In the digital age, big data and open data approach plays the key role in saving lives, securing livelihood, facilitating trade and investments, enhancing business resiliency in operations, raising disaster risk awareness for better emergency preparedness, formulating business continuity plan, maintaining resilient global supply chain, protecting critical infrastructure and safeguarding tourism industries.

In the case of the 2011 Great Japan Earthquakes and Tsunami, Using proper big datasets can facilitate interpret human behaviors and reactions to provide more comprehensive pictures and views to the shakings, warnings efficiencies and the traffic flow situation in different phases of disasters. From Pre-disaster to post-disaster phases, big data and open data approach can deliver just in time message to maintain the effective and efficient risk communication with higher level of public awareness through public private partnership to deploy emergency response effort and to deliver quality DRR assessments if situations.

APEC for a studies conclude the emergent needs to adopt big data and open data approach on large scale disaster with cross-border view of digital preparedness while emergency. To include whole society from public sectors to private industries and general publics, a comprehensive picture for emergency response using real time big data and open data is vital to succeed the collaborative interoperability operations from adopting DRR strategies, BCPs, deploying emergency relief missions and mitigating losses for sustainable economic growth and human security. A disaster-prone region, regional capacity building programs and training on BCPs and promoting big data and open data approach can ensure safer and smarter cross-border trades and investments in the booming economies of Asia.

The core value of the key objectives on enhancing digital preparedness against natural disasters is the real-time information sharing and interoperability with cross-border capacity building on crosscutting demands with synergies. The objectives are shown as below:

1. To picture the capacity building among APEC member economies in adopting big data and open data approach to build up a foundation for information sharing mechanism;
2. To interpret on-demand big data and open data through a region-wide survey to further identify shortfalls, challenges and opportunities that public and private sectors concerned the most;
3. To promote big data and open data approach to provide safer marketplace and enhance global supply chain resilience through quality BCPs, transparent real-time risk information disclosure and resilient critical infrastructure protection plan in position;
4. To formulate a collaborative real-time focal point network and mechanism on sharing cross-border big data and open data on better emergency preparedness to facilitate integrated actions and capacity building on DRR at regional level as a whole society.

Introducing science-and-technology based sharing mechanism through ICTs to enhance BCPs and digital preparedness on DRR is a global trend as the SFDRR highlighted in the third WCDRR. Without doubts, a solid backbone support via ICTs can benefit the stakeholders with synergy in all phases of disaster management from mitigation, preparedness, response to recovery in the Asia-Pacific region.

References

1. EM-DAT International Disaster Database. http://www.emdat.be/database
2. Asia-Pacific Economic Cooperation's Stats APEC: Key Indicators Database and Bilateral Linkages Database, November 2011
3. Asian Disaster Reduction Center (ADRC).: A Better Understanding of the Current Status of BCP Adoption and the Level of BCP Awareness among Private Sector SMEs in the APEC Region (2011)
4. Source: Asian Disaster Reduction Center (ADRC)
5. Guidebook on SME Business Continuity Planning. http://publications.apec.org/publication-detail.php?pub_id=1449/
6. Source: National Science and Technology Center for Disaster Reduction (NCDR)
7. Chunghwa Telecom Operation Report – the 1st Quarter, 2016 TSE: 2412 NYSE: CHT, 28 April (2016). http://www.cht.com.tw/ir/upload/content/20160428_1Q2016_presentation_CH_final.pdf
8. APEC Emergency Preparedness Working Group. http://www.apec.org/groups/som-steering-committee-on-economic-and-technical-cooperation/working-groups/emergency-preparedness.aspx
9. APEC Emergency Preparedness Working Group: In the category of 2011 outcomes of activities. http://www.apec-epwg.org/

10. APEC SME Crisis Management Center: Multiple-year Project on Disaster Resilience Building for SMEs in APEC. (M SCE 02/2011A_Improving Natural Disaster Resilience of APEC SMEs to Facilitate Trade and Investment) (2011)
11. Completion Report of Multi-Year Project: Improving Natural Disaster Resilience of APEC SMEs to Facilitate Trade and Investment. http://www.apec-epwg.org/public/uploadfile/act/2c0ca0199ba34676c3a21032d8e03918.pdf

A Comprehensive Decision Support System for Enhanced Emergency Decision Management and Training

Odd Steen[1]([✉]), Andrew Pope[2], Marion Rauner[3], Nicklas Holmberg[1],
Simon Woodworth[2], Sheila O'Riordan[2], Helmut Niessner[4],
and Karen Neville[2]

[1] Department of Informatics, Lund University, Lund, Sweden
{odd.steen, nicklas.holmberg}@ics.lu.se
[2] Business Information Systems, University College Cork, Cork, Ireland
{a.pope, S.Woodworth, sheila.oriordan,
KarenNeville}@ucc.ie
[3] Department of Innovation and Technology Management,
University of Vienna, Vienna, Austria
marion.rauner@univie.ac.at
[4] School of Business and Economics, University of Vienna, Vienna, Austria
helmut.niessner@univie.ac.at

Abstract. Emergency decision makers face a challenge taking rapid and high-risk decisions during an emergency situation, especially when the emergency is cross-border and requires multi-agency cooperation. The emergency decision makers use emergency management (EM) system and sometimes decision support systems (DSS) when responding to a crisis. To date the emergency decision makers have not had access to a system that supports them in all facets of the full EM cycle. This paper describes work in progress designing and building a comprehensive system of systems that intend to be that support for emergency decision makers. The system has successfully demonstrated its value from a technical and user perspective. Future tests will demonstrate if it will enhance decision management in reality-based emergency scenarios.

Keywords: Emergency management · Emergency management systems · Emergency decision making · Emergency decision support systems · Emergency management taxonomies

1 Introduction

Large scale emergency situations – be they natural, deliberate or accidental – are inevitable. They do not respect borders, a large number of people and animals, both domesticated and wild, die and the long-term consequences from economic to mental health can for years devastate the affected population.

When emergency decision-takers respond to emergency situations they are sometimes overwhelmed by decision-making [1]. They are required to, based on accessible

© IFIP International Federation for Information Processing 2017
Published by Springer International Publishing AG 2017. All Rights Reserved
Y. Murayama et al. (Eds.): ITDRR 2016, IFIP AICT 501, pp. 183–197, 2017.
https://doi.org/10.1007/978-3-319-68486-4_15

and available information, make rapid high-risk decisions when responding to an emergency situation. Quick decisions regarding allocation of strained resources, prioritizing casualties, while simultaneously trying to contain the level of impact are challenging.

To better manage and respond to emergency situations, emergency decision makers are often supported by disaster management systems that can e.g. provide graphical representation of relevant data about the emergency and its consequences. Even if decision support systems (DSS) have been used for emergency management [2, 3] a problem of disaster management systems is the lack of active decision making support needed for effective and efficient emergency responses.

Decision making under emergency situations requires special DSS to be prepared and account for often unforeseen, unique, complex, extreme, and evolving situations and issues that emerge during disasters [4, 5]. Emergency responders require real-time data and learning/modelling tools to best cope with such situations based on related disaster scenarios. Such a decision support would for instance need to provide capabilities to allocate available and often scarce resources to improve the identification and management of assets during an emergency response [6]. These systems need to integrate multiple components, such as: geographic information systems (GIS), storm tracking tools, damage projection and flooding models, and models for evacuating an affected population [4]. Also, the decision makers need training in emergency management to be better prepared for an emergency situation. Hence, not only is support for decision making in a live situation needed, but also for training of emergency decision makers.

These challenges are addressed by the S-HELP (Securing Health Emergency Learning and Planning) project [7]. With a Design Science Research [8, 9] approach the project researches and develops a comprehensive DSS for end-users to be better prepared, make better decisions, and perform better in emergency situations. The S-HELP DSS will provide support for rapid and effective decision-making for all stages of the emergency management lifecycle [10] from mitigation and preparedness (pre-disaster) to response and recovery (post-disaster).

The challenges for the S-HELP project is to design a DSS that:

- Is flexible enough to integrate with existing legacy systems and tools.
- Offer advanced capabilities and functionalities such as learning approaches based on taxonomies to increase semantic and organizational interoperability of cross-border multi-agency response.
- Facilitate emergency responders to overcome operational inefficiencies and delays regarding coordination and communication to best handle time critical major disaster situations.

Based on this the research question of the paper is: How should a system that meet these challenges be designed? The purpose of the paper is to describe and discuss work in progress designing and building the system of artefacts that will provide a comprehensive support for emergency decision-makers and thus be the DSS that hitherto has been missing.

In Sect. 2, the foundational emergency management taxonomies are discussed. Next, the S-HELP overarching system architecture and interoperability is presented in Sect. 3, followed by a more detailed description of the major system components in Sect. 4. How the system is tested is discussed in Sect. 5. Finally, the conclusion in Sect. 6 provides policy implications and further research.

2 Foundational Taxonomies for Emergency Management

In the S-HELP project, a DSS is developed for end-users to be better prepared, make better decisions, and perform better in emergency situations. For this reason, an SHELP strategic disaster management wiki to classify disasters (disaster risk, disaster types, extent of event, vulnerability) was created, to illustrate decision making, and to explain the emergency management (EM) environment, emergency management cycle, and the stakeholders involved [11, 12]. This content was expanded by emergency interventions/ tasks and emergency resources (emergency responders/skills, equipment and materials, information and data) under consideration of the EU civil protection mechanism (including the EU Civil Protection Modules, [13]). Furthermore, key terms for the three S-HELP disaster scenarios (chemical spill, flooding, biological hazard) were included. The S-HELP strategic disaster management wiki was implemented using the wiki platform of the University of Vienna, Austria which can be accessed via https://wiki. univie.ac.at/display/SHELP/. To enhance semantic and organizational interoperability of end-users [14], the above content was incorporated in the S-HELP DSS as described in Sects. 3 and 4.

The strategic disaster management wiki contains main figures, describes terms, links to essential EM organizations, and refers to key literature [11, 12]. The second release of the wiki incorporates 951 glossary terms and 33 figures based on 183 references to the literature.

In Fig. 1 the strategic disaster management wiki (#1; [11, 12]) represents an essential foundation for the skills taxonomy (#2; [15, 16]), resources taxonomy (#3; [17]), and skills/disaster taxonomy (#4; [18]). These three taxonomies were implemented into the S-HELP DSS as described in Sects. 3 and 4.

These components of the S-HELP DSS play a key role in training end-users regarding general strategic disaster management for more effective and efficient emergency management, communication, and operation.

The co-operation of different multi-disciplinary emergency responders in disaster management is highly complex in emergency preparedness, response, and recovery. End users want to know who of the emergency responders are needed for which emergency interventions/tasks by using what emergency equipment/material in order that emergency management can be better performed and interoperability is increased.

For the skills taxonomy (#2 of Fig. 1) main emergency interventions/tasks performed by emergency responders using emergency material/equipment and EU Civil Protection Modules were investigated. Based on this, a skills taxonomy was developed by interlinking emergency interventions/tasks and emergency responders/ skills [15, 16].

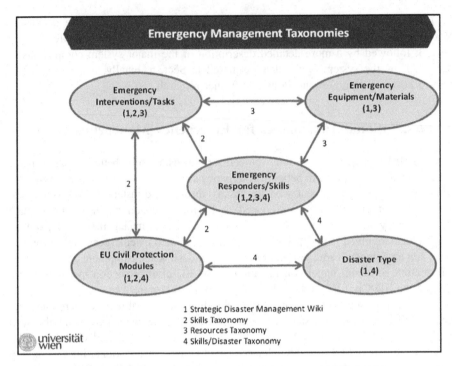

Fig. 1. Foundational emergency taxonomies for the S-HELP DSS

Eleven main interventions were considered including their related tasks: (1) general emergency management, (2) emergency communication, (3) forewarning, (4) evacuation management, (5) impact response, (6) search and rescue, (7) emergency transportation, (8) emergency engineering, (9) emergency shelter, (10) emergency food program, as well as (11) care of vulnerable and secure groups. Emergency responders were classified into: (1) core emergency responders (e.g., government, health care organizations, emergency services), non-core emergency responders (e.g., government, strategic health authorities, health care organizations, energy providers, food and beverage providers, information and communication services, transportation services, waste disposal services, water and sewerage undertakers), as well as co-operating bodies (military, communities, environmental agencies, media, voluntary sector).

EU Civil Protection Modules contain human and material resources of one or more member states and are able to perform pre-defined tasks in the areas of response [19, 20]: (1) advanced medical post, (2) advanced medical post with surgery, (3) aerial forest firefighting module using airplanes, (4) aerial forest firefighting module using helicopters, (5) chemical, biological, radiological, and nuclear detection and sampling, (6) emergency temporary shelter, (7) field hospital, (8) flood containment, (9) flood rescue using boats, (10) ground forest firefighting, (11) ground forest firefighting using vehicles, (12) heavy urban search and rescue, (13) high capacity pumping, (14) medical aerial evacuation of disaster victims, (15) medium urban search and rescue, (16) search and rescue in chemical, biological, radiological, and nuclear conditions, and (17) technical assistance and support team, as well as water purification.

In the resources taxonomy (#3 of Fig. 1) UNIVIE [17] interlinked emergency interventions/tasks and emergency responder/skills (skills taxonomy) to emergency equipment/materials needed including information and data.

The advantage of the S-HELP DSS to handle three emergency scenarios (chemical spill, flooding, biological hazard) in several example countries (Austria, England, Ireland, Israel, and Northern Ireland) was investigated. It was found that the emergency responders, i.e., core and non-core emergency responders as well as co-operating bodies, responding to a disaster differ according to the underlying disaster type. These were categorized into: (1) natural disasters (biological, cosmological, geophysical, hydro-meteorological), (2) man-made disasters (socio-technical disasters, human conflicts, (3) hybrid disasters (both natural and man-made disasters), and (4) sub-sequent disasters [12]. To enhance interoperability among end-users of different countries, a generic skills/disaster taxonomy which is applicable for any country was developed (#4 of Fig. 1; [18]). Such differences in emergency responders were illustrated for the three S-HELP scenarios (flooding $\rightarrow$ natural disaster $\rightarrow$ hydro-meteorological disaster $\rightarrow$ hydrological disaster; chemical spill $\rightarrow$ socio-technical disaster $\rightarrow$ technological disaster; biological hazard $\rightarrow$ natural disaster $\rightarrow$ biological disaster $\rightarrow$ epidemic) under consideration of the EU Civil Protection Modules. For the S-HELP flooding scenario, the primary and main core emergency responders are the emergency medical service, the fire brigade, and the police [21]. Several EU Civil Protection Modules are suitable for a flooding which might be called via the Emergency Response Coordination Centre: (1) emergency temporary shelter, (2) flood containment, (3) flood rescue using boats, (4) high capacity pumping, (5) technical assistance and support team, and (6) water purification [18].

3 The S-HELP DSS Overarching Architecture

The S-HELP architecture employs a modular design (Fig. 2). This ensures that components in S-HELP are broadly self-contained units that provide tools and decision support functionality around a specific area of the emergency management problem domain. For example, the situation component provides a high level management of the emergency situations modelled within the system.

The knowledge management component provides an interface and functionality relating to the large amounts of documentation and other knowledge assets that exists within the system. While each component on its own provides a level of functionality relating to its 'area of expertise', it is through the connection between components that the full power of the system may be realized.

3.1 Overview of the S-HELP System Components

As seen in the systems architecture model (Fig. 2) the comprehensive S-HELP DSS for emergency management and training comprises a collection of artefacts that together form an eco-system of vital components. Each component by itself is less important without the situational operability formed by interlinking the components into a whole system of systems. The overview below summarizes the components and their place and capability in the eco-system.

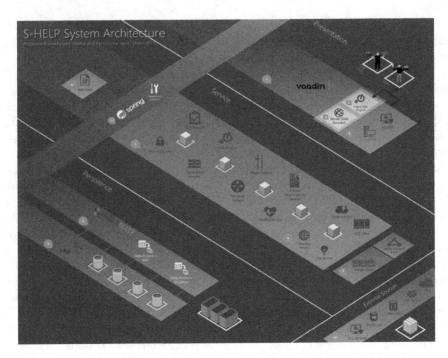

Fig. 2. S-HELP DSS Architecture [22]

Situation Component. Provides an overview of current live situations and associated incidents. Allows user to join situations based on access rights and role.

Current Recognized Situation (CRS) Component. The implementation of an EM information management system. Provides a high level reporting summary of data provided by other S-HELP components. Can be customized to accommodate alternative views and information management frameworks. This component provides the basis for a common operational picture that can be used by all agencies collaborating during an emergency situation.

Logging Component. Provides information managers with a system log of all content generated by S-HELP and external components and traditional data sources (e.g. telephone calls, weather alerts, media reports and e-mails). The information manager can choose data from the logging component and send directly to the CRS component as appropriate.

Learning Management System (LMS) Component. The S-HELP LMS platform provides admin tools, content authoring tools, communication tools, skills and performance management tools, and content management tools. The LMS platform facilitates the "End User Training Programme Concept" incorporating emergency management decision making and additional training content. Moreover, the LMS toolset integrates with the S-HELP modular architecture such that training and learning material can be surfaced and shared with other S-HELP components as appropriate.

Knowledge Management System (KMS) Component. A repository of organizational best practices incorporating standard operating procedures (SOPs), existing plans and past response structures, and GIS models. Content can be tagged using the S-HELP taxonomy and location information. As such, relevant content is surfaced automatically based on incident type and location. Surfacing relevant plans, case studies, models, and past incident responses plays a vital role in ensuring that trainees can acquire the experiential knowledge gleaned from past incidents. Moreover, an expert's database will ensure that users can identify, locate and contact those with expertise relevant to the current incident or training scenario.

Geographical Information System (GIS) Component. An INSPIRE compliant spatial database management system and front-end incorporating ArcGIS. Provides users with capabilities to visualize critical infrastructure and also assess hazard impact using rich datasets, modelling and spatial analysis tools. The GIS tool can also be used for training, exercises and response. The tool provides real-time visualization of hazards and incident response. The interactive features allow for end users to engage with the data for decision making and coordination purposes. The ability to import and export external models and shapes enhances multiagency coordination through the sharing of incident-specific critical information and data. Likewise, previous incidents and models can be geocoded such that relevant models are surfaced to the user based on the incident type and incident locale.

Twitter Component. The twitter component gathers information from the social media service Twitter. S-HELP users can search for tweets statically using location data (input manually or derived from location of current situation). Relevant tweets are displayed on a map and clustered accordingly. Relevant user information and tweet content will be displayed. Additionally, trending topics can be requested for given locations. A streaming service that reports and displays new tweets that relate to topics of given S-HELP users' preferences is also available. Using topic filters, the twitter module will display new tweets that meet the S-HELP users' filter queries, and it will do so in real time.

4 Major Backbone System Components

Essential for emergency decision making and training using the S-HELP DSS is the provision of generic and situational data consistent with the taxonomies (cf. Sect. 2), interlinked emergency management documents and Standard Operating Procedures (SOP) documents, and geographic emergency data. Four major components of the S-HELP DSS form a back-bone infrastructure: the Knowledge Management System (KMS) component, the Repository for Data Sets component, the Document Management System (DMS) component, and the Current Recognized Situation (CRS) component.

4.1 Knowledge Management System (KMS)

A key enabler of the S-HELP DSS approach is the creation of a Knowledge Management System to create, store and transfer the knowledge assets that comprise the experiential knowledge of emergency management practitioners. This will facilitate individual and inter- and intra-group learning in crisis management decision-making. The creation of a Learning and Knowledge Management Systems (LKMS) necessitates the integration of a Learning Tool-set and Knowledge Management System.

The LKMS comprises a repository for data sets realized as a relational database that stores emergency and disaster typology data consistent with the Emergency Management Taxonomies (cf. Sect. 2). Furthermore, it is integrated with a knowledge repository (Open KM) that supports the storage and transfer of knowledge assets in the form of standard operating procedures, emergency plans, business process models, expert yellow pages and other relevant documents. This powerful knowledge repository has been integrated with a learning platform (Moodle), and learning tools, that facilitate the training of key emergency management personnel.

4.2   Repository for Data Sets Component

Viewed from an enterprise architecture perspective [23, 24] the taxonomies discussed in Sect. 2 identify the inventory (row 1, column 1 in the Zachman Framework for EA v. 3.0) for the S-HELP LKMS, answering to the requirements set by the intentions (row 1, column 6 in the Zachman Framework for EA v. 3.0). Thus, the taxonomies specify the business concepts about which data needs to be managed in order for the S-HELP system to be able to fulfill the goals and intentions set by the planners of the system.

Based on the inventory identification the inventory specification (row 2, column 1 in the Zachman Framework for EA v. 3.0) was digitally transformed [25] into a Unified Modeling Language (UML) conceptual model (see Fig. 3).

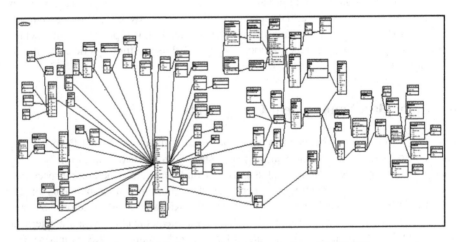

Fig. 3. S-HELP data repository conceptual model [26, 27]

The conceptual model was transformed into a relational logical model (see Fig. 4) for the data set repository, and then further to a physical data model implemented in MySql Server 5.6.

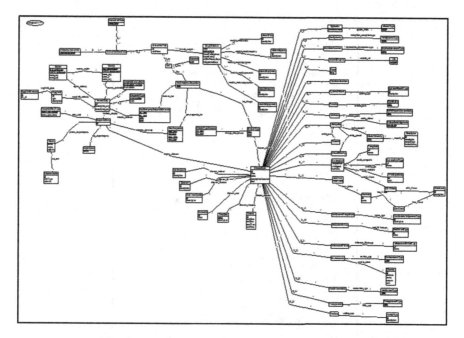

Fig. 4. S-HELP data repository logical model [26, 27]

Through this digital transformation, the data repository partly automates and digitalizes the foundational emergency management taxonomies.

The data set repository makes it possible to store and retrieve information about e.g. what kind of resources a generic emergency responder uses for one or more emergency tasks in responding to a specific type of emergency (e.g. a flood), as discussed in Sect. 2 (see Figs. 5 and 6).

When the data set repository is populated with generic and specific, real incident data it will be a knowledge base of both general and situated emergency information that could be queried by emergency decision makers during a live incident or fed as data into emergency responder training scenarios used for the Learning and Knowledge Management System (LKMS).

The output in Fig. 6 shows that in the 'London' region of the country 'UK' the 'County Police' acts as the generic key emergency responder (KER) 'Police', using e.g. the generic resource type 'Checklists/Plans' while performing the 'Evacuating' Intervention Task of the 'Evacuation Management' Emergency Intervention type in the 'Response' Intervention Phase to manage an emergency incident.

As each country have built up their own and nationally tailored organization and structure of emergency management, it is important that total flexibility is guaranteed in associating a national responder body to a generic responder in the taxonomy.

The Party Pattern [28] made it possible to record that a responder party (individual, organisation, or both) assumes the role of a national responder for a certain unique disaster event. The responder party type also assumes the responsibilities of a generic key emergency responder for a determined period. Modelling principles from [23]

```
SELECT
       `type` AS 'Resource Type'
       ,taskName AS 'Intervention Task'
       ,phaseName AS 'Intervention Phase'
       ,interventionName AS 'Emergency Intervention'
       ,u.label AS 'Key Emergency Responder'
       ,nk.rel_label AS 'Related Key Emergency Responder'
       ,nb.description_eng AS 'National Body'
       ,nb.NUTS_countrycode AS 'Country'
       ,r.name_eng AS 'Region'
FROM
       uses u
              JOIN
       InterventionTask it
              ON
       u.id = it.id
              JOIN
       InterventionPhaseTask ipt
              ON
       u.id = ipt.id
              JOIN
       natbody_kerstruct nk
              ON
       u.label = nk.label
              JOIN
       NationalBody nb
              ON
       nk.id = nb.id
              JOIN
       region_natbody rn
              ON
       nb.id = rn.id
              JOIN
       Region r
              ON
       rn.NUTS_regioncode = r.NUTS_regioncode
              AND
       rn.ISO_regioncode = r.ISO_regioncode
WHERE
       nb.NUTS_countrycode LIKE 'UK'
```

Fig. 5. An example data repository query in S-HELP

Resource Type	Intervention Task	Intervention Phase	Emergency Intervention	KER	Related KER	National Body	Country	Region
Checklists/Plans	Evacuating	RESPONSE	EVACUATION_MANAGEMENT	Police	Emergency Services	County Police	UK	London
Communication Devices	Evacuating	RESPONSE	EVACUATION_MANAGEMENT	Police	Emergency Services	County Police	UK	London
Communication Equipment/Materials	Evacuating	RESPONSE	EVACUATION_MANAGEMENT	Police	Emergency Services	County Police	UK	London
Communication Systems	Evacuating	RESPONSE	EVACUATION_MANAGEMENT	Police	Emergency Services	County Police	UK	London

Fig. 6. Output from the query in Fig. 5 (only a few lines showing)

made it possible to manage relations between super and sub entities through type entities, as well as maintaining dynamic hierarchical structures between data elements reflecting the taxonomies.

Combining all these connections gives the possibility to record what person and/or organization that acts as a national responder for a certain disaster event and also what person and/or organization that acts as a key emergency responder for the same disaster event (cf. Fig. 4).

Document Management System (DMS) Component. Open KM (OKM) was configured to fulfill the document management functionality of the LKMS. OKM provides managerial capabilities such as tagging, reading, writing, and storing useful emergency intervention documentation. Hence, OKM can facilitate individual and group learning, and the management (sharing/transfer/creation/use and control) of end user knowledge as part of the LKMS.

The document structure implemented in OKM (see Fig. 7) is in accordance with the taxonomies discussed in Sect. 2. Thus the structure of the data repository and the document management system are synchronized to accommodate easy integration of data sources in the LKMS.

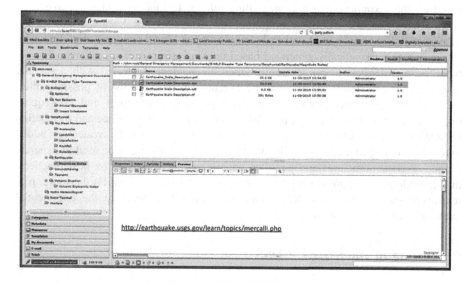

Fig. 7. Document structure in OKM

The KM is incorporated into the S-HELP KMS component using REST (REpresentational State Transfer) services and also provides facilities to build work flows in the jBPM Business Process Management suite. Based on the taxonomy in project deliverable D2.4 [16] a number of Business Process Model and Notation (BPMN: [29]) 2.0 models were developed in the project [26].

4.3   Current Recognized Situation Component

One important information management capability of the S-HELP system is the Current Recognized Situation (CRS) component. It was designed based on a work-flow identified by the S-HELP end-user group and incorporates lessons learned from Irish Framework for Emergency Management [30]. The CRS module provides an electronic implementation of current manual information management systems which often incorporate the use of whiteboards. However, the system goes beyond merely providing a digital implementation of manual information management techniques. Current manual EM information management systems are highly dependent on hand written input of information by qualified "Information Managers" on a single set of on-site whiteboards and markers. When the whiteboards run out of space for new entries, a picture is taken and the content is erased. If there are multiple incidents associated with a single emergency situation, then boxes are informally drawn onto the corners of relevant whiteboards.

4.4   Integration with Taxonomy

Beyond merely providing a means of facilitating manual data entry the development team has also been working on automatically generating content for the CRS panels based on the taxonomy and data modelling efforts. Unique Java classes have been created based on the collective output of the University of Vienna's Emergency Management Taxonomy and Lund University's Object Model representation. Resource entries can be automatically generated based on queries executed on different disaster types upon instantiation. For example, when an incident is created with a specific disaster type (e.g. flood), queries can be executed to derive a list of possible intervention tasks associated with the disaster type (e.g. evacuating) and consequent responder and resources required to fulfil the interventions (e.g. police and evacuation vehicles) will be identified. Once identified, new CRS entities will be created and added to the Resources panel automatically. Moreover, the taxonomy can be used to generate sample response structures and populate generic action lists based on best practices, thus providing an important decision support and training function. Furthermore, past responses, gleaned from the KMS, can be displayed to leverage the experiential knowledge of historical incidents.

5   Testing of the S-HELP DSS

The S-HELP system adheres to the S-HELP Quality Manual which specifies a valid test suite for any software artefact. For the S-HELP project, the test suite must coverall documented requirements of all types, it must fit into the accepted types of software tests (e.g., unit, integration, system), it must be reviewed and all specified tests must be executed, passed and reviewed. In practice, three different test types have been executed.

Unit Tests target a specific class. Objects are mocked and injected as necessary to test that class in isolation from other classes. The Maven build and dependency manager is used to drive test suites; such testing is tightly integrated with the build process. This is expected in an agile test environment. Unit Testing is fully automated.

Integration Tests are designed to test the interaction of a specific class with other classes or with a remote service or database. In all other respects Integration Tests are similar to Unit Tests. Like Unit Tests they can be run automatically as part of the Maven build process. Similarly test results are reported automatically.

User interaction and System Tests are manual in nature. User Interaction tests follow the use cases laid out for the S-HELP system and are documented in Excel spreadsheets. Failing tests are logged as bugs in the JIRA Software reporting system (https://www.atlassian.com/software/jira). The focus of these tests is to ensure that the User Interface behaves as designed and is productively useful to an emergency command center operator.

System tests to date have been limited in scope. So far the S-HELP build/ deployment process has been tested on multiple operating systems on Irish sites and also in a site in Austria. The test results demonstrate the deployability of S-HELP. Furthermore, the target platforms are diverse in terms of architecture and processing power (OS X and Ubuntu on Intel, Debian on ARM). These tests have demonstrated consistency of system operation and user experience across diverse platforms.

6   Conclusion

The S-HELP DSS will facilitate a better coordination and communication of multi agencies' emergency responders during major disasters to overcome operational inefficiencies and delays. This is especially essential and even crucial in times of increased susceptibility of our society to hazards and other threats caused by climate change, demographical change, political and economic instability, urbanization, migration, and flow of refugees (cf., e.g., [31, 32]).

The work on designing and building the S-HELP DSS is ongoing and tests carried out so far are promising. Work to be done is to test and demonstrate that the S-HELP DSS system of systems will provide the necessary emergency decision and training support for emergency decision makers. A series of three scenarios will be used to test this. These scenarios are being prepared to test incident intelligence, multi-agency response, what-if modelling, GIS capabilities, learning tool sets and post action evaluation. The scenarios will be used to test the system in a realistic operating environment across different disaster types. The scenarios comprise cross-border chemical explosion, biological hazard and widespread flood events. Future papers and articles will report on the outcome of these tests.

Acknowledgments. This project is funded by the European Union's Seventh Framework Programme for research, technological development and demonstration under grant agreement N° 607865.

References

1. Alexander, D.: Principles of Emergency Planning and Management. Oxford University Press, Oxford; New York (2002)
2. Egli, D.S.: Beyond the storms: strengthening preparedness, response, and resilience in the 21st century. J. Strateg. Secur. **6**, 32 (2013)
3. Whybark, D.C.: Co-creation of improved quality in disaster response and recovery. Int. J. Qual. Innov. **1**, 1–10 (2015)
4. Tufekci, S.: An integrated emergency management decision support system for hurricane emergencies. Saf. Sci. **20**, 39–48 (1995)
5. Turoff, M., White, C., Plotnick, L., Hiltz, S.R.: Dynamic emergency response management for large scale decision making in extreme events. In: Proceedings of the 5th International ISCRAM Conference, pp. 462–470. ISCRAM Washington, DC, USA (2008)
6. Kondaveti, R., Ganz, A.: Decision support system for resource allocation in disaster management. In: Annual International Conference of the IEEE Engineering in Medicine and Biology Society, EMBC 2009, pp. 3425–3428. IEEE (2009)

7. Securing Health Emergency Learning Planning, S-H.E.L.P.: Collaborative Project FP7-SEC-2013-1, Project no. 60786. European Union (2014)
8. Gregor, S.: Building theory in the sciences of the artificial. In: Proceedings of the 4th International Conference on Design Science Research in Information Systems and Technology. ACM (2009)
9. Gregor, S., Jones, D.: The anatomy of a design theory. J. Assoc. Inf. Syst. **8**, 312 (2007)
10. Alexander, D.: Principles of Emergency Planning and Management. Oxford University Press, Oxford, New York (2012)
11. Rauner, M., Pope, A., Niessner, H., Neville, K., Sasse, L., Tomic, K., O'Riordan, S.: Decision support for strategic disaster management: first release of a Wiki. In: Dawid, H., Doerner, K., Feichtinger, G., Kort, P.M. (eds.) Dynamic Perspectives on Managerial Decision Making – Essays in Honor of Richard F. Hartl. Springer, Heidelberg, Germany (2016)
12. University of Vienna, Austria: Glossary of terms and definitions and common grounds and standards for interoperability. Deliverable No. 2.1 (2014)
13. European Commission: Commission Implementing Decision of 16.10.2014 laying down rules for the implementation of Decision No 1313/2013/EU – Annex II- C (2014) 7489 final. European Commission, EC (2014)
14. Vernadat, F.B.: Enterprise Modelling and Integration. Springer, New York (2003)
15. Rauner, M., Pope, A., Niessner, H., Neville, K., Sasse, L., Tomic, K., O'Riordan, S.: Improving Decision Making in European Disaster Management: A Skills Taxonomy of Main Emergency Responders Needed for Key Emergency Interventions. Working paper (2016)
16. University of Vienna, Austria: Draft Skills Taxonomy Template. Deliverable No. 2.4 (2015)
17. University of Vienna, Austria: Draft Rescources Taxonomy Template. Deliverable No. 2.7 (2015)
18. University of Vienna, Austria: S-HELP Interoperability Standard. Deliverable No. 2.11 (2016)
19. European Commission: Decision 2010/481/EU Annex II, Euraton. Official Journal of the European Union 7 (2010)
20. European Parliament and the Council: Decision No 1313/2013/EU. Official Journal of the European Union (2013)
21. FLOODsite: Review Report of Operational Flood Management Methods and Models. FLOODsite (2007). http://www.floodsite.net/html/partner_area/project_docs/Task17_report_M17_1review_v1_1.pdf
22. Neville, K., O'Riordan, S., Pope, A., Rauner, M., Maria, R., Madden, M., Sweeney, J., Nussbaumer, A., McCarthy, N., O'Brien, C.: Towards the development of a decision support system for multi-agency decision-making during cross-border emergencies. J. Decis. Syst. **25**, 381–396 (2016)
23. Finkelstein, C.: Enterprise Architecture for Integration: Rapid Delivery Methods and Technologies. Information Engineering Services Pty Ltd, Australia (2015)
24. Zachman International®, Inc. http://www.zachman.com/images/ZI_PIcs/ZF3.0.jpg
25. Majchrzak, A., Markus, M.L., Wareham, J.: Designing for digital transformation: lessons for information systems research from the study of ICT and societal challenges. MISQ **40**, 267–277 (2016)
26. Lund University, Sweden: Learning and Knowledge Management System (LKMS). Deliverable No. 4.4 (2015)
27. Lund University, Sweden: Repository for Data Sets. Deliverable No. 4.2 (2014)
28. Fowler, M.: Analysis Patterns: Reusable Object Models. Addison Wesley, Menlo Park, Calif (1997)

29. Object Management Group: Business Process Model and Notation (DMN) Version 2.0. (2011)
30. National Steering Group: Principal Response Agencies. Framework for Major Emergency Management, MEM (2006)
31. Coppola, D.P.: Introduction to International Disaster Management. Butterworth-Heinemann, Boston (2011)
32. Neville, K.M., Doyle, C., Mueller, J., Sugrue, A.: Supporting cross border emergency management decision-making. In: Proceedings of ECIS 2013, pp. 1–7 (2013)

The Generation of a Situation Model, in Real-Time, as a Support to Crisis Management

Audrey Fertier[1]([✉]), Anne-Marie Barthe-Delanoë[2],
Aurélie Montarnal[1], Sébastien Truptil[1], and Frédérick Bénaben[1]

[1] Centre Génie Industriel, Université de Toulouse, IMT Mines Albi, France
audrey.fertier@mines-albi.fr
[2] Lab. de Génie Chimique, Université de Toulouse, CNRS, INPT, UPS,
Toulouse, France
annemarie.barthe@ensiacet.fr

Abstract. There are more and more data sources available in the world every day. This is the opportunity for organizations to improve their situation awareness in order to take better decisions, faster than ever before. The GéNéPi project was set up to help them: it aims to support their collaboration, in real-time, whatever the complexity or instability of the environment. To set up and test the solution proposed by the project's consortium, a crisis use case has been developed by official sources. This article shows a new approach to automating the creation and update of a situation model, in real-time to offer: (i) the decision-makers a common operational picture; (ii) the GéNéPi project a base on which a collaborative process is defined and maintained to the benefits of the decision makers.

Keywords: Modeling · Big data · Situation awareness · Crisis management · Common operational picture

1 Introduction

During a crisis situation, the inter-connection of networks compels the stakeholders to collaborate. To make this collaboration possible, on the field and between the several decisional levels, crisis cells are set up. Their main purpose includes the information sharing and a centralized decision-making. The number of incoming and outgoing communications of the crisis cells quickly takes up everybody's time. Moreover, the innate instability of the situation compels the decision-makers, far from the field, to obtain the best possible situation awareness in real-time.

The growing number of data sources over the last decade is the opportunity to quickly obtain information on the on-going situation. Unfortunately, if the crisis cells want to avoid drowning in raw data and information, they have to limit their investigation area on inner sensors, devices or internal reports. To support the stakeholders' collaboration on the field and relieve the decision-makers, the GéNéPi (The GéNéPi project is funded by the French national association for research. It considers using the

Y. Murayama et al. (Eds.): ITDRR 2016, IFIP AICT 501, pp. 198–213, 2017.
https://doi.org/10.1007/978-3-319-68486-4_16

innate granularity of the management levels in crisis context to better support coordination (cf. ANR-14-CE28-0029) project aims to design, orchestrate and monitor a response collaborative process in real time. One innovation involves the automatic generation of a situation model on the basis of raw data. This model is created and updated in two rounds: (i) A ground truth model comes first and describes fact coming directly from trusted data sources; (ii) New information is automatically deduced from the ground truths in regards with the knowledge base, thanks to deduction rules. During these two phases, the system instantiates a model called meta-model (A meta-model can be defined as "explicit specification of an abstraction" [1]. In the GéNéPi project, the meta-model is a model that describes the crisis collaboration domain.).

This paper presents a new methodology for supporting decision-makers in managing data and information, inside French crisis cells. The output is the situation model that will be used as an input for: (i) the inference and monitoring of the collaborative process; (ii) the generation of a common operational picture for every crisis cell.

To answer these topics, the second part of this article concerns the opportunities and threats brought by the amount of available data in crisis situation. The third one explains how to benefit from the particularities of crisis collaborations. The fourth one focuses on the features of events to be dealt with during a crisis response. Then, the fifth and last part presents two existing approaches answering to the 'how to?' question of the third part, along with a new methodology, answering to all the data features' issues presented in the fourth part.

2 Excessive Amount of Available Data to Be Processed in Real-Time

According to Ackoff [2]: data represents 'properties of objects and events', information is 'contained in descriptions' (Who? What? Where? How many?), and knowledge is 'conveyed by instructions' (How to?). This section explains where all this available data comes from, why is it important to manage it all, and how fast data needs to be processed by the crisis cells.

2.1 The Decision-Makers' Needs

Growing networks of people, devices, and organizations generate more and more data. These data sources are numerous and heterogeneous: they introduce complexity in crisis management at several levels. If the decision-makers want to take advantages of this new situation, they will need to: locate data sources; identify them; infer new information describing the situation; sum up and share their information and knowledge inside the crisis cell; etc. Their goal is to obtain the most reliable and accurate view of the situation, as a common operational picture, to be able to make well-informed decisions [3].

2.2   The Time Pressure

A shared situation awareness (SA) can be defined as "the degree to which team members have the same SA on shared SA requirement" [4]. This has to be achieved in real-time to fit the innate instability of crisis. To generate it, data and information have to be gathered from the stakeholders involved in the crisis response. Unfortunately, it takes significant and precious time to obtain and spread the right data or information to the right person or device at the right time. That's the reason why, the decision-makers choose to limit the number of their data sources.

2.3   Balance Between Swiftness and Quality

Limitations on data collection enable crisis cells to save time for decision-making but it also raises several issues as:

- **Outdated perceptions of the situation.** The instability of crisis situation makes things nearly impossible to predict. It is then critical to be informed, in time, of any on-going development. The stakeholders involved in a crisis expect systems to respect this 'on-the-fly' requirement and harshly judge failures. For instance, the SAIP application for smartphones [5] turns out useless because of a time lag of three (!) hours [6] during the Nice terrorist attack on July 15th, 2016.
- **Misjudging.** French crisis cells' emergency plans include meetings that are planned on a regular basis. One of the purposes of these meetings includes the sharing of information and the decision-making based on these information. Nevertheless, the order of the data arrival may lead to various interpretations that impact the resulting decision-making process. For example, the observations of: (a) a crowd movement, (b) few people injured, (c) loud noises can be interpreted in more than on way. If the order of the observations is (a, b, c), the situation can be understood as a classical crowd movement, whereas (c, b, a) where the situation could be due to gun shots.
- **Information loss.** Some data, as weak signals, is by nature not sufficient to attract the attention, as well as some other will not fit the information system of the crisis cells and will be lost for good.

To sum up, the growing number of available data is an incredible opportunity to improve the situation awareness of stakeholders, while facilitating decision-making through an always more accurate situation model. Meanwhile, the stakeholders have to face issues such as time lag, misjudging and information loss. Crisis information systems are then needed, in real-time, to both support the decision-makers [7] and generate the best situation model possible in order to generate the expected common operational picture.

How to automatically generate the best situation model possible describing the ongoing collaborative situation, while being on real-time update to match with the innate instability of a crisis?

3 The Generation of a Situation Model in Real-Time

Data mining may be considered as one of the relevant answers to the automatic generation of a situation model issue. A lot of data mining approaches are rather dedicated to business than to crisis situations, and there are huge differences between the two contexts of application. This section aims to highlight those differences and to define how data mining could be used to serve the management of huge amount of available crisis data, considering the challenging issues underlined in Sect. 2.

3.1 Particularities of Data Processing in Industry

Data mining approaches are frequently used by companies to monitor customers' relationships (CRM), or to identify the best market opportunities (BI), with the final objective to support business decision-making.

Wang and Wang [8] claim that one strong approach is to use data mining to bond the gap between: (i) the data gathering, data accessing and data analyzing; and (ii) the creation and exploitation of knowledge. They also propose a step that enables the data miners to extract and mine the data, while the business insiders learn from the results and take actions in consequence.

Three hypotheses have been made in this context:

- **Data sources known in advance.** Business insiders, in connection with data miners, plane data extractions according to their objectives. As the objectives are already known, it is somewhat easy to pick the most interesting data sources and analyze their streams with precise rules.
- **Narrow scope of decisions.** In most of the cases, companies have a precise decomposition of their functions: therefore, the scope of actions that can be taken to solve potential issues, or reach an objective, remains narrow.
- **Large timeline.** The data extraction may be conducted on a broad timeline to enrich the dataset and, hopefully, improve the accuracy and relevancy of the data mining results.

3.2 Particularities of Data Processing During the Crisis Response

Data extractions techniques depend on their field of application: objectives-conducted for industrial applications and 'data sources'-oriented for crisis response applications.

A wide scope of data sources has to be streamed during a crisis to prevent lack of information, information loss, misunderstandings and snap judgements. This represents a huge data volume as varied as satellite imagery, photographs, reports, social media messages, newspaper articles, GPS locations or sensors data that has to be processed in real-time. If only automated, such a data processing could infer precious knowledge. A valuable output could be a common operational picture consisting of a map where people, actors, risks, facts [9], sentiments [10] or on-going tasks have been localized on the crisis field.

However, crisis situations are far from the industrial cases and hypothesis:

- **Fuzzy, unknown data sources.** Data miners cannot predict the outcomes of their mining, nor the location of relevant and accurate data. Then, how to access data sources that are not known in advance, knowing that the more they are, the more reliable the result.
- **Unpredictable uses.** A data extracted from one data source may refer to several types of information, related or not to the decision-makers objectives. Hence, the classification rules have to be at once permissive to treat as many data as possible, and accurate to meet the decision-makers expectations.
- **Relevant actions hard to trigger.** The number of actions available to answer a risk or treat a bad effect is spreading as the number of stakeholders increases (whatever their operational/strategic level). In addition, performance indicators cannot be pre-established and the results of the response process are hardly assessable in short schedule.
- **Tight timeline.** One single event is enough to trigger or alter a crisis in a very short time. Under these conditions, the IT system should be able to detect such events within minutes.

3.3   A Three-Level IT System as a Basis to Data Management During Crisis Situation

The particularities of the industry and the crisis field reveal two important differences on: (i) the volume and quality of data that can be extracted in real time; (ii) the volume of possible actions to be taken. This is why there is a high interest in using data streams, not only to maintain a situation model, but also to define and monitor actions.

In this perspective, a three-levels IT system, as depicted in Fig. 1, is needed:

- **Data.** The raw data is directly extracted from heterogeneous and various data sources (such as GIS, sensors, social media...). In Fig. 1, the shadowed part illustrates the existence and needed use of unknown sources. Here, the extracted data are heterogeneous, numerous, more or less reliable and time dated.
- **Information.** This level corresponds to the contextualization of the previous data. Concretely, the information level aims at providing a state of the crisis situation in real-time. The common operational picture consists of a map where important instances are localized. Once implemented, this could support the decision making inside every crisis cells. A meta-model is used to standardize and facilitate this modelling. The information level is illustrated in white (see Fig. 1) to show that the modeled information can be easily recover.
- **Knowledge.** It consists of the actions to be taken, considering the crisis situation established at the information level. The actions are, for instance, part of the collaborative process that is: (i) deduced by the GéNéPi partners; and (ii) executed by the stakeholders. There is a wide range of possibilities in the action selection process. The shadowed part illustrates the fact that some actions, unknown at the beginning, have to be discovered in time to improve the quality of the crisis response.

The following sections focus on solutions to process crisis data in real-time and obtain the most relevant information to be put in the situation model.

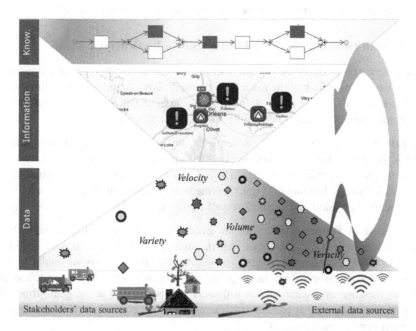

Fig. 1. Data, information and knowledge levels to support collaborations during crisis response.

How to automatically generate the best situation model possible describing the ongoing collaborative situation, while being able in real-time update to match with the innate instability of a crisis, thanks to a three-level IT system?

4 Particularities of Crisis Events' Data

Event can be understood as "the thing that happened" (as defined by Luckham and Schulte and Etzion and Niblett [11–13]). For example, it could be a tsunami, a water level reaching a threshold, the reception of an email, the new version of a web page, a comment on a Facebook status, etc. Here, they will be called field events. As a field event occurs or is about to occur, another one is created into an information system [14] in the shape of an object, a message or a tuple. In this paper, the last event will be called the IT event and it will at least contain:

- A unique ID
- The time of occurrence of the field event
- A description of the field event (data or information from the field)

To generate automatically the situation model representing the collaboration on the field, the system needs to describe the context, the partners and the crisis itself. Both the context and the partners can be represented in the preparation phase. That's why the system could focus, at first, on modelling the risks and effects of the crisis.

4.1 Overall Descriptions of the Field Events to Be Observed

To be able to avoid mistakes or delays in the generation of the common operational picture, based on the situation model, field events have to be observed through the entire Internet of Events (IoE) defined by van der Aalst [15]. It consists in four overlapping classes, as described in the following subsections.

The Internet of Things. This class embeds any physical object connected to the network through an Internet connection or thanks to unique ID tags such as barcodes or 'Radio frequency identification' tags. During a crisis, identification systems, like the 'Wireless internet information system for medical response in disasters', are used to report victims' position and medical record during triage [16].

The Internet of People. These data are generated from social interactions between people. It can be e-mails, messages sent through social networks such as Facebook, Twitter or Instagram. During a crisis, people tend to focus on social media to communicate, or to be informed on the on-going crisis, because of the 1 to n principle: post only one message on Twitter and n followers will be warned at the same time. This emergent crowdsourcing is particularly interesting in the context of crisis management to support context awareness [17].

The Internet of Locations. It includes any data with a spatial dimension. For instance, Tweets, Facebook posts, even pictures can embed geospatial attributes through the geolocation service provided by modern smartphones and cameras. During a crisis, a significant percentage (49% according to Kouadia [18]) of the potential victims has a smartphone and can be localized on a map. This crisis representation can therefore be used as a common operational picture to support local decision-making inside the crisis cells.

The Internet of content. It represents the information created by humans, like web pages, Wikipedia, YouTube, news feeds. During a crisis, official recommendations to assist victims could be transmitted directly to on-site people wanting to help, etc.

As van der Aalst [19] pointed out, event data is the major source of information. Therefore, all these available events are numerous and the data and information they contain is more or less reliable, comes from varied sources, in various types and format, and are time-dated.

4.2 Issues Due to the Volume, Variety, Velocity and Veracity of the Data Coming from the Field

Available events describe data and information coming from outside as from: the crisis field, upper crisis cells, lower crisis cells or the Internet. This section describes the characteristics of those heterogeneous inputs. It will focus on data features because an information from one person can be considered as a data by another [20].

The Volume. It refers to the quantity of data generated continuously per time unit. The volume is proportional to the size of the data [21] and therefore to the type of data [22]. A balance has to be found between widening the influence zone and spending energy to process data in time. Yet, the more data, the more creation of hidden information and patterns the decision makers will get [23]. And as the time passes by, the volume of available data continues increasing while the available capacity to process them stays the same [24].

The Variety. It refers to the diversity of data types, as videos or data logs [22–27], and data formats (Either structured, unstructured, semi-structured or mixed data set.), as structured or unstructured sets [21, 23]. Bypass issues linked to variety is possible thanks to metadata identifying what is contained in the actual data [22], even though a lot of details are lost in the process.

The Velocity. It refers to the speed needed to retrieve and process data in time [22, 24, 25, 27]. To avoid losing data, which could be essential to infer critical information for the decision makers, it is crucial to improve the swiftness of all the analysis' steps [28]. Velocity also refers to how quickly the data is generated [21, 24, 27].

The Veracity. It refers to the reliability, accuracy, consistency and security of data [20, 21, 29]. Lukoianova and Rubin [20] also identify objectivity, truthfulness and credibility as three complementary dimensions of veracity. As an illustration, the Fig. 2 represents four blind monks. If they keep their own data without sharing, they will see elephants as hoses, walls, trees or ropes…

Fig. 2. The blind monks and the elephant [30].

Rajaraman and Ullman [30] go further by assuming that the studied situation changes constantly (as a crisis situation should). The analysis process has then to aggregate heterogeneous data from as many diverse sources as possible (blind men) to generate the most reliable situation model (shape and gesture of the elephant) in real-time (because of the changes).

At last, one of the goals of event processing is to improve and favor the value of the data inside the system. This value generally decreases in proportion to the age, the type, the richness and quantity of the element in the system [28]. The veracity and variety should be considered when computing the value of the data or when analyzing the data [20, 28].

To sum up, in order to offer the decision-makers the best common operational picture possible, the three-level IT system will have to process numerous, varied, more or less reliable data, in time, during a crisis situation. This is known as Big Data issues.

How to automatically generate the best situation model possible describing the ongoing collaborative situation, while being on real-time update to match with the innate instability of a crisis, thanks to a three-level IT system that manages all the issues linked to crisis 'Big' data features?

5   Approaches to Generating Situation Models from Raw Data

According to the descriptions of data features above, a good analysis tool has to access as many events as possible (volume, velocity), from heterogeneous sources (variety). It also has to compute the veracity and value of every data inside the system. If not, the data will be used randomly. Methodologies covering at least one of these points already exist. This section presents two of them.

5.1   General Approaches Talking Down at Least One of the 4Vs' Issues

KDD – Fayyad [31]. The knowledge discovery in structured data base process has been set up to map low-level data, too voluminous to be easily aggregated. The process use patterns to link data together. These patterns have to be validated (veracity) and potentially useful (value). The whole process is made up of five main steps [29]:

- **Data selection:** Focus on a subset, on a sample to improve the performance of the system;
- **Data preprocessing:** Clean data by using pre-defined operations to remove noise, handle missing data, etc.;
- **Data transformation:** Identify useful features to represent data and achieve the users' goals;
- **Data mining:** Match the users' goals to a particular data mining method such as summarization, classification, regression, clustering, etc. Search for patterns by applying the closed method;
- **Patterns interpretation/evaluation:** Interpret mined pattern and resolve potential conflicts thanks to visualizations and the possibility of returning to any previous step.

SA – Endsley [32]. The situation awareness of a system is measured by its ability to perceive elements in a particular environment, to understand them and project them in the future. The whole situation awareness process is therefore made up of three main stages [30]:

- **Perception** of the elements: Observe and retrieve the status, attributes and dynamics of relevant elements on the field;
- **Comprehension** of the current situation: Gather retrieved elements and infer new elements that convey more and more meanings for the users and their goals;
- **Projection** of future status: Foresee the evolution of the elements' status to project its future dynamic in the environment.

The goal is to provide the knowledge and time (velocity) required by the decision-makers, in the sight of their objectives (value) (Table 1).

Table 1. Proposition of a particular classification along with some results (x: the V is taken into account by the methodology, -: the V is not considerate inside the methodology)

Name	Volume	Variety	Velocity	Veracity	Value
KDD	x	–	–	x	x
SA	x	–	x	–	x

These two tools partially cover the data features issues raised earlier. The three-level IT system can therefore combine these two methodologies to support the decision-makers in managing all the issues linked to a Big Data & crisis context.

5.2 A New Approach Taking into Account All the vs of Big Data

The GéNéPi project includes the Big Data management in the collaboration support system. Events are to be directly analyzed to generate up-to date situation models, in run time. During a crisis, these models will be used by:

- Other partners to deduce and orchestrate a collaborative process between the services on the field;
- Decision-makers through the generation of a common operational picture in each crisis cell to facilitate the decision-making.

The events treatment system has to take into account all the issues linked to the 'Big Data' features of crisis data. Thanks to the two approaches introduced in Sect. 5.1, three of the five types of issues can be solved, at least to some extent. The five 'operations' of the KDD approach should then be adapted to the three 'time steps' of the SA approach as to the three-level IT system features. Following this assumption, a new methodology has been set up inside the GéNéPi project.

The next subsections describe each step of the new approach illustrated in Fig. 3 and introduced by this paper.

Extract Raw Data from the Crisis Field. As underlined before, decision makers do not lack available data: it is recovered from the field through the reception of numerous events from diverse sources such as:

- The services involved (or to be involved) in the crisis response delivering ground truth data thanks to sensors dispatched on the field;

- The people taking part in the crisis response and victims of the crisis' effects come along with their smartphone full of sensors and, as the stakeholders, their own perceptions. For instance, Haiti, Japan or China are known for their citizen capability to ask for help or take part in the response through social media in times of crisis [33];
- The open data sources accessible through the Internet (objective or not).

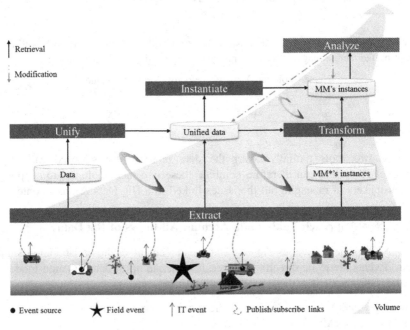

Fig. 3. Data deposition: five steps to counter the 4vs of big data

Only few sources are known from the crisis cells, while all the others are ready to be requested for, if discovered. Hence, to be able to discover new sources, along with their communication protocols, topics of emission and types of emitted events, a 'scan' of the crisis field has to be performed. The challenge is to find the key event sources [28] that is involved in inferring valuable (value) and reliable (veracity) information for the decision-makers on the crisis cells. The volume is also tackled thanks to rules that mainly filter and aggregate data. The goal is to avoid a pathological accumulation of data [28]: the "quantity vs quality" quest. As an output, the filtered and aggregated data is tagged with a use-by date to be defined for each type of event sent by the sources (velocity).

The 'Extract' box refers to the data selection step of the KDD approach and the perception phase of the SA approach.

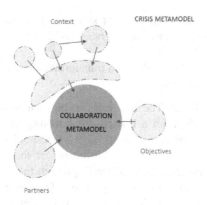

Fig. 4. MM meta-model

Unify the Data. The variety issue is solved thanks to a unified approach of interoperability [34]. This approach offers an unlimited access to the unified data from any part of the system and unable the 'Analyze' box to query the unified data set or the MM's instances set, regardless of all the variety issues. This transformation implies: (i) the identification of the type of data contained in the input event; (ii) the availability of a transformation rule concerning this particular type of data. If the rule does not exist in the system, the files' metadata can be used to get around the problem.

The 'Unify' box refers to the data preprocessing step of the KDD approach, adapted to unstructured data set.

Transform Instances. A data can skip the 'Unify' box if is already in the targeted type or if it is already contextualized, and in other words, if it is already an information. In the last case, if it is an instance of a known meta-model MM*, different from the system's meta-model MM, a model transformation has to be set up [35]. Else, the information is considered as a data. The target meta-model MM, used by the system (cf. level 2 of the three-level IT system), is composed of: (i) a core (see Fig. 4) that can describe any kind of collaboration; (ii) several layers inheriting from at least one core concept. The situation model, final output of the system, consists of all the instances stocked in the "MM's instances" set (see Fig. 3). They instantiates concepts form the triplet {Partners, Context, Objectives}:

- **The 'Context'** describes the surroundings as it appears with or without the crisis. To adapt the situation model to a particular risk (as flooding or road crisis), sub-parts have been developed around the main context.
- **The 'Partner'** describes the services (resp. people) available for the crisis response, along with their resources, sensors, and capabilities.
- **The 'Objectives'** describes the danger, effects and risks due to crisis events and affecting one part of the context.

As underlined before, the generation of situation model in real-time mainly concerns the 'Objectives' part, because the others are to be prepared in advance, before the crisis.

The 'Transform' box refers to the data transformation step of the KDD approach, adapted to unstructured data set.

Instantiate the Unified Data. The first rules to be applied on the crisis events are business rules. An example from a French crisis management plan can be: 'IF the predicted water level is higher than a 'level1' dike's threshold (which protects big cities from flooding) and IF there is, at least, 48 h left before the overrun, THEN the protected city has to be evacuated'. In the GéNéPi project, these rules are directly based on: (i) the French crisis response plans of several defense zones and counties; (ii) the experience of the actor that have already been involved in a crisis response; (iii) the doctrines of the services that are to be involved in a crisis response. All this knowledge, answering to 'how to respond to a crisis?', has been recovered from interviews conducted by the CEREMA (Study & expertise center of risks, environment, mobility and development), partner in the GéNéPi project.

The 'Instantiate' box refers to the data mining step of the KDD approach, and to the comprehension phase of the SA approach.

Analyze the instances. This last step enables the system to deduce information from others thanks to modeling rules. For example, if the danger 'Flooding' has been deduced from the 'Instantiate' box, several risks have to be added on the situation model. Depending on the context, one of the new instances could be a 'risk of victims' linked with a school or a hospital, or a 'risk of pollution' linked with industries. This is possible thanks to the existence of a knowledge base, where all the rules contained in the system apply.

The 'Analyze' phase is also the opportunity to monitor the generation and the projection of the situation model. Here, all the instances of MM and all the unified data are tag with veracity levels and value estimations. These iterations, between unified data and instances, are critical: without them, the system would be amnesic and unable to learn [21]. In this context, the research works of Lukoianova and Rubin [20] can be highlighted as they showed the possibility of measuring deception, subjectivity and credibility of certain data types. The iterations enable the system to:

- Improve 'unified data' and 'MM's instances' quality by optimizing their veracity value and value estimation;
- Check whether the situation model stocked in the MM's instances box, faithfully represents the crisis field reality;
- Put aside all the event sources judged as unreliable ones;
- Improve the MM meta-model's coverage by analyzing the veracity and value of unused 'unified data'.

The 'Analyze' box refers to the evaluation step of the KDD approach, and could serve for the projection phase of the SA approach.

The five boxes of the Fig. 3 enable a two-level system to deliver an organized set of information in the form of a situation model. Thanks to it, a common operational picture can be delivered and adapted to the context, objectives and resources of each crisis cells. Inner communications, and therefore decision-making, will be reinforced. Moreover, thanks to the GéNéPi project, collaboration processes (third level) will be deduced from this situation model, as orchestrated and maintain all along the crisis response. These two innovations will improve the decision-makers environment by maintaining the collaboration on the field (horizontal distribution) and by properly sharing information to the other crisis cells (vertical granularity).

6 Conclusion

Nowadays, more and more data sources produce more and more data each day. This is an opportunity for the crisis decision-makers to improve their own situation awareness. But, to avoid being drowned in data streams, they limit their number of accessible data sources. This situation could lead to data loss, data misjudging and outdated situation awareness. That is the reason why there is a need for data management support in the crisis response field.

The solution could be found in existing techniques coming from the industry. Alas, there is a big difference between: (i) known and unknown data sources; (ii) predictable and unpredictable use of data; (iii) finite and infinite number of relevant actions; (iv) minimize and maximize the time spent on the gathering part.

In this context, two approaches have been studied and valued considering the issues linked to crisis data features. The result of this study enables the implementation of a new approach, combining the qualities of both the Endsley's SA and the Fayyad's KDD.

This approach has now to be implemented in: (i) the IO Suite tool [36], enabling the collaboration support during crisis responses in the CGI laboratory of Mines d'Albi and in (ii) the GéNéPi prototype. In addition, more business rules have to be written thanks to the CEREMA partner, along with models transformation rules needed in the 'Transform' box.

In the future, such a tool, enabling the automatic generation of a situation model in real-time, whatever the complexity and instability of the context, will benefit, not only to crisis decision makers, but also to industries willing to quickly adapt in a day-to-day fashion.

References

1. Bézivin, J., Gerbé, O.: Towards a precise definition of the OMG/MDA framework. In: 16th Annual International Conference on Automated Software Engineering (ASE 2001), pp. 273–280 (2001)
2. Ackoff, R.L.: From data to wisdom. J. Appl. Syst. Anal. **16**(1), 3–9 (1989)
3. Dautun, C., Lacroix, B.: Placer "l'humain" au coeur des crises. LIREC **38**, 10–19 (2013)
4. Endsley, M.R., Jones, W.M.: A model of inter-and intrateam situation awareness: implications for design, training and measurement. New Trends Coop. Act. Underst. Syst. Dyn. Complex Environ. **7**, 46–47 (2001)

5. l'Intérieur, M.: de: Lancement de l'application mobile SAIP. http://www.interieur.gouv.fr/Actualites/L-actu-du-Ministere/Lancement-de-l-application-mobile-SAIP. [En ligne]. Disponible sur: http://www.interieur.gouv.fr/Actualites/L-actu-du-Ministere/Lancement-de-l-application-mobile-SAIP. [Consulté le: 29 juill 2016]

6. French Minister of the Interior, Mise en oeuvre de l'application SAIP le soir du 14 juillet 2016. http://www.interieur.gouv.fr/Actualites/Communiques/Mise-en-oeuvre-de-l-application-SAIP-le-soir-du-14-juillet-2016, juillet 2016. [En ligne]. Disponible sur: http://www.interieur.gouv.fr/Actualites/Communiques/Mise-en-oeuvre-de-l-application-SAIP-le-soir-du-14-juillet-2016. [Consulté le: 21 juill 2016]

7. Finn, R., Watson, H., Wadhwa, K.: Exploring big 'crisis' data in action: potential positive and negative externalities. In: ISCRAM Conference, Kristiansand, pp. 24–27 (2015)

8. Wang, H., Wang, S.: A knowledge management approach to data mining process for business intelligence. Ind. Manag. Data Syst. 108(5), 622–634 (2008)

9. Norheim-Hagtun, I., Meier, P.: Crowdsourcing for crisis mapping in Haiti. Innovations 5(4), 81–89 (2010)

10. Caragea, C., Squicciarini, A., Stehle, S., Neppalli, K., Tapia, A.: Mapping moods: geo-mapped sentiment analysis during hurricane Sandy. In: Proceedings of ISCRAM (2014)

11. Luckham, D., Schulte, W.R.: Event Processing Glossary - Version 2.0. EPTS, July 2011

12. Etzion, O., Niblett, P.: Event Processing in Action, 1st edn. Manning Publications Co, Greenwich (2010)

13. Chandy, K., Schulte, W.: Event Processing: Designing IT Systems for Agile Companies. McGraw-Hill Inc, New York (2009)

14. Luckham, D., Schulte, R.: Event processing glossary-version 1.1. Event Process. Tech. Soc. 2 (2008)

15. van der Aalst, W.M.P.: Process Mining: Discovery Conformance and Enhancement of Business Processes. Springer, Heidelberg (2011)

16. Koenig, K.L., Schultz, C.H.: Koenig and Schultz's Disaster Medicine: Comprehensive Principles and Practices. Cambridge University Press, Cambridge (2016)

17. Meier, P.: Digital Humanitarians: How Big Data is Changing the Face of Humanitarian Response. CRC Press, Boca Raton (2015)

18. Kouadio, J.S.: Les smartphones peuvent-ils aider à une meilleure remontée des données en cas de crue rapide pour améliorer les systèmes d'alerte? BSGLg 21, 57–68 (2015)

19. van der Aalst, W.M.P.: Data scientist: the engineer of the future. In: Mertins, K., Bénaben, F., Poler, R., Bourrières, J.-P. (eds.) Enterprise Interoperability VI. PIC, vol. 7, pp. 13–26. Springer, Cham (2014). https://doi.org/10.1007/978-3-319-04948-9_2

20. Lukoianova, T., Rubin, V.L.: Veracity roadmap: is big data objective, truthful and credible? Adv. Classif. Res. Online 24(1), 4–15 (2014)

21. Demchenko, Y., Grosso, P., De Laat, C., Membrey, P.: Addressing big data issues in scientific data infrastructure. In: 2013 International Conference on Collaboration Technologies and Systems (CTS), pp. 48–55 (2013)

22. Krishnan, K.: Data Warehousing in the Age of Big Data. Newnes, Burlington (2013)

23. Hashem, I.A.T., Yaqoob, I., Anuar, N.B., Mokhtar, S., Gani, A., Khan, S.U.: The rise of "big data" on cloud computing: review and open research issues. Inf. Syst. 47, 98–115 (2015)

24. Fan, W., Bifet, A.: Mining big data: current status, and forecast to the future. ACM sIGKDD Explor. Newslett. 14(2), 1–5 (2013)

25. Chalmers, S., Bothorel, C., Clemente, R.P.: Big data-state of the art (2013)

26. Ohlhorst, F.J.: Big Data Analytics: Turning Big Data into Big Money. Wiley, Hoboken (2012)

27. Power, D.J.: Using 'big data' for analytics and decision support. J. Decis. Syst. 23(2), 222–228 (2014)

28. Kaisler, S., Armour, F., Espinosa, J.A., Money, W.: Big data: issues and challenges moving forward. In: 46th Hawaii International Conference on System Sciences, pp. 995–1004 (2013)
29. Gantz, J., Reinsel, D.: Extracting value from chaos. IDC iView **1142**, 1–12 (2011)
30. Rajaraman, A., Ullman, J.D.: Mining of Massive Datasets, vol. 1. Cambridge University Press, Cambridge (2012)
31. Fayyad, U., Piatetsky-Shapiro, G., Smyth, P.: From data mining to knowledge discovery in databases. AI Mag. **17**(3), 37 (1996)
32. Endsley, M.R.: Toward a theory of situation awareness in dynamic systems. Hum. Factors: J. Hum. Factors Ergonomics Soc. **37**(1), 32–64 (1995)
33. Ling, C.L.M., Pan, S.L., Ractham, P., Kaewkitipong, L.: ICT-enabled community empowerment in crisis response: social media in Thailand flooding 2011. J. Assoc. Inf. Syst. **16**(3), 174 (2015)
34. Chen, D., Doumeingts, G., Vernadat, F.: Architectures for enterprise integration and interoperability: past, present and future. Comput. Ind. **59**(7), 647–659 (2008)
35. Wang, T., Truptil, S., Benaben, F.: An automatic model-to-model mapping and transformation methodology to serve model-based systems engineering. Inf. Syst. e-Bus Manage. **15**(2), 1–54 (2016)
36. Bénaben, F., Lauras, M., Truptil, S., Salatge, N.: A metamodel for knowledge management in crisis management. In: 49th Hawaii International Conference on System Sciences, pp. 126–135 (2016)

Improving the Involvement of Digital Volunteers in Disaster Management

Roberto dos Santos Rocha[1,2(✉)], Adam Widera[2],
Roelof P. van den Berg[2], João Porto de Albuquerque[1,3],
and Bernd Helingrath[2]

[1] ICMC, University of São Paulo, São Carlos, Brazil
rsrocha@usp.br, j.porto@warwick.ac.uk
[2] ERCIS, University of Münster, Münster, Germany
{adam.widera, roelof.vandenberg,
bernd.hellingrath}@ercis.uni-muenster.de
[3] CIM, University of Warwick, Coventry, UK

Abstract. Volunteered geographic information (VGI) has been seen as useful information in times of disasters. Several authors have shown that VGI is useful for coping with preparedness and response phases of disaster management. However, because it is still a young technology, the use of VGI remains uncertain, due to its lack of strong reliability and validity. It is our assumption that to improve reliability and validity the promotion of citizen engagement (CE) is needed. CE is not new topic, but in the digital humanitarian context, it involves important factors that are not yet considered by disaster managers, such as communication processes, motivation of volunteers, different media for production of information, etc. To fill this gap, we identified a set of preliminary factors which should be considered to promote the involvement of volunteers in disaster management. These factors were derived from critical review of CE literature and from an analysis of lessons learned from an experiment on interaction with citizens carried out in context of the EU-project "DRIVER – Driving Innovation in Crisis Management for European Resilience".

Keywords: Citizen engagement · Volunteered geographic information · Motivation · Crowd sensing · Disaster management

1 Introduction

Citizen Engagement (CE) refers to actions designed to identify and address issues of public concern [1]. Community participation can augment officials' abilities to govern in a crisis, improve application of communally held resources in a disaster or epidemic, and mitigate community wide losses [2].

Participatory community approaches in research and governance are not new [3, 4]. However, Web 2.0 platforms, mobile internet, and social networking access through smartphones have made a significant difference by encouraging the social responsibility and active engagement of citizens [3]. These technologies enable the public to contribute and participate on an unprecedented scale and have led to many diverse

Y. Murayama et al. (Eds.): ITDRR 2016, IFIP AICT 501, pp. 214–224, 2017.
https://doi.org/10.1007/978-3-319-68486-4_17

initiatives using information from citizens [3, 4]. Examples include, among others, participation of the public in event reporting, environmental monitoring, and providing information on natural disasters. This phenomenon is called volunteered geographic information (VGI).

VGI is the harnessing of tools to create, assemble, and disseminate geographic data provided voluntarily by individuals [5]. VGI has been increasingly recognized by researchers as an important resource to support disaster management [23–25]. The production of geographic information is predominantly made through social media (e.g. Twitter, https://twitter.com/), crowd sensing (e.g. citizens equipped with smartphones can report about local conditions using dedicated applications) and online mapping tools (e.g. OpenStreetMap, https://www.openstreetmap.org; Wikimapia http://wikimapia.org/; Google Map Maker, https://www.google.com.br/mapmaker) [5–7].

Whilst those platforms can be potentially used to provide useful information for dealing with disaster management, there are still many challenges to be addressed, for instance: (i) how can people be encouraged to provide valuable information; (ii) how can information from volunteers be validated; and (iii) how can this information be integrated with other sources of data [6, 8].

Many governments and agencies recognize the opportunities and challenges posed by informal volunteers, and many have developed strategies and resources for engaging and managing them. However, organizational culture, risks and liabilities impose significant barriers to greater involvement of informal volunteers in emergency and disaster management [2].

Different VGI categories – social media, crowd sensing, and collaborative mapping activities – require different strategies for promoting citizen engagement. It is our assumption that knowledge of the VGI categories is relevant for disaster managers to recruit and motivate users to utilize VGI-systems.

Additionally, works related to VGI in disaster management focus on production by volunteers and the use of this information by disaster managers. They disregard the fact that the production and consumption of VGI should be seen within a communication process, i.e., the communication among the stakeholders should be multidirectional.

To help fill this gap, we present in this paper a preliminary set of key factors to help promote the involvement of volunteers in the disaster management domain. These factors were derived from review of CE literature and from an analysis of lessons learned from a simulation exercise carried out in context of the EU-project "DRIVER – Driving Innovation in Crisis Management for European Resilience". The DRIVER project was launched in May 2014. This project, gathers the expertise of 37 organizations, and will jointly develop solutions for improved crisis management. Representatives from the security and defense industry, research and academia, SMEs, end-users and several European institutions, from 13 EU member states and 2 associated countries participate in this innovative venture.

With this work we aim to answer the following research question:

RQ. What factors should be considered by disaster managers to improve the involvement of digital volunteers?

The remainder of this paper is organized as follows. First, in order to set a ground on the different VGI approaches an overview is presented in Sect. 2. In Sect. 3 we present a review on the motivation and engagement of digital volunteers. In Sect. 4 we present factors to improve citizen engagement, based on lessons learned from an experiment on interaction with citizens carried out in context of the EU-project.

Finally, in Sect. 5, we conclude with final remarks and give potential directions for future works.

2 Volunteered Geographic Information

2.1 Volunteered Geographic Information VGI Source

In general, VGI in the context of disaster risk management can be collected through different collaborative sources [6]: (i) social media; (ii) crowd sensing; and (iii) collaborative mapping activities.

The first category of geo-information (i) involves the use of existing social media platforms to exchange information in an unstructured way. These platforms enable citizens to share self-produced content within a network of contacts or for the general public [6]. Common social media platforms include Twitter; Facebook, https://www. facebook.com/; Flickr, https://www.flickr.com/; YouTube, https://www.youtube.com/.

The second category of geo-information (ii) relies on citizens on the Web or equipped with smartphones to act as sensors and share observations [6, 10]. The term 'crowd sensing' is used to describe approaches that make use of specific software applications to provide more precise structured data [6]. Ushahidi-based platforms and mobile applications are the most commonly used in this category for data collection. GDACSmobile, for instance, is a tool that facilitates the self-organization of volunteers and improves the situational awareness of citizens by sharing an easy-to-understand overview of the state of affairs. At the same time, GDACSmobile also provides a feedback mechanism to the crisis manager/control center [11].

The third category of geo-information (iii) consists of a specific type of information and collaboration platform: the collaborative editing of geographic features to fulfill internet-based interactive maps. Well-known platforms like OpenStreetMap (OSM), Wikimapia and Google Map-Maker fall into this category [6].

Collaborative mapping activities are essential for disaster management, because they collect a very specific type of data – namely, georeferenced data about features like streets and roads, buildings etc. – and structures this information in the form of a map [23]. The OpenStreetMap (OSM) project has great potential in disaster scenarios, which was shown when a large number of volunteers provided their support in mapping events after the 2015 Haiti earthquake [26, 27] and the 2015 Nepal earthquake [23]. Collaborative mapping in OSM has emerged as a key mechanism through which individuals can provide information about affected areas, thus making a tangible difference to aid agencies and relief work without actually being physically present on-site [23].

2.2 VGI Types

Senaratne et al. [12], categorize the main types of VGI as (i) text-based VGI, (ii) image-based VGI, and (iii) map-based VGI.

Text-based VGI is generally produced implicitly on portals, such as Twitter or various blogs, where people contribute geographic information in the form of text by using smartphones, tablets etc. [12]. Twitter, for example is used as an information foraging source [12, 13]

Image-based VGI is generally produced implicitly within portals such as Flickr, Instagram, etc., where contributors take pictures of a particular geographic object or surrounding with cameras, smart phones, or any hand held device, and attach a geo-spatial reference to it [12].

Map-based VGI covers all sources that include geometries as points, lines, and polygons, which are the basic elements to design a map. Among others, OSM, Wikimapia, Google Map Maker, and Map Insight are examples of map-based VGI projects [12].

Table 1 presents the relationship between sources and the different types of VGI.

Table 1. A summary of the source and types of VGI

Source	Type		
	Text	Image	Map
Social media	X	X	
Crowd sensing	X	X	
Collaborative mapping			X

2.3 Typology of VGI

Craglia et al. [3] introduced the concept of typology in VGI. According to these authors, there are two modes through which individuals or communities contribute such information: first, the way the information was made available and second, the way geographic information forms a part of it.

Each of these two dimensions can be 'explicit' or 'implicit', with explicit denoting that the dimension is of primary concern to the piece of VGI, while implicit denotes that the dimension was not originally an integral part, and is of secondary concern [3]. Thus the topology of VGI proposed by Craglia et al. [3] is a matrix of four types of VGI as shown in Table 2.

Table 2. Typology of VGI [14] (adapted from Craglia et al. [3])

	Geographic information	
	Explicit	Implicit
Explicitly Volunteered	"True" VGI, e.g., OpenStreetMap	Volunteered (geo)spatial. Information, such as Wikipedia articles about non-geographic topics containing place names
Implicitly Volunteered	Citizen-generated geographic content (CGGC), e.g., Tweets referring to the properties of an identifiable place	User-Generated (geo)Spatial Content (UGSC), such as Tweets only mentioning a place in the context of another (non-geographic) topic

Geographic location is essential in disaster analysis [14]. Thus, only the explicit geographic category – explicitly- or implicitly-volunteered information – of the VGI typology is used in this paper.

Nevertheless, the typology of VGI proposed does not take in account the fact that different VGI types have different translation needs, which this may imply excess noise (e.g., many useless messages before a useful message to be found). For example, a picture of a flooded area is more effective (i.e., it has less translation needs) for disaster managers than a short message (tweet) describing the same flooded area.

Considering this aspect, we propose a new typology of VGI, which considers different levels of uncertainty – noise and translation needs. As can be seen, the explicit VGI sources – crowd sensing, and collaborative mapping activities – have fewer translation needs than social media data (Fig. 1).

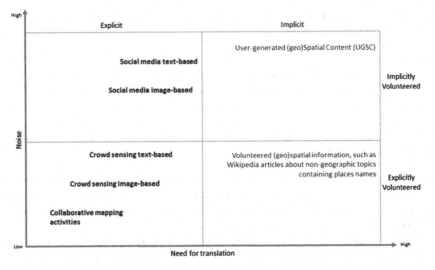

Fig. 1. Typology of VGI considering different levels of uncertainty - noise and translation needs

3 Motivation and Engagement of Digital Volunteers

A Digital volunteer or a digital humanitarian is an individual that applies and leverages their technical skills in collecting, processing and managing data in support of response efforts for disasters [30]. In most cases, he/she is not physically present at the place where the disaster has occurred. The Digital Humanitarian Network (DHNetwork) grew out of this ecosystem of emerging technical volunteer involvement based throughout the globe [29]. Since the 2010 Haiti earthquake, these communities have provided support to formal humanitarian operations [27], and more recently have provided a crucial compliment to operational organizations and governments active in the field [29].

However, it is still a challenge to keep digital volunteers motivated and engaged for longer periods, especially considering that they do not have strong connections to events due to their digital presence instead of physical presence in affected areas. This requires different ways to motivate and engage them to provide high quality contributions in future crisis/disaster situations.

To deal with this critical issue, we propose in this section a first attempt to understand how motivation of digital volunteers can be understood using, for instance, the Valence, Instrumentality, Expectancy (VIE) approach [17].

In general, volunteers are motivated by many incentives. Examples include, ideology, personal satisfaction, community, and humanitarian values. Particularly, in the context of a digital humanitarian, there is another factor that should be considered: the desire to apply and improve technical knowledge. Considering that many of these volunteers come from open source communities [28], why is it so important to understand the incentives of citizens in order for them share their observations from the field? Considering the 90-9-1-Rule [31], there is a so called "participation inequality". According to this rule, in a collaborative online environment, 90% of the participants of a community only view content, 9% of the participants edit content, and only 1% of the participants actively create new content [31].

In addition to such factors, it is important to understand two specific questions: (i) why does a citizen report an observation from the field, and (ii) does the information reported supports the decision making of disaster managers.

The first question is related to behavioral aspects, i.e., what are the incentives of citizens in order for them to want to share their observations from the field? Literature commonly understands incentives as instruments influencing the behavior of members of an organization or community in order to adapt to the organization wide system of objectives [18]. By creating incentives, certain desired modes of behavior from individuals are promoted, enabling specific situational conditions which in turn result in the activation of individual motives. In this case, a motive denotes a time-invariant psychological disposition, i.e. an isolated, not yet activated incitement for the behavior. Capelo et al. [28] highlight some important incentives:

- Encourage volunteers by giving feedback, recognition, appreciation and gratitude;
- Cultivate a sense of ownership and accountability. Team members have to know that they matter, and that they are making a difference in the humanitarian operation;
- Generate a feeling of inclusivity based on a system of collaboration, partnership and sharing with multiple stakeholders;
- Provide training and capacity-building opportunities for volunteers.

The second question is related to the contribution of effort input. For instance, the reporting of a flooded road is higher, if the reporter (or citizen) is affected or not. According to the VIE approach [17], the effort input of an individual is high when it expects that the contribution will yield results, which are first important to the organization or community, secondly, due to the expected instrumentality, show close relationships to individually aspired results from extrinsic incentives, and thirdly exhibit valences as high as possible.

4   Lessons Learned to Improve the Involvement of Volunteers

In this section, we summarize the lessons learned to improve the involvement of volunteers in the production of high-quality relevant information for disaster management. The elements presented here were derived from the VGI and citizen engagement literature reviews, as well as the analysis of lessons learned from a field experiment carried out in the EU-funded demonstration project DRIVER.

The selection process of the literature was based on the experience of the authors of this paper. Regarding the VGI literature, four main works were selected as an input to identify the main characteristics that may affect the digital volunteers' engagement: Albuquerque et al. [6], Craglia et al. [3], Klonner et al. [14], Senaratne et al. [12]. Regarding motivation and engagement of volunteers, we selected Nielsen [31], Lawler [17], and Capelo et al. [28] to understand the main aspects that should be considered in the digital volunteers' engagement.

The field experiment was based on a storyline designed by practitioners. They defined a fictitious disaster event based on past experience, which resulted in a more realistic and relevant scenario compared to a more tool-friendly situation designed by the tool providers. The experiments conducted in the DRIVER "Interaction with Citizens" campaign concentrate on the following functions (a more detailed description of this experiment can be founded in Havlik et al. [33], Middelhoff et al. [32] and van den Berg et al. [22]):

– Provision of context-aware and timely information tailored to the specific needs of different societal groups over various channels, in order to improve their understanding of the crisis situation and to minimize adverse impacts.
– Context-aware (micro-) tasking of non-affiliated volunteers to perform real and virtual tasks.
– Efficient gathering of situational information about an incident from volunteers.
– Efficient usage of received information from volunteers to improve the situational awareness of crisis managers and consequently their handling of the cri-sis.

In the following subsections, we will summarize the findings into two categories: (i) characteristics of VGI, and (ii) communication processes.

4.1   Characteristics of VGI

The characteristics of VGI – origin, type and typology – shown in Sect. 2 have an impact on citizen engagement.

In regard to the origin of VGI, crowd sensing and collaborative mapping activities have the potential to promote citizen engagement, due the ways in which the information is created.

Thus, we propose a typology of engagement based on five levels of involvement from volunteers in scientific work [20] and a typology of participation proposed by Pretty and Hine [21]. At the first level, citizens provide resources, while having only a minimal cognitive engagement. This level is called 'basic'. In second level, 'distributed intelligence' relies on the cognitive ability of the participants. After some training, the participants collect data or engage in minor interpretation activities. At this level, quality evaluation by the volunteers is crucial. The third level represents 'participatory engagement', where users take part actively in the problem definition and data collection. On the last level, 'self-mobilization', non-professionals collaborate with professionals, and together, decide on a problem they want to focus on and the methods for data collection. This allows for both the consideration of interests and motivation of the volunteers. On this level, volunteers are not only experts, but also have the role of facilitators [14, 20].

As shown in Table 3, social media presents a 'basic' level of engagement. This is because of the nature of its contribution, i.e., social media is provided implicitly. All other VGI sources, provided explicitly, require different strategies for citizen engagement, since many have volunteers with different levels of knowledge and motivation.

Table 3. Typology of engagement

Source	Typology of VGI		Levels of engagement			
	Explicitly	Implicitly	I	II	III	IV
Social media		X	X			
Crowd sensing	X		X	X	X	X
Collaborative mapping	X		X	X	X	X

Legend: I-Basic. II-Distributed intelligence. III-Participatory engagement. IV-Self-mobilization

4.2   Communication Process

The elements in the communication process determine the quality of communication. A problem in any one of these elements can reduce communication effectiveness [15]. For instance, different perceptions of the message, language barriers, interruptions, emotions, and attitudes can all reduce communication effectiveness. Therefore, a feedback mechanism should be considered to promote the involvement of volunteers.

The existing literature on VGI focuses on the production of geographic information, and the use of this information by disaster managers. It disregards the fact that the production of VGI should be seen within a more effective communication process, i.e., the communication among the stakeholders should have to include a mechanism for continuous feedback.

In the context of the DRIVER Project, tools were proposed that should address both objectives for the benefit of the community, and for individual members of the population according to the VIE approach. In a recent field exercise, the software tool GDACSmobile was used to communicate observations to crisis mangers (community-objective). The personal objectives of members of the population were addressed by sharing reports with the community as an information layer on a map of the environment around the user. In this way, the users could assure themselves of their safety in the situation and strengthen their situational awareness using map representation.

Consequently, by acknowledging the perceptions of community members, a common language visualizing interactions becomes a basic requirement for an appropriate crisis communication environment. One way to establish a common language is to use VGI systems in combination with commonly used information categories and according pictograms [22]. In the meantime, many different VGI tools are available, having different pros and cons regarding particular tasks. However, as mentioned above, the main challenge here is less a technical problem, but rather an organizational one. According to the discussion on incentives, we identify a trustful and open solution as most appropriate. However, it must be able to visualize benefits for the community, i.e. an easy- and fast-to-understand situation overview including a connection to responding authorities. In order to do so, the information should be structured and visualized respecting the communities' attributes (like age distribution, language, technical affinity, etc.).

5 Conclusion

Further research is still necessary for engaging volunteers in the production of high-quality relevant information for disaster management. For instance, how can we ensure that local communities are involved at a meaningful level in different phases of a disaster? This could be achieved, for instance, by initiating a community group or by providing training to volunteers to produce high-quality VGI. Moreover, how to improve collaboration between formal humanitarian organizations and volunteer technical communities (VTCs) should also be explored in future works.

Additionally, the different VGI categories require different strategies for promoting citizen engagement, given that the knowledge of the VGI categories is relevant for disaster managers to recruit and motivate users to utilize VGI-systems. Therefore, one of the expected outcomes will be the development of a new framework for promoting engagement of digital volunteers in the disaster management context.

Acknowledgments. The research that led to this work was funded by the European Community's Seventh Framework Programme: Marie Curie Actions/Initial Training Networks under grant agreement n° 317382 and FP7/ 2007-2013 under grant agreement n° 607798. João Porto de Albuquerque is grateful for the financial support from the CAPES Pró-Alertas (grant n° 88887.091744/2014-01 and n° 88887.091743/2014-01). The authors would like to thank Robin Mays and Lívia Degrossi for their helpful comments and suggestions, and the DRIVER "Interaction with Citizens" experiment team that has been working together for several months in order to prepare, conduct and finally assess the field exercise in The Hague.

References

1. American Psychological Association. http://www.apa.org/education/undergrad/civic-engagement.aspx
2. Schoch-Spana, M., Franco, C., Nuzzo, J.B., Usenza, C.: Community engagement: leadership tool for catastrophic health events biosecur. Bioterror 5(1), 8–25 (2007)

3. Craglia, M., Ostermann, F., Spinsanti, L.: Digital Earth from vision to practice: making sense of citizen-generated content. Int. J. Digit. Earth **5**(5), 398–416 (2012)
4. Weiner, D., Harris, T.M.: Participatory geographic information systems. In: Wilson, J.P., Fotheringham, A.S. (eds.) The Handbook of Geographic Information Science, pp. 466–480. Blackwell Publishing, Malden (2008)
5. Goodchild, M.F.: Citizens as sensors: the world of volunteered geography. GeoJournal **69** (4), 211–221 (2007)
6. Albuquerque, J.P., Eckle, M., Herfort, B., Zipf, A.: Crowdsourcing geographic information for disaster risk management and improving urban resilience: an overview of the lessons learned. In: Capineri, C. et al. (eds) European Handbook of Crowdsourced Geographic Information. Ubiquity Press (2016)
7. Haworth, B.: Emergency management perspectives on volunteered geographic information: opportunities, challenges, and change. Comput. Environ. Urban Syst. **57**, 189–198 (2016)
8. Horita, F.E., Albuquerque, J.P., Degrossi, L.C., Mendiondo, E.M., Ueyama, J.: Development of a spatial decision support system for flood risk management in Brazil that combines volunteered geographic information with wireless sensor networks. Comput. Geosci. **80**, 84–94 (2015)
9. Poser, K.: Dransch, D: Volunteered geographic information for disaster management with application to rapid flood damage estimation. Geomatica **64**, 89–98 (2010)
10. Ma, H., Zhao, D., Yuan, P.: Opportunities in mobile crowd sensing. IEEE Commun. Mag. **52**(8), 29–35 (2014)
11. Link, D., Widera, A., Hellingrath, B., Limbu, M.K.: GDACSmobile - an IT tool supporting assessments for humanitarian logistics. In: 2015 Annual Conference on the International Emergency Management Society (2015)
12. Senaratne, H., Mobasheri, A., Ali, A.L., Capineri, C., Haklay, M.: A review of volunteered geographic information quality assessment methods. Int. J. Geogr. Inf. Sci. 1–29 (2016)
13. MacEachren, A.M., Jaiswal, A., Robinson, A.C., Pezanowski, S., Savelyev, A., Mitra, P., Zhang, X., Blanford, J.: SensePlace2: GeoTwitter analytics support for situational awareness. In: IEEE Conference on Visual Analytics Science and Technology, Providence, RI, pp. 181–190. IEEE, Piscataway (2011)
14. Klonner, C., Marx, S., Uson, T., Albuquerque, J.P., Höfle, B.: Volunteered geographic information in natural hazard analysis: a systematic literature review of current approaches with a focus on preparedness and mitigation. ISPRS Int. J. Geo-Inf **5**(103), 1–20 (2016)
15. Keyton, J.: Communication and organizational culture: a key to understanding work experience. Sage, Thousand Oaks, CA (2011)
16. Ulmer, R.R.: Effective crisis management through established stakeholder relationships: malden mills as a case study manag. Commun. Q. **14**, 590–615 (2011)
17. Lawler, E.E.: Pay and Organization Development. Addison-Wesley, Reading (1981)
18. Grob, H.L., Buddendick, C., Albrecht, N., Widera, A.: Towards a holistic approach of E-learning incentive management. In: International Conference E-Activity and Leading Technologies, pp. 280–94 (2007)
19. Horita, F.E.A., Degrossi, L.C., Assis, L.F.F.G., Zipf, A., Albuquerque, J.P.: The use of volunteered geographic information and crowdsourcing in disaster management: a systematic literature review. In: 19th Americas Conference on Information Systems (2013)
20. Haklay, M.: Citizen science and volunteered geographic information: overview and typology of participation. In: Sui, D., Elwood, S., Goodchild, M. (eds.) Crowdsourcing Geographic Knowledge, pp. 105–122. Springer, Dordrecht (2013)
21. Pretty, J., Hine, R.: Participatory Appraisal for Community Assessment. Centre for Environment and Society, University of Essex (1999)

22. van der Berg, R., Widera, A., Lechtenberg, S., Middelhoff, M., Hellingrath, B.: Pictograms and assessment categories as crisis communication language: lessons from a field exercise with GDACSmobile. In: The 3rd International Conference on Information Communication Technologies for Disaster Management (submitted)

23. Poiani, T.H., Rocha, R.S., Degrossi, L.C., Albuquerque, J.P.: Potential of collaborative mapping for disaster relief: a case study of OpenStreetMap in the Nepal earthquake 2015. In: 49th Hawaii International Conference on System Sciences (HICSS) (2016)

24. Horita, F.E.A., Albuquerque, J.P.: An approach to support decision-making in disaster management based on volunteer geographic information (VGI) and spatial decision support systems (SDSS). In: 10th International Conference on Information Systems for Crisis Response and Management, Baden-Baden, Germany (2013)

25. Erskine, M., Gregg, D.: Utilizing volunteered geographic information to develop a real-time disaster mapping tool: a prototype and research framework. In: CONFIRM 2012 (2012)

26. Eckle, M., Albuquerque, J.P.: Quality assessment of remote mapping in openstreetmap for disaster management purposes. In: Proceedings of the ISCRAM 2015 Conference – Kristiansand, 24–27 May 2015

27. Zook, M., Graham, M., Shelton, T., Gorman, S.: Volunteered geographic information and crowdsourcing disaster relief: a case study of the Haitian earthquake. World Med. Health Policy 2, 7–33 (2010)

28. Capelo, L., Chang, N., Verity, A.: Guidance for collaborating with volunteer and technical communities

29. Humanitarian Response. http://www.humanitarianresponse.info/en/applications/tools/category/digital-volunteers

30. Liu, S.: Crisis crowdsourcing framework: designing strategic configurations of crowdsourcing for the emergency management domain. Comput. Support. Coop. Work 23(4), 389–443 (2014)

31. Nielsen, J.: The 90-9-1 Rule for Participation Inequality in Social Media and Online Communities (2006). http://www.nngroup.com/articles/participation-inequality/

32. Middelhoff, M., Widera, A., van den Berg, R., Hellingrath, B., Auferbauer, D., Havlik, D., Pielorz, J.: Crowdsourcing and crowdtasking in crisis management lessons learned from a field experiment simulating a flooding in city of The Hague. In: The 3rd International Conference on Information Communication Technologies for Disaster Management (submitted)

Disaster Reduction Potential of IMPRESS Platform Tools

Nina Dobrinkova[1]([✉]), Antonis Kostaridis[2], Andrej Olunczek[3],
Marcel Heckel[3], Danae Vergeti[4], Sofia Tsekeridou[4], Geert Seynaeve[5],
Andrea De Gaetano[6], Thomas Finnie[7], Efstathiou Nectarios[8],
and Chrysostomos Psaroudakis[8]

[1] IICT-BAS, Sofia, Bulgaria
nido@math.bas.bg
[2] SATWAYS, Athens, Greece
a.kostaridis@satways.net
[3] IVI-Fraunhofer, Dresden, Germany
{andrej.olunczek,marcel.heckel}@ivi.fraunhofer.de
[4] INTRASOFT, Athens, Greece
{danae.vergeti,sofia.tsekeridou}@intrasoft-intl.com
[5] ECOMED, Brussels, Belgium
geert.seynaeve@attentia.be
[6] CNR, Rome, Italy
andrea.degaetano@biomatematica.it
[7] PHE, Salisbury, UK
thomas.finnie@phe.gov.uk
[8] ADITESS, Nicosia, Cyprus
{nectarios,cpsaroudakis}@aditess.com

Abstract. In our paper we will present the IMPRESS Platform tools that have been used for tests and validation purposes in the case of Palermo Demo. The demo has been part of a national Italian field test exercise for civil protection authorities and all related services along. The system validation and tests procedures have been fulfilled in alignment with the authorities remarks. The outcomes and results from each tool in the platform will be described and the added value for the users who worked with them.

Keywords: IMPRESS project · INCIMAG · INCIMOB · WARSYS · Medical resources · Reaction in mass emergency

1 Introduction

In our paper we will describe a system which final test phase is still in process. However it has been partially tested on a big scale exercise in Palermo, Italy on 7th June 2016, but further final tests will be completed in February 2017in Sofia, Bulgaria. We will now focus on description and the system capabilities and designed functionalities which give opportunities to the emergency medical teams on the field and in the operational rooms in cases of mass emergencies. Some of the achieved results in the first tests will be also described.

Y. Murayama et al. (Eds.): ITDRR 2016, IFIP AICT 501, pp. 225–239, 2017.
https://doi.org/10.1007/978-3-319-68486-4_18

IMPRESS platform communication tool can be used for faster decision support and many saved lives in cases of mass emergencies. The IMPRESS project platform as designed can be used in assistance to support emergency medical teams on the field, that require involvement of diverse actors and deployment of various ICT systems to achieve the ultimate goal of efficient decision making and provision of a consolidated operational environment. This need comes to support various public safety agencies who are involved in a mass emergency response in their respective knowledge domains. To support these agencies a comprehensive ICT system with specific editions has been designed in the framework of FP7 call for Security with project acronym IMPRESS. The different systems or editions identified are targeting the needs of Emergency Medical Services (EMS), Law Enforcement, Fire Brigade, Coast Guard, Crisis/Civil Protection and Hospitals. Each edition is based on a core software platform whose purpose is to provide the standard command and control functions, the management of the required business processes, role based communications based on the organization's incident command structure, while at the same time being interoperable in a loosely coupled manner by exchanging open standard messages (e.g. alerts, resource requests, availability requests) in an intelligent way. These public safety agencies or organizations might have existing legacy systems with which interfacing occurs via another IMPRESS component, the core database responsible for all incoming data from different sources called - WARSYS.

The system operates in two directions on the field with mobile application called INCIMOB and on the dispatch center with desktop application called INCIMAG. Since the most significant operations take place on the field, first responders are equipped with a fully functional mobile data terminal which provides the chain of command with common situational awareness and the current reality on the field and act as their gateway to decision support tools. Patient tracking, situational reporting, resource messaging and geographical mapping are the primary functions of the first responder's mobile application. The structure of the system gives ability to the field teams and the teams in the hospitals or dispatch centers to communicate between each other through mobile devices bi-directionally. Field responders could have the capability to communicate via voice to the command center notifying them in real-time as to their status using their traditional telecommunication radios.

Decision Support Tools accessed by the Control Center application (INCIMAG) provide forecasting and recommendations to the incident commander and Emergency Operational Center (EOC) operators/logistic officers on what are the best course of action during an incident.

Drawing upon and combining all these layers of information, a Common Situational Picture and Situational Awareness well connected can provide regional, public health or ministerial authorities with what is occurring (severity, location, progress) and resource utilization. This provides a Common Situational Awareness (CSA) between the various public safety agencies (across command structures) and deep understanding and realization what can help in the detection of resource depletion depending on the mass emergency. The incident management tools are combined under the name INCIMAG and the incident management tool for the field operator is named INCIMOB.

The design of the system follows the IEEE1016 [1] standard of decomposition, dependency, interface and detail description of the components that constitute each subsystem as well as their interconnection with other IMPRESS modules and devices. The system is partitioned into various subsystems and components that match up with the user requirements in order the appropriate tools to be available for the end-users in a health emergency situation. The components address the user-requirements directly but also provide ancillary tools that are required behind the scenes to make these user-requirements viable.

2 System Overview

The system designed under the project contains the following components:

- Reference Semantic Model, which defines an ontology related to the health emergency management in mass emergency
- Data Harmonization Component (DHC), which makes the harmonization between the WARSYS (data base) component and the Reference Semantic Model
- WARSYS is the data base, which extract data from various sources and homogenize it for the use of the different components
- LOGEVO provides the logistics of health care resources, in hospital surge, when it comes to available medical care during events that exceed the limits of the normal hospital infrastructure
- SORLOC is a SOuRce LOCalization module which can support decision making in cases of biological released desease giving information of the resulting disease outbreak
- PATEVO component allows the simulation and prediction of the physiological/ health state of casualties, including the effects of medical treatments
- INCIMAG component includes the tools and environment to manage emergency incidents (it is a desktop solution)
- INCIMOB part of the platform and refers to the mobile extension of the INCIMAG system, for on-field operations, patient tracking, receiving notifications, etc. INCIMOB has also INCICROWD option for regular people inputs
- The training Component is an online training platform based on Moodle architecture providing to the users and operators useful information what tools and components can be found under the IMPRESS system platform.

2.1 WARSYS Component

WARSYS data base is the core of the IMPRESS system responsible for importing and storing structured data in the rest of the modules. It provides data importing capability from medical and logistics repositories (such as hospital information systems), while it has also the ability to store data by listening to the IMPRESS Messaging Bus (ActiveMQ) module. WARSYS then provides the homogenized data stored, to the data harmonization component (DHC) module.

WARSYS incorporates technologies and knowledge extracted by various national Database projects in the past, but it's a totally new component designed and implemented for the IMPRESS Platform.

The innovation in WARSYS lies in the cooperation of various licensed and open source products integrated to a database system that support many different kind of data sources. In addition, this capability of WARSYS gives the opportunity to handle many different types of resources and data in the future.

The EDXL files family manipulation and importing is another innovation of IMPRESS and WARSYS as its subcomponent.

WARSYS architecture is represented in Fig. 1.

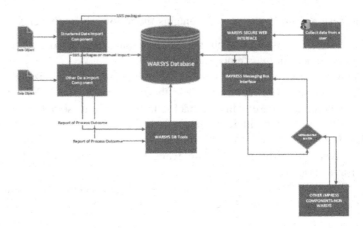

Fig. 1. WARSYS architecture

WARSYS architecture main component is the WARSYS Database where storage utilities are provided that make stored data available to the rest of WARSYS subcomponents as well as to other IMPRESS components. To support the operation of WARSYS Database the WARSYS DB Tools component is used. This component provides several administration tools and are used by authorised database administrative personnel (DBA) in order to manage import and export processes, provide maintenance, check WARSYS system health and connections to other IMPRESS components.

The rest of WARSYS architecture components are used to import (manually or automatically) and store data from different sources, as well as communicate with the other IMPRESS components through the message bus interface.

The Structured Data Import Component (SDIC) component is a set of visualised import stored procedures, called on demand by a user who has the relevant access privileges, in order to insert Hospital data into to the WARSYS Database. The SDIC component can be automatically called when data on the messaging bus become available.

The data import process is mainly handled by (SQL Server Integration Services) SSIS packages procedures. The first step is to validate the integrity of the files to be imported and append timestamp information, for security, validation and tracking purposes. Then the system identifies what this file is about and triggers the relevant import stored procedure. The stored procedure calls, the WARSYS SSIS mechanism and the file content is imported to the database on tables specified in the stored procedure. Apart from structured data, WARSYS can import data from other sources without using SSIS packages. This capability is mainly supported by python scripts. These scripts accept an XML as input, use the XSD schema file and insert data in MySQL tables. Using MSSM for MySQL, or other python scripts data from the MySQL databases are inserted to the MS SQL database.

Beyond the data import of EDXL files and other sources, WARSYS provides two more interfaces: one of the communication with the end user through the WARSYS Secure Web Interface and one for the interconnection with other IMPRESS components through the WARSYS IMPRESS Messaging Bus Interface.

Through the WARSYS Secure Web Interface component, and upon successful authentication, hospital personnel are able to connect to WARSYS and upload files or provide data manually regarding Hospital Availability, through web forms.

2.2 LOVEGO Component

The LOGEVO component main goal is to forecasts the evolution of the provision of resources to the hospital and to the field (Hospital Surge and similar) determining the time-curve of the amount of resources that can be provided to the system by exploiting the incremental capacity of the health structures involved in the crisis. In a Mass Casualty Incident (MCI) [2] the health care resources which are necessary to treat the large number of patients exceed the resources available. The system's resources deployed in the field in normal situations are insufficient and are often quickly depleted. The management of an Emergency situation requires therefore putting into action plans capable to quickly and efficiently enhance the health care response. The ability of the health services to scale up their resource provision becomes a key point for decision support. The LOGEVO component is one of the Decision Support System (DSS) elements in the IMPRESS system, set up to provide logistic support to the decision makers. The logic of LOGEVO was designed and samples were prototyped in Matlab [3] and the consensuses of medical doctors on the preliminary test results were obtained. LOGEVO component concerns hospital capacity, the hospital surge [4] capability and timing as well as the capacity and capability of the health service in general involved in a crisis event. By using this component, the imbalance between care needs, resources availability and the on-going modifications in the levels of both can become more optimized. The overall description of LOGEVO is depicted in Fig. 2.

2.3 SORLOC Component

The rapid determination of a source of biological contamination in time and space is essential for a coordinated response to "Extra-Ordinary Public Health Challenge" (EOPHC). Determination of the source of contamination is harder for biological threats compared with incidents typified by physical trauma as they are expected to come to official attention several days after exposure and infection. SORLOC is responsible for

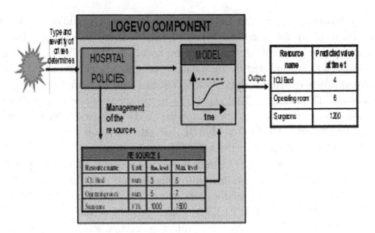

Fig. 2. General architecture of the LOgEVO component

determining the likely exposure source in time and space or simply time given field observations of a covert release of a biological contaminant. SORLOC component functionalities can provide observations that as a result return a probabilistic inference of the location of a release of a pathological biological agent. SORLOC is not an epidemiological surveillance system. A fundamental assumption of the models used is that the cases arise from a single confirmed outbreak of a known pathogen. SORLOC has been created to assist the decision makers in choosing where to focus resources (manpower and remediation measures) in the event of such an incident and arises from foreground work within Public Health England (PHE) on 'back-calculation' of epidemics or 'reverse epidemiology'.

SORLOC therefore has a single scope: determine a SOuRce LOCation. This determination has two facets, one temporal and one spatio-temporal [5]. Each facet has two subcomponents:

- Locate a source in time or time and space
- Provide an estimate of epidemic progression

In keeping with the one-task one-component philosophy it was decided to split SORLOC into a set of discrete sub-components each of which would provide a single function to the greater SORLOC component. The natural subdivision was that of models and interface. This is because the models are (relatively) short running; very computational resource intensive processes while the interface is a long-running process that requires very few computational resources. Dividing the models into temporal and spatio-temporal comes from a similar decision based on the fact that these models are likely to be grounded in different mathematical frameworks.

Treating the models as separate sub-components allows us to develop the interfacing technology with a known model before we investigate novel techniques for the spatial analysis. Part of the challenge in construction of the interfacing comes from ensuring a consistent run-time environment and placing and retrieving data from a shared high performance computing cluster in an automated way. The other part of the challenge is the specification of the data for input and output as before this project no standard for the transmission of epidemiological data. However the work on SORLOC component is still ongoing and the listed challenges can be met within the whole architecture of IMPRESS system.

2.4 PATEVO Component

PATEVO is a DSS component in the IMPRESS system which predicts the patient's physiological status evolution over time, predicting therefore the scenario evolution in terms of victim physiological status. PATEVO has complementary functions, which support the functionality of the component and those functions are: SCENGEN, SYMPTSCORING, STATSCORING, GAUGER, DAMAGER, SYMPTER, RESE-STER, aiming to implement logically distinct tasks necessary to complete the architectural design for the description of Scenario evolution in cases of emergencies. PATEVO is one of the DSS components designed to assess the evolution of patient health status with respect to evolving time, modelling both the effect of injuries and the effect of delivered treatments. To complete the picture of the Scenario evolution, a series of other functions are designed and implemented in order to test the functionality of the component in a real or simulated environment. The simulation environment will be also able to reproduce the two test-scenarios (the Palermo Scenario and the cross-border Scenario) against which the IMPRESS solution will be measured, as well as other different crisis scenarios. Each real or simulated crisis scenario produces a certain number of "affected" individuals (patients) among the existing "bystanders" (people exposed to risk), producing for each individual a set of anatomical lesions (with different levels of seriousness). Patients have to be triaged and appropriate care has to be delivered in the field, as first aid, or in definitive care structures, in order to restore their vital physiological conditions in an efficient way.

Each simulation instance starts with the generation of a CRISIS EVENT. The DSS PATEVO component predicts the evolution over time with physiological dimensions, which are called the Physiological State Variables (PSVs). The evolution is determined by the initial variable status (the initial defect), the initial rate of worsening and by the therapeutic maneuvers (if any) delivered. In the present formulation, medical care (treatments) is delivered by structures, which are called medical Assets: while an isolated surgeon, however good, will not be able to deliver effective care without instruments, drugs and assistance, an Operating Room (OR), endowed with all necessary human and instrumental accoutrements (surgeons, anesthesiologists, nurses, defibrillators, blood, IV sets etc.), is actually able to deliver a given standard of care. So is, for instance, an Ambulance. In the current terminology, therefore, isolated medical personnel are not considered, while OR's and Ambulances are health assets which can be employed and can be subject to competitive allocation (to some victim or to some other victim), to gradual increase via Hospital Surge mechanisms, etc. Clearly, not all Assets deliver the same Treatments: while an OR can administer oxygen, fluids, blood and vascular repair, an Ambulance can only administer oxygen and fluids. Each Asset is therefore characterized by the set of Treatments it can deliver. The row connecting the PSVs to the Score codes box (STATSCORING function) allows the system to have, in the simulation phase, a global vision, the "true" one, of the affected victim's status, determining the "true" scoring from the "Expected Time of Death", which represents the time at which one of the PSVs reaches a value indicating death. Moreover, from the Symptoms (observed in the field), medical personnel or volunteers make their own triage and are able to then test their performance in the triage procedure by comparing their scores with that automatically performed by the system (implementing appropriate scoring algorithms) from the detected symptoms (the SYMPS-CORING function) (Fig. 3).

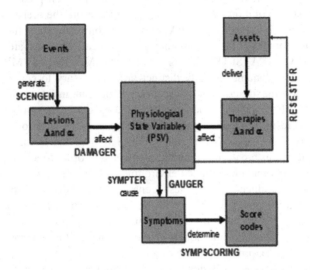

Fig. 3. General architecture of the PATEVO component and its collaborative functions

The Reference Semantic Model is an ontology defined as the IMPRESS Ontology, whose objectives are interoperability, data harmonization and linked data provision. The IMPRESS Ontology design and implementation process follows the METH-ONTOLOGY [6] steps and is implemented in OWL. The IMPRESS Ontology upper layer contains the following four main concepts:

- EOPHC (ExtraOrdinary Public Health Challenge): The concept refers to the emergency events and incidents that take place and require response.
- Person: The concept refers to the human individual.
- Resource: The concept refers to anything that is used to support or help in the response during a health emergency.
- Activity: The concept refers to any activity that takes place in order to reduce the impact of an emergency event.

The temporal aspects of the ontology have also been taken under consideration describing the evolution of the data through time. The data fact includes various sets of code lists described in SKOS as well as properties that are associated with user roles and geospatial data. The IMPRESS Ontology is further aligned with the TSO standard.

2.5   Data Harmonization Component

The Data Harmonization Component implements the data harmonization procedure that is required in order to harmonize the multidisciplinary and heterogeneous datasets of the IMPRESS Platform and provide a semantically homogenized view of the data. Also, these data are provided as linked data to the rest of the IMPRESS Components. Thus, Data Harmonization is also responsible for the linking of the RDF data [7] with other third party linked data resources.

The Data Harmonization Component implements data harmonization using the IMPRESS Reference Semantic Model which covers the respective domains of knowledge of the domain of health emergency management.

The main tasks that are realized by the Data Harmonization Component are the following:

1. Provide a real-time RDF view of the IMPRESS data stored in the WARSYS database, based on a specific mapping file
2. Provide access to RDF data views via a SPARQL endpoint
3. Execute SPARQL queries to RDF data and process the results, if necessary
4. Links the IMPRESS RDF data with specific linked data resources using a specific mapping file
5. Handle and serve the requests for data from the Message Bus

Based on the above, Data Harmonization Component includes four main sub-components: the Mapping Generator which is responsible to generate the mappings between the database data and the RDF view, the RDF Viewer which provides access and exposes the RDF views, the Query Handler subcomponent which handles the requests for data and the Data Linker.

As shown in Fig. 4, the DHC Manager receives requests for data from the Message Bus and based on the type of request calls the DHC RDF Handler which is responsible of querying the Mapping Generator for native RDF data or the RDF repository for linked data, through a SPARQL [8] endpoint. The Mapping Generator produces the dynamic harmonized view of the data that exist into the WARSYS database, while the DHC Data Linker generates RDF data linked with other Linked Data provided online. The results of the linking process are stored into an RDF repository in order to resolve issues of resources unavailability or low performance due to network latency issues.

The Data Harmonization Component uses the D2RQ server [9], an RDB2RDF technology, as well as, the SILK framework [10].

2.6   Recommendation Component

The Recommendation Component produces recommendations/suggestions on how to distribute the patients over hospitals. The component, based on the patient status (and status forecast, using the PATEVO component) and on available resources (ambulance vehicles and hospitals bed availabilities in different categories; also forecast of avail-abilities using the LOGEVO component), gives a recommendation about the order of patients, the destination hospitals, and optimal routes to the hospitals. This component can be used in every day incident patients dispatching and case of mass casualty incidents (MCI).

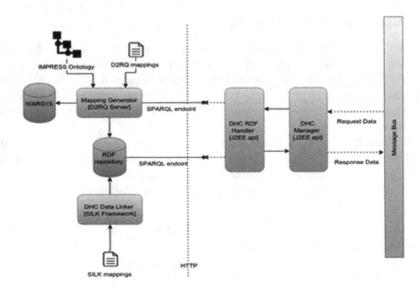

Fig. 4. Architecture of the DHC component

The Recommendation Component consists of the Distribution Service and the Optimisation Services: The distribution computation is based on routing on a street network that will be loaded from a database (the street network parameters used for the routing can be adjusted manually, to reflect traffic information like max speed or road closures). Each patient has a transportation priority that determines the order of transport. In addition, patients have a set of needed Assest that determine the hospitals that come into consideration. The amount of available Assest of a hospital may increase over time, so additional patients can be brought to it subsequently.

The optimisation computation tries to find an optimal order for the patient transport. For this, it uses LOGEVO to determine the increasing Asset availabilities of the given hospitals. In addition, PATEVO/STATSCORING is used to get the health status of the patient, how its health status will evolve over time and how the treatment (Asserts) will influence the health status. Based on this an initial priority and needed Assets for each patient is determined which is used to compute the prehospital time of each patient via the distribution computation explained before. Based on the resulting prehospital time PATEVO is used to check the health status at arrival time. If a patient would be dead or if other constraints are not met, adjustments on the patient priorities are done and the computations are repeated.

2.7   INCIMAG Component

During mass casualty incidents and disaster, Public Safety Agencies rely primarily on voice over radio communication along with pen and paper notes for situational awareness. The Integrated Incident Management System called INCIMAG that functionalities are to interconnect stakeholders, decision makers, operators, first responders through standardized data interoperability for incident coordination and shared situational awareness. Although the system capabilities are to support different Public Safety Agencies our primary focus is for Emergency Medical Services by implementing payloads that include data specific to Emergency Medical Services such as incident representation, unit tasking, triage, treatment and transport tracking of emergency patients (Fig. 5).

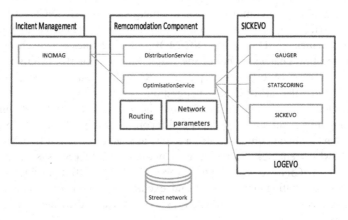

Fig. 5. General architecture of the recommendation component and relation to other components

The core existing geospatial platform (CEF - Chameleon Enterprise Foundation) of Satways Ltd. provided the Enterprise Application Open Service Gateway Initiative (OSGi) framework on top of which additional modules in the form of OSGi bundles were developed. With the final goal of a Multi-agency system for emergency call taking, incident and resource management and coordination, this initial round of implementation includes various client side plugins as well as server side components and services for call taking, address geocoding, resource management, and communication with field resources, hospital availability and patient tracking. An application server, database, back-end services and messaging middleware provide the necessary multi-tier infrastructure for the rich client application to visualize and manipulate data according to the various standard flows for incident and resource management determined by a Public Safety Standard Operating Procedures (SOPs). The interaction between agencies during normal operations and in mass casualty incidents takes place through an intelligent message router, designed and implemented for this purpose. Its aim is to route messages to the proper recipients who have declared their interest in particular messages, roles, or geographic areas. A subset of the Emergency Management Exchange Language (EDXL) family has been implemented: the Common Alerting Protocol (EDXL-CAP), the Hospital Availability Exchange (EDXL-Have), the Situational Reports (EDXL-SitRep) and the Tracking of Emergency Patients (EDXL-TEP) which can all be wrapped in the Distribution Element EDXL-DE) planned for the final phase of of development of the system. This subset provides the interconnection of agencies which is very important in cases of emergencies. Finally a

Mobile Application Programming Interface has been developed that will facilitate the interaction between INCIMAG instances and the related INCIMOB mobile application.

2.8 INCIMOB Component

The IMPRESS system comprises the mobile application INCIMOB that is connected to an INCIMAG desktop solution. INCIMAG is a full-featured command & control system to be deployed in command posts or emergency centres. INCIMOB is defined as mobile interface for INCIMAG and is therefore only connected to this system. INCIMAG provides an SDK-API to INCIMOB, which defines data exchange formats and communication channels. One of the major functions of INCIMOB is the registration and tracking of emergency patients. Recorded data will be processed by INCIMAG and the IMPRESS integration layer used as input for the PATEVO/LOGEVO components. In addition, the app provides up to date information about the ongoing event, status updates and recommendations from the DSS tools.

Further development comprises also a public available version of INCIMOB, called INCIcrowd, which enables the public to support the IMPRESS system in terms of crowdsourcing. INCIcrowd will be a light version of INCIMOB, to enable the public to receive alerts, submitting observations and exchanging resource offers/needs. INCIcrowd will be connected to the IMPRESS system via a dedicated server and the IMPRESS message bus.

Both applications have a general common architecture, depicted in Fig. 6.

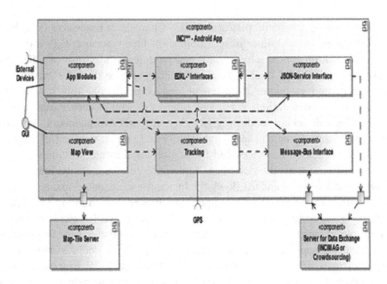

Fig. 6. General architecture of the IMPRESS smart applications

Each application contains of a set of modules. Furthermore, each module provides a set of features and uses a set of interfaces to communicate with the IMPRESS system. Each application can provide a set of features: some are similar in both apps, while others are unique for the specific app. Multiple related features can be bundled in one module. To switch between the modules, the applications use a design pattern that is called 'navigation drawer'. This pattern is used in a wide range of mobile applications and is intuitive for persons that are using smartphones in their everyday life.

The modules, and with that the applications, use a set of communication channels to communicate with the rest of the world, in this case with the IMPRESS systems. To get data from the application to a server, a RESTful- or SOAP-Service is used to transfer data messages serialised in JSON or XML format. To get data from the server to the application without the need for the application to permanently asking for new data, another communication channel is necessary. This channel has to provide the possibility of pushing messages to the application. A message bus is used as solution for sending messages to the mobile application devices (smartphones). Furthermore, the application needs access to a map tile server, to display features on a map. All these communication channels need an internet connection. Therefore, access to WLAN/Wi-Fi or 3G/4G mobile networks is mandatory.

3 Palermo Test Case and Achieved Results

The IMPRESS system tests started in the beginning of the project's third year and on 7th June 2016 in Palermo, Italy the first tests of the described components were done. The use scenario take place in Plarmo, a city with 700,000 inhabitants located in the Mediterranean Area of Southern Italy, and simulates the sudden liberation of high concentrations of toxic compounds from a fire developing on-board of a ship moored in the Palermo harbor.

The concept of the tested scenario moves from the availability of actual data from a historical fire, which developed in the Palermo waste dump of Bellolampo (Fig. 7) between July 29 and August 17, 2012.

Fig. 7. Palermo waste dump of Bellolampo

All the parameters about the toxic cloud that has been transferred above Palermo city center have been extracted from the past event in 2012. The designed scenario for IMPRESS system testing on 7th of June 2016 included sudden event consisting of a fire occured in a ship moored just outside the Palermo harbor (in Fig. 8 the red circle indicates the location of the ship).

Fig. 8. Palermo district involved called "Kalsa" plus the boat location in the gulf (Color figure online)

The ship has mainly a cargo of plastic materials that, during the combustion, releases different toxic substances such as dioxins, hydrogen cyanide, hydrogen chloride, and phosgene. Dioxins are unintentionally, but unavoidably produced during the manufacture of materials containing chlorine, including PVC and other chlorinated plastic feedstocks. Dioxin is a known human carcinogen and the most potent synthetic carcinogen ever tested in laboratory animals. A characterization by the National Institute of Standards and Technology of cancer causing potential evaluated dioxin as over 10,000 times more potent than the next highest chemical (diethanol amine), half a million times more than arsenic and a million or more times greater than all others. World Health Organization state that "Once dioxins have entered the environment or body, they are there to stay due to their uncanny ability to dissolve in fats and to their rock-solid chemical stability".

The presence of a wind from North East carries the toxic cloud in the direction of the urban area. This produces sudden release of toxicants in a place close to a very populated city area. The scenario involves the District "Kalsa" of about 0.8 km^2, indicated by the shaded area in Fig. 8.

The systems tested during the Palermo demo were oriented towards deployment of INCIMAG suit and INCIMOB mobile version for immediate triage on the field with injured people. The desktop application of INCIMAG was installed in all involved authorities and hospitals in order to have cluster of involved actors. The INCIMOB operators were thought how to operate on the field with the mobile application. The simulation final results were quite optimistic, so on the second stage in Sofia, second half of February 2017 the full capacity of the system with recommendation engine will be included and the Decision support part of the system will be fully tested.

4   Conclusions

In this article we have described how the IMPRESS Incident Management Tools can work fully together to enhance and support the functions of the agencies involved in an everyday emergency situation, mass emergency incident and crisis situations. Each actor in such a situation requires technological support. If this on field support is timely provided and the basic activities are fulfilled the injured people and saved lives can increase its percentage. The Incident Management tools designed target the Emergency Medical Services, Law Enforcement, Fire Brigade, Coast Guard, Crisis/Civil Protection as well as Hospitals by empowering them with an information system (field and command center) which will provide a Common Situational Awareness and deep understanding and realization of the severity in the mass emergency. With IMPRESS ICT tool which can help in the detection of resource depletion or depending on the emergency situation evacuation or escalation of efforts on the field can deal better with Extra Ordinary Public Health Challenges.

Acknowledgement. This work has been partially funded by the EC in the 7th Framework Programme, (SEC-2013.4.1-4: Development of decision support tools for improving preparedness and response of Health Services involved in emergency situations) under grant number FP7-SEC-2013–608078 - IMproving Preparedness and Response of HEalth Services in major criseS (IMPRESS).

References

1. IEEE 1016–2009 Standard for Information Technology – Systems Design – Software Design Descriptions (2009)
2. Committee on Guidance for Establishing Crisis Standards of Care for Use in Disaster Situations, Institute of Medicine: Crisis Standards of Care: A Systems Framework for Catastrophic Disaster Response. National Academies Press, Washington (DC) (2012)
3. MATLAB and Statistics Toolbox Release 2009b. The MathWorks, Inc., Natick, Massachusetts, US (2009)
4. http://www.calhospitalprepare.org/healthcare-surge
5. Kernighan, B.W., Pike, R.: The UNIX Programming Environment. Prentice-Hall, Upper Saddle River (1984)
6. Gomez-Perez, A., Fernández-López, M., Corcho, O.: Ontological Engineering: With Examples from the Areas of Knowledge Management, e-Commerce and the Semantic Web. Springer Science & Business Media, London (2006). METHONTOLOGY: From Ontological Art Towards Ontological Engineering
7. Resource Description Framework (RDF). https://www.w3.org/RDF/
8. SPARQL Query Language for RDF. https://www.w3.org/TR/rdf-sparql-query/
9. Accessing Relational Databases as Virtual RDF Graphs. http://d2rq.org/
10. Volz, J., Bizer, C., Gaedke, M,. Kobilarov, G.: Silk-a link discovery framework for the web of data. LDOW, vol. 538. http://dc-pubs.dbs.uni-leipzig.de/files/ldow2009_paper13.pdf

M&S Support for Crisis and Disaster Management Processes and Climate Change Implications

Orlin Nikolov[1](✉), Nikolay Tomov[2], and Irena Nikolova[3]

[1] Crisis Management and Disaster Response Centre of Excellence,
Sofia, Bulgaria
orlin.nikolov@cmdrcoe.org
[2] Bulgarian Modeling and Simulation Association - BULSIM, Sofia, Bulgaria
nikolay.tomov@bulsim.org
[3] Space Research and Technology Institute,
Bulgarian Academy of Science, Sofia, Bulgaria
irena.nikolova@mail.space.bas.bg

Abstract. This paper addresses the efforts of NATO, EU and other regional initiatives to support education and training for better understanding the Crisis and Disasters Management processes (CDMP) and Climate Change Implications (CCI) on Military activities. The article tackles the question of applying Modeling and Simulation systems, tools, software and practises as a complex combination of live, virtual, and constructive environment not only to predict the trends, but to identify the source in a particular situation. Currently in NATO (according the Action plan on M&S in support of military training) there is a significant gap in estimation, forecast, and response plan generation capabilities related to crisis and disaster management and climate change implication. The development of a specific technical platform for CDMP & CCI will provide NATO & EU with a unique comprehensive training and analytical capability. This platform is expected to enable the support of large scale crisis management and disaster response distributed exercises and analysis with specific tools and simulations for different types of Crisis and Disasters situations. This would enhance the quality of training of the militaries and will provide a critical new capability for Allies.

Keywords: CAX · Crisis management · Disaster response · Comprehensive approach · NATO-EU cooperation · Civil-military interoperability · Interagency cooperation · Multinational exercise · Smart defence · Pooling and sharing · Risk reduction · Technical architecture · Simulation

1 Introduction

The responsibility for crisis management and disaster response differs for every nation and may involve various ministries and agencies. It is also a core task of the Alliance. Today, the Alliance is able to make decisions in crisis and emergency situations and to act under significant threats and time pressure. NATO develops capabilities to be

© IFIP International Federation for Information Processing 2017
Published by Springer International Publishing AG 2017. All Rights Reserved
Y. Murayama et al. (Eds.): ITDRR 2016, IFIP AICT 501, pp. 240–253, 2017.
https://doi.org/10.1007/978-3-319-68486-4_19

prepared, on a case-by-case basis and by consensus, to contribute in effective crisis and disaster prevention. This enables the Alliance to engage actively in crisis management and disaster response referring to non-Article 5 for crisis response operations. The Alliance therefore encourages the joint training of military and civilian personnel for building trust and confidence.

NATO's role in crisis management and disaster response goes beyond military operations and includes crisis and disaster response operations against natural or manmade disasters. A crisis can be political, military, social or humanitarian, and therefore NATO Crisis Response System covers different resources and capabilities of dealing with diverse types of crises, including disaster response.

Based on the perception that military intervention alone cannot resolve a crisis or ensure recovery after disasters, the NATO Summit Declarations and the Strategic Concept emphasizes the need for NATO to enhance its contribution to the Comprehensive Approach to crisis management. The goal is to enhance the Alliance and Nations' civilian and military capabilities for crisis management and disaster response.

Virtual reality, artificial intelligence algorithms, simulation of alternatives based on different scenarios, add high potential to risk analysis and assessment. With the support of modeling and simulation, various conditions could be created for: a holistic analysis, further development of existing methodologies, models, infrastructure, validation of working hypotheses by means of creating the environment for designing, testing and managing architectures of different systems, building models of systems, testing of specific criteria, running process optimisation, experimentation, assisting informative decision-making, etc.

Design and development of a simulation environment for natural disaster risk assessment include the need for realistic visualization of the impact from the concrete natural disaster, visualization of the affected groups and their capabilities (reaction time, scope of the disaster and potential negative impact, available resources, etc.) and precision in forecasting. Additionally, presenting the effects and impact on the population and on the environment as a result of real-time decision-making is almost impossible to be executed with traditional means. A very important activity is the analysis of the cooperation among all responsible stakeholders, dealing with natural disaster risk assessment.

Applying modeling and simulation for the preparation of all-levels authorities in disaster management becomes one of the most effective methods for education and training, which allows, with the use of minimum resources, the evaluation of the current level of preparedness and readiness of the national and institutional forces and resources.

The challenges that the Integrated Natural Disaster Risk Assessment Information System faces create the need for new preparation methods aiming to ensure maximum results with the use of minimum resources. This imposes the adaptation of available forces and resources to work in a joint multinational environment consistent with the requirements for speed, precision and flexibility. Subsequently, the requirements towards the system, considering the work in a joint multinational environment, will continue to increase demanding full interoperability. New doctrines and procedures concerning risk assessment and the mitigation of the negative impact caused by natural disasters have to be developed alongside the new systematic preparedness programmes.

Modeling and simulation in crisis management and disaster risk assessment is applied in order to recreate imaginary critical situations. Modeling and simulation are becoming even more popular nowadays given the current level of societal development and the penetration of modern technologies in all academic, applied and socio-economic areas. Modern technologies enable the recreation of the reality into virtual reality with training purposes. Virtual reality is used to recreate specific events (terrorist attack, natural disaster, social anomaly) which is to serve the users to assess and be prepared in case similar potential real events occur.

2   Disasters Impact on People

In recent years, an increase in the number and the magnitude of man-made or natural disasters has been recorded around the world and particularly in Bulgaria. An increase in the negative effects of disasters on the social relations, the economic growth and the sustainable development of the countries is also registered.

According to the type of hazard, disasters can be generally classified in the listed groups bellow (The Human Cost of Weather-Related Disasters 1995–2015). The report focus on hydrological, meteorological and climatological disasters, which are collectively known as weather-related disasters (see Fig. 1).

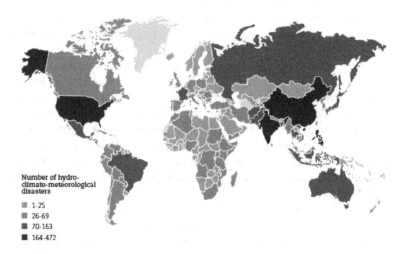

Fig. 1. Number of weather related disasters

- Natural Hazards by Disasters type
  - *Geophysical*
    - Earthquake
    - Mass movement (dry)
    - Volcanic activity
  - *Hydrological*
    - Floods
    - Landslides
    - Wave actions

- *Meteorological*
  - Storms
  - Extreme temperatures
  - Fog
- *Climatological*
  - Drought
  - Glacial lake outburst flood
  - Wildfires
- *Biological*
  - Epidemic
  - Animal accidents
  - Insect infections
- *Extra-Terrestrial*
  - Impact
  - Space weather
- Human costs and impacts of weather related disasters
- Manmade disasters
- Climate Change Implications.

The human losses caused by weather-related disasters depend on multiple factors, including the type of hazard, its location, duration and the size and vulnerability of the population. The basic economic impacts, including homes and infrastructure damaged and destroyed, must also be considered. Other costs, including repairs, rehabilitation and rebuilding expenditure, plus lost productivity and increased poverty, are harder to quantify but nevertheless must be taken into account when analysing the overall economic burden of disasters.

The Fig. 2 shows that people are mainly affected by disasters such as flooding and drought.

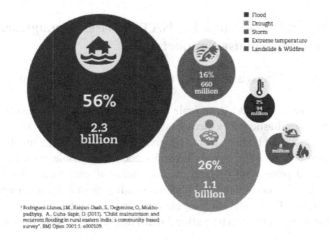

¹ Rodriguez-Llanes, J.M., Ranjan-Dash, S., Degomme, O., Mukho-padhyay, A., Guha-Sapir, D. (2011). "Child malnutrition and recurrent flooding in rural eastern India: a community-based survey". BMJ Open 2001;1: e000109.

Fig. 2. Number of people affected by disasters

When causes for deaths are analyzed the situation is completely different. Storms and Extreme temperature are main "killers". Storms, including hurricanes, cyclones and storm surges, killed more than 242,000 people between 1995 and 2015 (see Fig. 3), making storms the most deadly type of weather-related disaster in the last 21 years.

Scientific results suggest that climate change will increase the upward trend in the numbers of floods and storms worldwide, while the population that needs protection will increase at the same rate as population growth in disaster-prone regions. On the positive side, weather forecasting has made extraordinary progress in recent years, with predictions highly reliable within a 48 h period. In the face of climate change, we may not be able to stem the increased frequency of storms, but better risk management and mitigation could reduce deaths and other heavy losses caused by those predictable hazards.

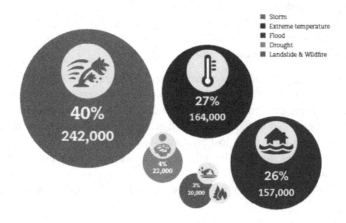

Fig. 3. Number of people killed in disasters type

3   Modeling and Simulation for NATO Crises Management and Disaster Response Support

Managing crisis situations is a priority not only at national level, but also at NATO and EU level.

Crisis situations may entail large-scale incidents forcing the evacuation of civilian population and other drastic safety measures. Due to the scale of crisis situations a great number of managing bodies from different institutions are involved in the decision-making process. The actions taken by each responsible organisation - army force, police, civil protection, fire and medical units, as well as the voluntary units, have to be adequately coordinated and planned in advance in order to ensure rapid and effective response. To reach optimal effectiveness and efficiency in the actions undertaken, these forces have to be well-trained. The preparedness of the forces and the rapid allocation of resources during crisis situations cannot be achieved without regular training and exercises.

At the same time, the rapid development of modern technologies has led to a broad application of modeling and simulation methodologies and tools in risk assessment, disaster management and training of teams and decision-makers. Simulation possesses high potential serves as a catalyst in the process of human capacity-building using innovations and experiments in training, evaluation of alternatives and validation of concepts, methodologies and procedures.

Their main purpose is to create, based on high-level architecture and technology, the specific conditions for individual training, coordination of actions at any level, as well as support decision-making on risk reduction and eliminate the impact of disasters.

The successful application of simulations in disaster risk assessment and the improvement in the preparation and qualification of staff members could enable various scenarios analyses, put the focus on preventive actions and enhance decision-making during natural disasters and emergencies. The analysed information allows higher precision in risk and impact assessment of emergency situations and increases the effectiveness of the rescue and recovery activities.

However, the capabilities of the CMDR Training and Climate Changes preparedness can be greatly enhanced by the utilization of the application of crisis management and disaster response tools, software and simulation systems.

The developed M&S environment will have its initial operational capability (IOC) established and operational in time to support the planned NATO Crisis Management Exercises, as well as any regional Network projects or exercises and trainings.

The integration of all mentioned aspects will add value to NATO force structure in order to be well prepared for the next conflict by supporting capability building; improving interoperability and support of capability development with education and training for NATO and partner leaders and units; testing doctrines; developing and validating concepts through experimentation; providing lessons learned, evaluations and assessments.

4 Integrated (Distributed) CDMP & CCI Simulation Platform

The combination of Live, Virtual and Constructive simulation is expected to form the Integrated CDMP & CCI Simulation Platform. In the context of an architecture for a CMDR Simulation & Training Environment we can identify the main "modules" of such a Platform as:

- Management Framework – the Management Framework includes the Integrated Management Cycle. Considering the specific training features and the best practices, the framework has been developed on the conceptual basis of the project management.
- Simulation Framework – application of a federated approach based on High Level Architecture (HLA), but could also include Distributed Interactive Simulation (DIS) and Test and Training Enabling Architecture (TENA);

- Modeling and Simulation Tools - tools including modeling and simulation of CBRN, flooding and earthquake effects during crises, crowd movement models and modeling of civil emergency services, etc.;
- Environment Representation - including terrain, weather conditions and infrastructure;
- Training Audience with their C4I real tools including decision and situational assessment tools, also visualization, simulation control and analysis tools;
- ICT Infrastructure – including hardware, basic software and connectivity for supporting the functioning of the Training Environment.

These six main "modules" of the CDMP & CCI Simulation Platform will enable a powerful Integrated (Distributed) Training Environment for CMDR.

Adapted to NATO's Concept Development and Experimentation Policy and processes for capability development the Integrated Environment for CMDR Training could be schematically presented as three main functional labs (see the figure bellow):

- Concept Development Lab – provides a framework for identifying existing ideas and solutions or developing new ones to overcome capability shortfalls and gaps in CDMP & CCI;
- Experimentation Lab – its role is to determine, with the means and tools of experimentation, whether a concept under development will achieve its main aim;
- Training Lab – a place for exercising the approved concepts, tested and validated with experiments (Fig. 4).

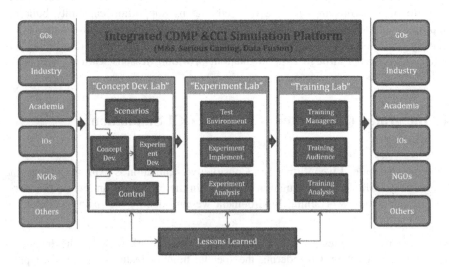

Fig. 4. CDMP & CCI Simulation Platform

5 Project Management of CDMP & CCI Simulation Platform

The realization of a CDMP & CCI simulation platform from the management point of view is a complex activity which requires specific efforts in the area of the management and planning. In this regard, the Platform development should be planned and executed according to the Project Management Approach, using PRINCE2 as a specific organization dedicated to deliver its specific results/objectives.

PRINCE2 (PRojects IN Controlled Environments) is the most widely practiced project management methodology, based upon project management best practices and used in over 150 countries and NATO. PRINCE2 provides common systems, procedures and language.

The achievement of the objectives of the CDMP & CCI simulation platform design, development and realization is ensured by good project management, which defines the exercise goals, organises the work packages and assigns the workload to highly motivated, qualified and experienced teams.

The specific benefits are as follows:

- CDMP & CCI simulation platform implementation in scope, in time and in budget;
- Transparency, distinct distribution of responsibilities and assessment of deliverables and achieved results at each stage;
- More effective and efficient resource management;
- Storing data and knowledge bases.

6 Trends in the Simulation Solutions for Disaster Risk Assessment

Tendencies in the development of simulation solutions for disaster risk assessment are focused on the improvement of standards, services, communication, equipment and software, training, education and technical knowledge, necessary for the successful design and maintenance of a complex modeling and simulation program and for achieving maximum benefit from their utilisation.

A common technical environment enables the identification of standards for the use of modeling and simulation software which determines the technical architecture, including the type of interface of the additional programme applications.

The simulation architecture consists of main functional elements, interfaces and programming rules applicable to all simulation applications. It provides the general framework within which specific system architectures and higher-level architectures can be defined and made functional.

Data standards are used in creating, publishing and guiding the actions, procedures and the methodologies for defining the data requirements used in modeling and simulation. These requirements include data exchange, verification, validation and accreditation standards, and also standards for authorisation data sources and ensuring data security. Data standards improve the interoperability between modeling and simulation providing data and command, control, communication, computer and intelligence (C4I) systems.

7 Knowledge and Expertise in Simulation Development Technologies

The acquisition and development of simulations with the aim of meeting a wide spectrum of users' needs is a very challenging task. The possibility of simulating exercises at any level, where the switching between different levels is performed in different simulation systems and simulators, reaching the demands of the individual training, is a highly complex task.

The usage of simulation systems ensuring Live Simulation, Virtual and Constructive Simulation brings to a qualitative new level the process of modeling and simulation. Each simulation is applied to different trainings, exercises and games. The 'Serious games' type will contribute to the specific procedures and missions of the training.

Technology evolves quickly and enables the increase in general effectiveness of the modeling and simulation. In order for the Integrated Natural Disaster Risk Assessment Information System to benefit from modern technologies, a constant research on their development has to be conducted. This process includes gaining knowledge on modeling and simulation, creating education database by referring to periodicals, participation in conferences, international programs, expert exchange and participation in international exercises conducted in a distributed manner.

8 Remote Training and Distributed Exercises

Conducting distributed CAX using a simulation module enables financial and material savings to be made as trainees will participate in the trainings from different locations. Effectively, the new joint capabilities enable the conduct of joint exercises run by various structures of different institutions and organisations without the need of physical presence at a specific location.

The goal is to establish a joint information system for training capabilities development, analysis and assessment using the entire spectrum of real, virtual and constructive simulations.

9 Capability Analysis of Simulation Instruments for a Natural Disaster Risk Assessment

Analysis conducted with the use of simulation provides the opportunity for almost comprehensive risk assessment, applying various probability and intelligent methods, with integrating diverse types of data and expertise in a context of subjectivity and incomplete certainty. Through simulation the theory easily turns into practice and enables people to use the pragmatic method in analysing and improving their work.

In order to create a 'Simulation' module as part of the Integrated Natural Disaster Risk Assessment Information System the necessary software and simulation systems have to be selected and to be connected into a common environment. The expectation that a single software can encompass all natural disasters is a more or less unachievable task considering the current state of the technologies. Globally, a number of simulation systems and software exist, which are designed to solve different tasks for anticipating and mitigating the risk of various natural and man-made disaster and for crises management in case such events occurred.

Exploring the simulation systems and software, with the aim of selecting the most appropriate combination for the purpose of training staff members in a close to the reality environment during a specific type of a natural disaster, and connecting them in a common environment in which different scenarios can be simulated, is a promising approach that could save time and resources.

The current practices shows that it is almost impossible, and unnecessary for that matter, to create a simulation model that includes all levels - from tactical to strategic. Overall, the trainees exercise different types of activities and it is not necessary for the high level authorities to be able to manage local finances, but rather to know what has to be the contribution for achieving a positive result.

Last but not least, attention should be paid to the fact that disasters are diverse and cyclic as well as differing from one geographic latitude to another. If, for the region of North America, typhoons and hurricanes are a widely spread disaster, for Europe these are floods, for Asia – earthquakes, and droughts for Africa.

The common trait of all these is that they are measured against material, financial and, almost in all cases, human life losses.

Due to the aforementioned reasons, to design and develop a stand-alone product for an integrated risk assessment covering all types of disasters is a heavy and unpractical task.

The integration of software products in a common environment is expected to contribute for tackling the aforementioned issue. Transferring scenarios, forces and resources, which may be observed on different simulation systems is an easier option for solving the generality issue of the task.

Solving this problem is imperative also because disasters know no borders and can easily spread from one country to another, and because the responsibilities for different disasters are shared by different ministries and institutions. Therefore, interagency cooperation and interaction is of crucial importance and simulation products provide the best result in training the management staff from different ministries in a realistic uniform environment.

10   Criteria for Selection of Simulation Instruments and Solutions for Disaster Risk Assessment

Well fitted simulation instruments suitable for risk assessment of various types of natural disasters on the territory of the Republic of Bulgaria - flood simulation, fire simulation, CBR contamination, evacuation simulation, etc. have been identified.

The analysed simulation products and solutions, covering specific areas, were ranked in the following manner:

- Selected simulation solutions applicable to the natural disaster risk assessment for the territory of the Republic of Bulgaria based on historical data on the frequency of occurrence of these and other anticipated disasters as a result of climate change;
- Selected simulation solutions on the basis of the criterion 'available open source solution information';
- Selected simulation solutions on the basis of 'information received from providers of simulation solutions';
- Selected simulation solutions on the basis of 'expertise'.

11   NATO Computer Supported Capabilities Dealing with CDM & CCI

The 2015 Gap Analysis Report serves as the foundation for the development of the 2015 Action Plan (AP) on M&S in support of military training. The Science, Technology, Modeling & Simulation Branch NATO HQ SACT and the Crisis Management and Disaster Response Centre of Excellence (CMDR COE) staff realized that there is a gap in NATO computer supported capabilities dealing with large scale events with negative impact on human society such as crisis and disasters, as well as in the evaluation of Climate Change. CMDR COE's staff has started a project for developing a technical platform using M&S for conducting experiments, tests, CAXs and training in the CMDR and Climate Change domain.

The project was endorsed by the NATO Science and Technologies Board and started in February 2016 with an end date February 2019 under MSG-147 with lead nation Bulgaria and participation from Austria, Bulgaria, Germany, Sweden, USA, M&S CoE, CMDR CoE, JFTC, and companies as IBM, MASA Group, C4IS. The project is open to Industry and NATO Partnering Nations.

The aim of the project is to develop a reference architecture and demonstrate a technical platform that enables prompt, reasonable and effective verification and validation of Crisis/Disaster and Climate Change Implication (CCI) Response plans.

The development includes scientific researches, concept development and experimentation, standardization and interoperability improvements.

The expected Deliverables from the projects:

- Investigate, categorize and catalogue data sources available for Disaster Response.
- Analyze existing standards in common vocabulary and adapt existing ones for NATO purposes.
- Categorize existing M&S solutions for CMDR & CCI and develop missing ones.
- Computer formalization of Command and Control logic for Crisis/Disaster Response (DR).
- Reference architecture/platform for proof of concept.

- Demonstration (contribution to multinational exercises) as a test bed for Analysis and Trainings in order to support Crisis/Disaster Management and Climate Change Implications.
- Synergies and Complementarities

The project combines NATO Crisis Response Process with industrial theory for system control in predefined parameters. The task is of significantly large scale and is divided into subtasks and spread among NATO Nations, bodies, organizations and partners.

The three phases of the project will be synchronized to move forward at the most rapid pace possible.

Phase 1 is planned to take 12 months and will result in the development of a Master Plan to guide and direct this project. It would also identify all the requirements, products and specifications for support of the crisis management and disaster response technical platform for M&S.

Phase 2 is planned to take twelve months and will result in building the initial operational capability (IOC) of the crisis management and disaster response technical platform. Planning of the experiments, verification and training for CMXs would be conducted as well during this phase.

Phase 3 is planned to take twelve months aiming to achieve successful execution of CM exercises and analysis efforts as part of the operational support of the crisis management and disaster response technical platform. During this phase, experienced subject matter experts will support the improvement of the platform. They would also conduct advance training for using the fielded simulations and tools.

The technology matureness has reciprocal effect to the command and control logic. Implementation of such developed technical products in NATO Crisis and Disaster Management process will smarten up it and that is one of the aims of MSG-147.

The project has three main directions for analyzing CDM in NATO in order to improve the E&T and support of the decision making process in the Alliance:

- First one is the analysis of the Disaster Risk Management (DRM) processes, preceding the development of the Operations Plan:
  - Fast and accurate Disaster Risk Analysis;
  - Comprehensive approach and correlation assessment among hazardous events;
  - Prevention and Preparedness Measures proposals.
- Second one is the assessment of the Disaster Response, during NATO operation:
  - Fast and accurate Disaster Assessment (DA);
  - Dynamically generated proposal for Response Plan.
  - Lessons Learned process
- Third one is the development of module for a realistic modeling and representation of different types of disasters for the purpose of education and training, experimentations, verification and validations.

The following components should be developed in order to achieve the above mentioned results:

- Input Data Module - database for statistical (history) and real-time data. The database should have standard properties and interface.

- Disaster Model Engine – combines input interface (accept data from the database), disaster model repository (as many as possible mathematical representations of different types disasters), output interface.
- Decision-Making Support Module – database with fragmented SOPs and defined triggers for disaster alerts and response. To each elementary action of the SOPs, will be added metadata containing: relevance to event, priority and sequence, dependences, etc.
- Filtering and Distribution Module – will filter the relevant elementary response actions and will dynamically generate proposal for Response Plan or Prevention and Preparedness Measures proposal (Fig. 5).

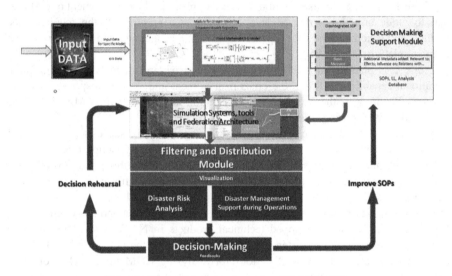

Fig. 5. Technical Architecture for CDMP & CCI

12   Conclusions

The development of M&S architecture specific for the needs of the CMDR Training and Climate Change preparedness would provide NATO with a unique comprehensive training and analytical capability for non-military type of operations. This M&S architecture would be able to support large scale CDM distributed exercises and analysis with specific crisis management and disaster response tools and simulations. Experienced and highly trained personnel will operate this newly established technical environment. This new crisis management and disaster response environment will be supported by operationally experienced simulation subject matter experts to ensure successful operations, exercises and support activities from the beginning of the operations.

The close cooperation in the crisis management and disaster response domain requires the involvement of the appropriate military and civilian capabilities. These capabilities will include information and intelligence sharing, developing and operating early warning systems (in support of building common situational awareness), as well as conducting crisis and disaster planning and response, and preparedness for Climate Changes.

The establishment of a CMDR M&S Platform should have its initial operational capability established and operational in time to support the planned NATO Crisis Management Exercises, as well as any regional Network projects or exercises and trainings.

References

1. Nachev, M., Nikolov, O.: Multinational Initiatives and Training in Support of Regional Defense Cooperation – BG (2015)
2. Technical report MSG 068 "NATO Education and Training Network"
3. ACT Directive for Operating JWC, JFTC and JALLC (80-3), version: Latest, March 2004
4. ACT Directive for the Implementation of JWC, JFTC and JALLC Plan of Action and Milestones (80-6), version: Latest, December 2004
5. Joint Training, Experimentation and Interoperability Development Capabilities (CP 9B0401), version: Latest, June 2004
6. JWC and JFTC Training and Experimentation Facility AIS Concept User Requirements Analysis, version: 1.1, December 2005
7. BI-SC 75-3 Collective Training and Exercise Directive, version: Latest, OKT (2010)
8. MSG-068 NETN TAP, version: Latest, April 2007
9. STANAG 4603
10. IEEE Standard 1516–2010 (2010)
11. Huiskamp, W., Wymenga, R., Krijnen, R., Harmsen, E.: Network Infrastructure Design Document for NATO Education and Training Network (NETN), (2009)
12. JFTC Presentation to SEEETN Balkan Bridges MPC – Charles M. Stibrany, CIV US Program Manager; Gultekin Arabaci CIV TU
13. Nikolov, O.: Training for success. Joint Training initiatives improve security in the Balkans – Per Concordiam, vol. 6, no. 1 (2015)
14. Integrated Environment for Crises Management and Disaster Response Training. In: CMDR CoE Proceedings, vol. 1, Sofia (2015)
15. The human cost of weather related disasters report – Centre of research of epidemiology of disasters (CRED) (2015)

Assessment of Flood Vulnerability Using Fuzzy Logic and Geographical Information Systems

Valentina Nikolova[1] and Plamena Zlateva[2(✉)]

[1] Department of Geology and Geoinformatics, MGU, Sofia, Bulgaria
v.nikolova@mgu.bg
[2] Institute of System Engineering and Robotics - BAS, Sofia, Bulgaria
plamzlateva@abv.bg

Abstract. The assessment of river flood vulnerability requires analysis of the whole physical-geographical environment, and taking into account the interaction between all natural and social–economic components of the study area. In the current paper a flood vulnerability map is elaborated in Geographical Information Systems (GIS) environment using fuzzy logic overlay analysis. Precipitation, distance from streams, flow accumulation, lithology, land use, slopes and altitude are considered and analysed as factors influencing the floods. In particular, the proposed methodology for an assessment of flood vulnerability by fuzzy logic is applied for the catchment of the river Luda Kamchia. This river is situated in the Eastern Bulgaria, Europa. It takes about 1600 km^2. The relief is mainly low-mountainous and the annual amount of precipitation is between 600 and 800 mm, influenced by the Black sea in the eastern part of the river basin. Proposed methodology for the assessment of river flood vulnerability and elaboration of maps of flood vulnerability by fuzzy logic overlay analysis in GIS environment is a first step in development of the information system for integrated risk assessment from natural disasters.

Keywords: River flood vulnerability · GIS · Overlay analysis · Fuzzy logic

1 Introduction

The increasing cases of river floods in global scale and damages caused by them determine the importance of the problem. For these reasons, it is need for more detailed study of the floods factors. The floods are one of the most widespread natural disasters with natural and social components. The assessment of flood vulnerability requires analysis of the completely physical-geographical environment and taking into account the interaction between all natural components of the area [1]. Social and economic infrastructures also should be taken in consideration, particularly in flood risk assessment and mitigation. A large amount of quantitative data about river runoff, precipitation, river basin hydrological and morphometric features have to be processed. The interpretation of available data and analysis of hydro-climatic factors of floods are in relation of lithology, soils, relief and land use of the river basin. In this regard, the used methods in investigation of river flood susceptibility could be divided in the three groups: mathematic-statistical; geographical-spatial analysis and modelling. The use of

Y. Murayama et al. (Eds.): ITDRR 2016, IFIP AICT 501, pp. 254–265, 2017.
https://doi.org/10.1007/978-3-319-68486-4_20

GIS technology allows processing of large amounts of data and optimization of the decision-making process [2]. The application of remote sensing gives information as about difficult accessible areas as well as about large areas and could be shortened the research time.

There are many researches about flood susceptibility, flood vulnerability/hazard and risk assessment using GIS and remote sensing [3, 4]. The development of technology and seeking more detailed investigation of flood parameters, even in areas that are difficult to access, determine developing of the research of flood susceptibility, flood hazard and risk, and wider application of remote sensing methods and GIS [5–7].

Different floods influencing factors are considered in the publications, for example distance from the river, lithology, rainfall, land use/land cover (LULC), soil type, stream power index, topographic wetness index, rainfall, slope, morphometric parameters of the catchment and also socioeconomic impacts of flooding. The factors are chosen depends on expert's view on the natural processes and having regard environmental properties of the research area, interaction between natural components and morphometric features of the drainage basin. One of the main question in flood investigation is which factors have significant influence on flood occurrences and flood parameters and how to determine the weights of each factor. Other important question considered in the literature is about the meaning of the main concepts: flood suscep-tibility, vulnerability, hazard and risk. Often susceptibility and vulnerability are used with the same meaning though the susceptibility is considered as a possibility that the event could be happen and the vulnerability is the sensitivity degree toward a natural hazard, associated to the exposure to a catastrophic event and combined with the human ability to resist. Flood hazard is associated with the probability of a flood event. According to the Directive 2007/60/EC on the assessment and management of flood risks "flood risk" means the combination of the probability of a flood event and of the potential adverse consequences for human health, the environment, cultural heritage and economic activity.

There are many qualitative and quantitative methods for the flood vulnerability assessment. However, it is necessary to point out, that the assessment of the flood vulnerability is done under the subjective and uncertain conditions (for example, there are short records or only few measured points) [8]. The fuzzy logic approach is an appropriate tool for flood vulnerability assessment [9]. This approach provides ade-quate processing the expert knowledge and uncertain quantitative data [10, 11]. The fuzzy logic, implemented in GIS environment is used as an overlay technique when there are inaccuracies in attribute and in the geometry of spatial data [12–15].

The aim of the current research is to show the advantages of the fuzzy logic approach and geographic information systems (GIS) in assessment of flood vulnera-bility and to build a GIS data base to be used in decision making for flood vulnerability/flood hazard management. The flood vulnerability map will be elaborated in GIS environment using multi-criteria analysis and fuzzy logic. Precipitation, distance from streams, flow accumulation, lithology, land use, slopes and altitude will be considered and analysed as factors influencing the floods.

2 Data and Methodology

The flood assessment and flood vulnerability map of the river basin are done in GIS environment (ArcGIS, ESRI Inc.). ArcGIS Spatial analyst tools – Overlay is used for determining areas prone to floods in different rate. Data about relief, precipitation, lithology, drainage network and LULC is used for that purpose. The analysis is made for the whole river basin. Using the basin approach is the most logical approach in flood assessment because all hydrological and geological-geomorphological components of the area strongly interact in the frame of the catchment.

In this study, the flood vulnerability model is constructed through following two main etaps:

- Determining the river catchment area
- Determining the factors with significant influence of the floods

2.1 Determining the River Catchment Area

The drainage network and watershed are delineated on the base of ASTER GDEM (a product of METI and NASA) with 30 m horizontal resolution using Hydrology tool of ArcGIS Spatial analyst and following the sequence: Quality of data raster; Project raster; Filling sinks and removing inaccuracies; Flow direction; Basin; Flow accumulation; Stream raster.

Stream raster is calculated applying Map algebra (ArcGIS Spatial Analyst Tools) on flow accumulation raster. The main question in stream raster generation is: what is the threshold value of the area from which a stream could be formed. The value could be different depends on the relief of the area and the factors of erosion. The horizontal resolution of the digital elevation model (DEM) has also to be taken into account. All cells with a value less than the determined threshold value receive a value 0 (they don't form a stream) and others 1 (there is a stream).

2.2 Determining the Factors with Significant Influence of the Floods

Having regard the researches published in this field there are many factors that could cause the floods. Floods are complex natural phenomena depending on hydrological, geological-geomorphological, soils and land use/land cover peculiarities.

Taking into account the specific features of the research geographical area and limited available data, the following seven parameters are considered as main flood influencing factors: rainfall intensity, flow accumulation, distance from stream, lithology, LULC, slope and altitude.

Rainfall intensity. Rainfall and particularly intensive rainfall have a major role for flood occurrence. An intensive rain even for a short time can cause floods more that light rain during several days. Of course, the time for drainage of surface water is in the relation of the form of the river basin, stream density, soil/rock permeability and vegetation. The rainfall intensity is presented by modified Fournier index (MFI), calculated as the sum of monthly average amount of precipitation divided to the average annual amount of precipitation [16].

Flow accumulation. It is an indicator for the water quantity of the area. Flow accumulation is determined on the base of the DEM and presents the accumulated flow in each cell of the raster. The value of the cell shows the number of the cells from which the flow is accumulated. If the flow accumulation is 0 then there is no runoff. The runoff is increased at greater values of flow accumulation.

Distance from stream. The distance from streams as a flood factor should be assessed in relation to the possibility the high waters to flood adjacent areas and to the time for which the surface (slope) flows reach the riverbeds.

Lithology. The rocks composition, their grain-size and physical properties determine the rocks permeability, which is of great importance for flood occurrences. High permeable rocks favor water infiltration and ground flow while less permeable rocks favor surface flow and at horizontal or low slope areas are factors for high flood vulnerability.

LULC. The type of land cover influences the time to drain the slope runoff. Forests favor the infiltration of rainwater in soils and prevent fast surface runoff. In this way, they decrease the probability of floods. Arable lands, grasslands and sparsely vegetated areas have less hydrological role and could favor floods occurrence in case of appropriate topographic conditions and intensive rains.

Slope and altitude. The altitude and slope of the catchment area determine the hydro-climatic conditions. Usually high elevated areas have more precipitation which is a prerequisite for higher river runoff, but on the other side valleys and lowlands (with altitude less than 200 m) are more prone to floods because they facilitate the river overflow in case of high water. The elevation and slope influence on the most of cases on the speed of the water flow and development of erosion processes. It is need to point that the prerequisites for floods are more in cases of low and flat areas in comparison with the elevated areas with high slope.

3 Fuzzy Logic Overlay Analysis

The concept of the fuzzy logic is proposed by Zadeh in [17]. It is developed around the basic idea of so-called fuzzy sets or membership function. Fuzzy set theory is regarded as an extension of classical set theory. It enables the processing of imprecise information by means of membership functions, in contrast to Boolean transformations. Usually the membership functions is assigned 0 to false values and 1 to true ones, but fuzzy logic also allows in-between values [10].

Here, the main idea is to assess the flood vulnerability by applying fuzzy logic in respect to the several flood factors. As a result, a flood vulnerability map is created in GIS environment.

According proposed methodology the fuzzy logic overlay is applied in GIS environment each one of flood factors is entered in GIS database as a separate layer. All vector layers (rainfall intensity, lithology, LCLU, etc.) are converted in raster surfaces. The next step is to create fuzzy membership raster at which the input raster is transformed a 0 to 1 scale, indicating the strength of a membership in a set, based on a specified fuzzification functions. These functions are applied to the initially created rasters for rainfall intensity, distance from streams, flow accumulation, slope and altitude. For lithology and LULC which present qualitative information (not quantitative) the reclassified rasters (values from 1 to 5 according to the susceptibility of floods) are used as membership input rasters. A reclassified distance from stream raster (rates from 1 to 5) is also used to create a membership raster. The applied membership type for slope and altitude is "small" and for the other factors we applied "large" taking into account the nature of the modelled feature and spatial distribution of the values. After creating fuzzy membership layers a fuzzy overlay is applied. The values of the resulted flood vulnerability, presented in the output raster, are classified in 5 classes (1 very low vulnerability to 5 – very high vulnerability) using natural breaks classification method.

3.1   Case Study: The River Luda Kamchia Basin

The above described methodology is applied for the river Luda Kamchia basin. It is situated in the Eastern Bulgaria and is a part of the river Kamchia basin (see Fig. 1).

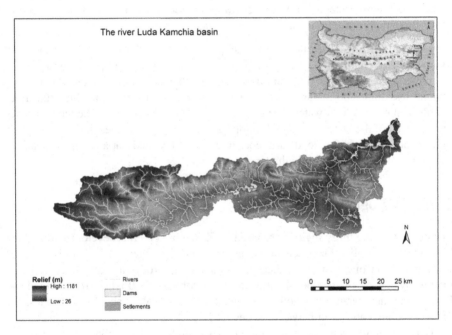

Fig. 1. A case study: the River Luda Kamchia basin.

The river Kamchia is the largest Bulgarian river which flows into the Black Sea. The study area is about 1600 km^2. The form of the basin is long and narrow, and it is a bit larger in the low part which could be a prerequisite for floods in the low part of the river basin. The relief is predominantly low-mountainous (600–1000 m above sea level) and includes Kotlenska, Varbishka and Karnobatska mountains. The highest point of the watershed is peak Bulgarka (1181 m). About the lithology the most part of the river basin is built of alternation of carbonate and non-carbonate rocks. The drainage network of the river Luda Kamchia catchment is well developed. The streams density is about 1–1.5 km/km² and it increases to 2 km/km² in the western higher part of the study area. The annual amount of precipitation is about 600 to 800 mm. The maximum is observed in May – June and November – December. Forests cover about 88% of the total area of the river basin. Non-irrigated arable land takes nearly 4% of the area and other types of land use are less than 2% each of the river basin. Settlements have 0.45% of the investigated area. In this relation forests are the land use/land cover type with the highest influence for runoff and water quantity of the catchment.

3.2   Flood Factors for River Luda Kamchia Basin

Rainfall intensity. In the current research the precipitation data for 30 years period is taken from precipitation reference book, published by Bulgarian National Institute of Meteorology and Hydrology. There are only 4 meteorological stations in the river Luda Kamchia basin and other 5 stations, located near to the investigated area are also used in the analysis. The spatial distribution of the MFI is done by inverse distance weighted (IDW) interpolation. The results show not very high intensity of rainfall. The values of the MFI are between 50.64 and 70.12. In this case we reclassified the output raster in 3 classes using natural breaks classification method: 1 – with very low importance for flood occurrence; 2 – low and 3 – moderate.

Flow accumulation. The flow accumulation map is elaborated on the base of digital elevation model (see Fig 1). The values of flow accumulation in the generated raster for the river Luda Kamchia basin are from 0 to 2 294 333. Taking into account the relief of the catchment it is considered that the threshold area to create a stream is 5 km². The number of cells corresponding to this area at 30 m DEM resolution is 5556. In this case the new stream raster includes cells with value greater than 5556. After checking the results, reviewing the surface and making tests with different values of the pixels it is accepted 2500 as a threshold value to be able to include also smaller lines with temporal flow. In this regard and taking into account natural breaks it is reclassified the flow accumulation raster from 1 to 5 where all cells with value less than 25 700 received value of 1 (very small importance for flood occurrences) and these with value great than 1 700 300 received value 5 (very high importance for flood occurrence). The values between 25 700 and 1 700 300 are divided in 3 classes (with rates 2, 3 and 4) using natural breaks method.

Distance from streams. Five flood vulnerability intervals are set according to the Table 1. The stream density and the type of the relief are taken into account in determining the distance from streams as a flood factor. The distance zones are determined using ArcGIS Analysis Tools – Proximity – Multiple Ring Buffer and evaluated to the flood vulnerability. The values of 1 to 5 are added to the generated polygons to show the vulnerability of each polygon to floods.

Table 1. Flood vulnerability according to the distance from stream

Distance from stream (m)	Flood vulnerability
0–50	5 – very high
50–150	4 – high
150–300	3 – moderate
300–500	2 – low
more than 500	1 – very low

Lithology. The information about the lithology is taken from the geological map, scale 1:200000 and is entered in the GIS environment as a polygon layer. Having regard the physical-mechanical properties and chemical composition of the rocks they are divided into 5 groups: unconsolidated non-carbonate rocks; consolidated carbonate rocks; consolidated non-carbonate rocks; alternation of carbonate and non-carbonate rocks; volcanic rocks [18]. These groups are rated to flood vulnerability as follow (see Table 2).

Table 2. Flood vulnerability determined by lithology

Rocks	Flood vulnerability
Unconsolidated non-carbonate rocks	4 – high
Consolidated carbonate rocks	2 – low
Consolidated non-carbonate rocks	5 – very high
Alternation of carbonate and non-carbonate rocks	4 – high
Volcanic rocks	4 – high

Unconsolidated non-carbonate rocks (gravel and sand) are accumulated in the lower part of the river valleys. Though the high permeability of sand they have high flood vulnerability rate because of the high level of ground water. The gorge nature of Luda Kamchia River is a reason for weak accumulation and limited distribution of the alluvial deposits in this part of the catchment area. Consolidated carbonate rocks (limestones, dolomites, sandy and marlly limestones) have limited distribution in the river Luda Kamchia basin, mainly in Kotlenska mountain (the Northern high part of the catchment) and in some areas to the East, in the low part of the river basin. Karst relief could be a prerequisite for flash floods but having regard the morphometric properties of the river basin and limited area of these rocks they are rated as low flood suscep-tibility. Consolidated non-carbonate rocks are presented by clay-sandy slates, sand-stones, conglomerates and clays, and they are a good condition for surface runoff. These rocks are slightly spread in the Luda Kamchia River catchment. Larger areas could be found in the low part of the basin after the Kamchia dam. A considerable part of the river Luda Kamchia catchment is built by alternations of carbonate and non-carbonate rocks (slates and sandy limestones, clayey marls and limestones, clayey-sandy slates). Volcanic rocks are presented by tuffs and andesites. They have limited distribution at southern slopes of Kamchiiska Mountain, the low part of the drainage basin.

LULC. The information about the LULC types in the catchment of the river Luda Kamchia are given in Table 3. The types are determined by CORINE Land Cover 2012 project. The largest area of the basin is covered by forests take (about 88%). This fact significantly decreases the vulnerability to floods. Arable lands, vineyards, pastures and shrubs which are not big obstacle for surface runoff and could facilitate floods have around 6% of the area. The sparsely vegetated areas which are rated as high vulnerability to floods areas takes less than 1% of the investigated basin. Urban areas, industrial sites are not taken into evaluation because of the scale of the research and lack of information about the infrastructure. Water bodies (dams) also are not evaluated.

Table 3. LULC flood vulnerability

LULC	Flood vulnerability
Urban areas	Not evaluated
Industrial or commercial units	Not evaluated
Mineral extraction sites	Not evaluated
Sport and leisure facilities	Not evaluated
Non-irrigated arable land	3 – moderate
Vineyards	3 – moderate
Fruit trees and berry plantations	2 – low
Pastures	3 – moderate
Complex cultivation patterns	3 – moderate
Land principally occupied by agriculture with significant areas of natural vegetation	3 – moderate
Broad-leaved forest	1 – very low
Coniferous forest	2 – low
Mixed forest	1 – very low
Natural grassland	3 – moderate
Transitional woodland/shrub	3 – moderate
Sparsely vegetated areas	4 – high
Water bodies	Not evaluated

Slope. The slopes are calculated in ArcGIS on the base of DEM. For the most of the catchment of the river Luda Kamchia they are in the interval 3 – 10° followed by 0 – 3°. Steep areas 25 – 44° take a limited part of the basin. Five slope intervals are determined having regard the morphometric features of the river basin and rated to flood vulnerability (see Table 4).

Table 4. Flood vulnerability determined by slopes

Slopes in degree	Flood vulnerability
0–3	5 – very high
3–10	4 – high
10–18	3 – moderate
18–25	2 – low
25–44	1 – very low

Altitude. The relief of the river Luda Kamchia basin is predominantly low mountainous. The highest point is 1181 m. The altitude zone of 200 to 600 m is 65% of the whole basin. The areas elevated above 1000 m are nearly 0.55%. The hilly lands favor fast surface runoff to the river beds and could be considered as areas with high to moderate vulnerability to floods. In this regard and taking into account the relief of the area we determined 5 altitude intervals rated to the flood vulnerability (see Table 5).

Table 5. Flood vulnerability determined by altitude

Altitude (m)	Flood vulnerability
<100	5 – very high
100–200	4 – high
200–600	3 – moderate
600–1000	2 – low
>1000	1 – very low

3.3 Results and Flood Vulnerability Map

Application of fuzzy logic overlay analysis allows to consider the combined effect of flood factors. As a result a flood vulnerability map is created (see Fig. 2). The fuzzy logic overlay analysis shows moderate flood vulnerability in the predominant areas of the river basin. The values of the flood vulnerability rate are a bit higher in the low part of the river basin and also in the central part, at the drainage area of right tributary of the river Luda Kamchia, after Kamchia dam. This is related with the horizontal topographic surface (slope between 0° and 3°) and also with the physical properties of the rocks – consolidated non-carbonate rocks. The high flood vulnerabiity on the limited part of the slopes of Kotlenska mountain (western part of the river basin) could be explained mainly with the higher rainfall intensity and lithology presented by alternation of carbonate and non-carbonate rocks. Applying fuzzy logic overlay shows in generally higher flood susceptibility near to the river beds. The form of the river basin, which is narrow at the central part and wider in the low part is a prerequisite for accumulation of higher water quantity in the low part of the river basin which could cause floods.

The results about the flood susceptibility in the river Luda Kamchia catchment are subject of future investigation. More attention should be given to the removing data

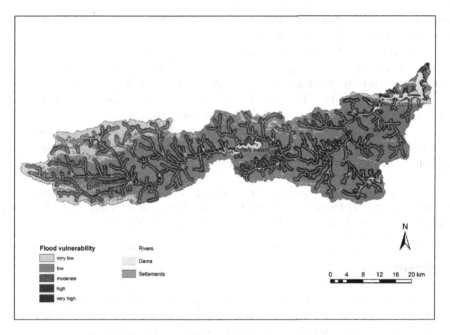

Fig. 2. Flood vulnerability map using fuzzy logic overlay.

imperfection and interpreting the results of the analysis of flood influencing factors. The number of factors is not limited and additional factors could be considered too. The built GIS data base is open and other information could be entered. About the flood cases in the past periods the published data is not enough and it does not present the time and spatial characteristics of this nature phenomenon. The analysis of the flood influencing factors show that they could facilitate flood occurrence. The questionnaires about floods in the river Luda Kamchia basin show the floods happen often in the valley of the river Luda Kamchia. The lack of the published data about big floods in the investigated area could be explained with the geomorphological features of the river basin which are not favorable for wide floods and also with the experience of the local people to organise their activity out of the risk zones.

4   Conclusions

The river flood vulnerability map created by fuzzy logic overlay analysis shows that the river Luda Kamchia basin is not under the great threat of floods though there are different segments of the river valleys with high flood vulnerability. In this regard the flood influencing factors should be taken into account in regional development and planning. The both big dams (Kamchia, in the central part of the basin and Tsonevo, in the low part of the river basin) control the river runoff and decrease the risk of floods but have to be properly managed. More attention should be given to the determining of flood factors and their weights, taking into account their importance for flood occurrences and interaction between different factors.

Application of GIS technology allows processing of a large amount of data and optimizing the decision making. The built GIS data base includes information about drainage network, river basin boundary, relief, slopes, lithology, precipitation, flow accumulation and LULC. The system is open and could be completed with other environmental and economic features that effect on the foods.

The assessment of river flood vulnerability and elaboration of maps of flood vulnerability by fuzzy logic overlay analysis is a first step in development of the information system for integrated risk assessment from natural disasters.

Acknowledgement. The authors express their gratitude to the Bulgarian National Science Fund for the partial financial support under the Grant No. DFNI - I02/15 from 12.12.2014, titled "Information System for Integrated Risk Assessment from Natural Disasters".

References

1. Kazakis, N., Kougias, I., Patsialis, T.: Assessment of flood hazard areas at a regional scale using an index-based approach and analytical hierarchy process: application in Rhodope-Evros region, Greece. Sci. Total Environ. **538**, 555–563 (2015)
2. Kourgialas, N., Karatzas, G.: Flood management and a GIS modelling method to assess flood-hazard areas—a case study. Hydrol. Sci. J. **56**(2), 212–225 (2011)
3. Kundu, A., Kundu, S.: Flood vulnerability assessment using participatory GIS approach. J. Remote Sens. GIS **2**(1), 8–22 (2011)
4. Kafira, V., Albanakis, K., Oikonomidis, D.: Flood susceptibility assessment using G.I.S. An example from Kassandra Peninsula, Halkidiki, Greece. In: Proceedings on 10th International Congress of the Hellenic Geographical Society, Thessaloniki, Greece (2014)
5. Wang, Y.: Using landsat 7 TM data acquired days after a flood event to delineate the maximum flood extent on a coastal floodplain. Int. J. Remote Sens. **25**, 959–974 (2004)
6. Lacava, T., Filizzola, C., Pergola, N., Sannazzaro, F., Tramutoli, V.: Improving flood monitoring by the robust AVHRR Technique (RAT) approach: the case of the April 2000 Hungary flood. Int. J. Remote Sens. **31**, 2043–2062 (2010)
7. Mallinis, G., Gitas, I.Z., Giannakopoulos, V., Maris, F., Tsakiri-Strati, M.: An object-based approach for flood area delineation in a transboundary area using ENVISAT ASAR and LANDSAT TM data. Int. J. Digit. Earth **6**, 1–13 (2013)
8. Papaioannou, G., Vasiliades, L., Loukas, A.: Multi-criteria analysis framework for potential flood prone areas mapping. Water Resour. Manage **29**, 399–418 (2015)
9. Yeganeh, N., Sabri, S.: Flood vulnerability assessment in Iskandar Malaysia using multi-criteria evaluation and fuzzy logic. Res. J. Appl. Sci. Eng. Technol. **8**(16), 1794–1806 (2014)
10. Zimmerman, H.: Fuzzy Set Theory and it Applications. Kluwer Academic Publishers, Norwell (1996)
11. Zlateva, P., Velev, V.: Complex risk analysis of natural hazards through fuzzy logic. J. Adv. Manage. Sci. **1**(4), 395–400 (2013)
12. Leonardi, G., Palamara, R., Cirianni, F.: Landslide susceptibility mapping using a fuzzy approach. Procedia Eng. **161**, 380–387 (2016)

13. Jiang, W., Deng, L., Chen, L., Wu, J., Li, J.: Risk assessment and validation of flood disaster based on fuzzy mathematics. Prog. Nat. Sci. **19**, 1419–1425 (2009)
14. Fotis, M., Georgia, V., Apostolos, V.: Estimation of the prefecture of Evros vulnerability in flood cases using GIS and fuzzy set algebra. In: Proceedings on Sixteenth International Water Technology Conference, IWTC 2016, Istanbul, Turkey (2012)
15. Perera, E., Lahat, L.: Fuzzy logic based flood forecasting model for the Kelantan River basin, Malaysia. J. Hydro-Environ. Res. **9**, 542–553 (2015)
16. Arnoldus, H.: An approximation of rainfall factor in the universal soil loss equation. In: Boodt, M., Gabriels, D. (eds.) Assessment of Erosion, pp. 127–132. Wiley, Chichester (1980)
17. Zadeh, L.: Fuzzy sets. Inf. Control **8**, 338–353 (1965)
18. Nikolova, V.: Determining of the morpholithology types in the Kamchia River Basin (Eastern Bulgaria) by means of geographic information system (GIS). Geogr. Pannonica **14**(3), 76–82 (2010)

Author Index

Printed in the United States
By Bookmasters